# ARCHITECTURE Santa Fe: a guidebook

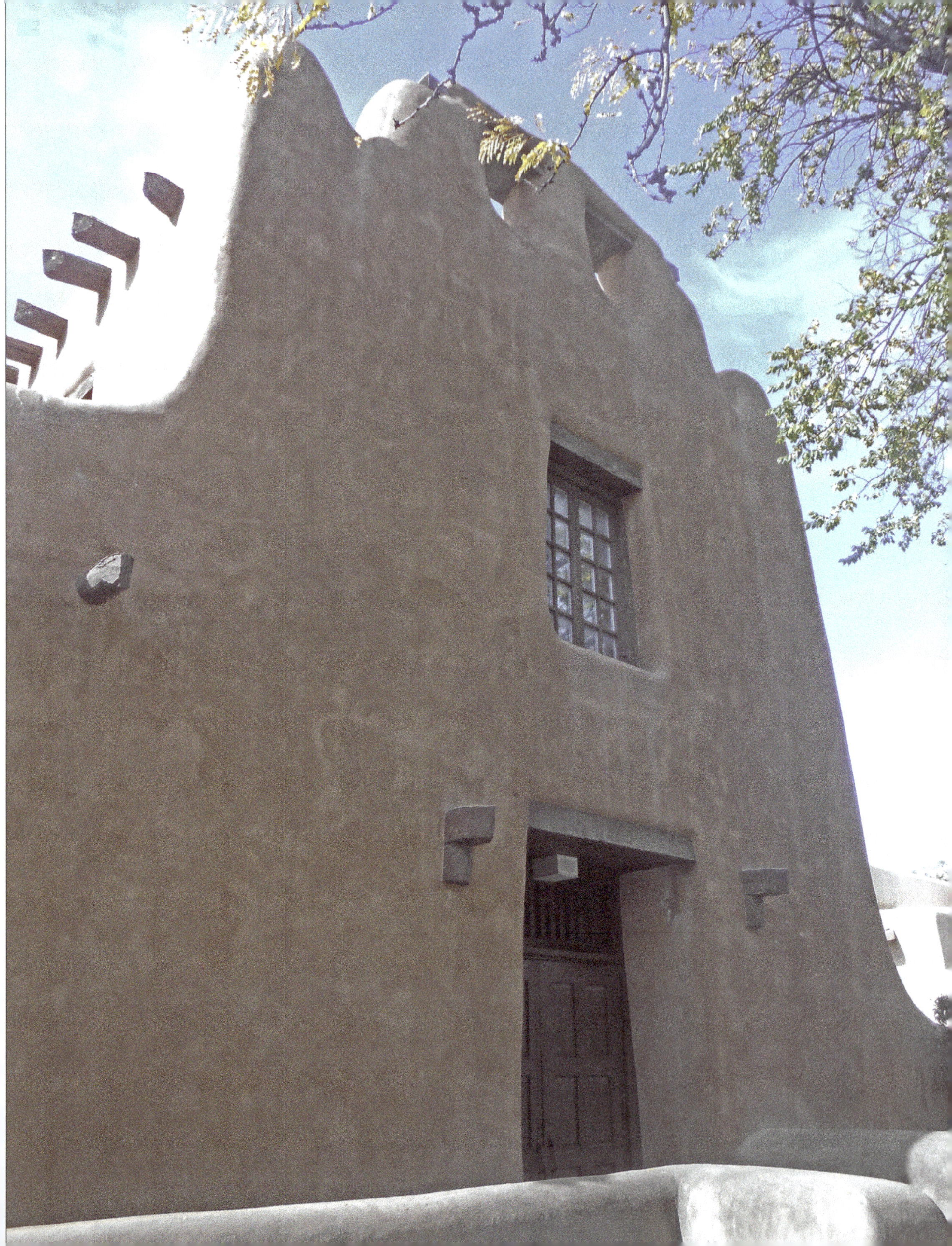

# ARCHITECTURE
# Santa Fe: a guidebook

Paul Weideman

Running Lizard Press
Santa Fe, N.M.

ISBN: 978-0-578-60690-3

*Cover photo-illustration: Gross Kelly Warehouse, 1913*
*Cover designed by Taura Katerina Costidis*

*Frontispiece: New Mexico Museum of Art, 1917 (Lincoln Avenue elevation)*
*Back cover photo: Casa Tutti residence, 2015*

(All photos in this book by Paul Weideman unless otherwise noted)

Running Lizard Press
Santa Fe, N.M.

To Mary Margaret, for inspiring and nourishing me while enduring, and often encouraging, the predilections, compulsions, and foibles of an obsessed photographer and writer; and to all lovers of good architecture old and new.

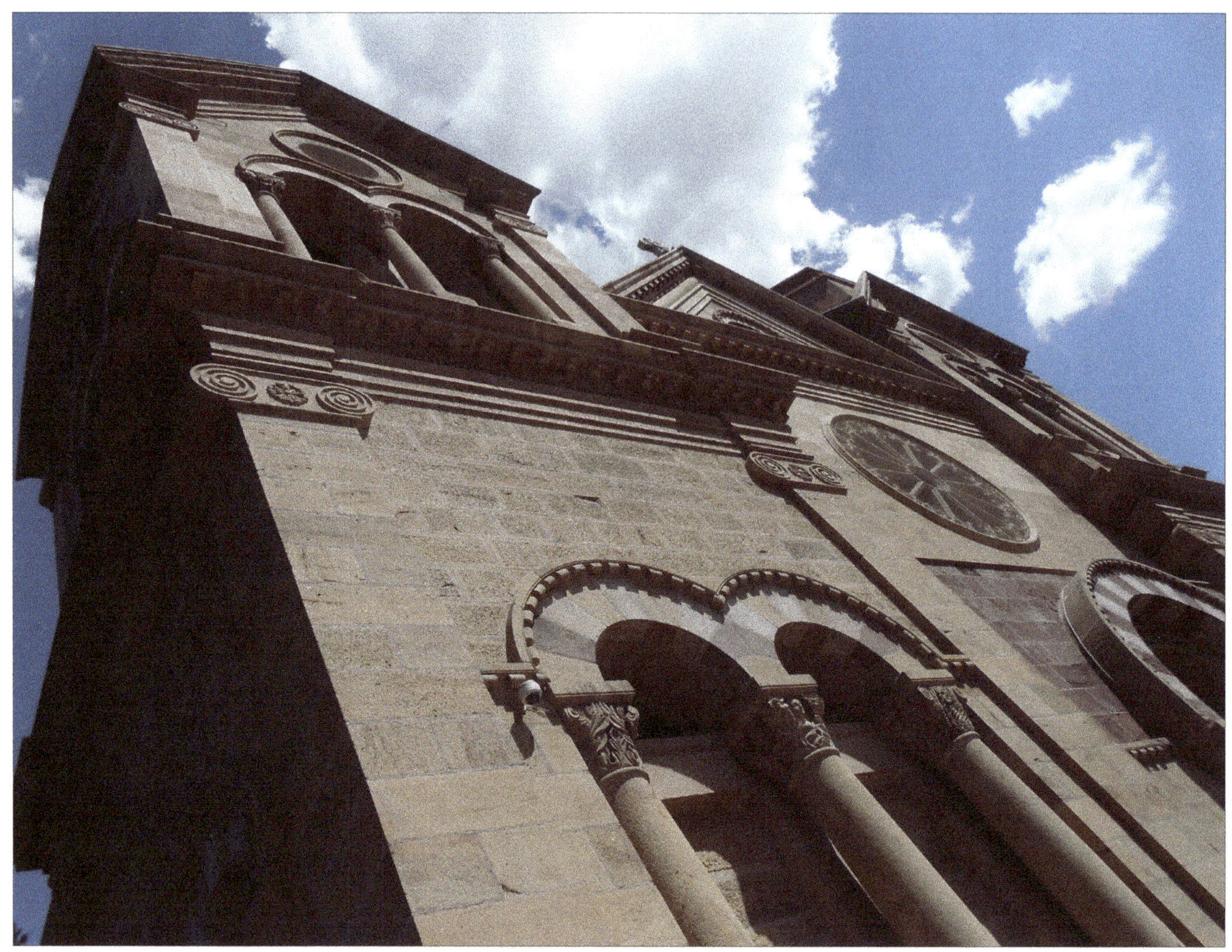

Cathedral Basilica of St. Francis of Assisi (1886)

# TABLE OF CONTENTS

# FOREWORD

by Gayla Bechtol, AIA

As the world of technology, artificial intelligence, and perhaps a reimagined internet, take shape and impinge on our collective and individual psyche, we must still live somewhere, an actual place where we rest our heads at night, that is livable and equitable. Santa Fe is such a place, created over the last 400 years: a real place, and also an imagined place.

Paul Weideman takes us on a tour of these homes and buildings made during the past four centuries or so. It is a great overview, and food for thought and further study about the buildings and the politics of building in oftentimes complicated Santa Fe. The chronological order of the lovely photos is helpful to all of us to remember what is at stake in the continued preservation of Santa Fe.

I arrived in Santa Fe in love with the walls: their form as well as their texture. I already understood Santa Fe as a place, as a typology — a plaza surrounded by institutions, and the roads/houses/fields leading along the waterways to distant towns, and the subsequent suburbia-influenced additions. Life and the practice of architecture are meaningful here because the friction created between past and future matters, and everyone has an opinion and can agree to disagree, almost always respectfully.

Our challenge, as our city becomes more and more popular, is that the expense of tearing something down and rebuilding is no longer an obstacle. Every generation thinks it is the smartest, the greatest, and the most talented. We don't have to look very far back in time to see our mistakes, and to understand how easy it is to destroy urban fabric, for example changing narrow roadways to wider highways along our rivers in our towns.

Fortunately, most of our urban fabric survived the Urban Redevelopment years. And the community rose up to reject a redevelopment project that would have destroyed our past at the Railyard. I think *poco a poco* (step by step) is the way to keep our city vibrant. If we don't understand and ultimately keep our context, this conversation is moot.

In Santa Fe we talk about these kinds of issues, out loud and often, in real time, real space, with each other, person to person. Architecture is about relating to the City with a capital C. If we erode the City by taking away too much of our past, we lose our context. Then the styles really do become irrelevant.

There are many roads to the truth and this book reveals the arguments, pro and con, of preservation versus style, and best of all helps answer the question, "Why does it look like this?"

Weideman explores the necessary arguments, as he always does in his articles. He understands that the "integrity of the historic district," as he puts it, is at stake, that some buildings need to survive that are an "honest tribute to the lineage" of our built environment that actually began in ancient times.

This book is a fantastic discourse on the accumulation of history, theories, personalities, and community desires that are embodied in Santa Fe Style. I find references to books and articles for me to add to my library and knowledge. Until now, I had not heard Carlos Vierra quoted, in describing the New Mexico Museum of Fine Arts, as "expressing as much of the freedom of line and information of the original, as modern material and methods have so far been able to allow. It is hard for workmen whose training has held them down to accuracy and rigid mathematical line to accept the freedoms of what might be described as a free-hand architecture."

Architects who practice in Santa Fe are lucky we have someone with the sensitivity of Weideman, who understands that the builder and the architect work together to create the building. Only someone who understands this architecture, and the creation of it, can ask the meaningful questions of the experts. With his unique access he is able to describe changes in technique and opinion, and describe what this means to Santa Fe style, and to the urban design of our community.

*Gayla Bechtol is an active member of the Santa Fe chapter of the American Institute of Architects and (in the fall of 2019) secretary/treasurer of the Friends of Architecture Santa Fe board of directors. One of its goals is to help our citizens answer the question, "How may I help Santa Feans have a meaningful land-use conversation without demonizing the other side?"*

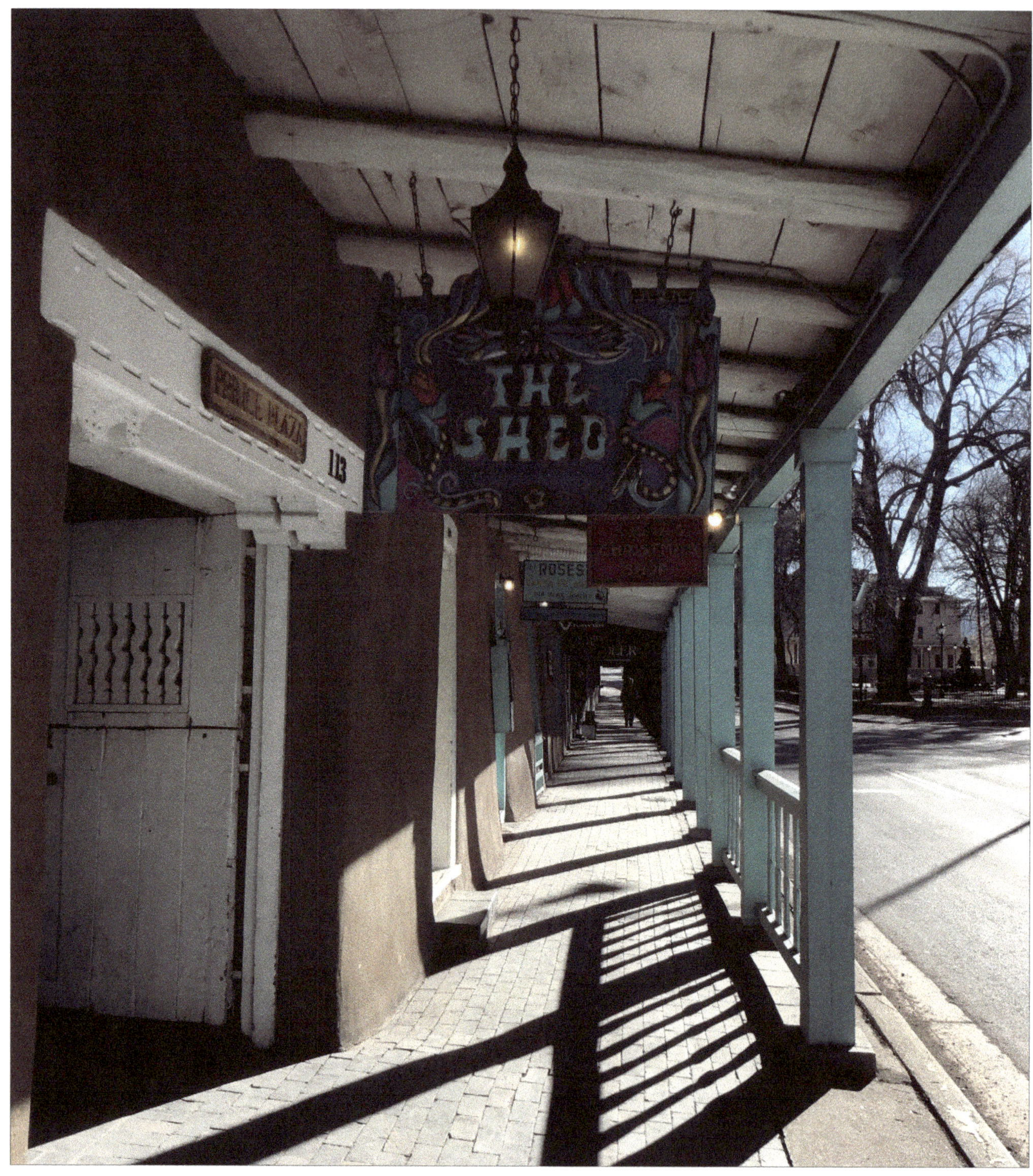


A part of the Arias de Quiros *portal* "tunnel" along E. Palace Avenue

# INTRODUCTION

**THE NEARLY ORGANIC** character of an old Santa Fe home can be riveting, and soothing. Run your hand slowly along the mud-plastered wall and feel its age; let your mind recall the stories of Native people living their lives on this land a thousand years ago, of nervous bold Spanish settlers on this frontier in the 1500s, and of excited Anglo "explorers" arriving via the Santa Fe Trail and the railroad from Missouri, Kansas, and points east three centuries later.

Most of that mud plastering — even on the ancient Palace of the Governors — was long ago replaced by cement-based stucco, so that tactile experience is pretty hard to find. On the other hand, if you exult in the satisfaction of hunting down rarities, those buildings do exist. And in any case, the wonderful, unique quality of Old Santa Fe can still easily be experienced in other significant ways.

Early residents were experts at finding the best kind of earth to make mud plaster to provide protection to the walls that were also made of earth: adobe bricks. Many of the city's buildings are made of other materials that only look like adobe, but hundreds of venerable, real adobe buildings still stand. And you will understand Santa Fe's treasured character in other ways when you spend time in certain areas of the downtown.

Virtually every weekday for more than 15 years I have walked, fascinated, down the *portales* (long covered porches) of what is called the Arias de Quiros Site on East Palace Avenue. What's so intriguing about this place? For one thing, its glorious unevenness. Many of the walls on this collection of storefronts and courtyard entrances, forming a continuous street facade nearly 400 feet long, are not plumb; they often cant in toward the top.

The sidewalk is paved with old bricks that are not consistently flat, and if you drag your feet you may stumble. The entrances into the shops vary from two steps up from the sidewalk to straight in — and the variation is somewhat sporadic, not strictly a matter of a gradual difference in elevation along the block. The entire walk is shaded by this series of *portales*. From the two-story Sena House east, these are brown and capped at the street edge with brick cornices. Along the western half of the block, the *portales* are painted blue, as are the occasional wood-spindled railings at the street. And if you view this block from the sky (or via Google Earth), you'll see that behind the street elevations lie several *placitas* (courtyards); the largest is Sena Plaza, about a quarter-acre in size.

These aren't just any buildings. Originally the Prince, Trujillo, and Sena houses, the block represents "perhaps the most important group of Spanish Colonial buildings" in the city, according to a 1988 city-sponsored survey of neighborhoods by historian Corinne Sze and architect Beverley Spears. Some foundations, and perhaps walls, may date to the 1600s, as do some at the Palace of the Governors just to the west.

Now, about this subject, some perspective. Santa Fe's architecture is neither as ancient as what can be encountered on a few other continents nor as exciting, perhaps, as Wright's Fallingwater cantilevers or Saarinen's flying roofs, and of course there's nothing close to the jarring, soaring or jutting fantasies of Liebeskind, Gehry, and Koolhaas. The feeling here instead is about a direct and respectful relation to the ancient past in this place, and that shows up generally in a softly geometrical solidness and an emphasis on the horizontal.

There is a quietness about it, and not only because these older buildings are adobe — houses with thick walls made of dense adobe bricks are very quiet inside. It's also a collection of design qualities that are as earthy as the color of the local mud plaster.

The general paucity of ornamentation lends a strong, silent vibe to the structures. Of course this relates to the fact that the dominant Spanish-Pueblo Revival and Territorial Revival styles (both of which we call "Santa Fe Style") harken back to ancient and frontier times when there was little to ornament *with*. Many exteriors nonetheless demonstrate owners' tastes for at least touches of color and ornamentation and refinement, examples including brightly painted woodwork, hand-carved beams and corbels, pedimented lintels over windows and doors, and fancy-cut brackets.

As you hopefully will not have guessed, I have had no formal training in architecture, but, over the last 30 years, the more I have paid attention to it — to Santa Fe's well-designed buildings new and old, and to the materials used — the more artistically alive this realm seems to be.

This book is intended as no more than a primer or sampler, and hopefully as a trigger to your own inspiration and positive experience in the city. My avenue has two lanes: one is of words, sentences, and paragraphs, my credentials grounded not only in enthusiasm but in the fact that I have been writing about our architecture for the *Santa Fe New Mexican* for 20 years.

The second avenue is photography, which actually was my first impulse for this book project. In the volume's second, larger, section, I offer "snapshots," made with my vintage Rolleiflex film camera, of 114 Santa Fe houses and institutional and commercial buildings dating from the 14th century to the 21st century. That gamut includes examples (built before the profession of "architect" existed) from pre-Historic Era times and on the frontier of northern New Spain. The newer, architect-designed house is certainly a different species, although many of the finest pay honest tribute to the lineage. (The best architects are also artists and, hopefully, advocates of joy in their buildings.)

In one sense, there is in the famous Santa Fe Style no architecture, since the historic antecedents were plainly practical vernacular; however, Isaac Rapp and John Gaw Meem — the Santa Fe architects/designers who collectively functioned from the 19-teens into the 1950s as what we think of today as the archetypal exponents of the style — did more than merely ape what existed in the humble owner-made homes of old Santa Fe and the Spanish-built churches at, for example, the pueblos of Acoma and Laguna.

Another all-important facet of the city's vaunted "difference" is the survival in some areas of a medieval street pattern. These are districts within which the visiting drivers of RVs and large trucks may either get lost, stuck, or both. But these narrow, winding streets do accommodate residents, and they are indispensable to the integrity of the historic district (and thus to tourism).

For me, the experience of Santa Fe is so enriched by its bells and smells: the ringing of bells at the Cathedral Basilica of St. Francis of Assisi and other 18th- and 19th-century churches downtown, and the bells at train crossings in the Santa Fe Railyard; and the transcendent waftings of Northern New Mexico, of chiles roasting in the late summer, of piñon wood burning on winter evenings, and of fresh tamales steamed in restaurants in the mornings year-round.

All of these qualities resonate with the warm palette of earth-tone buildings in the Capital City. And when you have developed a fine feeling for those, you may also enjoy seeing some of the city's well-designed buildings that boast more contemporary styling and materials, and that at least abstractly honor the building language of old Santa Fe.

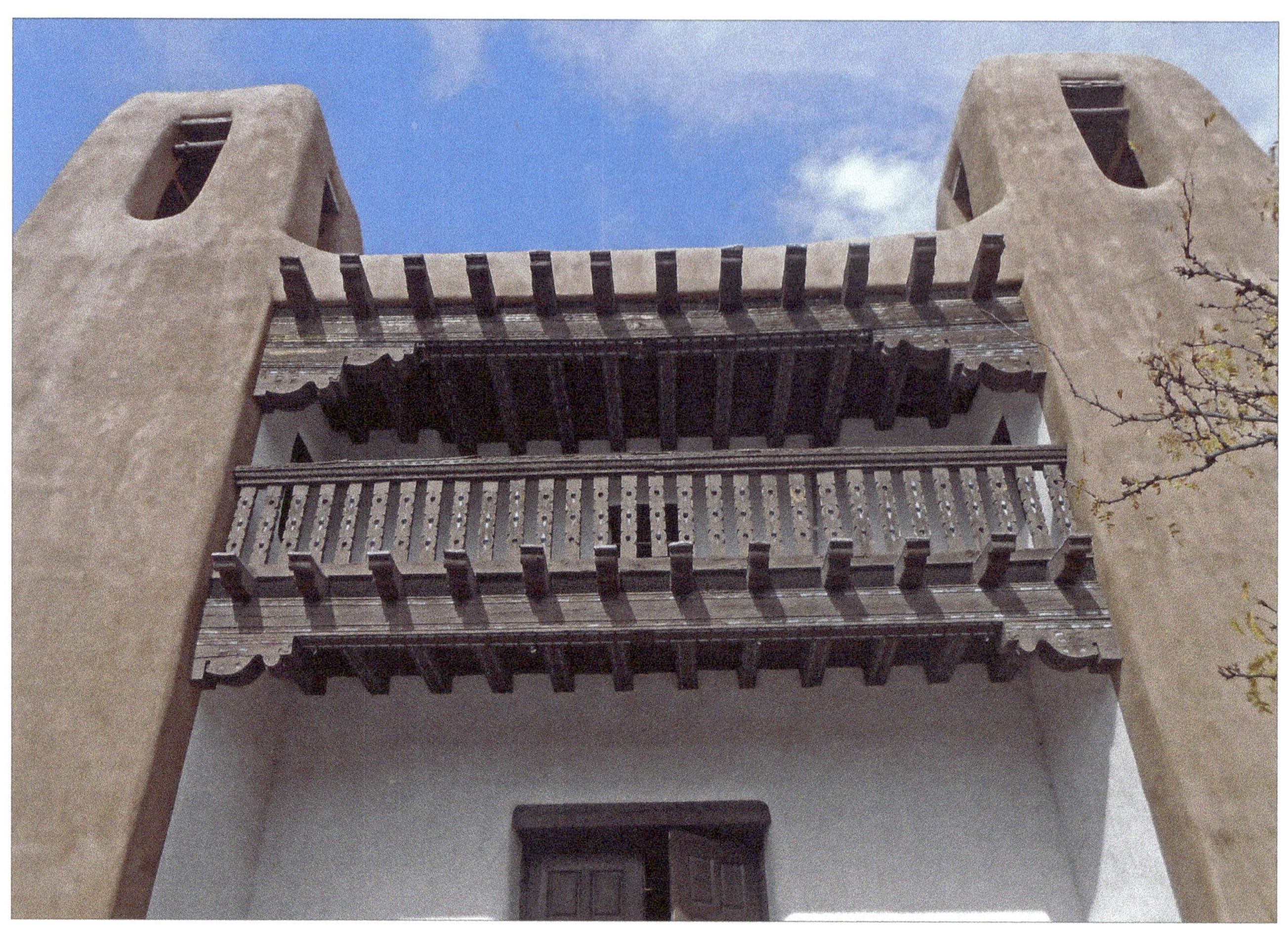

Towers at the west end of the 1917 New Mexico Museum of Art on E. Palace Avenue.

*"You must... get rid of your burros and goats: I hope ten years hence there won't be an adobe house in the Territory. I want to see you learn to make them of brick, with slanting roofs. Yankees don't like flat roofs, nor roofs of dirt."*

**— Commanding General of the U.S. Army William Tecumseh Sherman, speaking in Santa Fe on Oct. 28, 1880**

# Chapter 1
# FROM PUDDLED ADOBE TO 'SANTA FE STYLE'

IT IS AMAZING how often, and intensely, has been debated the character of Santa Fe's appearance — how citizens, builders, architects, writers, historians, planners, preservationists, and the practitioners of boosterism have passionately deliberated about and expounded on this or that aspect of the city's architectural personality over the last century or so. One fundamental reason it is remarkable is that the styles that are still popular, and some important aspects of today's building construction, relate directly to the area's built environment in ancient times.

What is Santa Fe Style? The term has been used to describe many things about New Mexico's capital city. At its lower end is a visual tableau that includes jackalopes; chile ristras hanging somewhat caricaturelike by the dozens from the facades of hotels; tourists ultrabedazzled with fringe, silver, and turquoise; wooden models of singing coyotes wearing colorful kerchiefs; and comestibles overadorned with chile, piñon nuts, and chipotle — not to mention the rows of tacky plastic "farolitos" that some business owners put on their parapets at Christmastime and leave up evermore out of laziness or a weird sense of ritual adornment.

In architecture, Santa Fe Style broadly refers to the revival versions of the Pueblo, Spanish-Pueblo, and Territorial styles. The phrase also brings to mind a host of details, often bursting with folk-art qualities — think carved and painted beams, corbels, and window frames, and many of these are actually on a continuum begun decades and even centuries ago that tell vivid stories about the creativity and individualism of the residents.

**Looking back a bit**

At the end of the Pleistocene era (around 9500 BCE), hunters wandering in this part of the world followed herds of mastodon and other large mammals. They lived in camps for short periods of time — archaeologists know of only one Paleoindian site in the Santa Fe area, in part because of the scanty record deposited by nomads — but they left behind projectile points, including of the famously ancient Clovis and Folsom types.

Through much of the Archaic Period (5,500 BCE - 600 CE), people visiting this region were hunter-gatherers. But by the later Archaic, because the climate had shifted and there was more precipitation, the nomads would return to campsites year after year. They began to build dwellings, partially dug into the earth.

From 2004 to 2008, the site known as Ogapogeh ("White Shell Water Place"), a few hundred feet north of the Santa Fe Plaza, was excavated by archaeologists in advance of the Santa Fe Community Convention Center construction. Among the more than 600,000 artifacts discovered at the site of the ancient Tewa village, there were stone flakes and pieces of charred corn and wood dating back as far as 400 CE The Office of Archaeological Studies' Stephen S. Post said at the time that it was the earliest evidence of domestic life ever found in the downtown area. The people of Ogapogeh grew crops and traded corn, clay pots, and animal skins for shells and parrot feathers from Mexico.

In the early Developmental Period (600-1200), Native people built circular pit homes with walls made of puddled adobe and/or rock or *jacál*, with central hearths. By about the year 1000, they were building with hand-molded ("puddled" or "coursed") adobe and establishing permanent communities in the valley of the Santa Fe River. Over the next two centuries or so, the Indians inhabited the piedmont areas north of the Santa Fe River, then they gradually moved to lower-elevation sites in the river's floodplain and built multistoried adobe roomblocks around plazas. A typical domestic unit during the Coalition Period (1200-1325) had one or two pit structures, each one about six feet deep and 12 feet in diameter, associated with 10 to 20 surface rooms.

The advantages of living collectively were realized by the inhabitants of villages such as Pindi and Agua Fria Schoolhouse, which were located on either side of the Santa Fe River about six miles downstream of what

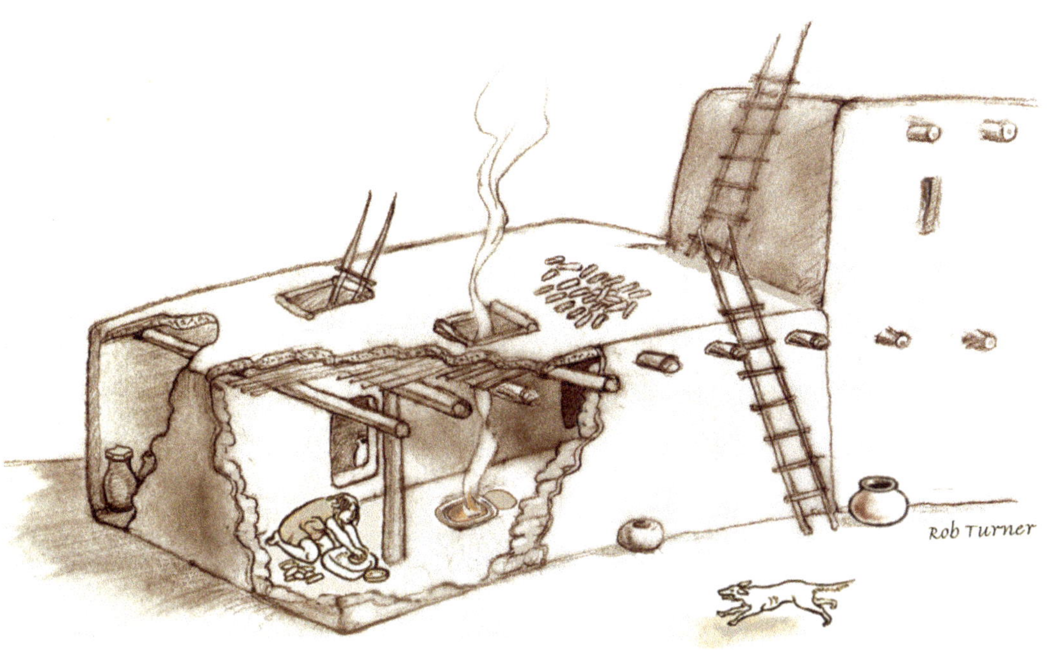


Sketch of an early Pueblo dwelling, illustrating the puddled-adobe construction

Courtesy Rob Turner, illustrator

is now downtown Santa Fe. Those pueblos were occupied from about the early 13th century to the early 15th century and at their zeniths had perhaps 2,000 people living in housing blocks up to three stories high. Arroyo Hondo, five miles south of the Plaza, grew to an urbanscape of 10 plazas and 24 roomblocks, accommodating as many as 800 Puebloans.

For defensive reasons, there were no doors on ground floors. Ladders were an important innovation, brought into service daily to enter homes via rooftop openings. Doorways were fashioned in the interior adobe walls for circulation among rooms on the ground floor, and, in the higher stories, for access to rooftop spaces that were used for domestic activities.

Ogapogeh, Pindi, Agua Fria Schoolhouse, and Arroyo Hondo were long abandoned by the time the Spanish conquistadors arrived. That happened in 1598 as Don Juan de Oñate of the Viceroyalty of New Spain established his force at Río Grande Pueblo of Ohkay Owingeh, which he promptly renamed San Juan de los Caballeros. Oñate was the first governor of distant Spain's province of Nuevo Mexico. His successor, Don Pedro de Peralta, had instructions to found and settle a city.

The plan of La Villa Real de Santa Fe de San Francisco de Asís (the Royal City of Holy Faith of Saint Francis of Assisi) generally followed King Phillip II's 1573 *Ordenanzas de Descubrimiento*, which have been termed the "Laws of the Indies." Based on them, the early development of Santa Fe occurred in two halves: the Spaniards' Barrio de San Francísco on the north side of the Santa Fe River and the Barrio de Analco — developed for the Indians who came with the Spanish from Mexico — on the south side.

The latter barrio developed along De Vargas Street was full of character of a type that would prove amusingly unfamiliar to Anglo newcomers in the late-19th century. "The tourist wishing to see real Mexican life of the average type will find it best exemplified in the street running parallel to the river on the south side," says *Berger's Tourists' Guide to New Mexico*, which was published shortly after the 1880 advent of the railroad in Santa Fe. "Everything here has such a foreign aspect that it is difficult to realize that one is within the limits of the United States."

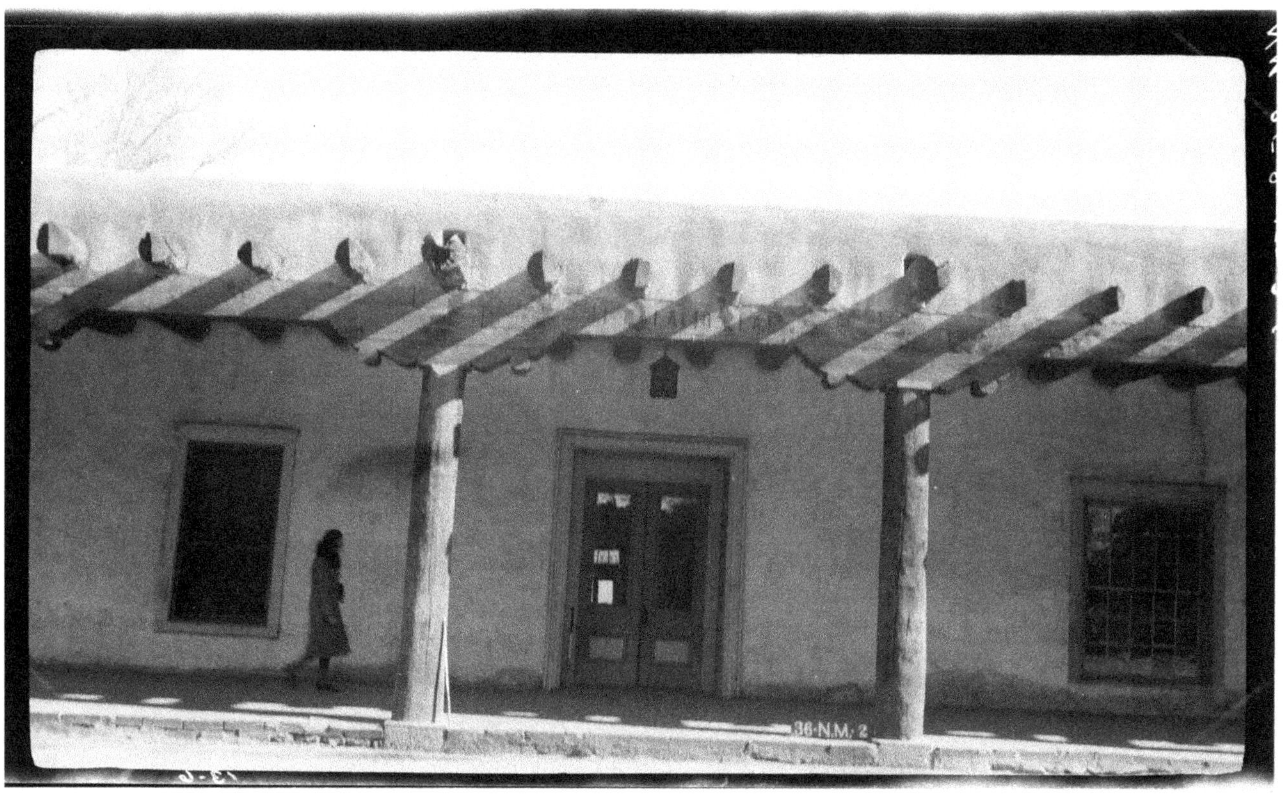


Palace of the Governors, 1934

Courtesy Library of Congress

Interestingly, we have no description or evidence of the actual form of the original plaza or of the original *casas reales* (the royal houses that were later known as the Palace of the Governors) because the relevant documents did not survive the Pueblo Revolt of 1680. But the first plaza probably occupied a much larger parcel than we see today — it likely extended not only east to the ground of the original *parroquia* (parish church) and the site of today's Cathedral Basilica of St. Francis of Asissi, but south almost to what is now Water Street.

The 1680 Pueblo Indian revolution was led by Po'Pay of Ohkay Owingeh following eight decades of persecution at the hands of Spanish soldiers and priests. The Hispanic residents under Governor Antonio de Otermín fled to El Paso del Norte (most of which is today Ciudad Juárez, Mexico). Thirteen years later, Don Diego de Vargas led the resettlement of Santa Fe. New Mexico endured as an outpost of the Spanish Empire for another century and a quarter, until Mexican Independence in 1821 — coincidentally the same year as the founding of a major commercial link with the East: the Santa Fe Trail.

Mexico's reign in Nuevo Mexico only lasted 25 years, succumbing to yet another invasion. In August of 1846, Brigadier General Stephen Watts Kearny, at the head of the U.S. Army of the West, took control of Santa Fe. Two years later, Mexico ceded New Mexico to the United States with the Treaty of Guadalupe Hidalgo, and in 1850 it became a United States territory. Another entry in the parade of flags that have flown over the Palace of the Governors came in 1862: the colors of the Confederate States of America flew in Santa Fe, but for just a few weeks before a series of defeats by Union forces.

**The Spanish-Pueblo building**

Spanish-Pueblo describes the building type adapted by the European settlers in the 16th and 17th centuries based on the earthen dwellings of the Pueblo Indians. The adobe walls and the roof structure — a thick layer of insulating earth (the *torta*) packed onto a bed of light plant material (twigs, bark, straw, chamisa) over *latillas* (poles) laid on *vigas* (debarked logs) — were adapted from those of the native peoples.

"Spanish and Indian builder alike, on reaching the house-site, laid the *vigas* across the walls with the excess length left to take care of itself by protruding from the outer wall," wrote Kate Chapman and Dorothy N. Stewart in their 1930 book *Adobe Notes or How to Keep the Weather Out With Just Plain Mud.* "Thus developed a fortuitous feature that sets apart the New Mexican house in the eyes of the visitor: for what is lovelier than viga shadows slanting along the weathered surface of an adobe wall?"

Besides the adobe brick-making technology and the adobe oven known as the *horno* — both of which had been brought to Iberia by the Moors — the Spanish introduced stone footings for buildings, doors (hung by means of pintle hinges) replacing ladder-accessed roof hatches, and the *fogón*, the

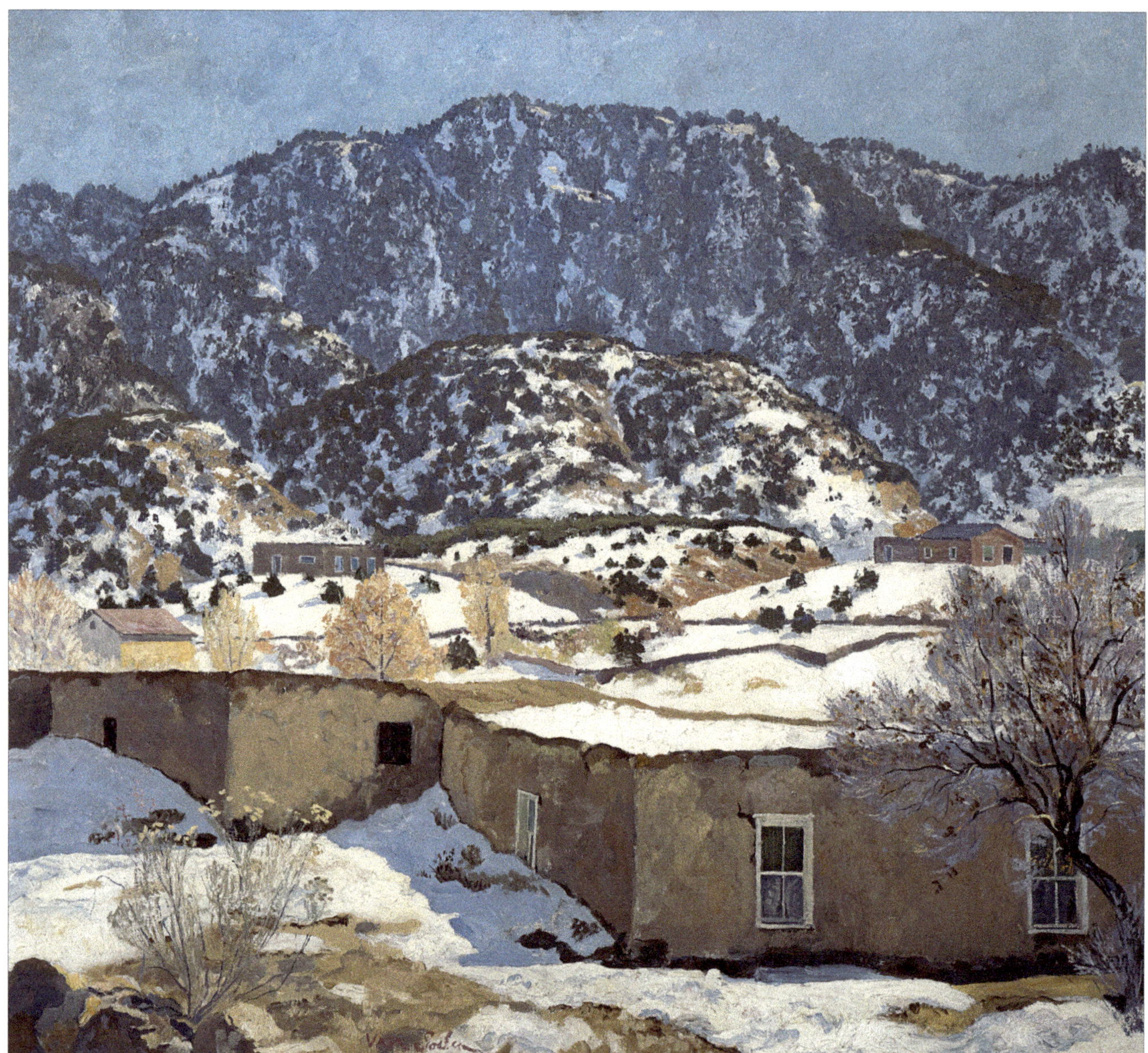

Theodore Van Soelen, *A Santa Fe Hillside*, circa 1924, oil on canvas, 34 x 26 inches

Collection of the New Mexico Museum of Art. Gift of Henry Dendahl in memory of his mother Johanna S. Dendahl, 1946 (137.23P)

shallow, bell-shaped fireplace with chimney. "Three sticks of wood standing on end in an adobe *fogón* … throw off a surprising amount of heat, and as the adobe itself also gives heat they are very economical," scholar E. Boyd wrote in "Domestic Architecture in New Mexico" in a 1973 issue of the journal *El Palacio*. "The small space taken up by these corner fireplaces, their efficiency and picturesque look have all led to their continued construction in the Southwest today." (These have for some reason come to be known locally as "kiva fireplaces.")

Doors and windows on Spanish Colonial buildings were set in untrimmed openings. The earliest windows were small and placed high on the walls. They

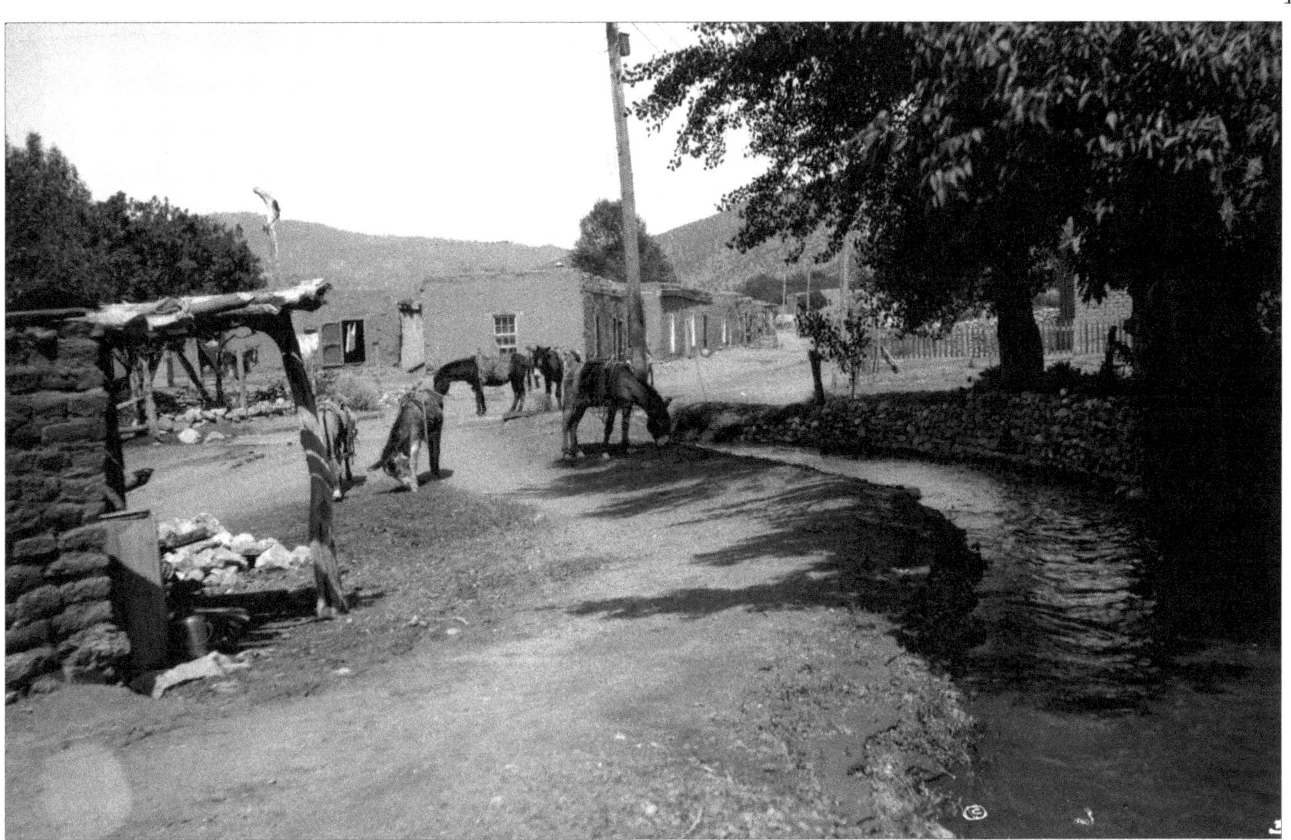

were either open or were glazed with sheets of selenite, a transparent, crystalline variety of gypsum that could be found on the surrounding mesa lands.

Selenite was also employed on transverse clerestories in the mission churches. The Franciscan friars, who designed and built at least 50 churches at area pueblos by the middle of the 17th century, were basically self-trained architects; Alonso Peinado was possibly one of the earliest of these, working in the Santa Fe area before 1620. For their churches, the Franciscans evolved a vocabulary that included several types of bell towers, curvilinear or stepped parapets, front inset balconies, wall buttresses, and the ingenious *claraboya* or transverse clerestory. Created by constructing the roof of the sanctuary above that of the nave and glazing the resulting vertical gap, the clerestory flooded awe-inspiring light upon the altar in the otherwise dim interior of the church.

Burros at the Acequia Madre, the main irrigation ditch that is as old as the city of Santa Fe. The Acequia Madre ("mother ditch") is one of about 700 acequias in New Mexico that have for centuries diverted irrigation water from the Rio Grande and other streams and delivered it to the gardens, orchards, and fields of the member irrigators or *parciantes*.
Photograph by T. Harmon Parkhurst, circa 1915

Neg. no. 011047 courtesy Palace of the Governors Photo Archives (NMHM/DCA)

**THE HOUSES OF THE SPANISH SETTLERS** were small, typically having three rooms at most — not quite the elegant and spacious hacienda too often depicted in old movies and romantic novels set in the American Southwest. The width of the house was limited to the roof load borne by the *vigas* and so was usually 15 feet or less. Defense against marauding Indians was a powerful design incentive on the frontier, and Spanish houses turned a solid wall to the street, with doors and windows opening onto the *placita*. The domicile was often accessed through a gate and a *zaguan* large enough for the passage of a horse and perhaps a wagon.

As Ralph Emerson Twitchell wrote in his wonderful 1925 book *Old Santa Fe: The Story of New Mexico's Ancient Capital*, the residences in the old Spanish days were built in a "hollow square" form. "This method of building gave to each residence a courtyard or patio with only one exit, a large door or gate opening into the street. The rear rooms were used for kitchen and store-house purposes. The apartments opened into the patio which had a fine *portal* or porch on all four sides. The walls of some of these ancient dwellings exceeded three or more feet in thickness and usually were from twelve to fourteen feet in height."

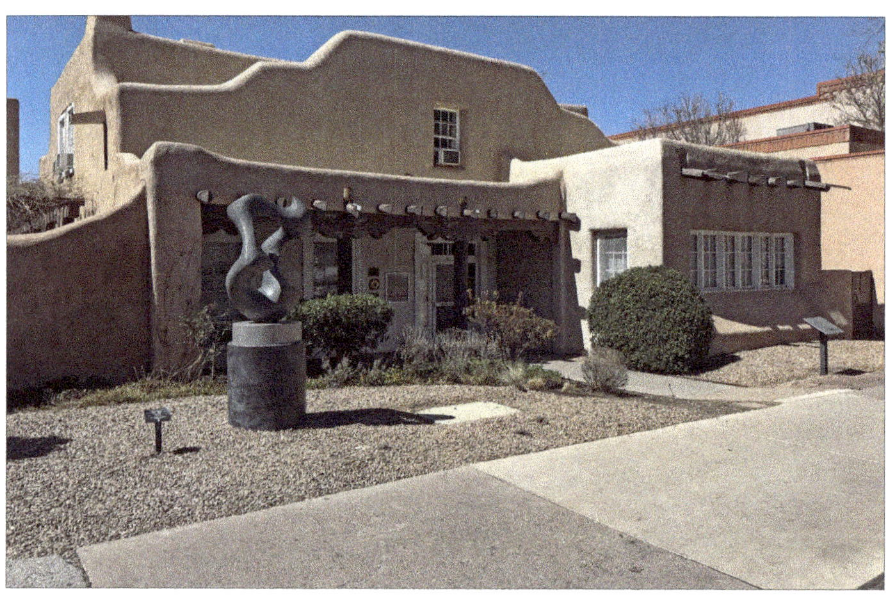

Hewett House

Inside the house of a family of modest means, there were few if any chairs. In a custom dating back to the Moors, a *colchón* or mattress was folded or rolled up against the wall and covered with Indian blankets to provide daytime seating. The more prosperous residents had beds, chests, benches, the standing closets and built-in cupboards known as *trasteros* and *alacenas*, respectively, and *fogóns*.

Street-front *portales* date back at least to the early 19th century. U.S. Army Captain Zebulon Pike wrote in 1807 that many of Santa Fe's houses "have a shed [roof] before the front, some of which have a brick flooring." The long, shady porch was a hospitable addition to blocks of commercial buildings. Army engineer J.F. Gilmer's 1847 map of Fort Marcy and Plaza of Santa Fe shows *portales* all around the Plaza and extending along the south side of San Francisco Street east and west of the Plaza.

### The Territorial building in Northern New Mexico

The Territorial style was a frontier variation of the Greek Revival style that had been popular during the first half of the 19th century in the eastern United States. It was instituted in Santa Fe primarily after the U.S. entry in

1846, making use of tools and building materials imported from the East along the Santa Fe Trail, as well as bricks and sawn lumber from the earliest local kilns and sawmills. Among the neoclassic features were white-painted *portales* (often with balustrades) and square columns (sometimes decorated with chamfered edges or bead moldings); milled-lumber doors and windows topped with pedimented lintels; and brick coping along the roofline, many examples built in imitation of the Greek dentil, but always added primarily to protect adobe parapet and wall surfaces from erosion.

There are no unremodeled examples of early Territorial (pre-1865) buildings extant in Santa Fe. Most of the structures of the Army's Fort Marcy compound — which once included houses, barracks, shops, and storehouses boasting Greek Revival details — are long gone. However, two of the early-1870s adobe officers' houses still exist, although in remodeled form: the Edgar Lee Hewett House, 116 Lincoln Avenue, and the A.M. Bergere House at 135 Grant Avenue.

In 1916, Frank Springer, the owner of 116 Lincoln (and a rancher, lawyer, amateur paleontologist, and Museum of New Mexico backer) had the house modified in the Spanish-Pueblo Revival style to serve as a home for museum founder and director Edgar Lee Hewett. The Grant Avenue building (whose guests included President Ulysses S. Grant in 1880) housed Adelina Otero Warren, a suffragette and Santa Fe County superintendent of schools, and Alfred Maurice Bergere, court clerk and musician. In 1926, the cross-gabled roof on the original house was removed and a flat roof was added in compliance with the Santa Fe style. Then, 75 years later, Gluckman Mayner Architects, New York, was employed to remodel the building as the Georgia O'Keeffe Museum Research Center.

Bainbridge Bunting (*Early Architecture of New Mexico*, 1976) wrote that houses in the late 1800s — after the Indian threat had subsided — more often opened outward, and the *placita* accordingly began to be rare. Following the 1880 arrival of the railroad in Santa Fe, the flow of building materials increased in both quantity and variety compared to what had been transported in wagons over the Santa Fe Trail during the previous 60 years.

John P. Conron and R. Patrick Christopher, writing about the Territorial period in a 1978 issue of *New Mexico Architecture*, mentioned the difficulty of dating New Mexico buildings from the late 19th century by style alone, because newer materials and architectural elements had so often been applied to older structures. They enthused that this "mix-up of current fashion along with continuing historical building styles and techniques" make the architectural milieu "of Santa Fe — and indeed all of New Mexico — charming and unique."

During this period, many of the buildings being erected in Santa Fe were the result of designers who consulted published pattern books and simply evolved their design sensibilities from experience as builders on the local scene. However, the number of professional architects rose steadily after the coming of the trains, and in 1897-1898 a field-related course in "Drawing and Higher Mathematics" was taught at the University of New Mexico by Edward Buxton Cristy (who in less than a decade would be designing buildings in the "Santa Fe Style" before that term existed).

By 1895, as Bunting, Conron, and Boyd Pratt told it, "Santa Fe was catching up! The local definition of progress then was an eradication of the 'Mexican' past." During the late Territorial period, many of the important new buildings bore styles having little or nothing to do with Northern New Mexico architectural precedents. Among them were a series of Classical Revival government buildings — the double-domed 1886 capitol, the 1889 U.S. Courthouse, and the single-domed 1900 capitol — as well as the Gothic Revival or Romanesque Revival Loretto Chapel (1878), Church of the Holy Faith (1882), and St. Francis Cathedral (1884); the Italianate Catron Block (1891); and the French Second Empire St. Michael's College (1878), Loretto Academy (1880), St. Francis Sanitorium (1880), and Palace Hotel (1881).

**The Spanish-Pueblo Revival**

The story of the inception of the architectural concept known as the Spanish-Pueblo Revival is a fascinating one, dating back a little over a century. It can be seen as essentially stemming from a desire for increased tourist revenue, but that appraisal demeans a set of qualities for which Santa Fe is justly renowned: a tradition based on a specific type of earthen architecture, one that today really does reflect on the three cultures for which Santa Fe is famous.

The first was the puddled-adobe dwelling of the pre-historic Pueblo Indian. The term "puddled adobe" describes an ancient and effective process of making walls by adding, and letting dry, successive layers of mud. The Spanish came to this area in the mid-1500s and established the provincial capital La Villa Real de Santa Fe de San Francisco de Asís in 1610 or perhaps two or three years earlier. (Santa Fe is the oldest capital city in the United States, but St. Augustine is several decades older and Jamestown may be a year or two older.) (Santa Fe is also the highest capital city at 7,000 feet above sea level.)

Similar to the arrivals of other Europeans in other parts of the country, the coming of the Spanish explorers was not a joyous event for the people who had lived here for hundreds of years. There were of course battles, and atrocities committed by both conquistador and Indian, including during the

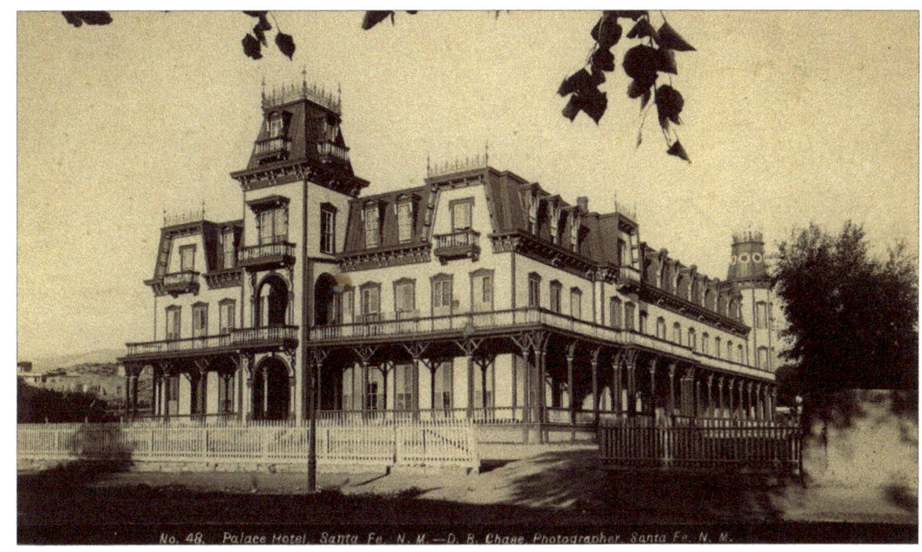


Palace Hotel, Santa Fe, N.M., by Dana B. Chase, circa 1888

Negative No. 56984 courtesy Palace of the Governors Photo Archives (NMHM/DCA)

1680 Pueblo Revolt. Not least was the effort to obliterate Native spiritual beliefs and practices in the name of "Christian" indoctrination. However, something that has rarely been mentioned in histories of the colonial period is that after the drastic early troubles, Spanish settlers and Native peoples coexisted on an arid frontier for centuries. Once the challenging nature of the landscape and climate was apparent, the newcomers must have welcomed every bit of technology and knowledge about wild plants and animals and agriculture and architecture that was known by the indigenous people.

The third culture, made up of what are today referred to as "Anglos" in Northern New Mexico, is the real newcomer. With a few significant exceptions, this second wave of Europeans — the non-Hispanic whites and people of color — arrived in a privileged set of circumstances: if the main influx of people can be tied to the arrival of the railroad in 1880, the West had already really been won, in truly hardscrabble form, by their predecessors. Now truly began the tourist trade. It was time for people to come and *partake* of Santa Fe. One famous example was the Fred Harvey Company's "Indian Detours" program. Travelers from other parts of the country and from around the world could step off the train at the Lamy Depot or exit La Fonda in Santa Fe to board large touring automobiles for day trips out to see the "exotic" landscape and visit Indian pueblos and archaeological sites.

In 1912, New Mexico was admitted to the United States of America, and Santa Fe's leaders decided to pay attention to heritage. Departing from the general American trend to modernism, Santa Fe, it was decided, should attract attention in virtually an opposite vein: by focusing on the sorts of things that visitors loved, including the old buildings that were characterized by soft lines and earth tones.

A vital re-examination was under way. A little more than three decades before, there had been great excitement about the coming of the railroad. But when the Atchison, Topeka & Santa Fe Railway bypassed the city, stopping nearest in Lamy, 15 miles south, the capital's dominant trade position at the crossroads of the old Camino Real and the Santa Fe Trail quickly faded. All the plans for a vibrant new residential district with a trolley operating between the rail yards and the Plaza withered. The people of Santa Fe managed to raise funds to pay for a spur line from Lamy, but the hoped-for surge in population and business did not quickly follow. Museum of New Mexico founder Edgar Lee Hewett and other local leaders hatched a plan to tap into tourist interest in the town's historic character, its plaza-centered downtown, and its narrow, twisting lanes lined with adobe homes.

### New-Old Santa Fe exhibition

Soon came a new push to preserve those old buildings and to model new ones after the vintage Spanish-Pueblo homes. This revival style would be tailored to Santa Fe. The museum's Jesse Nusbaum canvassed the town, taking pictures of the older houses. His photos were a featured attraction in *New-Old Santa Fe*, an exhibition that opened at the Palace of the Governors on Nov. 18, 1912. The city, according to a flyer for the show, would become the "tourist center of the Southwest."

The *Santa Fe New Mexican* waxed still more optimistic, with a reference to the January admission of New Mexico to the Union: "The Old, New idea of planning for the future of the oldest and the newest city on the soil over which floats the stars and stripes will be pictured tonight," proclaimed a story on the newspaper's front page that day. It added that "all those who have ideas as to the future of what is destined to be the great tourist city of the Americas are asked to visit the assembly room and there discuss this interesting and important subject. The plans proposed for the beautification of Santa Fe are to be exhibited ... accompanied by maps, by plaster of paris models, by wash drawings, and by photographs showing scenes in and about the ancient city that will astonish many lifelong residents ot Santa Fe."

In a 1912 report, the city's Planning Board wrote that "the attraction of Santa Fe can best be preserved and increased by developing the town architecturally in harmony with its ancient character." The *New-Old Santa Fe* exhibition was mounted to advance what the board termed the "Santa Fe style," and also to promote tourism.

The other result of this work by the city's leaders was the positing of a building form based on a synthesis of architectural details seen in many of Nusbaum's photographs of the old houses. The idea was for a long, low profile with flat roof, earth-colored adobe walls, a recessed *portal*, the roof drains known as *canales*, and *vigas* projecting through the front wall. Sylvanus Morley, who supervised the exhibition, stressed that Santa Fe's design idea should avoid too much similarity with California's Mission Revival style.

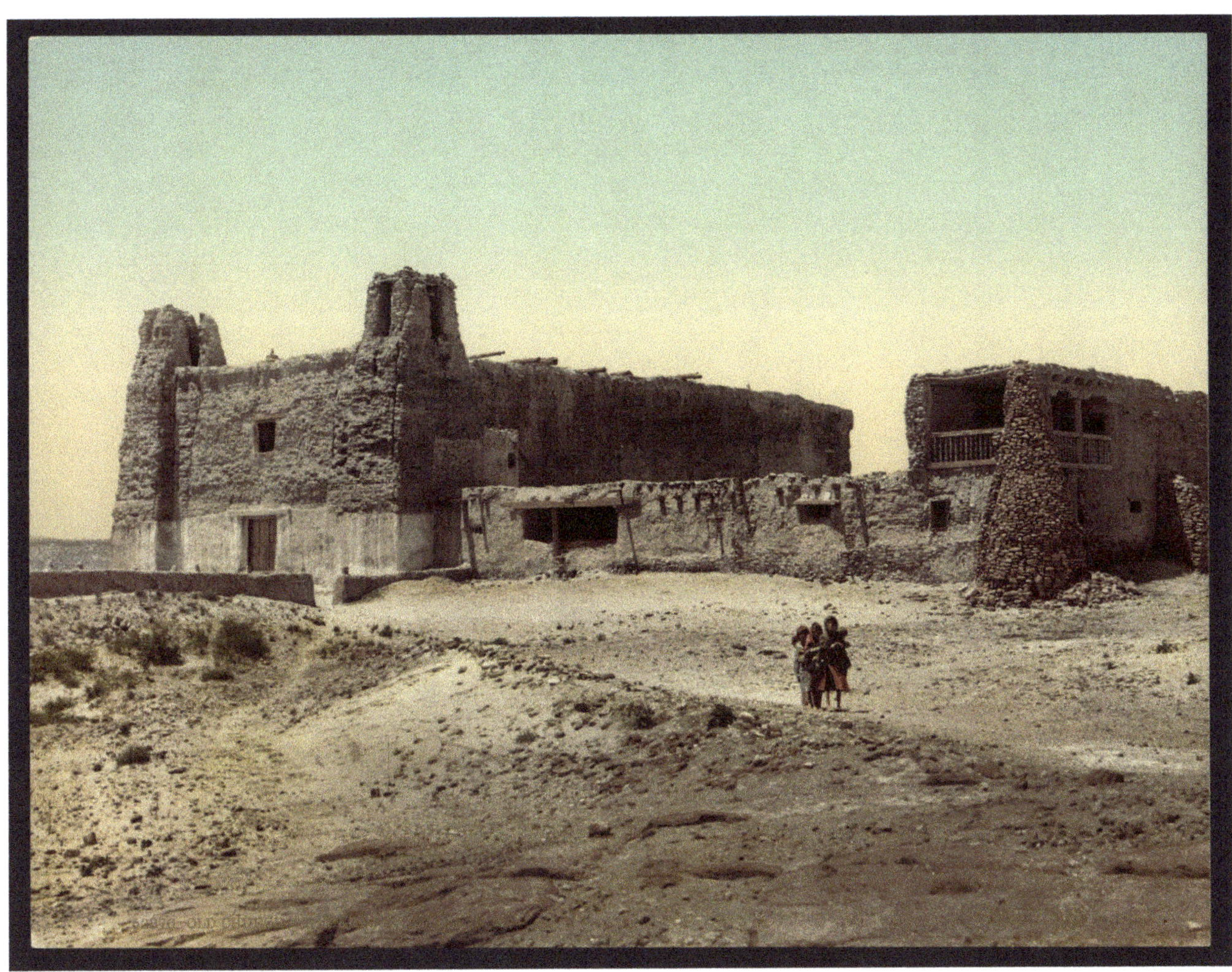

Old church [San Esteban del Rey] at Pueblo of Acoma, 1902, copyright Detroit Photographic Co.

Courtesy Library of Congress

Conron and Christopher have the Spanish-Pueblo Revival style first expressed in 1905-1907 at the University of New Mexico (the Central Heating Plant and two dormitories, Kwataka Hall and Hokona Hall, all designed by E.B. Cristy under president William G. Tight) in Albuquerque. One of the first obvious examples of the new style in Santa Fe was Nusbaum's 1909-1913 remodel of the Palace of the Governors. Under his direction, the classical balustrade along the front edge of the *portal* — a 19th-century conceit — was taken off and replaced by *vigas* projecting through a new, high parapet; and the porch support system was traded out for heftier posts and *zapatas*.

**MANY OF THE NOW-RENOWNED ARTISTS** who came to Santa Fe in the early 20th century (often for tuberculosis treatment at Sunmount Sanitarium) loved the old buildings. The houses with their sensuous lines and earthy adobe colors that blended with those in the arid plateaus and mesas of the surrounding landscape were popular subjects for painters. One of the first was

Carlos Vierra, who thought Santa Fe's simple adobe homes were rapidly yielding ground to bungalows and other modern styles and who helped persuade city officials to foster a revival of the traditional Spanish-Pueblo style. He aided Nusbaum in the restoration of the Old Palace and, by the end of that decade, Vierra and architect Trent Thomas were finishing the artist's own adobe house (at the corner of today's Old Pecos Trail and Coronado Road).

In 1915, portions of the *New-Old Santa Fe* exhibit were featured in the sprawling Panama-California Exposition staged in the city of San Diego, Calif. The exposition's director-general, D.C. Collier, hired Hewett as its director of ethnology and curator of Southwestern exhibits. The architectural firm Rapp, Rapp & Hendrickson designed the expo's New Mexico Building primarily based on the early-17th-century mission church San Esteban del Rey at Acoma Pueblo, 60 miles west of Albuquerque. This borrowing from historic forms was repeated immediately after the exposition in the primary (Palace Avenue) facade of the Rapp firm's design for the Museum of Fine Arts in Santa Fe. The building's masterful conglomeration of forms also echoes the Laguna Pueblo church on its Lincoln Avenue facade.

The downtown museum, along with the Gross Kelly Warehouse completed several years earlier in the railroad yards, offered a major kick-start for the city's newly christened architectural style. It would be cemented during the next decade or so with the construction of La Fonda, the new U.S. Post Office (now the Museum of Contemporary Native Arts), Connor Hall at the New Mexico School for the Deaf, and the Laboratory of Anthropology, as well as significant residences such as the Spitz Gardesky House, the Fenyes Curtin Paloheimo House, Martha and Amelia Elizabeth White's El Delirio (now the School for Advanced Research administration building), and the Laboratory of Anthropology director's residence. (*All of these buildings survive, and are included in the second section of this book.*)

The beauty of Santa Fe's new museum silenced most of the critics of the now vaunted Spanish-Pueblo revival. The Rapp edifice "brought home even to the most obtuse a realization that Santa Fe had an American architecture and an American art," according to Twitchell. He added that the style was evidenced in a number of lovely new houses, "notwithstanding the opposition of local contractors and builders who, for purely selfish purposes, endeavored to bring to Santa Fe the modified Hindu bungalow, so popular in southern California."

In January 1917, when the School for the Deaf and Museum of Fine Arts were being completed, Vierra wrote in *El Palacio* about "Our Native Architecture in its Relation to Santa Fe." He described the School design as "expressing our strong tendency toward formality" but of the Museum "expressing as much of the freedom of line and informality of the original as modern material and methods have so far been able to allow. It is hard for workmen whose training has held them down to accuracy and rigid mathematical lines to accept the freedom of what might be described as a free-hand architecture."

The casual appearance of early owner-built adobe houses was gospel to some 20th-century homebuilders in Santa Fe. Betty Stewart reportedly forbade her workmen from employing plumb bobs and chalk lines. And in their wonderful little *Adobe Notes* volume, Kate Chapman and Dorothy Stewart wrote, "The uneven or hand-made surface of indoor walls, so much admired, is best produced as the old-timers produced it — by the use of a smallish, primitive trowel, wielded by a not-too-expert hand, with entire lack of a mechanical guide. Even the most accomplished workman, thus equipped, will be unable to plaster with too great a degree of regularity."

Another common feature of the early homes — and one that was gloriously mimicked by architect John Gaw Meem and has been a part of the vocabulary of many Santa Fe Style homebuilders ever since — is the *portal*: simply a long, covered porch (but in Santa Fe most often held up by substantial beams on corbels and *zapatas* atop substantial wood posts.) *Portales* afforded shady places for relaxing — and, in front of business blocks, for merchants and their customers to stroll and visit with sheltering protection from sun, rain, and snow.

Chapman and Stewart explain, "Whether a house is of the earliest and most primitive, the middle, or the latest and most sophisticated period, there is a general rule that was never broken, and that contributes to the restfulness of the Santa Fe 'effect': the *portal* is either inset, with rooms on three sides of it, or it must cover the entire length of the house, or the length and one side, or the two sides of an L, or the four sides of a patio; but it is never tacked on the house around the front door, like a porch or stoop."

Vierra, who moved to Santa Fe in 1904, was passionate about his adopted city's distinctive architectural fabric, and he was nervous about its preservation. In a 1926 paper for the School of American Archaeology, he wrote that Santa Fe had already suffered an "immeasurable" loss. "Nothing will push Santa Fé off the map, to lie protestingly among the forgotten places, so quickly or so easily as the majestic mansion, the modern cottage, the 'cute' bungalow (should be spelled bungle-o in Santa Fé) or the old adobe with the new razorback roof [probably a reference to the pitched roof with gables], if we persist in building them until they strangle our own architecture and individuality."

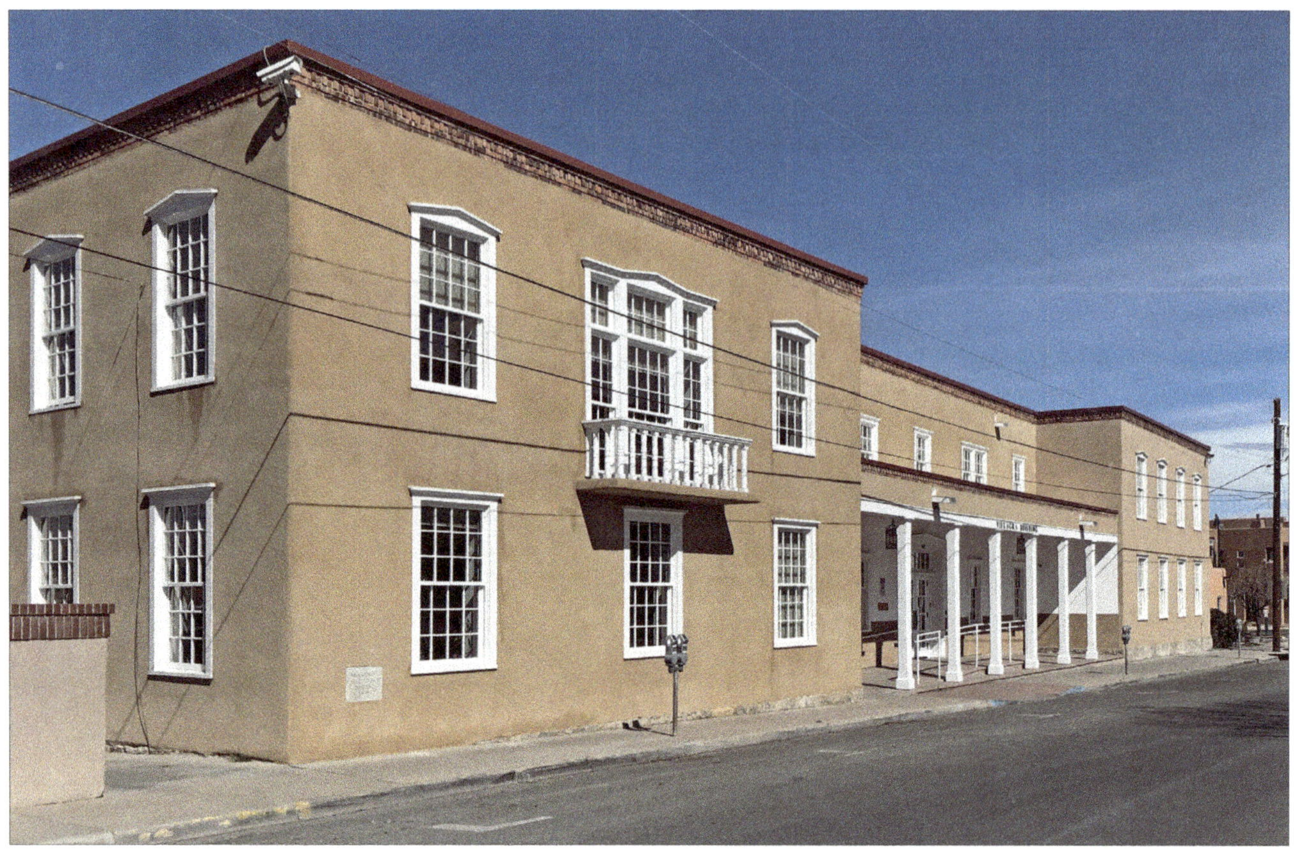

The 1934 Villagra Building, designed by John Gaw Meem: a splendid example of the Territorial Revival style

**The Territorial Revival style**

The other building type that traditionally has qualified as "Santa Fe Style" is Territorial Revival. Such buildings retain the "adobe" look of the flat roof and earth-toned walls, but modify it with sharper corners; white-painted window and door frames, pedimented lintels, and *portales;* and brick coping along the roofline — often with the bricks in one row alternately set inward and outward to simulate the decorative dentil course of a classical cornice.

Meem began to recall 19th-century Territorial detailing in his 1928 Manderfield School. At that time, according to David Kammer, who wrote an extensive survey of Meem's work for a 2002 National Register of Historic Places nomination, "some clients, particularly those seeking residences conveying both a regional flavor yet a more formal appearance than they felt the Spanish-Pueblo Revival style offered, began to favor the Territorial Revival style."

It is thought that Meem finalized the style with a pair of 1932 commissions: La Quinta at Los Poblanos in the Río Grande Valley near Albuquerque, and the Federal Emergency Recovery Act Building (now known as the Villagra Building) in Santa Fe.

*"The outstanding quality of the Architecture of this region is simplicity. The earth, poor or rich, makes the walls, the forest trees the ceilings; so that the house of the Pueblo and the house of the Millionaire are not so very different. It is the only place in the world where this is so."*

**— Kate Chapman and Dorothy N. Stewart in their 1930 book 'Adobe Notes or How To Keep the Weather Out With Just Plain Mud'**

*"What's really neat is that form follows function. See that hand-scorped lintel over a window? Well, it holds up the wall above. And those vigas that have been stripped of bark are holding up the roof. It's not phony; it's real, and it takes a lot of skill to do."*

**— Santa Fe homebuilder Sharon Woods**

# Chapter 2
# ABOUT MATERIALS

**BY THE 500s AND 600s,** the Ancestral Puebloan people in this area began changing from a primarily hunter-gatherer lifestyle to a more settled existence. They built pit houses, partly excavated dwellings with walls of mud and sticks and boughs of chamisa, juniper, piñon, and similar material. By the 13th century, at pueblos such as Ogapogeh, Pindi, Agua Fria Schoolhouse, and Arroyo Hondo, Native people typically lived in villages. The settlements consisted of clusters of roomblocks up to three stories tall, built around plazas and made using the puddled-adobe technique, sometimes incorporating stone.

"When Spaniards came to New Mexico they found sedentary Indians living in communal buildings several stories high with underground ceremonial rooms," E. Boyd wrote in the journal *El Palacio* in 1973. "These were sometimes of undressed ledge stone and pebbles, but where soil conditions were suitable they were made of mud laid up in courses, or of hand-shaped turtlebacks (mud patted into loaves)." Footings for walls were adobe, river cobbles, or andesite slabs. The walls themselves were sometimes made of flat stone, where it was available, but most were coursed adobe; here the homebuilder added globs or basketfuls of mud along the extent of the wall, smoothing it out top and sides before it dried. The base course of such dwellings was 9 to 13 inches thick and 15 to 24 inches high, according to Winifred Creamer's *The Architecture of Arroyo Hondo Pueblo.* After the mud dried, another course of slightly smaller dimensions was added on top. Four or five courses were laid before roofing.

Rooms ranged from about 45 square feet to 115 square feet, with an average dimension of about 8 by 10 feet. The roof *vigas* (debarked logs of native ponderosa pine) were set across the shorter dimension. On top of those were laid pole or plank *latillas.* When poles were used, the builder added layers of brush — which could include reeds, grass, leaves, juniper bark, corn stalks, cholla, and pine or piñon branches — on the latillas, then a thick layer of waterproofing, insulating clay (the *torta*) on top. If plank *latillas* were used, the clay could be smoothed right on top.

Residents made small excavations in their packed-earth floors. Some were hearths used for cooking, heat, and light. Others were cists used to mix adobe, process grain, and for storage. In archaeologists' explorations of 700-year-old ruins in the Santa Fe area, it was not too uncommon to find evidence of handsomely plastered walls, plank shelving, wall niches, and hanging pegs.

Although there is evidence that the American Indians were already using form-molded adobe bricks in some places as early as the 1300s, the conventional wisdom is that New Mexico's adobe-brick construction harkens to Spain, where it was introduced by the Moors (medieval Islamic Arabs), who invaded the Iberian Peninsula in 711. Some of the earthen structures that were found by the Spanish when they adventured into the northern frontier of New Spain (today the state of New Mexico) in the 16th century were on a grander scale than what they left in Iberia. The Franciscan missionaries soon set about building dozens of monumental adobe churches; one imposing example that remains is San Esteban del Rey at Acoma Pueblo (100 miles southwest of Santa Fe), which was built between 1629 and 1642.

To make adobe bricks, the local soil, which often has a high percentage of clay, is mixed with sand for the ideal material: too much clay and the bricks crack, too much sand and they crumble. Chopped straw is added to help the bricks dry evenly. Mixed with water, the earth mixture is shoveled into wooden forms on the ground. The forms are removed and the bricks dry for several days, then they are turned onto their sides and allowed to dry completely over at least 10 days.

The typical adobe brick today is 4 by 10 by 14 inches, according to Cornerstones Community Partnerships' excellent *Adobe Conservation Handbook*, from which much of the detailed information in this chapter was gleaned. In former times, adobes could be closer to two feet long, although 14 inches is plenty heavy when you're hefting one after another to build a wall. (The author first had a taste of this experience in 2000, helping, with his wife, to build an adobe house as part of a Santa Fe Habitat for Humanity "First Ladies Build" project.)

"Two bricks of the old size laid end to end across a wall with mud mortar made a wall four feet thick," E. Boyd wrote. "Spanish adobe walls found in early historic sites are easily distinguished from those built by the Indians, even when they are side by side, by the greater width of Spanish walls, the presence of molded bricks and, often, of river cobble foundations."

Smaller buildings for storage or to shelter animals were sometimes made using another ancient technique: mud and/or manure applied on posts and sticks, which was termed *jacál* in New Mexico but is known as wattle-and-daub elsewhere in the world. Another construction method was *terrón*, in which the builder built up walls with blocks of grassy sod cut from floodplains.

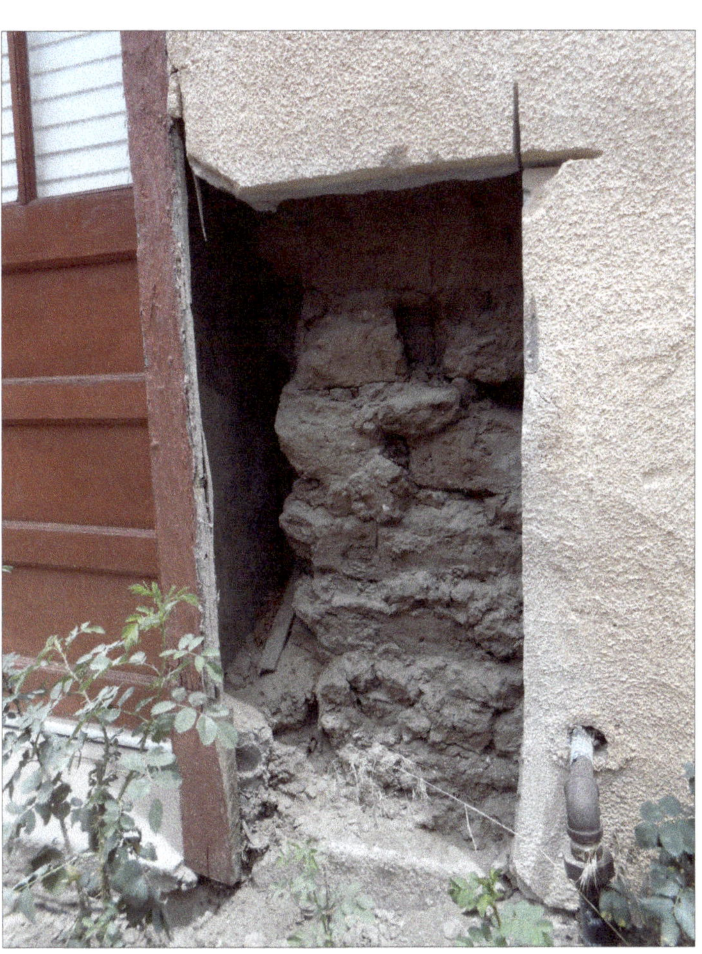

Water-eroded adobes revealed after cutting away a section of cementitious stucco during 2016 restoration work on the Garcia House on Alto Street

SPANISH SETTLERS built adobe walls with mud mortar, the bricks laid to alternate the joints. They set down three or four courses during a work day, then allowed it to dry for a few days before continuing with another few courses. Mud plaster was applied to finished walls in several layers totaling up to three inches thick. The builders added finely chopped straw to the mud for the final coat; applied by the *enjarradora* primarily with horizontal strokes, the straw pieces helped break up the flow of rainwater and prevented channeling and erosion. Mud plaster must be patched every year or two, and the whole building should be re-mudded every five to 15 years, depending on the regularity of maintenance. In a June 2016 interview, Cornerstones director Jake Barrow talked about mud-plastering maintenance at San Miguel Chapel. "We know we have to revisit those parapets once a year, and we do. How much labor is that? Two

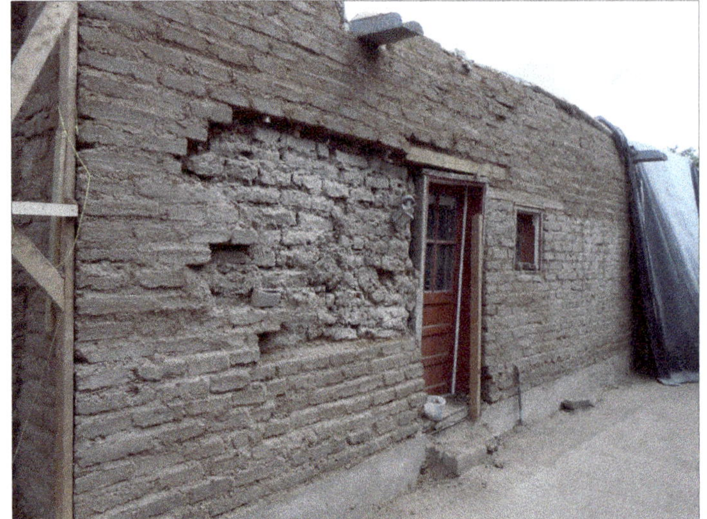

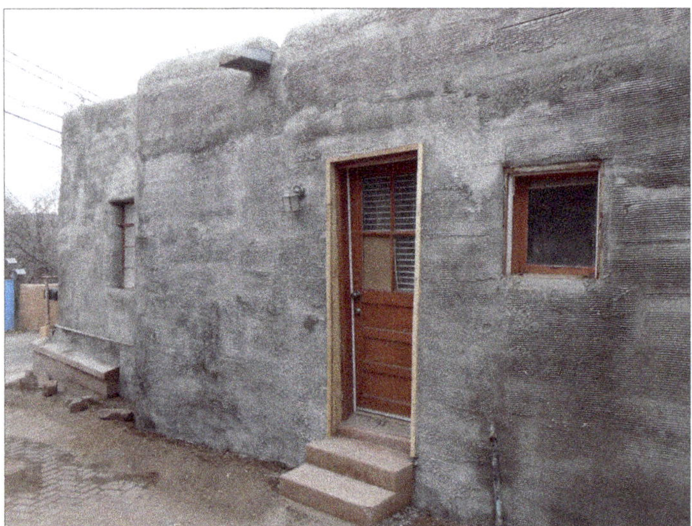

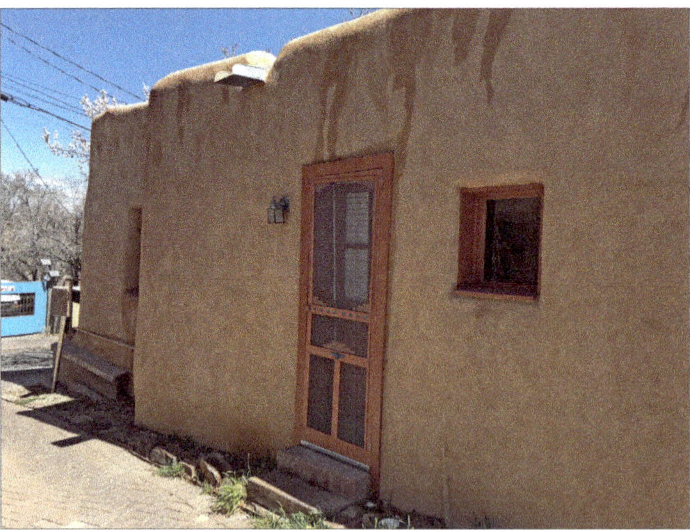

or three people for a day. And every now and then you have a little problem, like some erosion at the base, and you have to work for an hour or two on that.

"We do testing, for example we have a test wall we're working on with the National Park Service at Pecos National Historical Park. Our theory is if you do this right, you can get some longevity out of these mud plasters. It's easy to do and easy to learn, but it's also easy to do it poorly."

For plastering maintenance at San Miguel, Cornerstones uses a light-colored clay from a site in Pojoaque, about 15 miles to the north. The material is not just sitting there, waiting to be shoveled into a pickup truck. It comes from a rocklike material that must be harvested by the organization's volunteers using muscle, sweat, and mattock.

The clay chunks are crushed to powder, then the material is hydrated in a Walker pug mill and finally mixed at the ratio of two parts clay to five parts concrete sand. The fine material from this particular site is reserved for mud-plastering at San Miguel.

In her journal, Charlotte White detailed the plastering work in her rehab of the old Donaciano Vigil House on Alto Street. In the spring of 1961, she had two women from Cañones mud-plastering exterior walls.

The west wall of the historic Garcia House is shown in the middle of adobe-rebuilding work (top), when adobe work was finished and covered with the first ("scratch") coat of stucco (center), and complete — the water marks along the top are from melting snow on the parapet

For the final coat, they used fine-sifted earth added to tortilla-flour paste. "It fits in all the cracks and looks gorgeous," White wrote.

While the primary color of adobe buildings always was in the range of earthy browns, residents found many ways to augment that tonal set. A subtly glimmering finish was sometimes obtained through the use of micaceous clay. Interior adobe walls, and outside walls underneath *portales*, historically were finished with a gypsum whitewash known as *jaspe* or with calcimine paint made from pigmented lime. Alternatively, people used a thin clay wash colored with *tierra amarilla*, *tierra azul*, *tierra bayita*, *tierra colorada*, or *tierra blanca*, earth colors available on the New Mexico landscape.

In one of his columns for the *Santa Fe New Mexican*, historian Marc Simmons recalled Amado Cháves, who was born on the New Mexico frontier in 1851 and became the territory's first superintendent of public instruction and a mayor of Santa Fe. In a 1927 letter, Chavés recalled that "interior walls in old houses had all been covered with whitewash made from local gypsum. That presented a problem since those who brushed the wall came away with white smudges on their clothes. To remedy that, a band of tierra amarilla was painted on the lower part of the wall. This was a yellow clay with mica flakes that provided a permanent surface. The town of Tierra Amarilla near Chama took its name from a nearby deposit of this clay."

Another way that people solved the *jaspe*-smudging problem was to tack several feet of cretonne, calico, or red-cotton cloth around the lower part of the walls. Besides the practical value, this created a colorful wainscoting effect.

*Tierra amarilla* must have carried a degree of cachet, since its appearance was sometimes copied simply through the use of yellow paint. One instance shows up in a 1934 Historic American Buildings Survey of the Palace of the Governors; the participating architects (who made wonderfully accurate measurements and drawings) noted a fireplace surround "painted with Yellow Ochre Water Paint in Imitation of Tierra Amarilla as found in the Old Buildings."

Another example is El Zaguan on Canyon Road. In the mid-2000s, the Historic Santa Fe Foundation removed the various layers of finishes from the *zaguan*, in order to restore an earthen finish, and discovered a bright yellow calcimine paint had been applied — probably during Margretta Dietrich's ownership between 1928 and 1961 — to mimic the building's traditional *tierra amarilla* wainscot.

**A SLIGHTLY MORE MODERN** wall finish than finely mixed local mud is lime plaster, which has been used in Northern New Mexico since the mid-1800s. "As far as I've been able to determine, lime technology didn't make it to

Northern New Mexico until the U.S. Army arrived," said Alan "Mac" Watson, a Santa Fe conservation professional, in a March 2016 email exchange. "I think that the first lime kiln in New Mexico was built at Fort Union. The first one was built of adobe to make the bricks for the second one."

One of the advantageous traits of lime is that it is self-healing: small cracks soon disappear when moisture dissolves the newly exposed "free lime," and that tends to seal the cracks upon drying.

The community of Lamy had a kiln for firing limestone to produce quicklime, which was then slaked in water for months, or perhaps years — the longer the slaking, the better the quality of the material. Lamy lime was used to produce the moldings and archivolts for the Cathedral of St. Francis of Assisi and Loretto Chapel, the wall plaster at Loretto, and the mortar to set the quoins and ashlars at the cathedral, according to adobe conservation expert Ed Crocker.

Santa Feans during colonial times likely had a closer source of lime. In 2011, Museum of New Mexico archaeologists discovered a Spanish Colonial slaking pit between the cathedral and Marian Hall, about 750 feet east of the Plaza. Watson believes that quicklime for the cathedral was brought in from the Lamy lime works — built by French masons Monier and Coulloudon — and slaked on site. "The amount of mortar and plaster would require a lot of slaked lime in putty form," Watson said, "and it is common elsewhere — in colonial Mexican churches — for there to be a slaking pit behind the church where slaked lime putty could be kept for years, waiting for use to repair plaster and to re-point masonry."

In *Adobe Notes*, Chapman and Stewart wrote, "This house [here the booklet offers a small linoprint of a simple adobe building] was plastered in the eighties, with a thick coat of old style, slow-to-set lime, which had probably been slaking in a pit for a year. There is a brick coping at the top which keeps water from running between the adobe and the lime. It had only just begun to peel off around the canales in 1924, in which year the canales were made waterproof and the plaster patched. One doesn't mind patching after forty years."

The details of a recent lime-plastering job point to the challenges of maintaining old adobe buildings. This involves El Zaguan, which is owned by the Historic Santa Fe Foundation. In early 2014, HSFF restoration specialists Charles Coffman and Bobby Wilson compared the ground along the 150-foot wall facing on Canyon Road to a century-old photograph and realized the surface is more than two feet higher than it was — one result was that water was virtually being pushed into the adobe wall by hydrostatic pressure.

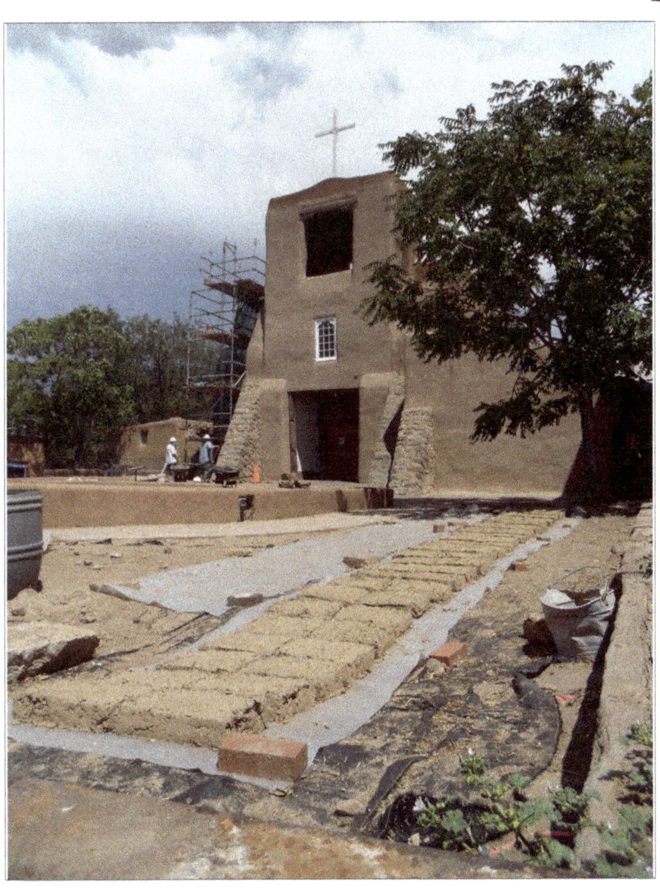

Sun-drying adobe bricks for repairs to San Miguel Chapel. The bricks are for the building's walls; the buttresses visible on either side of the entrance are made of stone

Coffman and Wilson hand-dug a trench all along the wall and installed a rubber waterproofing material. They also removed about four layers of old paint (including a hideous pink epoxy) and replaced wood trim pieces at the tops of the windows. The existing trim was actually helping water get into the walls. They put in new trim that flanges up at the rear, then metal lath to anchor plaster patches in advance of replastering the entire wall. In work on the adobe buildings it owns, the foundation has wanted to use natural, traditional finishes, but these are sometimes problematic because water can soak up from the ground and degrade them. Nevertheless, HSFF planned to use mud plaster such as El Zaguan would have had originally — at least two centuries ago.

That plan changed after 2007 rehabilitation work on the front facade. When cement stucco was removed, the crew uncovered a *rajuelar* system — small pieces of rock inserted into the mortared joints that help bind lime plaster to an adobe wall. With that discovery, the foundation decided to finish the job with lime. The new coat of lime plaster was applied in July 2015. Visitors can see the old adobe bricks and the mortar with *rajuelar* stones in a small "truth window" near the north end of the El Zaguan street wall.

Some *adoberos* go to the length of adding mucilage from prickly pear or cholla cactus to improve the adhesive and water-repelling characteristics of lime plaster. Jake Barrow, program director for Cornerstones Community Partnerships, said that technique is "still very common in the south, particularly in Mexico. It's never been that common up this way."

So, from prehistoric times and through the colonial and Mexican periods, Indians and Spanish settlers used the local earth to construct buildings. Adobe was also quickly used by the next settlers, the Americans.

In 1846, Lt. J.F. Gilmer had an adobe-and-timber "star fort" built by 100 Army laborers and 20 local masons at Fort Marcy. But a shift from adobe to brick buildings — hastened by the 1880 arrival of the Atchison, Topeka & Santa Fe Railroad and its infusion of people, ideas, and building materials from the eastern United States — occurred most rapidly among the newcomers, the Anglos.

Sister Blandina Segale, an Italian-born nun who grew up in Cincinnati, arrived in Santa Fe in mid-September 1865 and described the accommodations: "Imagine the surprise of persons coming from places where houses are built with every convenience and sanitary devices, suddenly to find themselves introduced into several oblong walls of adobes, looking like piled brick ready to burn, to enter which, instead of stepping up, you step down onto a mud floor; rafters supporting roof made of trunks of trees, the roof itself of earth which they were told had to be carefully attended, else the rain would pour in ..."

Another viewpoint on the accommodations, from some decades later, was recounted by Richard Bradford in John Pen La Farge's book *Turn Left at the Sleeping Dog: Scripting the Santa Fe Legend, 1920-1955*. "The houses that I knew were from the nineteenth century," Bradford wrote, recalling his earliest visits to the town in the 1930s. "They were low-ceilinged, they were thick-walled, and they were badly wired and badly plumbed, and I just loved them. The new ones are not particularly Santa Fe-ish because the real Santa Fe house isn't designed by an architect. It's designed by the man who builds it. He builds one room at a time, as he needs it, so they have an informal, rambling, unplanned quality. That's what makes them Santa Fe houses — they're built by amateurs."

Now about those roofs. The historic roof used on dwellings during colonial times was flat, incorporating a thick layer of compacted earth (the *torta*) laid on willow saplings, yucca, cattail, or chamisa brush on top of juniper *latillas* or *rajas* set crosswise, diagonally, or in a herringbone pattern (sometimes painted in bright colors) over pine or spruce *vigas*. This fairly weatherproof "sandwich" of local materials was adapted from the roofs that Native peoples historically used on their homes.

Such an "adobe roof" with up to 18 inches of earth provided excellent insulation, and its weight stabilized adobe walls — up to a point. Perennial additions of fresh earth could ultimately result in a weight that brought down the building. This is one more reason to value historic adobes: they're survivors!

"When a roof begins to leak," W.W.H. Davis wrote in 1857, "it is repaired by putting a few sacks of dirt upon it; and after a heavy dash of rain, it is usual to see every family upon the roof giving it a thorough examination and carrying up fresh earth to mend the breaches."

Earthen roofs also had the bad habit of leaking dirt. This was sometimes controlled by the addition of a *manta*, a cloth "drop ceiling" stretched and attached to the vigas. When painted with lime, the cloth shrank and became firm, taking on the appearance of a plastered ceiling.

By 1900 or so, people had access to catalogs from which they could order stamped-tin panels to create handsome drop ceilings; one of these is a treasured feature of the historic Our Lady of Light Catholic Church in Lamy.

Sawn lumber was not available until the 19th century, shipped in on the Santa Fe Trail or produced at local sawmills; the first was built in 1847 by the U.S. Army at what is now the Randall Davey House at the end of Upper Canyon Road. Milled lumber was brought in larger quantites by train after 1880. Wood planks sometimes replaced the *latillas* in roofs, and were also employed for floors instead of the traditional dirt floors sealed with ox blood and covered with a length of the ruglike *jerga* material.

Metal roofing sheets brought from the East over the Santa Fe Trail and then the railroad allowed people to erect a lower-maintenance pitched roof; these were often simply added over the existing flat *torta* roof. This convention of adding gable and hip roofs, and often dormers, transformed the appearance of small towns and villages during the first half of the 20th century. Beverley Spears' wonderful 1986 book *American Adobes: Rural Houses of Northern New Mexico* offers a deep excursion into this realm.

THE ARRIVAL OF THE RAILROAD at the end of the 19th century meant not only a dramatic expansion of the "store" of building materials, but a substantial increase in the use of items prized for their convenience. One of these was Portland cement, which quickly displaced mud and lime plasters as the favored material to finish building exteriors.

The railroad also brought corrugated-tin roofing material; pressed-metal and cast-iron products; brick of various colors and sizes; factory-made wood products; metal items such as hinges, which took the place of wooden pintle hinges on doors, windows, and shutters; and greater quantities, and larger panes, of glass. The old, small windows that both Indians and Spanish had glazed with local selenite (sheets of translucent mica) began disappearing.

The manufacture of brick, which was used for wall-parapet coping on adobe houses and later as a wall material, did not begin until well into the American period, in the 1860s. During the previous few decades, limited quantities were imported on the large wagons traveling the Santa Fe Trail from Missouri. Kiln-fired brick figured into several of Santa Fe's grand building projects of the late 19th century. One was the elaborate 1882 St. Vincent Hospital. It was built by Sister Blandina — although she began the project as an industrial school to teach trades to local girls. "We have started our own brickyard," she wrote about the project in her 1932 book *At the End of the Santa Fe Trail.* "250,000 bricks will be burnt at the first firing. We have eight gentlemen pledged to send workingmen to wait on the bricklayers."

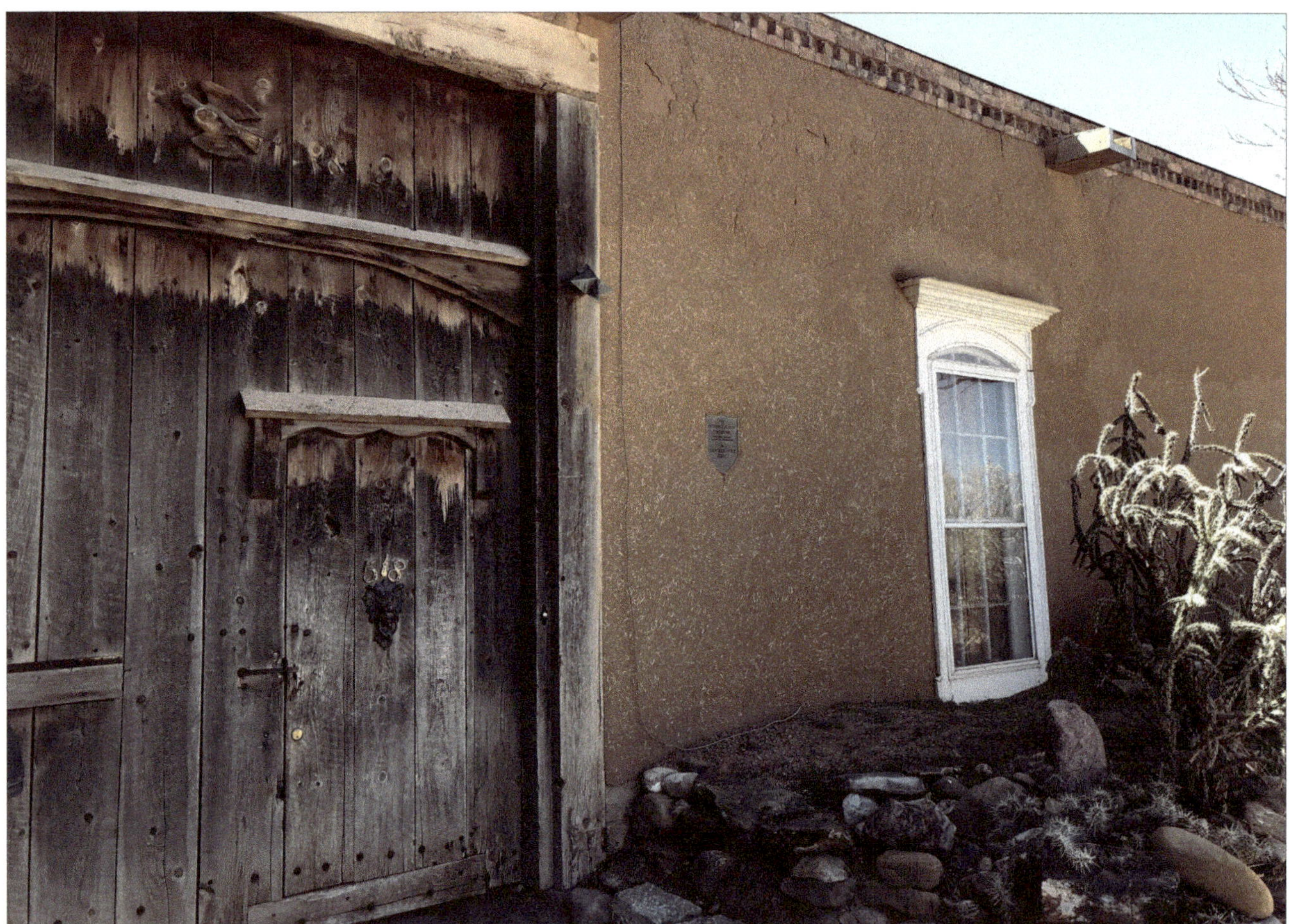

The Donaciano Vigil House. You can see a Mexican-style gate to the *zaguan* (and a walk-in door cut into the gate); a beautiful window salvaged from the old Loretto Academy; protective brick coping on the parapet; and, on the wall, genuine mud plaster that is unfortunately a rarity in Santa Fe today.

The traditional building material of Northern New Mexico was also part of the construction recipe for the New Mexico Territory's first hospital. "The intersecting interior walls are to be of adobe laid in mortar. This will make the school cool in summer and warm in winter," Sr. Blandina wrote in her journal. As the three-story building went up, with the help of architect Projectus Mouly (who was simultaneously at work on Loretto Chapel), the nun established both a quarry and a brick-making facility. Some lumber for the school was hand-sawn in Santa Fe, but she also made use of a sawmill in Glorieta and a planing mill in Las Vegas. Shortly after the railroad arrived in Santa Fe in 1880, Sr. Blandina took a train to St. Louis. She returned with roofing material and a workman to lay the slate on the building's mansard roof. "Our roof will be the first slate roof in the territory," she wrote.

Charlotte White and Boris Gilbertson incorporated a good quantity of brick in their early-1960s improvements to the Donaciano Vigil House. These bricks were obtained from the old territorial penitentiary; in her journals, White says that the pen began manufacturing red brick the year after its 1885 opening.

"Millions of Bricks to Build Up Santa Fe!" read an ad in the local paper on June 18, 1886. "No Experiment! No Burnt Adobes! No Convict Labor!" The company was Donoghue & Monier, Santa Fe.

In the mid- to late-19th century, some of the more progressive citizens and merchants dressed their pitched roofs in terne brought in on the Santa Fe Trail. "Preceding the manufacture of corrugated metal, flat sheets of metal roofing called terneplate were small enough to be carried on wagon trains over the Santa Fe Trail," historic preservation consultant Catherine Colby wrote in a 2013 report for the Historic Santa Fe Foundation. Several types of metal roofs have standing seams running down the roof faces, but the additional horizontal seams between the small sheets give terne roofs their distinctive look. Terne ("dull" in French) was composed of steel sheets dipped in a molten alloy of lead and tin.

The terne roof of the 1891 Felipe B. Delgado House on East Palace Avenue was likely installed by local tinner Alexander Irvine. A reporter for *The New Mexican* at the time witnessed the intense heat endured by Irvine in the midst of a roofing job at the west end of the Palace of the Governors and noted, "Such men are truly martyrs to progress."

Back in the day, glinting silver atop houses and commercial buildings was a mark of prestige. Metal roofs — durable and fireproof — were welcomed as "a solution to the age-old problem of the traditional flat earthen roof that leaked water and dust," Corinne P. Sze wrote in a piece for the Autumn 2002 Bulletin of the Historic Santa Fe Foundation, but then she added that, by the early decades of the 20th century, they were "banished as 'a hideous monstrosity of tin' by advocates of the historical 'Santa Fe style.'"

The Delgado roof lasted more than a century before being replaced in 2011 by its owner at the time, the Historic Santa Fe Foundation. The terne (no longer made with lead) was supplied by a venerable West Virginia company, Follansbee Steel. The horizontal seams were soldered, just as on the original roof, then the locking crimps for the standing seams were completed using a little robotlike machine that crawled up the roof on rollers. The job cost almost $140,000, but if it lasts anywhere near the 120 years of the original, it was money well-spent to honor the building's history.

**IN THE EARLY 20TH CENTURY**, concrete and cement became popular building materials. Cement-based plaster was seen as a low-maintenance alternative to mud and lime and was widely used. Brown cementitious stucco was sometimes applied in pebble-dash fashion, one surviving example being the Second Ward School. But although cement is widely available, easy to apply, and renowned for its permanance, it does not breathe and does not help to moderate temperatures and humidity inside the house as do natural plasters. Also, if water does find its way underneath, it is trapped there and tends to deteriorate the adobe bricks. Cement stucco does not adhere to adobe — rather than "marrying" with the structural earthen wall, it can lift off, exacerbating water-infiltration impacts.

Such degradation was seen in 2015 when the Historic Santa Fe Foundation moved to address concerns at its 19th-century Garcia House on Alto Street. As sheets of the inches-thick concrete stucco were carefully cut away, substantial voids were discovered where water had washed down — from a *canal*, in one dramatic instance — and eroded the adobe-brick wall structure. The very permanence for which the concrete was chosen also hid the extent of the malady beneath the stucco. For several months, contractor New Mexico Earthworks worked to cautiously remove the old stucco and then rebuild the walls with new adobe bricks and mud mortar before replastering.

In the early 20th century, inmates at the old state penitentiary, which was located just a mile southwest of the Plaza, manufactured a set of much-used building materials. They used locally quarried limestone and clays to produce bluish-black bricks of standard size; thick, 12 x 12 paving tiles; and hollow "pentile" blocks that have grooves on the outside surfaces that functioned as mechanical keys for mortar.

Santa Fe pentile goes back at least to 1915. Contractor Watson recently dug up a notice in *The New Mexican* from September 9 of that year that reads, "The new $10,000 building which [banker] Levi A. Hughes is erecting on Federal Street and Washington Avenue [for a U.S. Forest Service office] will prove to the people of the Southwest that hollow tile, as now manufactured at the state penitentiary, is the ideal building material for this country. This is the opinion of Mr. Hughes, who has just received some of the fist [sic] hollow tile turned out by the convicts. 'It will be more expensive than adobe but cheaper than brick,' said Mr. Hughes today, 'and it will cause the structure in which it is used to be cool in summer and warm in winter. The hollow chambers in the tile, filed [sic] with air, will provide the ideal wall for any type of building. I am convinced that hollow tile will become very popular.'"

Two days later, the newspaper had another report that positively establishes the timing of this material's production: "The first lot of the high-grade hollow tile manufactured at the penitentiary, which institution will make a specialty of tile making, was delivered to L.A. Hughes for use in his new Forestry building. It is said that these tiles lay into the wall at a less cost than either brick or adobe and beyond a doubt they make a better wall."

In modern times, walls made from the dense, brittle blocks are universally despised by builders working on remodeling projects. "It's murder to work with," contractor Richard Connerty wrote to me once. "Pan-tile, 'pentile' in the local vernacular due to its association with one of the penitentiary's industries, was invented over two and a half thousand years ago by the Roman builders. Its ribbing on the top and sides provides handy 'keying' for masonry and plastering, respectively."

Another example of the material's legacy of difficulty: an exterior wall must be covered with wire mesh before applying stucco, but pentile just bends the nailclips that are typically used. Larry Wilson, who owned the foam-insulation company TC&I, had to design a special glueclip to anchor the chicken wire when he was stuccoing old pentile houses. Nor is pentile the insulation wonder for which it was touted: just ask any resident of Santa Fe's South Capitol distict, where many of those homes tend only to keep folks cooler in the winter and warmer in the summertime.

There are actually hundreds of Santa Fe homes and larger buildings made of pentile (or similar, imported hollow-tile blocks). Members of the esteemed Bergere family used it to build a second story on their home on Grant Avenue (now the Georgia O'Keeffe Museum Research Center). The Lensic Performing Arts Center and the New Mexico School for the Arts (built as Santa Fe Builders Supply and operated until recently as Sanbusco Market Center) are also pentile. The New Mexico Museum of Art was constructed with 750,000 kiln-fired bricks produced at the state penitentiary, as well as steel and cement.

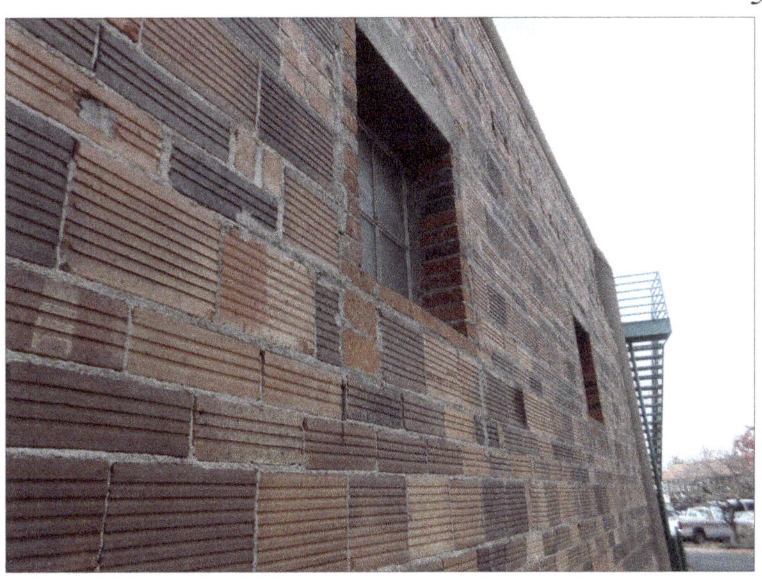

Unusual unstuccoed-pentile wall at the New Mexico School for the Arts

Below, pen pavers bordering a sidewalk on East Palace

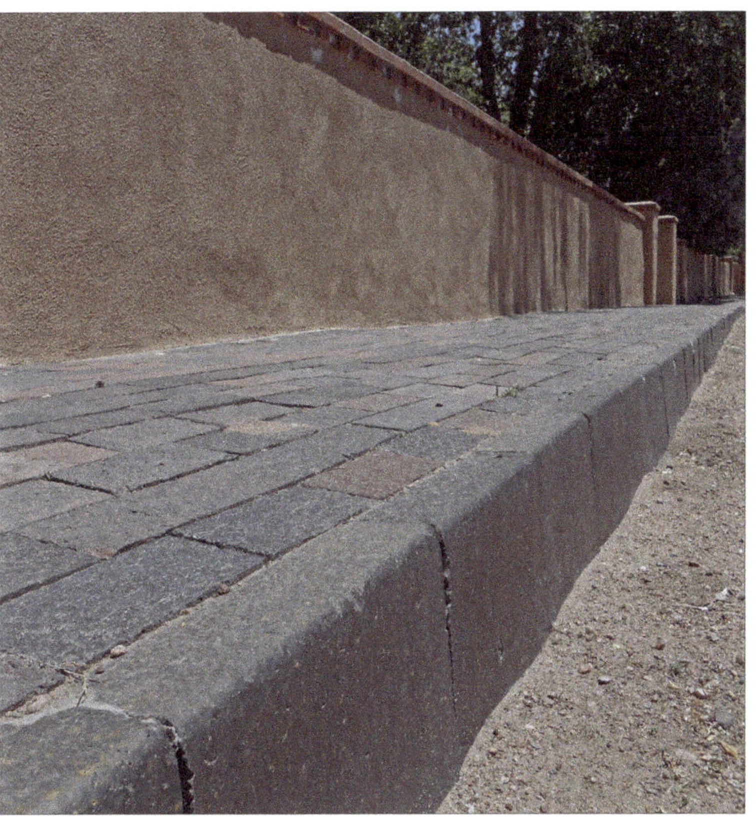

John Gaw Meem used pentile on the Laboratory of Anthropology, Manderfield School, Greer Garson's Forked Lightning Ranch house in Pecos, his own studio and early residence on Camino del Monte Sol, and many other projects.

Some of the 12 x 12 penitentiary tiles can be seen bordering sidewalk segments on East Palace Avenue. "Those are wonderful blocks," said Ed Crocker. "They were built to be curb tiles. Thirty-five years ago, when they tore up Palace Avenue for sewers, all the curbs were those: about four inches thick and fabulous in terms of mass. I'd go up every day and load up my truck. It is very heavy, but you can cut it with a diamond saw very easily."

Crocker is a principal of Crocker Ltd. Architectural Conservation, Santa Fe, a trustee of the International Council on Monuments and Sites, and a writer. He said the pen-produced tiles are a breeze to work with, but he had the opposite opinion of the hollow pentile blocks. "They're hideous, god-awful things. If you try to drive a nail in, it shatters; you have to drill holes to put an anchor in. It used to be that power [for heating homes] was cheap, but these have the worst insulative properties of anything on the planet. I hate them."

Concrete has been a common building material in Santa Fe for about a century. According to the city's 1997 Historic Building Inventory Manual: A Citizen's Guide to Conducting Architectural Survey in Santa Fe, reinforced concrete was used beginning in about 1920, concrete block was produced starting in 1945, and slump block — a concrete masonry unit having what can be described as "a slightly relaxed, Santa Fe Style, appearance" — since 1970.

ONE POSSIBLE OVERVIEW of this subject is that Santa Fe's architectural fabric consists of a range of building types:

• Historic adobe buildings with mud/lime plaster, such as the San Miguel Chapel and the Donaciano Vigil House;

• Historic adobe buildings with concrete stucco, examples being the Palace of the Governors and Nuestra Señora de Guadalupe;

• Historic non-adobe buildings like the Santa Fe Depot and the New Mexico Museum of Art;

• Non-historic but distinctive non-adobe buildings, such as the Santa Fe Opera theater and the Warehouse 21 teen center; and

• Thousands of ordinary non-historic, non-adobe, and perhaps non-distinctive buildings.

No one who loves Santa Fe architecture would deny the importance of preserving the valuable historic buildings — and their contexts, their streetscapes. But it is true that the real, traditional mud-plastered adobes today represent a very small minority in Santa Fe's fabric, even looking only at the historic district.

The late architect Jeff Harnar adored Santa Fe's historic architecture, loved contemporary design, and tried to blend them in ingenious ways. He had compelling ideas. A few years before he died, he suggested that it would have been very interesting if, instead of directing that everything in town should look like a Pueblo-style adobe, the 1957 Historic Styles Ordinance had mandated that all new buildings had to be made of adobe — honor the historic material, but allow the appearance of buildings to evolve in whatever (hopefully tasteful) directions the material allowed!

John Gaw Meem was an early champion of traditional design but using new, longer-lasting, more maintenance-free materials. Speaking at a Santa Fe meeting of the American Institute of Architects in 1953, he said the modern client had little patience with maintenance and added that that "demand has been met in various ways: by covering the adobe with earth-colored waterproof stucco, by chemically treating the adobe itself with bitumen or similar substances, or by using brick, tile and concrete shaped to resemble adobe."

Eleven years later, Meem was interviewed by Sylvia Loomis as part of the New Deal and the Arts project for the Smithsonian Institution's Archives of American Art. He noted that when he arrived in Santa Fe in 1920, the Museum of Fine Art (now the New Mexico Museum of Art) on the Plaza was just three years old. And that beautiful Santa Fe Style building, made of bricks from the state pen, "established a precedent for doing building similar to adobe building in a permanent material — masonry and stucco...

"In those early days, when we first started, the effort was to make these buildings as closely imitative as possible of the [Pueblo Indian and Spanish-Pueblo] prototypes. But then as time went on... I became very conscious of the fact that there was a possibility of expressing these forms in a way that wasn't completely imitative yet would suggest the architecture and would blend in with our architecture rather than be exactly like it...

"The question has come up whether it's legitimate to use shapes that recall something else," Meem said. "That comes up in connection with whether it is right to cover a real adobe building with stucco because with stucco — especially when you color it — is no longer adobe. And yet if you don't do that you would have lost the Palace of the Governors."

The house Meem designed for Bishop Everett Jones in 1951 is architecturally modest, and elegant, and it incorporates some of the architect's favorite details. Among those are the beautiful carved beams and corbels at the living-room junctions with the dining room and with a three-sided sunroom or bay window, and, on the exterior, a few battered walls that accentuate the appearance of solidity. His mantel for the living-room fireplace — a rope-carved wood feature that is attached to the wall but seems to float above the firebox — is a marvelous blend of the traditional and the contemporary.

The Jones House also is an example of Meem's belief that modern, long-lasting materials could be employed to perfect effect in continuing the "adobe-look" appearance of the Spanish-Pueblo Revival style. "Yes, I think there was clear recognition that contemporary, affordable materials should be used," his daughter, Nancy Meem Wirth, said in a 2013 interview. "He was really turned on by that idea, that it wasn't going backward, but forward, still respecting the vernacular and the historic by battering those walls."

AS THE TREND of using more permanent materials became standard, another realm in the building trades evolved: insulation, employed for increased comfort and to reduce heating and cooling expenses. In the 1970s, foam (both rigid polystyrene panels and sprayed polyurethane) began to be widely used as an alternative to glass wool. One example comes from the New Mexico School for the Deaf, where architect Kenneth Clark headed a $4.3 million campus renovation in 1978. Apparently this included addressing the rotted, original wood windows on Cartwright Hall and Connor Hall, and improving the thermal characteristics of campus buildings.

"A new process was used to insulate the buildings," said an article in the September 1978 issue of the school magazine, *New Mexico Progress*. "They were encased in styrofoam insulation, and a new coat of stucco was applied over it." The modernization, which addressed fire-code issues, was done without compromising the "traditional Santa Fe/Southwest charm."

Today, foam is widely used to insulate Santa Fe Style houses across the price spectrum. Homewise, Inc., uses both rigid foam panels and blown-in cellulose in the walls of its affordable homes. And the builders of multi-million-dollar adobe homes spray a thick layer of foam onto the exterior walls before applying stucco.

Expressions of craftsmanship are exhibited in many of the old Santa Fe houses — even those dating to colonial times, when this area was a frontier and there must have been precious little time to devote to anything artistic. (Then again, there is a rich and prolific tradition of painted and carved santos [saints] dating to the 17th and 18th centuries.) Santa Fe Style is still in demand, and (at least when the new-home market is humming) local sawmills Hansen Lumber Co. and Spotted Owl Timber work heavy shifts producing *vigas*, corbels, posts, and beams. Locally based furniture companies create *trasteros*, tables, chairs, and beds in the old way, using Northern New Mexico woods like ponderosa pine, and their craftsmen are busy cutting and fitting joints and doing detailed carving.

The fact is that Santa Fe Style "keeps a lot of craftsmen alive," long-time homebuilder Sharon Woods said in a 2007 interview. "People come here and see the carved, braided posts, what it takes to lay adobes, plasterers, guys who build kiva fireplaces. These are dead arts in other parts of the country."

Most of the adobe-look buildings in the capital city today are not made of earth bricks, although there are a few high-end homes every year whose builders still use adobe for its excellent qualities. It is an ironic truth that this was once the most affordable building material: newlyweds and their families and friends dug the earth, often from the very site, and made the bricks and built the walls of their new home themselves.

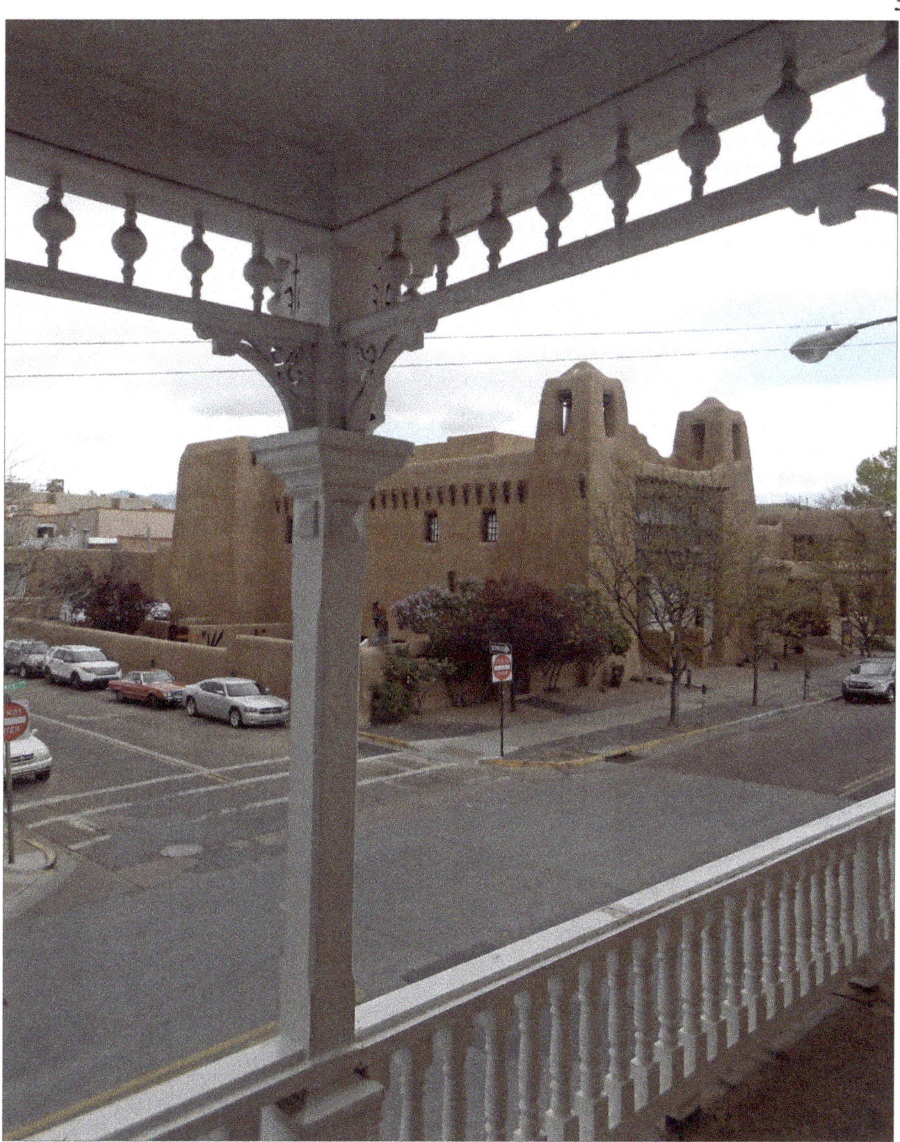

The 1917 New Mexico Museum of Art (penitentiary brick) seen from the front balcony porch of the 1891 Felipe Delgado House (adobe)

This was still true long after frontier times. "No country affords a better opportunity for the industrious and frugal man to own a home than New Mexico," said a front-page piece titled "Owning a Home" in the July 21, 1874, edition of *The Daily New Mexican*. "He procures his lot for a small sum, or, as in community grants, by mere occupancy, and the material with it, except the vigas and windows and doors, with which to build his house. Labor, in the construction of adobe dwellings, is abundant and cheap; indeed, nearly every laborer in the country is skilled more or less in this class of work, and in very many cases can himself at least complete the adobe work. It is one of the privileges in this free country; and the universal desire to own a house, as has been well remarked, constitutes the strength of the American republic."

However, today adobe is one of the most expensive building methods, employing increasingly rare *adoberos* to raise walls using asphalt-treated adobes transported from a different city. More commonly, the wall materials of choice are wood framing, steel framing, concrete, pumice-crete, and even recycled polystyrene — all finished with sheathing, vapor barriers, and either cementitious or elastomeric stucco to achieve the desired Santa Fe Style appearance. Elastomeric stucco is more waterproof than cementitious stucco, and you can see this after a rain. Houses finished with cement-based stucco have a darker, soaked appearance on the upper part of the walls. Those with elastomeric stucco are rather monotonously shiny across the entire wall surface — a plastic look.

The contrast is not unlike the difference between painted and plastered interior walls. Many local Realtors have witnessed potential buyers from outside express confusion at the subtly mottled or dappled appearance of hand-troweled plaster — in some of the best examples sporting a final finish of polished beeswax. This is one of the aspects of traditional architecture that, once understood, is considered among the most beautiful. It also is one that survives in many of the most contemporary expressions: homes with hard edges, larger expanses of glass, exposed steel, integral-color concrete floors, modern appliances, and engineered-quartz countertops, yes, but still graced by interior walls of hand-troweled plaster for an elegant touch of earthy aesthetic. (And if you find yourself in a venerable house where wonderful plastered walls have been covered in paint, you have just witnessed a travesty.)

Whatever the non-adobe material used today, builders have evolved a set of practices designed to mimic adobe. In some of his grander, non-residential buildings, John Gaw Meem added decorative buttresses of the type historically built onto large adobe buildings to provide added wall support. In others, the walls were battered, mimicking the natural construction of adobe buildings — especially those taller than one story — to support the great weight of all those earth blocks with thicker walls at the base tapering to slightly thinner above.

Today's builders often take special measures to give the corners of a non-adobe house the rounded appearance of adobe. They construct cagelike wood-framed forms to soften the edges along the tops of the walls; finished with stucco along with the walls, they quite resemble adobe parapets.

Some Santa Fe-area citizens who have an affinity for natural materials build houses using straw bales — not load-bearing, but as tremendous-insulation infill for walls in a post-and-beam structure — or form-poured pumice crete or rammed earth. But a building methodology that has really taken off in the past two decades is the insulating concrete form. With these hollow ICF blocks (most of which are made of recycled polystyrene), walls are assembled,

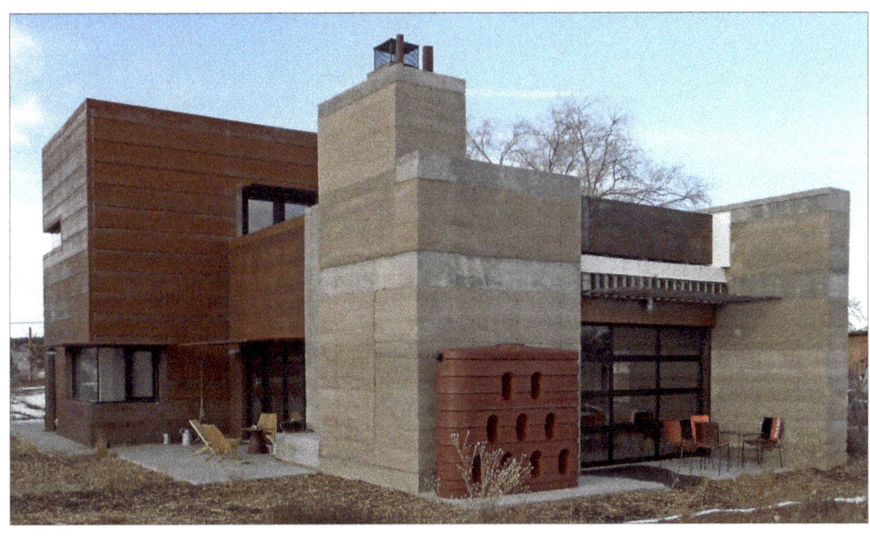

Zane Fischer abode designed by Fischer and architect Alexander Dzurec

Lego-like, on rebar anchored in the stem walls, then concrete is poured through their centers to create a sturdy and self-insulated structure.

OF COURSE, NOT EVERYTHING IN SANTA FE is done in the Spanish-Pueblo Revival and Territorial Revival styles. The 1957 ordinance only governs buildings in the central, historic district. Among the recent buildings that contrast strikingly from the norm are the Zane Fischer residence and the Molecule Design showroom. Adriana Siso recycled and modified 11 international shipping containers for her stunning, silvery Molecule furnishings showroom in the Baca Area of the Santa Fe Railyard. And Fischer collaborated with architect Alexander Dzurec on a home in Agua Fria Village (a few miles southwest of Santa Fe's historic district) that won the top prize in the 2013 AIA-Santa Fe awards. It's a remarkable concerto of forms: articulating off a central concrete tower, clad in rusted steel, are two wings — one a long, prefab-metal studio/carport and the other a boxy construction of metal and rammed earth holding the living spaces.

Pisé de terre or rammed-earth construction was employed by architects Conron & Woods, Santa Fe, and Leo A. Caly Co., Phoenix, as the wall material for a new building for the New Mexico Public Employees Retirement Association. The 2009 structure satisfied the PERA board's desire for a contemporary structure that also reflects the regional earthen-architecture heritage. Roy Woods said the layered construction method also relates to prehistoric puddled-adobe walls. The Lockwood Construction team on the PERA project searched for a type of dirt that would be best for the rammed-earth process and found it in Abiquiú. It was amended with a small percentage of cement; the 24-inch-thick walls were constructed around steel framing.

For a house in Lamy, Mark Giorgetti, principal of the design-build firm Palo Santo Designs, chose pumice-crete construction. The walls, which were poured in temporary forms, are full of light, porous pumice rock that boasts high insulation value. The 16-inch walls yield handsomely scooped windows, similar to those on an adobe house. They're finished on the inside with lovely earth plaster from the Albuquerque company American Clay. An interior wall was made with 80-year-old adobes recycled from a historic remodel in Santa Fe. The interior adobe wall is a more and more popular green-building feature because it provides thermal mass, helping to moderate indoor temperatures and reduce reliance on heating and cooling equipment. The Giorgetti house also harkens back to colonial times when floors were dirt, sealed with ox blood — these are also earth, but with linseed oil as the sealer.

The 2008 Santa Fe Community Convention Center by Spears Architects and Fentress Architects, Denver, is a good example of a recent, very large, adobe-look building. The grand but welcoming structure has steel-framed walls but boasts stamped-tin lamps, sconces and chandeliers by Santa Fe artists William and Luann García, and exterior *portales* and lintels made of salvaged timber from a New Mexico forest fire. The convention center won a "Gold" certification in the U.S. Green Building Council's Leadership in Energy & Environmental Design (LEED) program.

For a new downtown hotel, Drury Southwest chose AMVIC blocks, an ICF produced in Canada, for an addition that includes the hotel entrance. The larger part of the Drury job was an adaptive re-use project to transform the old St. Vincent Hospital that was designed by Meem and built on a budget a few years after World War II. The walls facing the old parking lot were quite plain compared to those on Paseo de Peralta and East Palace Avenue, which sport sections of ornamental brickwork and facades punctuated by a few strategically placed doors with pedimented lintels and balustraded balconies. To create the Drury Plaza Hotel, the old hospital's interior walls were demolished and new, steel-frame walls with better insulation were constructed.

The 96,000-square-foot New Mexico History Museum, completed in 2009, has walls of Nudura ICFs. The History Museum was constructed on a sort of "keyhole" infill site and had to mesh with existing buildings. Because it is directly behind the Palace of the Governors, special techniques were employed to minimize vibrations that could damage the centuries-old adobe walls.

*"The rectangular terraced masses, the flat roofs, the protruding vigas, the wood ceilings, the white interior walls, are all a part of the contemporary scene, a heritage from time immemorial and the earth and people of New Mexico."*

**— John Gaw Meem, addressing a 1953 meeting of the American Institute of Architects in Santa Fe**

# Chapter 3
# RAPP, MEEM, AND HISTORIC PRESERVATION

ISAAC RAPP AND JOHN GAW MEEM are the two architects most identified with Santa Fe Style as well as the two with the most significant designs still standing in the city. But many came before.

Who designed the Palace of the Governors? Professional designers or architects did not arrive in New Mexico until the coming of the Army of the West in 1846, Boyd Pratt wrote in 1989 in the journal *New Mexico Architecture.* We picture the people who built the Old Palace and other buildings in the frontier town in the two centuries or so before that year as concentrating on program — designing and building structures that would serve the anticipated needs of their inhabitants — but of course all but the most conservative or unimaginative would also have added some degree of aesthetic embellishment.

We do not know exactly what the original Palace looked like, but its design and construction in the second decade of the 17th century likely was the responsibility of Governor Don Pedro de Peralta. Among the other designers of buildings in Santa Fe before the 1900s were master mason Andres Gonzales, who directed the 1710 rebuilding of San Miguel Chapel; Gerónimo López, who likely built the Canyon Road building now known as the Borrego House later in the 18th century; the firm Dofflemeyer & Grace, which remodeled the Spiegelberg store on the Plaza in the 1860s; Antoine and Projectus Mouly, Quintien Monier, and François Mallet, who built St. Francis

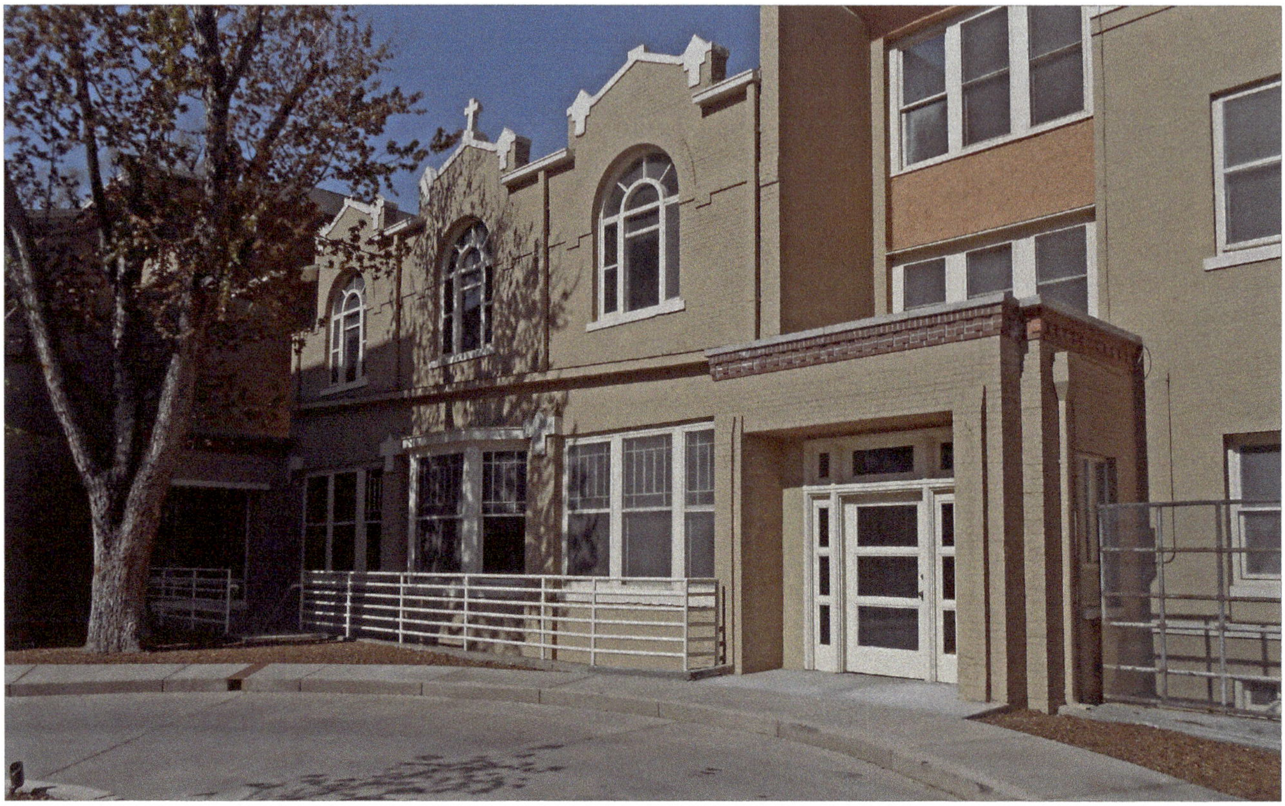

Marian Hall, 1908, by Isaac Hamilton Rapp

Below, a Marian Hall fireplace

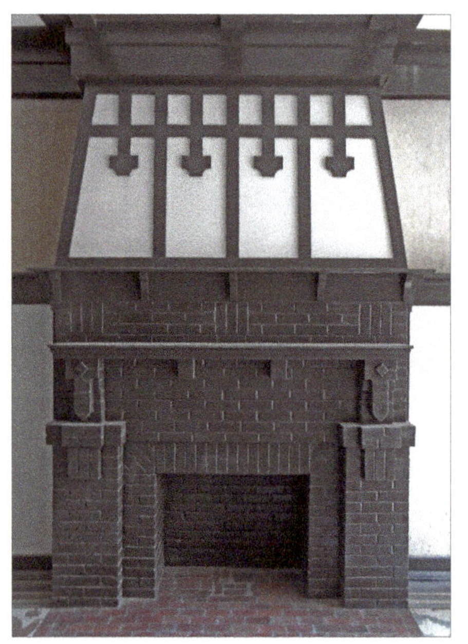

Cathedral; Chas. Wheelock, probably the designer of the Palace Hotel; J.B. Randell, designer of the 1882 University of New Mexico Whitin Hall; E.S. Jenison of Chicago, the 1886 capitol building; H. William Kirchner, the 1887 Santa Fe County Courthouse; and Philip Hesch, the 1888 Hesch and 1890 Eugenie Shonnard houses.

Isaac Hamilton Rapp was working in the area before the start of the 20th century. Born in New York City, he moved to Trinidad, Colorado, in his early 30s. He and his brother, William Mason Rapp, opened an architecture office in 1901; they were joined by Arthur C. Hendrickson three years later. Specific projects bear the names Rapp & Rapp, or Rapp, Rapp & Hendrickson, but Isaac was the firm's leading figure.

He designed most of Trinidad's important buildings, in many styles, according to the Colorado Historical Society. He was also responsible for more than a dozen buildings in Las Vegas, New Mexico, among them the 1894 Masonic Temple and the 1903 Carnegie Library.

His 1908 Territorial Executive's Mansion, described by Rapp biographer Carl Sheppard as a "white-trimmed Georgian brick box topped with balustrade and modillion cornice, and with a half-round entrance portico of Corinthian columns," was an example of the architect's pre-Santa Fe Style work in the New Mexico capital.

Rapp's first important Santa Fe job was the city's third territorial capitol building — the first to serve that purpose was the Palace of the Governors and the second was the double-domed Jenison building that burned down in 1892, six years after its completion. Rapp's capitol was finished in 1900. A half-century later, it was severely remodeled by the W.C. Kruger Co. to conform to the Territorial Revival style that had become the norm for state government buildings in Santa Fe. Both the grand entrance portico and the dome were removed, the roof was flattened, and a 105-foot tower was built on the north side, creating what we know today as the Bataan Memorial Building.

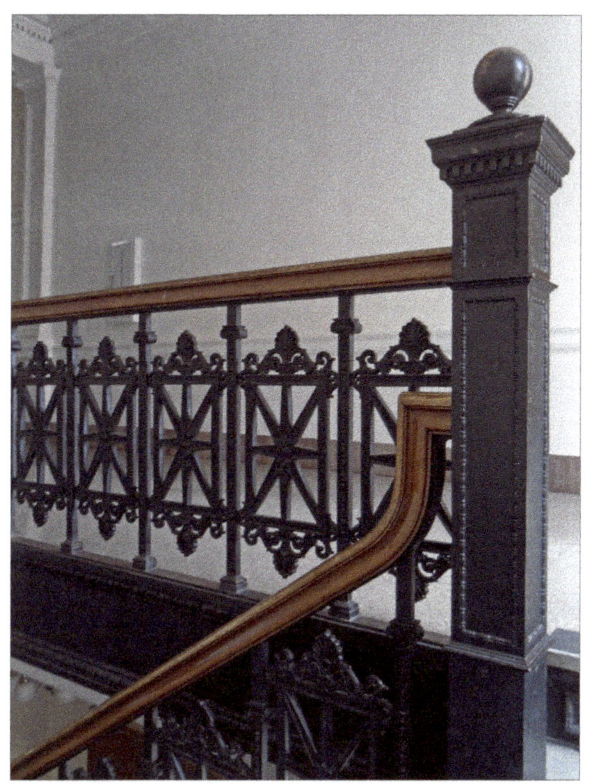

Stairway railings in Rapp's 1900 state capitol, now the Bataan Memorial Building

Three other early Rapp buildings in Santa Fe are gone — the 1904 Catron High School, the 1908 Executive's Mansion, and the Ionic-columned 1911 First National Bank that was on the east side of the Plaza — but two more are extant, and pretty much in their original state: the 1905 First Ward School (now Ventana Fine Art) and the 1908 St. Vincent's Sanitorium for the Sisters of Charity, known today as Marian Hall.

RAPP WAS THE FIRST significant interpreter/exponent of Santa Fe Style after the city decided in 1912 to prioritize an essentially synthetic design based on its oldest existing buildings. In that year, Museum of New Mexico archaeologist Sylvanus G. Morley, who was a leader in the effort to brand the city based on those historic precedents, wrote an admiring letter to Rapp about his design for the Colorado Supply Company store in Morley, Colo. Morley said that building, with towers based on San Esteban del Rey at Acoma Pueblo, was "so absolutely in the spirit of 'The Santa Fe Style.'" This is one of the first known uses of that term.

Isaac Rapp actually worked in a variety of styles, but his powerful role in establishing the Spanish-Pueblo Revival stands out today. His 1914 Gross Kelly Warehouse was the first substantial commercial building done in the revival style. Next came his New Mexico Building for the 1915 Panama-California Exposition in San Diego. Then, two years later, the same basic design was enlarged and expanded upon stylistically for the Museum of Fine Arts (since renamed the New Mexico Museum of Art) on the Santa Fe Plaza.

Both the expo pavilion and the museum were modeled after the Acoma mission church with a two-story, two-towered church form (but adding a balustraded balcony similar to those seen at historic churches in Las Trampas and San Felipe Pueblo) on the left and a smaller mass with open loggia (living quarters at the Acoma feature) on the right, separated by a long, one-story section (part of the cloister that surrounds San Esteban del Rey's large *placita*). For the museum, Rapp, Rapp, and Hendrickson also added — around the corner facing Lincoln Avenue — another dominant mass, the front of which is a recreation of the Laguna Pueblo mission church facade, complete with a curvilinear parapet punctuated by twin *espadañas* and flanked by "horn" projections at the corners, plus a centered window and door.

Among the other distinctive attributes of the impressive museum building are deeply set windows and exterior buttress masses that intensify the impression of "adobe solidity"; rows of projecting *vigas* whose parallel shadows play on the earth-colored surface; bullet-carved corbels and beams; and a fully enclosed *placita.*

Other extant Rapp buildings include the Sunmount Sanitarium (today's Carmelite Monastery), the New Mexico Asylum for the Deaf and Dumb (its modern name the New Mexico School For the Deaf), and, facing on Old Santa Fe Trail and San Francisco Street, the original section of La Fonda.

The hotel was Rapp's last major commission. The main entrance is in a facade structure strongly related to the Lincoln Avenue feature from the museum on the other side of the Plaza. It still has the horns, but here he simplifed the parapet to just one bell opening and then added a balcony in the center of the structure. (Other design professionals who have worked on additions and renovations to the Rapp hotel over the past nine and a half decades include Meem, Mary Colter, William Lumpkins, Holabird & Root & Burgee of Chicago, W.C. Kruger, and Barbara Felix.)

Rapp designed La Fonda in 1920, the same year as the arrival in Santa Fe of John Gaw Meem. Later in the century Rapp was all but forgotten as Meem became famous for his Laboratory of Anthropology and Director's Residence, the Santa Fe Municipal Building (now the Santa Fe Public Library), the County Courthouse, and numerous residences, schools, and churches — most notably the adobe Cristo Rey Church — as well as Fuller Lodge, a grand log structure an hour away in Los Alamos.

MEEM'S FIRST APPEARANCE in Santa Fe was as a seeker of a tuberculosis cure at age 26. He contracted the disease in Brazil, where his father worked as a missionary and where John was born and raised. In one of the classic "Why I came to Santa Fe" stories, Meem was walking on a New York street,

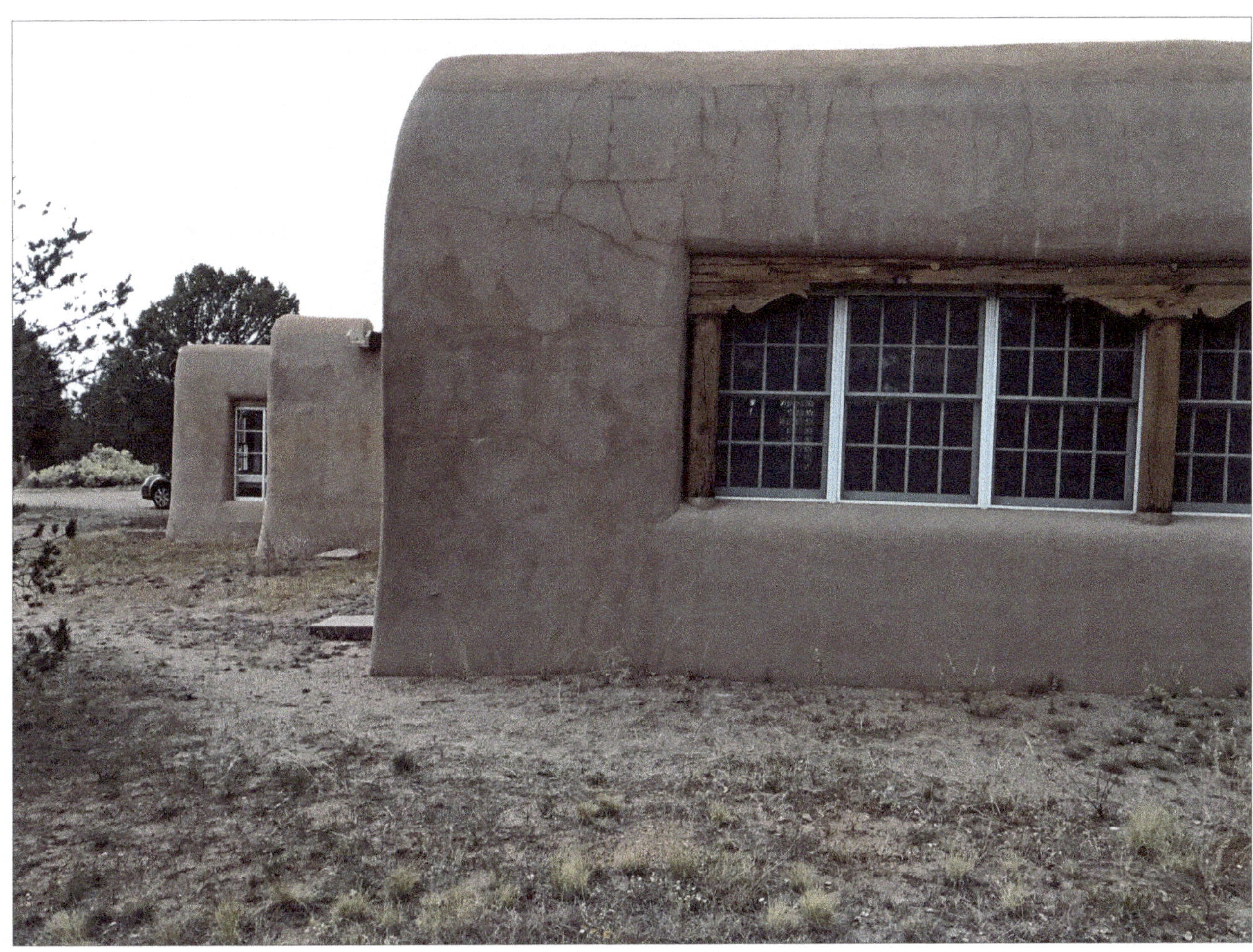

Staggered masses: John Gaw Meem's architectural studio and early "bachelor pad," now the art building for Santa Fe Preparatory School

despondent over the doctor's diagnosis of TB, when he noticed a colorful poster. Upon closer examination, he saw it was an advertisement for the Atchison, Topeka & Santa Fe Railroad. The pictures of the newly completed art museum in Santa Fe and of the desert landscape fascinated him. He came to Santa Fe to avail himself of Dr. Frank E. Mera's treatment regimen at Sunmount Sanitarium.

Meem had no formal training in architecture, but he did have a degree in structural engineering from the Virginia Military Institute. More and more interested in building design, and feeling better, he took a position with the Denver architectural firm Fisher and Fisher in 1922. He also attended evening courses in the Atelier Denver, a studio affiliated with New York's Beaux-Arts Institute of Design. The tuberculosis brought him back to Sunmount in 1924. There he basically started his office in bed, entering into a partnership with fellow patient Cassius McCormick that would last for several years.

The majority of their designs fell firmly within the Santa Fe Style construct, both the old-fashioned-looking Spanish-Pueblo Revival type and the Territorial Revival style, which Meem innovated beginning with the 1925 Ashley Pond house and the 1927 Manderfield School. But two important projects were not related to either style. Palen Hall, an annex to the stone Church of the Holy Faith, has a steeply pitched roof and a stucco/half-timbered facade. Designed by Meem in 1925, the hall was built by Antonio Windsor, whose resumé included the Women's Board of Trade Library and the Scottish Rite Temple. The second project, 1928's Fuller Lodge at the Los Alamos Ranch School, was constructed of huge pine logs — 771 of them.

When Meem began work on Fuller Lodge, he had already designed 10 Santa Fe houses, including his first complete project, the East Palace Avenue residence of Hazel Pond. In the five years before he worked on another Ranch School project — the half-timbered Arts and Crafts Building — Meem designed 11 more Santa Fe homes as well as Las Acequias, the country estate of Cyrus McCormick Jr. in Nambé; the Laboratory of Anthropology and the lab director's residence (today's Museum of Spanish Colonial Art) on Camino Lejo; and the first buildings for Santa Fe Indian School.

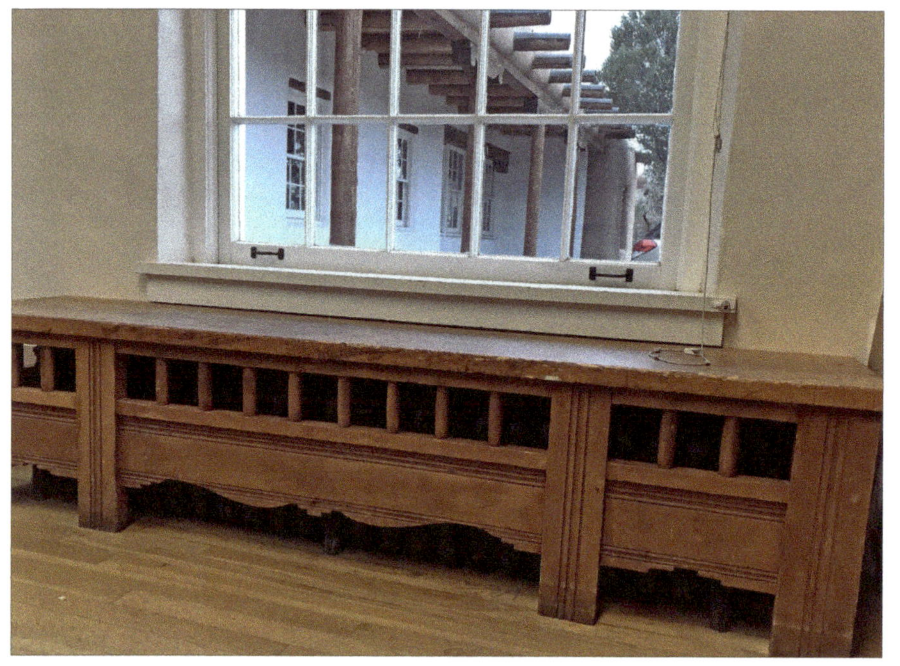

A carved-wood radiator cover in John Gaw Meem's studio

Meem's prolific career took off in part because he was in the right place at the right time. He arrived in Santa Fe eight years after New Mexico achieved statehood (in 1912) and eight years after Museum of New Mexico director Edgar Lee Hewett and his associates began shaping Santa Fe's architectural aesthetic along strict Spanish-Pueblo Revival lines. The result, according to Albuquerque architectural historian David Kammer: "Nowhere in the United States is a regional architecture more evident than in New Mexico."

Speaking before a gathering of architects in 1953, Meem said of the region's early Spanish houses that "certain features were common to all: the uneven contours of the earthen walls, the rectangular masses, the flat roofs,

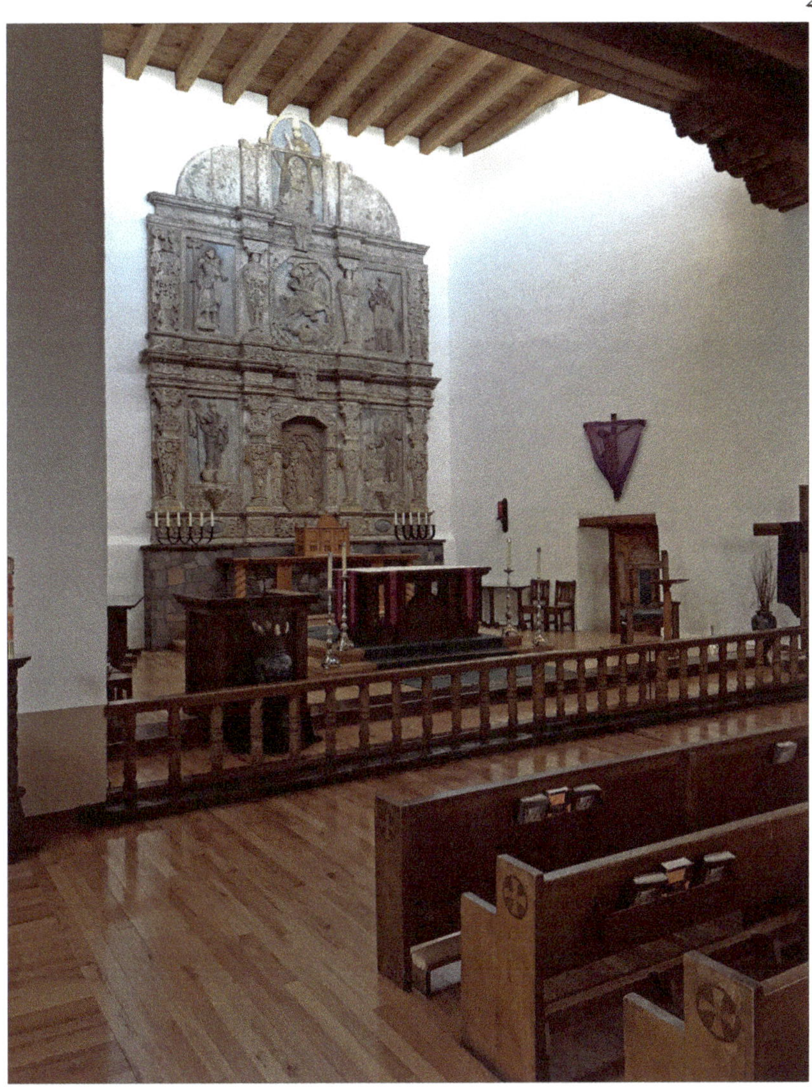

Meem designed Cristo Rey Church with a transverse clerestory in the roof structure. He had seen examples of this device, which floods light onto the altar, in his work with the Committee for the Preservation and Restoration of New Mexico Mission Churches.

the wood ceilings and white interior walls, the same as in pre-Columbian times." And about the regional style, he said, "One of its chief characteristics is that it is a wall-bearing post and lintel style ... [Another] is the extraordinarily intimate relation between structure and its site.

"This is exemplified by the flat roofs which seem to reflect the mesas of New Mexico (one of the most prominent features of our landscape), by the color of the walls, which is identical with the surrounding soil, and finally by the softness of the contours caused by erosion which with the resulting batters make the buildings seem integral parts of the earth itself."

He was emphatic about one point: "We are more impressed with clarity and cleanness than with the picturesque." And, in his 2001 book *Facing Southwest: The Life and Houses of John Gaw Meem*, Chris Wilson points to the success of that strategy: "By calming the overly picturesque details and compositions of the style as practiced before his arrival in 1920, and instead emphasizing the sculptural massiveness of adobe, Meem imbued Santa Fe style with a dignified monumentality."

The creative energy of Meem's mind shows in the ideas he advanced to invigorate the Santa Fe Plaza. His prize-winning plan in a 1931 competition on that subject suggested two solutions. In the first, a rebuilding based on early Santa Fe would begin by razing all buildings that were over two stories tall. Also, the post office (today's Museum of Contemporary Native Arts) and the other buildings in that block would be taken down to restore the original rectangular plaza with the main church (the cathedral) fronting on its east side. The plaza, with *portales* on all four sides, would be transformed from a commercial center to "an exhibit of early architecture."

The second idea was much less drastic. It called for the installation of *placitas* within business buildings facing on the south side of the Plaza, opening up shops along arcades to increase store frontages, and increasing building heights but with setbacks to guarantee adequate sunlight into the Plaza from all sides. "Portales similar to the one at present on the Governors' Palace should be constructed over the sidewalks on the east and west sides," according to Meem's plaza-improvement plan. "Those two sides have ample sunlight and in fact awnings or marquises [marquees] are essential at certain times of the day; which means that the portales would not materially affect the shops in back. They would however tie the plaza in with the Governors' Palace in a delightful way and give the whole a most interesting appearance."

Curiously, no *portales* were recommended for the south side of the town square. "On account of the fact that the south side has very little sunlight, the portale [sic] here has been eliminated. Instead, a system of recessing in certain instances and in others of building directly on the property line is shown."

It was more than three decades before the Plaza *portales* (which had been removed in the late 19th century) were rebuilt in a collaboration between Meem and architect Kenneth Clark.

One of the iconic projects in Meem's career was his large addition to Santa Fe's oldest hotel, La Fonda. Bunting wrote that Meem was in agreement with Harvey House architect Mary Colter's opinion that Rapp's design was "too nervous and indented." She "preferred simple lines to the wavy lines of the old hotel." Meem's exterior would be "in the Spanish-Pueblo type of architecture matching the present portion of the hotel, except that the emphasis will be more on mass than ornament. Its numerous setbacks and recesses will recall the terracing in the more ancient Pueblos of Taos and Acoma." He was also concerned that the "tall mass of the enlarged hotel not compete with the cathedral towers when seen from afar nor destroy the scale of the city."

That "tall mass" is Meem's tower at the hotel's southwest corner. He worked out its form while he was wrestling with the restoration design of a pair of towers 100 miles to the southwest: on San Esteban del Rey, the centuries-old Spanish mission church at Acoma.

In 1921 Meem had visited the 18th-century church San José de Gracia in Las Trampas and was attracted to the movement to protect and restore the state's historic churches, which he later described as "characterized by a massive dignity and simplicity." He co-founded the Committee for the Preservation and Restoration of New Mexico Mission Churches, an organization that focused on San Esteban del Rey beginning in 1924. The massive Acoma church, built between 1629 and 1644, was in bad repair. The restoration began under the guidance of Burhnam Hoyt, architect for the CPRNMMC, with

Meem assisting as coordinator of the work. During the last three years of the five-year project, Meem led the restoration, which included replacing the vast roof and reconstructing the two towers flanking the entrance.

The original plan for rebuilding the deteriorated towers was advanced by Meem and Santa Fe artist/preservationist Carlos Vierra, but the committee also consulted Acoma elders. "Meem's eye for lines and curves was really, really good, but oral history was also important to them," said Kate Wingert-Playdon, author of *John Gaw Meem at Acoma: The Restoration of San Esteban del Rey Mission*, in a 2013 *Santa Fe New Mexican* interview. She added that it is not known for certain which came first, the final design of the Acoma tower or that for the La Fonda tower.

In 1933, Meem received a commission for the University of New Mexico administration building — the first of more than 30 structures he and his firm designed on the UNM campus. In 1934, he was appointed regional director of the Historic American Buildings Survey. And in that year he penned an article for *American Architecture*, in which he stated, "Some forms are so honest, so completely logical and native to the environment that one finds — to his delight and surprise — that modern problems can be solved and are best solved by the use of forms based on tradition."

THE WORD "FORMS" stands out in the John Gaw Meem story, because he focused on the use of materials more permanent than adobe while maintaining what was considered the all-important *look* of the adobe building. "In our contemporary regional architecture," he said during a May 1953 Phi Kappa Phi banquet at UNM, "design must conform to all requirements of modern usage, but in interpreting these requirements, elevation and ornamentation are consciously composed of symbolic forms to provide additional emotional or spiritual value. It is for this reason that walls are slightly battered and that bricks on parapets are sometimes clipped to accentuate the curve of contoured outline. This is done not to imitate adobe, but to recall by means of a conventionalized symbolic form the heritage of ancient buildings or the characteristic shapes of the landscape."

Architectural historian Bunting, who wrote *John Gaw Meem: Southwestern Architect* in 1983, was of the opinion that Meem's Zimmerman Library (1936) at UNM was the Southwest's best example of Pueblo Revival architecture, period. However, when Frank Lloyd Wright saw the structure, he said, "This is imitation and all imitation is base," according to a 1977 School of American Research leaflet about Meem's work. "That's a dubious and incorrect criticism," Meem reportedly responded. "An imitation of what? If by imitation is meant the recalling or reflection of the past, he would condemn the whole of the Renaissance."

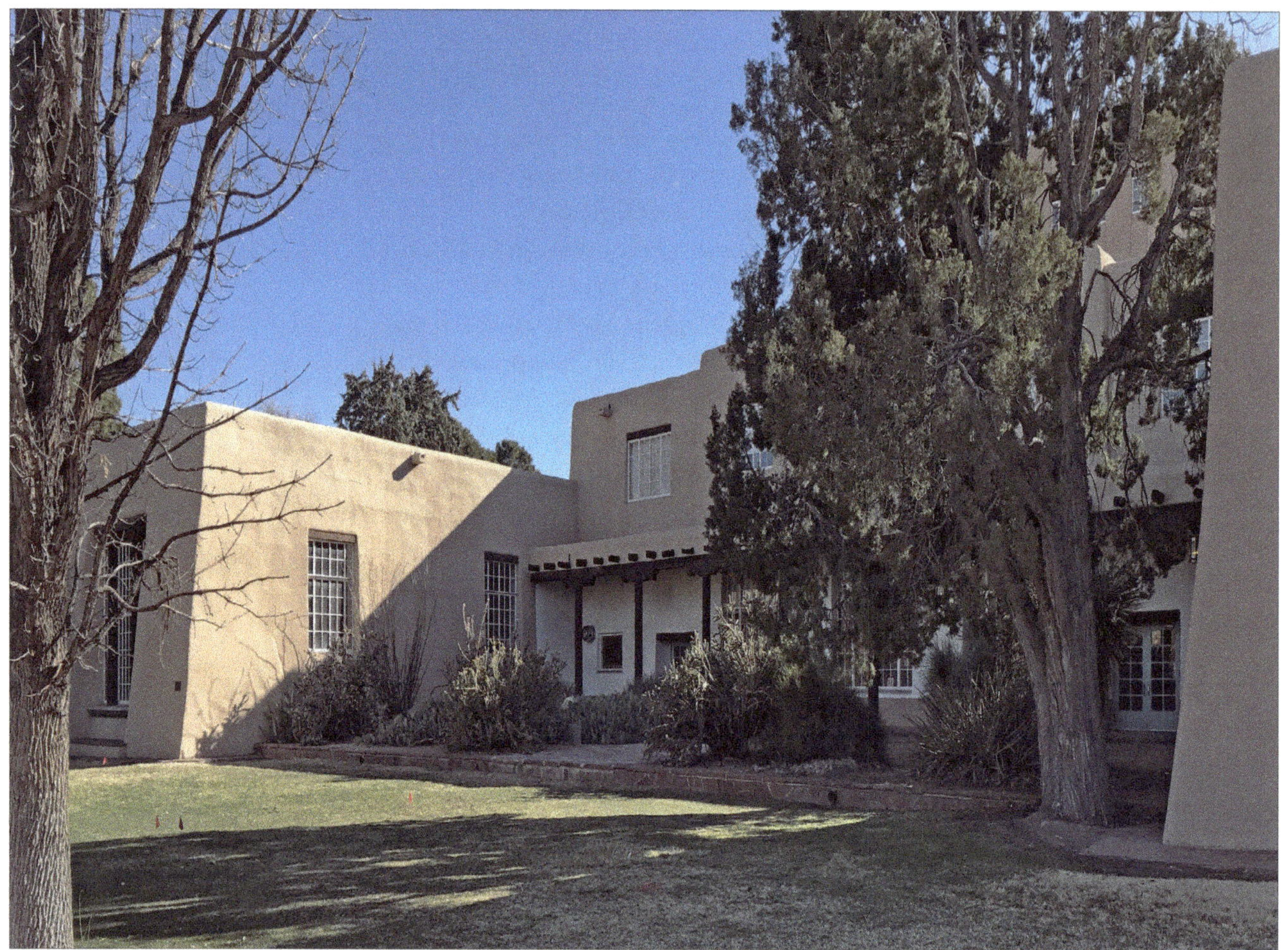

Zimmerman Library, University of New Mexico, Albuquerque, by John Gaw Meem

During his career, Meem designed perhaps 80 houses. A strong segment in his portfolio of institutional buildings was the church. He designed 32 of them, including the 1939 First Presbyterian Church with its grandly (or exaggeratedly) buttressed facade, and the more modest 1947 Immanuel Lutheran Church. The naves of both buildings boast ceilings of *vigas* and carved corbels, and both have front facades symmetrically topped with stepped parapets and bell gables. But his most famous is the monumental Cristo Rey Church.

The 350-foot building, completed in 1940, involved the diversion of an *acequia* to aid in the manufacture of more than 180,000 adobe bricks, but Meem also employed a steel frame. This building is wonderfully asymmetrical, the two towers that frame the entry of different size and form. Meem designed the chancel to accommodate an oil painting of Our Lady of Light and a singular *reredos*, a marvel of carved-stone saints; the piece was made in 1760 for La Castrense, an adobe military chapel that once stood on the Plaza's south side.

In the years after the end of World War II, Meem's firm designed or remodeled eight buildings on or near the Plaza: the Renehan Building, the

Franklin store, and the Santa Fe Publishing Company, all reworked in 1946; the Sears store, 1948; two buildings owned by the Seligmans, 1949; and the Masonic Lodge in 1952. Two years later, the office did a drastic Santa Fe Style remodel of Rapp's 1911, white-columned, First National Bank on the east side of the Plaza.

Meem drew plans for, but never saw built, homes that represented quite an evolution of the city's famous style. One was a 1943 model-house commission from the Santa Fe Builders Supply Company (Sanbusco) and the other a 1946 model solar house plan for the Libby-Owens-Ford Glass Company. With their cantilevered roofs and curtain walls, both look a bit like Mies van der Rohe houses but with projecting vigas.

Other highlights from the Meem portfolio are the Mary Vilura Conkey Residence (1928), the Robert Tilney Residence (1929), the Amelia Hollenback Residence (1932), the Santa Fe Municipal Building (1936; today housing the Santa Fe Public Library), the County Courthouse (1938), the Museum of International Folk Art (1950), and Santa Fe High School (1951; now the Santa Fe City Hall building).

For 35 years, Meem's practice was a design laboratory with a staff that numbered in the dozens. Among the most important of his associates was Gordon Street, who came into the firm in 1927 and opened his own office five years later. Hugo Zehner joined Meem in 1931 and became a partner in 1940. Zehner was a structural, rather than design, genius, and it was he who supervised a challenging stabilization of St. Francis Cathedral in the late 1930s. Denver native Bradley P. Kidder joined the firm in 1934 and remained until 1947, when he went out on his own.

Edward Obert "Bung" Holien moved to Santa Fe in 1944 and became an associate in Meem, Hugo Zehner & Associates. By 1949, Holien was made a full partner and chief designer in the firm. The office was called Meem, Zehner, Holien & Associates from 1944 to 1956. John McHugh joined the Meem practice for a decade beginning in 1946. William R. Buckley, whose wife, Madge G. Buckley, was also an architect, became the office's chief draftsman in 1952 and stayed with the firm until Meem retired in 1959, at which point Buckley formed a partnership with Holien.

### Saving the old and valuable

Adobe buildings are rugged and if well-maintained last for centuries. However, a vacant adobe is particularly vulnerable to death by water. Under unrelenting erosion, many venerable abodes have reverted to piles of dirt with logs on top. In fact, there is a longstanding tradition of recycling vigas: neglect, weather, and gravity bring them slowly down to the ground as the walls dissolve, then man recycles the valuable timbers into the roof of a new building. An interesting side-effect is that practice is that an ancient beam or lintel on a building may be dated by dendrochronology testing (tree-ring analysis) but who knows if it's always been part of that building?

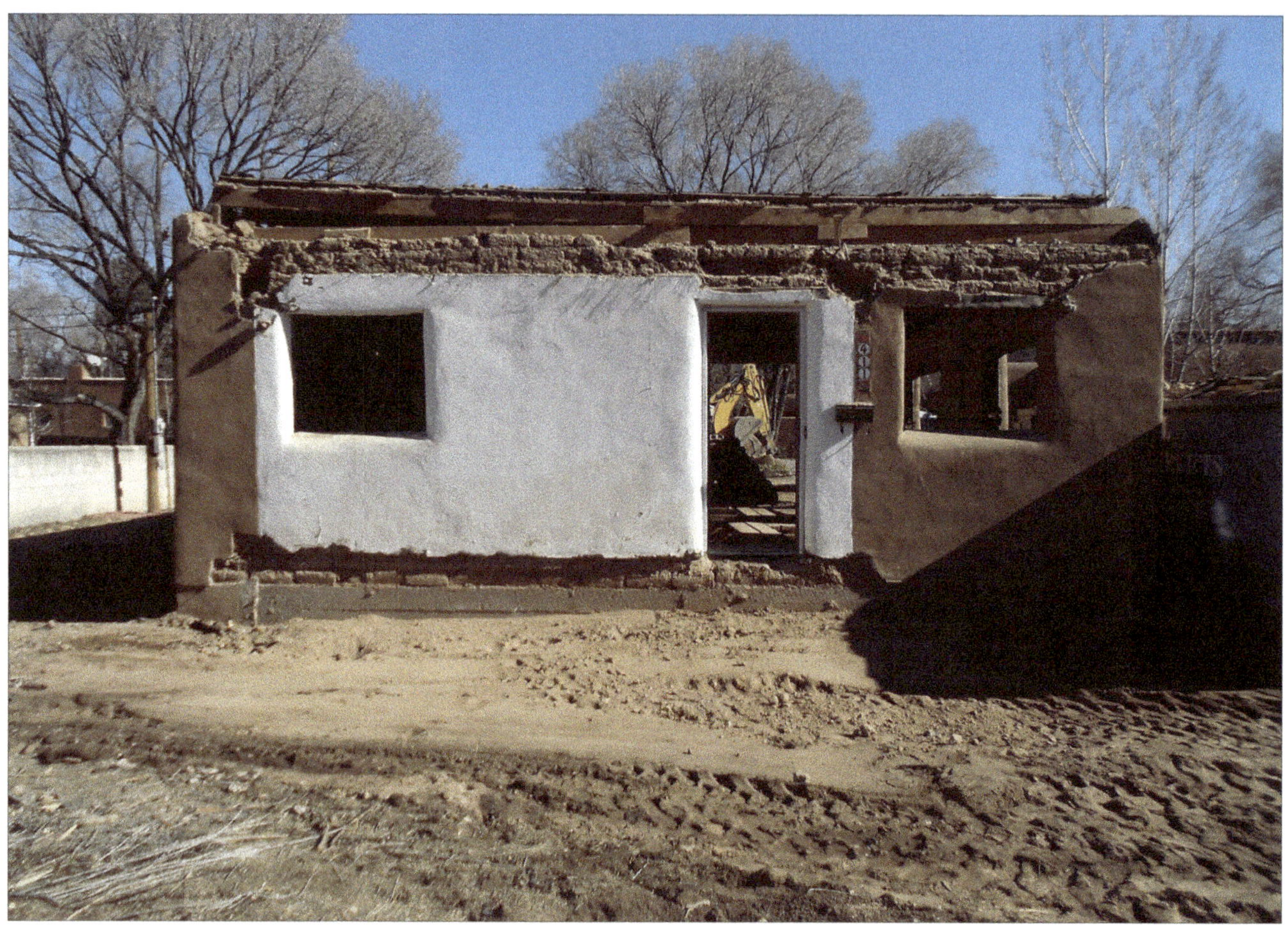

A recent example of an old Santa Fe adobe home that was demolished to make way for a new house. When this photo was taken midway through the job, the owner and builder thought the basic adobe structure could be preserved and incorporated into the new house, but it was subsequently razed.

Meem was one who believed that historic preservation was of supreme importance in this area. For a time he chaired the Committee for the Preservation and Restoration of New Mexico Mission Churches, which rehabilitated dozens of historic edifices, including those at Acoma, Laguna, and Zia pueblos. He was also a co-founder of the Old Santa Fe Association and a member of the Historic Santa Fe Foundation.

Meem, the artists Vierra, Gustave Baumann, and William Penhallow Henderson; and writers Mary Austin and Alice Corbin were among those who established the Old Santa Fe Association in 1926. Their first priority was

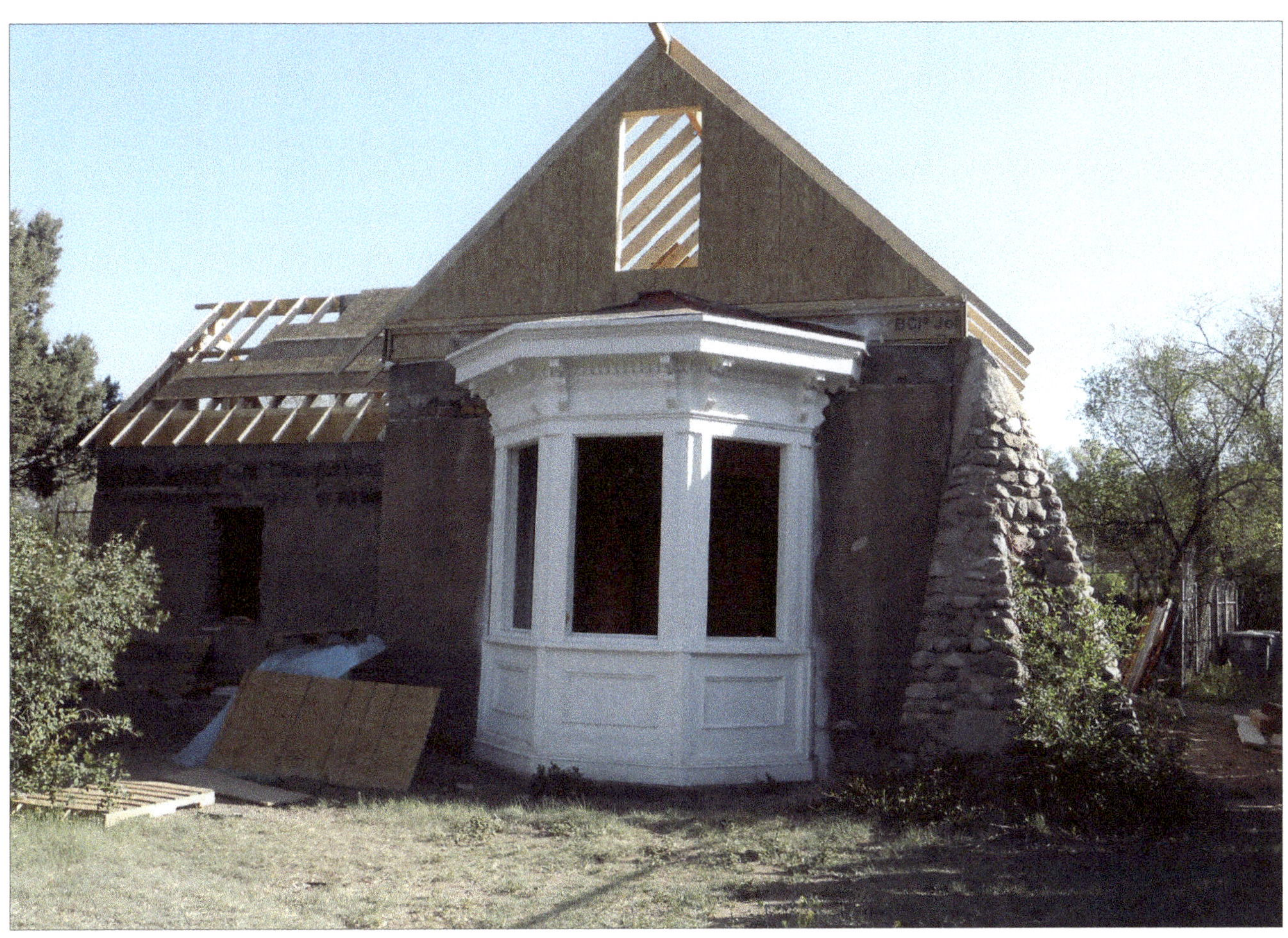

organizing to prevent 3,000 acres near the present-day location of St. John's College from becoming an elitist seasonal colony. OSFA has functioned as the city's preservation activist ever since. According to the group's website, it "takes an active role in guiding the growth and development of our city by advocating appropriate city policies that will maintain and strengthen the unique character of Santa Fe."

The association recently spearheaded an effort to protect three of Santa Fe's historic bridges. One of the three, the Delgado Street Bridge, was subsequently named to the National Register of Historic Places — as was the entire campus of St. John's College, established in Santa Fe in 1964. The foundation of the National Register nomination was the master plan and core buildings by Bung Holien and William Buckley.

The properties on the OSFA watch list (in mid-2019) included

• The Santa Fe County Courthouse on Grant Avenue, planned to be restored using the original John Gaw Meem courtyard conformation.

• The Vladem Contemporary art museum, a remodel and addition to the Halpin Building on Montezuma Ave.

Many Santa Feans were saddened when the 19th-century Fransisca Hinojos House was severely damaged by fire in 2013. Most of the adobe walls survived, as did the distinctive bay-window element and the stone buttress. The city's Historic Districts Review Board denied a bank's demolition request, then allowed contractor John Wolf to rebuild and improve the house as his own home, including (mostly) "in-kind" replacement of the roofs and other fire-compromised features.

• St. Michael's Drive corridor, the focus of a potential pedestrian-friendlier remake.

• Proposed hotel or other commercial building in the vacant lot adjacent to Loretto Chapel.

• St. Catherine Indian School, a campus founded in 1894 by Katherine Mary Drexel, a Catholic nun who was canonized in 2007. Since 1998, the buildings have been vacant and facing what is appropriately termed "demolition by neglect."

• Old Pecos Trail corridor slated for "improvements."

THE HISTORIC SANTA FE FOUNDATION was established in 1961 in reaction to the demolition of the lovely, 19th-century Simon Nusbaum House to build a parking lot (on land that presently accommodates the Hotel Chimayó de Santa Fe and Rosewood Inn of the Anasazi). The nonprofit HSFF has owned and protected several historic houses and the 1920 Cross of the Martyrs and has plaqued nearly 90 features — mostly buildings but also the Acequia Madre, the Fairview Cemetery, the 1895 Hydroelectric Plant, and El Puente de los Hidalgos — on its Registry of Resources Worthy of Preservation.

The foundation sponsors a Faith and John Gaw Meem Preservation Trades Intern every summer, presents occasional mud-plastering workshops, and administers a significant preservation-easement program.

In 1998, John and Merry Schroeder, owners of a downtown building that once housed J.S. Candelario's Original Old Curio Store, were the first to grant a historic-preservation easement after a new state law allowed such protections. The HSFF has since negotiated preservation easements for 10 other buildings. The easement strategy is flexible. In the case of the Shuster Mian House, only three doors and the streetscape are covered. On the William Penhallow Henderson House, the easement applies to beams, windows, doors, cabinets, radiator covers, and Henderson's characteristic flower carvings on the woodwork, as well as maintaining open space between the house and the street. Historic-preservation easements are attached to the building deed and thus legally binding in perpetuity. HSFF has responsibility for monitoring and enforcing the terms of the easements.

Now, one of the bottom lines in this discussion is that, overall, Santa Fe's core looks pretty much as it did decades ago. That's kind of the point of historic preservation, at least in the broader sense: the community's historic fabric is just about as important as the historic integrity of each building. But this is also the fulcrum of the argument for some critics. If a place appears as

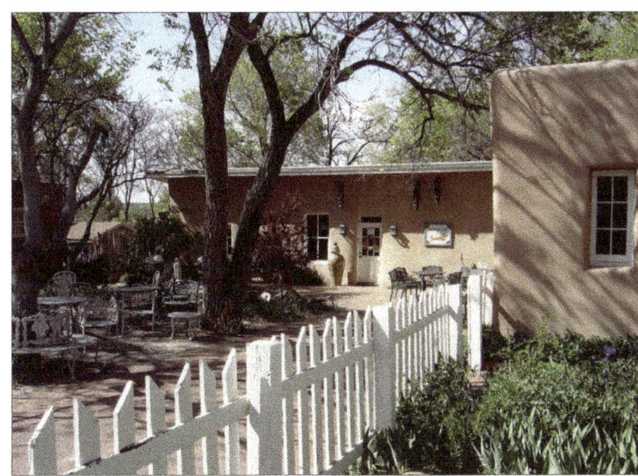

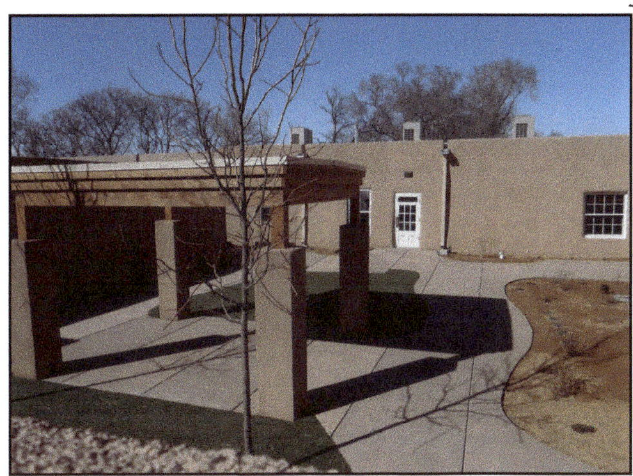

The historic Manuel Valdés House was last seen by the general public in its Mission Café incarnation (left) from 2006 to 2010. The El Castillo retirement center purchased it, did a drastic exterior remodel to the building and the landscaping (right photo — but this view does not include the building mass seen projecting toward the camera in the left photo) and hid it behind a tall street wall. The Historic Santa Fe Foundation subsequently removed the house from its Register of Resources Worthy of Preservation. This is an example of city government facilitating the gradual demise of Santa Fe's historic fabric with inappropriate development approvals.

if the 21st century — and even the 20th century — have not happened, "you actually make it more difficult for people to understand that the past leads right up to them," said Daniel Bluestone, author of the 2010 book *Buildings, Landscapes, and Memory: Case Studies in Historic Preservation*, in a 2010 interview with *The New Mexican*. "I think we should do everything we can to help people understand that preservation is not only about preserving the past but about helping people engage the past in the context of the present — and in a way that lets them think critically about what they're doing today and where we're headed in the future."

In the interview with Bluestone, I commented that so much of what's happening with modern architecture in the city — including the proliferation of pseudoadobes — is shaped with tourism in mind. Bluestone responded that the problem is people "who think they know what tourists want and desire and think and need. It is the people that set out to coddle and swaddle tourists at every turn, not realizing that they really want some connection to authenticity."

Fortunately, Santa Fe offers a spectrum that includes faux-adobe buildings — including beautiful examples like Rapp's New Mexico Museum of Art and Meem's Laboratory of Anthropology — as well as newer adobes such as Cristo Rey Church and (precisely because of the efficacy of historic preservation) real, old adobes including El Zaguan, the Lamy Building (formerly the main St. Michael's College building), and the four-centuries-old Palace.

Though the level of debate about historic preservation in general has been relatively low-key (and arguably *too* low-key) in recent years in Santa Fe, nationally there are strong voices cautioning against preservation for the sake of preservation. Some of them "worry that architecturally undistinguished buildings and neighborhoods are winning landmark status for political or sentimental reasons," according to Ben Adler, writing in the February 2012 *Architectural Record* (a commentary forwarded to me by renowned Oklahoma

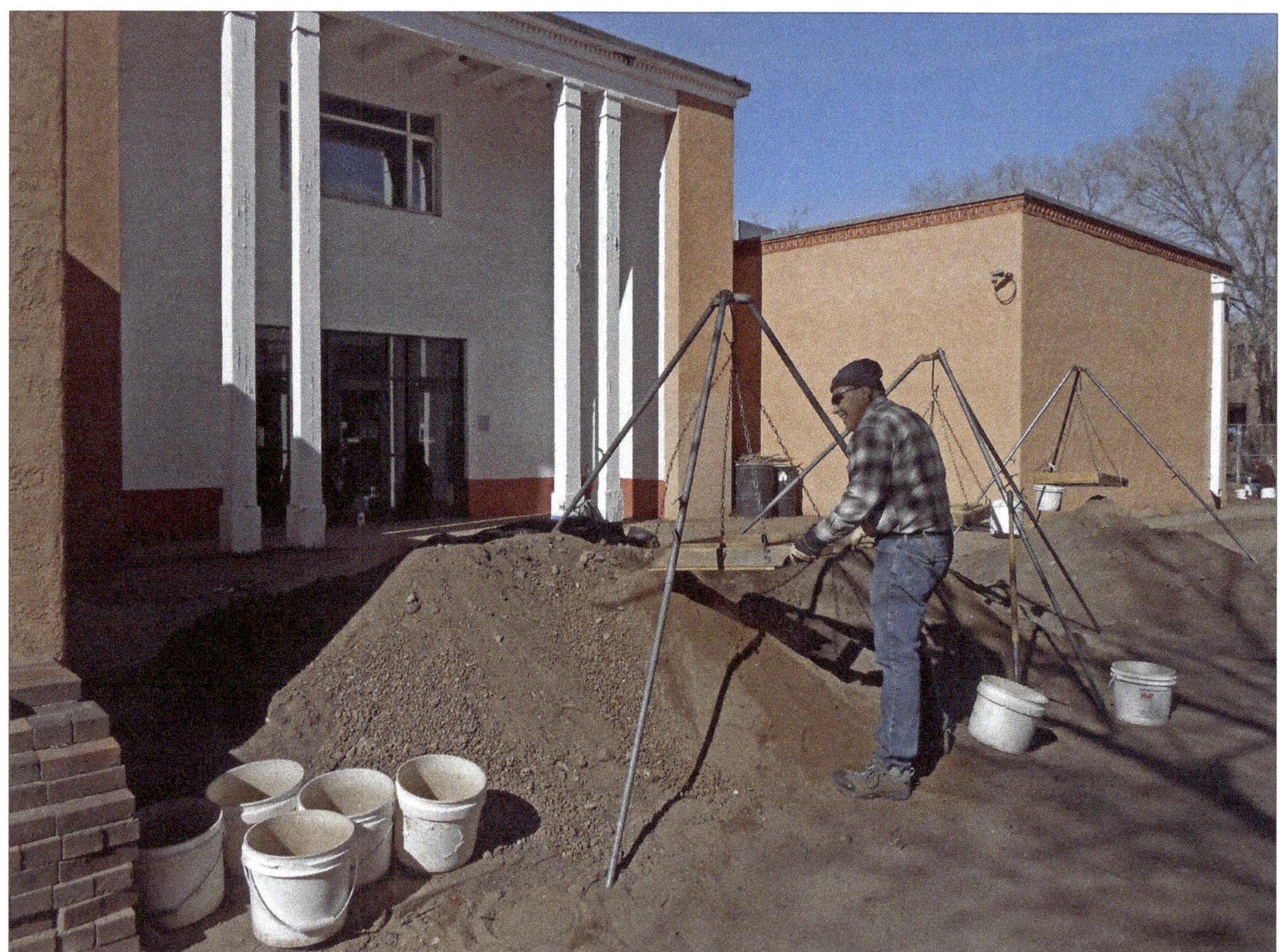

Tim Maxwell, the former longtime director of the State Office of Archaeological Studies and president of the Old Santa Fe Association, sifts earth for artifacts in January 2017 during city-mandated excavations at the 1860s Allison School site. The building before him was built in 1938 as a junior high school, then was converted for use as a district court building. The excavations were required in advance of demolition and the construction of a new Santa Fe County administration annex.

architect Robert Lawton Jones, who retired to Santa Fe in the late 1990s). "The result, they say, is a public that embraces architectural nostalgia rather than innovation."

Harvard economist Ed Glaeser, in his 2012 book *Triumph of the City: How Our Greatest Invention Makes Us Richer, Smarter, Greener, Healthier, and Happier*, attacked landmarking, saying, "The cost of restricted development is that protected areas become more expensive and exclusive." Well, that is often true, but it must be balanced by another fact: that there is great demand to reside in Manhattan and Charleston and Santa Fe — and they are all wonderful places to live or visit — precisely because of the protected architectural quality in core areas of the built environment in these places.

One of Santa Fe's recent success stories was the preservation of the Jane and Gustave Baumann House. Early in 2009 the Historic Santa Fe Foundation announced that it had acquired the house to "document, evaluate and conserve" the distinctive adobe dwelling built in 1923. Careful rehabilitation work on various aspects both interior and exterior was performed from 2009 to 2011. It was then placed on the market with a preservation easement in place. The easement protects many built features of the home and many hand-carved and painted accents by artist Baumann — including fingerpainted marks on doors and cabinets and a painted band, high up on the walls of the octagonal foyer/gallery, of stylized shapes based on Pueblo Indian motifs. Baumann is renowned for his colorful woodcut prints and is remembered for the shows he and his wife and friends would stage in their living room featuring his elaborate, handmade marionettes. The ceiling hooks that suspended parts of the marionette theater are still there.

The house was subsequently purchased by Nancy Meem Wirth, a community leader in historic preservation and conservation.

**Archaeology**

The significance of a historic building in Santa Fe — where basements are rare — can be thought of as beginning at the foundation and ending at the apex of the roof. But the city's heritage-protection mandate extends deeper, into the realms of early American, early Spanish, and very early Native American artifacts that are often in place several feet below the surface.

An archaeological clearance is required before significant downtown construction projects can proceed. The hundreds of thousands of artifacts that have been discovered over the years in various excavations around town range from animal bones, nails, beads, and majolica found in an 18th-century Spanish colonial midden (trash heap) in the old rail yards to pottery sherds, tools, whistles, skeletal remains, and lithic and architectural remnants from Native American deposits dating back more than 1,500 years.

Scientists with the Museum of New Mexico's Office of Archaeological Studies turned up some interesting material during required excavations in advance of the Drury Hotel project. The digs were performed along a 100-foot stretch of ground between Marian Hall and the Cathedral Basilica of St. Francis of Assisi. They discovered many potsherds, in most cases from pottery made in the 1600s and 1700s by Native people for Spanish "customers," and they found the remains of a lime-slaking pit that may have been used to make plaster for the 1714 *parroquia.*

Right next to the Palace Avenue sidewalk, archaeologist James Moore and his crew dug down and found material that he believes came from earth-leveling work just after the 1896 fire that burned down the beautiful St. Vincent Sanatorium. Then, at about four feet down, Moore's crew found a subterranean surface of large river cobbles that were laid so as to drain water to the sides. Moore told the *Santa Fe New Mexican* that he thought it could well have been the oldest cobblestone street ever discovered in Santa Fe.

*"It is my conviction that within the terms of the proposed Ordinance there is still room for contemporary expression... But there are limitations. They are a price I believe the majority of architects will be willing to pay for this act of conservation."*

**— John Gaw Meem, "Proposed Historical Zoning Ordinance, 1957," evidently presented at a city meeting**

# Chapter 4
# A PRESERVATION ORDINANCE AND THE ROQUE LOBATO HOUSE

SANTA FE'S DISTINCTIVE APPEARANCE is guarded by citizen committees and by the city itself. The primary tool wielded by the municipality is the Historic Districts Ordinance, an updated version of the Historic Styles Ordinance that was adopted in 1957. At that point, city leaders' preferences for the Spanish-Pueblo and Territorial revival styles had already been exercised for three or four decades, but more and more they worried that Santa Fe was drifting toward an "Everytown, U.S.A." aesthetic. A local stimulus for giving those design preferences the force of law was the protest arising from the construction of a new building on Lincoln Avenue in 1955.

Designed by John Conron and David Lent for their furniture store and architecture office, the glassy Centerline building probably added weight to the arguments against anything remotely modernistic in the downtown area. The business had a decidedly contemporary appearance, and Conron and Lent fostered a progressive atmosphere within its walls. In June 1957 a newspaper notice urged citizens to visit Centerline (which it called a "contemporary general store") to see an exhibition of about 60 photographs by Ellen Auerbach and Eliot Porter. The Centerline controversy is perhaps ironic in two respects. First, the remodeled building was chosen as "a good example of modern commercial" and "a cleverly executed remodeling job" in an *Art Week* architecture judging event in November 1957. Second, the somewhat hysterical excitement over the Centerline contrasts with Conron's dedication to heritage buildings in Santa Fe — including serving as preservation architect for decades at the Palace of the Governors.

John Gaw Meem spoke about the proposed style ordinance at a 1957 city meeting. Wondering whether the town's historic appearance would survive, he said that "the Twentieth Century is in a hurry... Modern architecture, so much of which one is thrilled by, is tremendously influenced by prefabricated machine products, whose use inevitably, in its more commercial aspects, tends to sameness and monotony," he said. "If London and Rome are having trouble with this dominating sameness, how long do you think little Santa Fe can retain its unique and delightful character?"

Meem, Oliver La Farge, Sam Montoya, and Irene von Horvath authored the ordinance that was unanimously approved by the City Council on Oct. 30. Architect John McHugh reacted with the pronouncement that the ordinance was "against the tradition of Santa Fe" and would become "the first shadow of the dark cloud of conformity." Another opponent condemned the new law as a "sign that Santa Fe has lost faith in the future."

Thirteen years later, in an article in *New Mexico Architecture*, McHugh admitted that everybody would be sad to see the charm of Santa Fe lost, adding that "each year we are losing a little ground." In his article titled "Old Santa Fe and What to Do About It," he stressed an important attribute not often discussed: "The most rapidly disappearing aspect of Santa Fe's charm is the Medieval street pattern. This is something that is especially ours. Only Santa Fe and Boston have this fascinating variety of twisting streets of varying widths."

McHugh also advocated that the ordinance should be made "more flexible with more emphasis on general architectural character and harmony with the traditional buildings which constitutes our heritage. The Committee [the city's historic-review board] must be given much more discretion, be less bound by rigid rules." It can be argued that the distinctiveness of the city, its sense of liveliness, depends to a degree on a variety of architecture. Yes, these can be built in other parts of the city, and have been — witness, for example, Molecule Design, SITE Santa Fe, and the homes by Robert Zachry and Jon Dick — but one or two buildings with some degree of energetic modernity could possibly "fit" in the historic district.

Trey Jordan, a local architect with a modernist bent, hinges part of his position on the fact that there should be houses built in the historic district in the early 21st century that will be particularly valued, *and merit preservation*, a hundred years from now. An architect-designed building should be special, and should make a statement about the ideas of the day, rather than merely blending in. And architects should be challenged to respectfully update the Santa Fe Style vocabulary; otherwise, its evolution is left up to technicians.

There have been several approved projects that likely violated the city ordinance in terms of style or massing or impact to the streetscape (and thus to the town's historical identity). Each one, unfortunately after the fact, was considered by local preservationists as a wake-up call to vigilance and to what could be irrevocably lost. And each arbuably added to the long-term erosion of central Santa Fe's character.

Among these projects were the construction of the Eldorado Hotel, the First Interstate Building, the La Esquina Building, the Inn at Loretto (a gargantuan structure, but the Tulsa developer worked with the Old Santa Fe Association on an "appropriate" design), and the First Judicial District Courthouse, as well as the intemperate remodel of the 19th-century Valdés House as part of the El Castillo retirement complex.

TWICE A MONTH, the Historic Districts Review Board — colloquially referred to as the H-Board — rules on a vast array of cases in the city's historic district. The cases involve proposed new-home projects and a myriad of remodels, where the board rules on exterior wall colors, height increases, and other design impacts, as well as on the minutiae of wall, window, door, roof, *portal*, and fence forms and materials. Many of the buildings in the district have been surveyed and assigned a status — landmark, significant, contributing, or noncontributing — and each project is considered accordingly by the H-Board when owners want to make changes. The city is obligated to deny proposed alterations that would cause a downgrade in historic status.

It is interesting that once upon a time, when an owner wanted to perform restoration work on a historic building, the concept across the country was that the new work should match the old as closely as possible. Now, according to the Secretary of the Interior's Standards & Guidelines for the Treatment of Historic Properties, the repair or restoration work should be "differentiated from the old" and even "clearly identified as a contemporary re-creation."

The rules in the city of Santa Fe are similar. They encourage repair over replacement, but where replacement is necessary, the new material "shall match the material being replaced in composition, design, color, texture, and other visual qualities." On the other hand, additions "shall not duplicate those of the existing structure in a manner that will make the addition indistinguishable from the existing structure."

The challenge of making decisions with both of those strictures in place illuminates the complexities faced by the H-Board members on a continu-

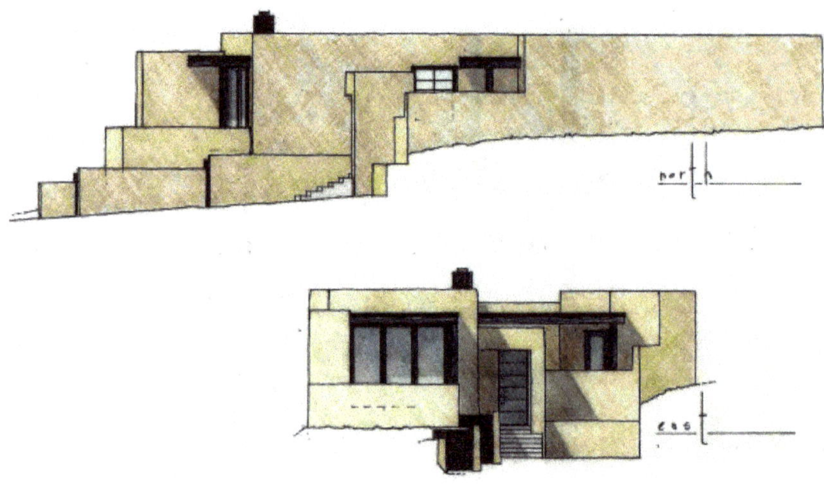

Trey Jordan has been designing homes in Santa Fe since 1990, but this proposal for what can reasonably be considered as contemporized Santa Fe Style, for a lot on Camino Cabra, was denied by the Historic Districts Review Board.

ing basis — although the real task simply involves judging whether the proposed change will accommodate the owner's desire to improve the property but not damage the historic character of the building, the neighborhood, and the historic district.

The "historic district" is actually composed of five districts that occupy approximately 4,000 acres in the old part of town. (Santa Fe in 2019 totaled about 33,600 acres.) They are the Downtown and Eastside Historic District, the Don Gaspar Area Historic District, the Westside-Guadalupe Historic District, the Historic Transition District, and the Historic Review District.

The standards in the Don Gaspar Historic District are fairly lenient, reflecting the diverse styles and materials employed in this part of town beginning in the post-railroad era. Thus construction with brick, slump block, and stone is often allowed, as are hip, gable, and shed roofs.

By contrast, the rules are quite restrictive in the Downtown and Eastside Historic District, in which exist many of the best examples of Spanish-Pueblo buildings. Here flat-roofed adobes are king. In this subdistrict, there are two categories. The most protected realm is "Old Santa Fe Style," which is characterized by construction with adobe. Here builders and remodelers generally are allowed to build with brick, masonry block, and other materials as long as the end result looks very much like an adobe building or addition.

Three firm guidelines point to the fierceness of the protections in place: exterior walls must be at least eight inches thick; the builder must avoid "geometrically straight façade lines"; and the area of solid wall space in any façade must be greater than the window and door space combined.

Somewhat less rigidly controlled are buildings that fall within a "Recent Santa Fe Style" description. The intention here is that they be in harmony with historic buildings. "No less than 80 percent of the surface area of any publicly visible façade shall be adobe finish, or stucco simulating adobe finish," the code reads. "The balance of the publicly visible façade may be of natural stone, wood, brick, tile, terra cotta, or other material, subject to approval."

THE RECENT RISE of sustainable building — Santa Fe passed its Green Building Code in March 2009 — poses extra challenges for the H-Board, homeowners, and architects and builders in the historic district, where a proliferation of visible banks of photovoltaic panels (to mention the most obvious example) would subtract from the treasured historic visage. A strong example of the debates swirling around Santa Fe Style at the beginning of the 21st century are recalled in Trey Jordan's designs, and the reactions to them. In early 2004, some H-Board members were displeased with a house on Armijo Lane — a design they had approved — in the historic Cerro Gordo neighborhood. They pointed to the grayish stucco, a visible glass door, and the crisp edges of the corners and parapets that were noticeably different from the rounded edges of the standard Spanish-Pueblo Revival buildings.

It can be argued that the house is a perfect example of how something more contemporary can fit in. The differences are relatively subtle, but it is obviously different from the houses around it; however, if those homes can be described in a collective way at all, the term "vernacular whatevertecture" may be appropriate because there are so many variations from lot to lot.

The exterior stucco of the Armijo house is a bit grayer, but it's still brown. There are definitely "crisp" edges at the tops and edges of the walls, and there are various recesses and projecting planes — different geometries. But the neighboring houses can be seen as a jumble of brown boxes with rounded edges but otherwise having very little similarity from one to another. There are all sorts of windows, doors, ornamentations, roofs, and fences. Another reason for the natural, haphazard arrangement of these homes is that the topography is so uneven; and the distance from house to house varies greatly. These are all precisely the attributes that give this neighborhood a singular character. There is no reason to expect more regularity.

Age is another pertinent factor in this argument. Except for a 3-acre parcel to the southwest that was built by the city housing authority as a planned complex, this neighborhood developed naturally. The houses were built as needed, and this Armijo Lane house fits in as simply one of the most modern — *recent* — additions to the neighborhood. So it just adds to the basic honesty of Cerro Gordo.

In July 2006, the Historic Design Review Board shot down plans for another Jordan house on Camino Cabra. Like the Armijo Lane domicile, this design was for a house with hard edges, but it also was traditionally asymmetrical and had a *portal.* The design could simply have been read as a gently contemporized Santa Fe Style home.

A moderate number of such well-designed houses could co-exist with the thousands in the district that more closely conform to the idealized Santa Fe Style of yesteryear. Some of the nervousness has to do with quantity.

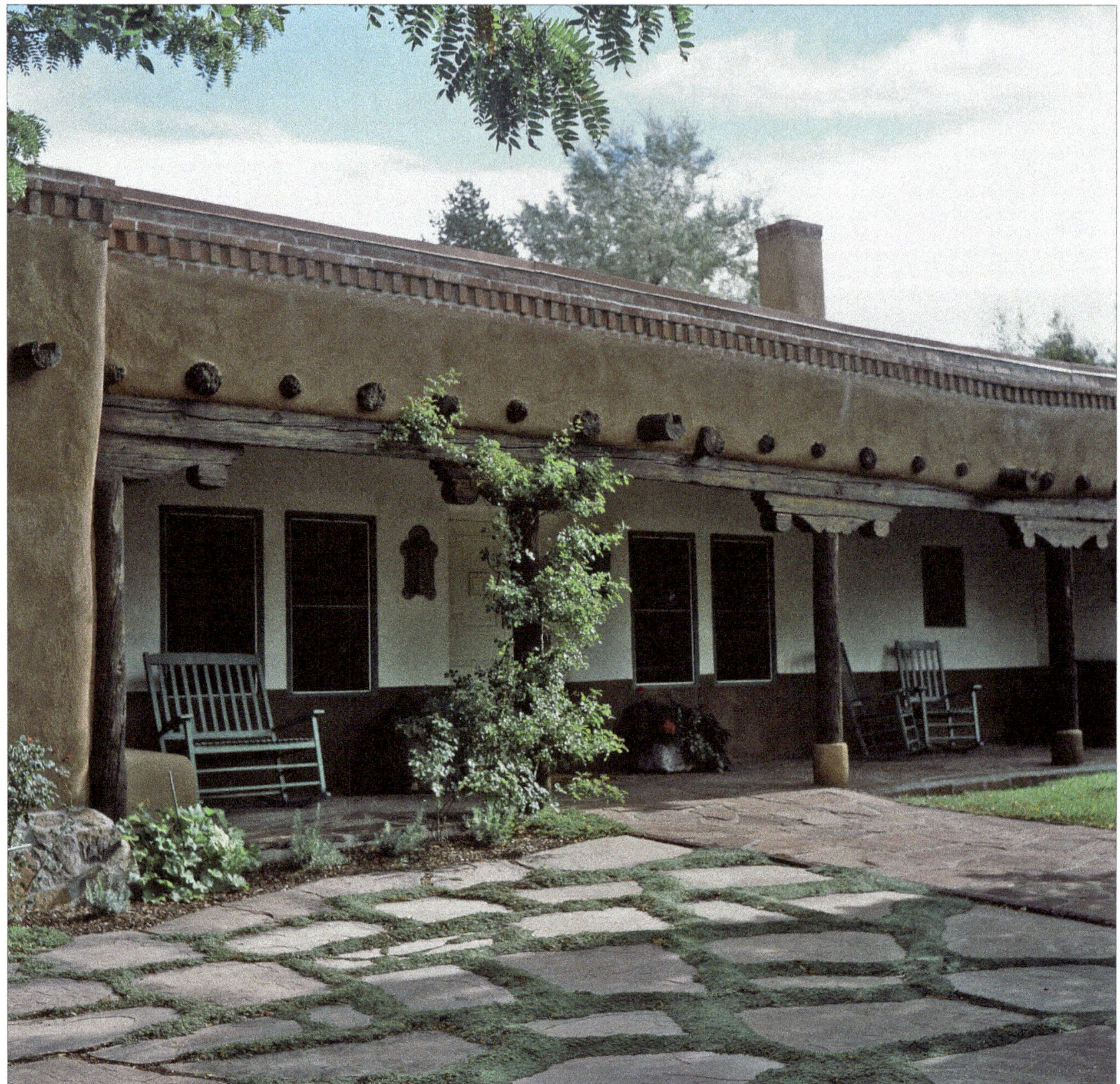

The Roque Lobato House: old projecting *vigas* and more recent brick coping, abbreviated *portal*, and attractive but modern thyme-bordered flagstone paving

Too many contemporary-design houses punctuating the streetscapes in old neighborhoods could be deleterious, just as Santa Fe will lose its quality if its historic adobes one by one are erased by thoughtless, dollar-driven remodels.

There are always citizens weighing in on both sides of this issue. One example was a letter-writer who responded to a news story about the Armijo Lane house. He bluntly suggested that Jordan go elsewhere if he didn't like the rules, adding, "We have a contempt for most contemporary architecture because it is visually cold, boring, sterile, arrogant and just plain ugly."

Another commenter from the public, after coverage of the Camino Cabra proposal, called Jordan's design "a very tasteful interpretation of many of the elements we all love about the architecture of Santa Fe, without blindly copying every little detail over and over."

At the time of the Armijo Lane case, David Rasch, the city's historic preservation officer and chief staff member for the H-Board, said the architect's designs were too modern for the historic area. A decade later, he had moderated his appraisal. "When the board approved this, they were looking at two-dimensional drawings," Rasch said in a September 2015 interview. "But once it was built, people were complaining about the color and the crisp edges, saying, 'This isn't Santa Fe Style.' But when I started doing more research into the Santa Fe Style vocabulary, you see human-scaled masses that fit nicely on the earth, and there's a mass with a corner *portal* just like the White sisters [today's School for Advanced Research administration building] and a slatted wood window cover that's basically a variation on an early type of window grille, so he's got many of the elements of Santa Fe Style. I believe this is the 21st-century evolution of Santa Fe Style, because it has the vocabulary. But the preservationists and the board don't agree yet."

Jordan maintained that his work respects the city's architectural history and is in agreement with the ordinance. "David Rasch has really come around, and the H-Board is getting there," he said later that month. Frank Katz [board member] has been a real good voice and I think he understands how to broker some sort of middle ground with people who don't really want to see the vernacular evolve."

SOME PEOPLE MAY SAY it is obvious whether or not a house is historic, but the issues can be knotty. Many venerable adobe buildings have been changed significantly, but aren't they still "historic"? The case of the Roque Lobato House is an intriguing one in this conversation.

Lobato was a soldier and armorer to the Royal Spanish Garrison of Santa Fe, according to the 2014 book *The Roque Lobato House, Santa Fe, New Mexico* by Chris Wilson and Oliver Horn. The abode, which dates to 1785, adjoined the northern approach to the city. Close by on the north were a gunpowder storehouse for the garrison and a small fort that was known as La Garita. To the southwest were the Spanish presidio fortifications.

Lobato's house originally was a simple line of rooms with an inset *portal* in the center of the front façade. Most of the rooms opened directly onto the *portal*, which was 16 feet deep. The domicile was purchased in 1910 (from its fifth owner, A.B. Renehan) by Museum of New Mexico archaeologist and Santa Fe Style evangelist Sylvanus G. Morley. He later described its condition as having been "very much down at the heel" and after the purchase he engaged himself in a renovation and expansion.

He created a courtyard in the rear by adding a wing at the east and a robust, handsome pergola on the west and by bolstering the existing stone wall along the north. Morley appended *portales* to the east and south facades, incorporating in the latter a very old carved-beam element that Wilson believes may have first been installed in a courtyard *portal* at Santa Fe's 17th-century *parroquia*. Morley also built up the firewall above the front *portal* and restored the house's windows to a type he considered more appropriate to the building's pedigree. Although he certainly made substantial (if sensitive) changes during his ownership, the house's character was severely compromised in the 1960s and 1970s — if the judgments of the City of Santa Fe and the Historic Santa Fe Foundation are to be honored.

The offending modifications include the addition of brick coping to that tall firewall over the front *portal*, which gives the house a "Territorial Revival" stamp. Even more egregious to the aforementioned arbiters of historic authenticities was the abbreviation in the depth of the front *portal* as the owners built a new wall to provide an inside hallway. In reaction, the Historic Santa Fe Foundation lifted the property from its Registry of Resources Worthy of Preservation, and from the next edition of its book *Old Santa Fe Today*, and the city downgraded the house's status in the historic district to "noncontributing."

**IN THE NEW MILLENNIUM**, owners Karl and Susan Horn worked with architect Craig Hoopes and artist Sergio Tapia on a renovation. Whenever they could, they followed Morley's Arts and Crafts aesthetic. While honoring his house's historic bones and details, Karl Horn simultaneously counterposed the renovation work against the ideas of strict preservationists who would sacrifice virtually nothing for livability. He invoked 19th-century art critic John Ruskin, who famously said that the heritage value of a building "was not in its stone and mortar but rather in its ability to bear witness to the passing waves of humanity."

In considering this house's history, we can understand that there are two "periods of significance," which correspond to the ownerships of Lobato and Morley. It is easier to look at the house today and say you can't discern 18th-century character, but surely Morley's stamp survives. So it is certainly historic, right?

These matters occupied a panel before a modest audience at the New Mexico History Museum on May 31, 2015. That afternoon, the museum sponsored a forum titled "Lively Discussion of The Roque Lobato House,

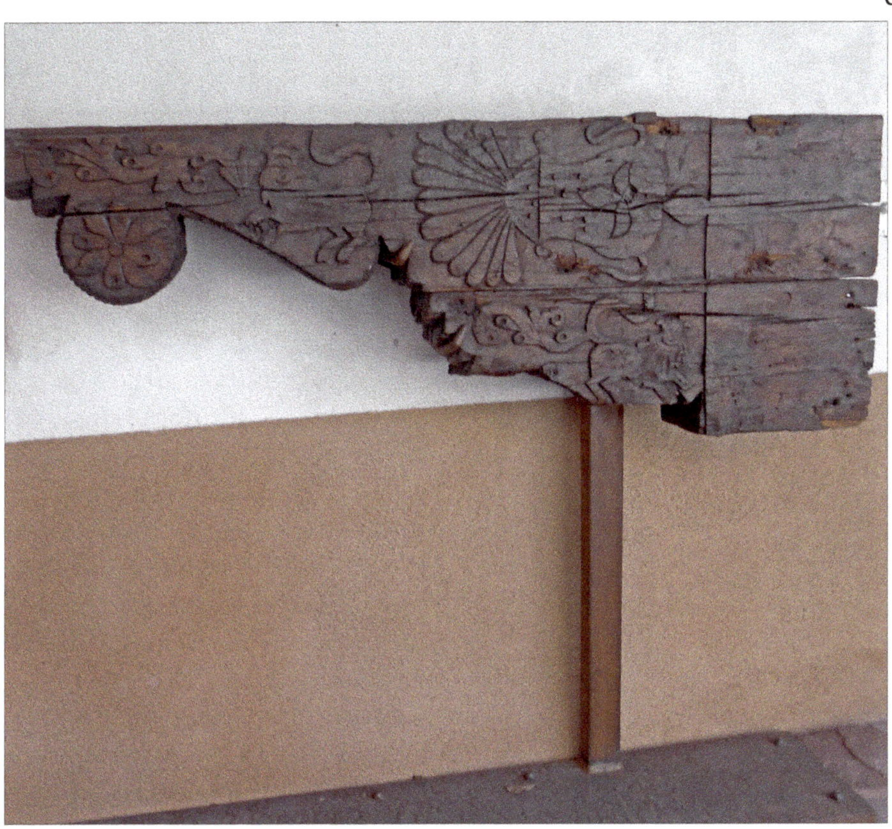

This corbel on display at the Lobato House was originally part of the rear *portal*. Architecture writer and University of New Mexico professor Chris Wilson believes it may have been carved for the first *parroquia*, the town's 17th-century parish church

a Santa Fe Landmark since 1785." Architectural historian, UNM professor, and author Wilson moderated; the panelists were architect Beverley Spears; historian and writer John Pen La Farge; and longtime historic-adobe contractor Alan "Mac" Watson.

Speaking about that important change to the front *portal*, Wilson told the gathering, "Most porches on Spanish Colonial houses were six, maybe eight feet deep and were primarily to provide covered circulation between the rooms. There were no interior hallways, and in the 20th century the most common remodel of Spanish Colonial houses, after the addition of kitchens and bathrooms, was figuring out how to add interior corridors.

"Why did the Historic Santa Fe Foundation react so vehemently to this one change? My best guess is that the house's deep porch had emerged in the minds of the art colony as their historic precedent for something they had begun to do in the 1920s and 1930s. They viewed the porches as not merely circulation corridors but as outdoor rooms."

In other words, as a more modern purpose for the *portal*.

Regarding the 1960s addition of brick coping to the roofline, Wilson said that such a modification "in fact was in keeping with the way people historically protected parapet walls."

Spears said she thought Morley was "heavy-handed in his height of the parapets" and that the house's original historic integrity "was further damaged by the addition of the brick coping."

La Farge, who was president of the Old Santa Fe Association at the time, affirmed that "Santa Fe houses evolved, including because of the availability of new materials." He then referred to the logic of the *portal* remodel with a statement about another of Santa Fe's venerable dwellings. "My grandmother's house, which she built in the 1930s on Upper Canyon Road, had her bedroom in the middle of the house, and to get to another part of the house one had to walk through my grandmother's bedroom. That's very Santa Fe, but it's not very convenient."

Watson discussed several "aspects of integrity" that the state's Cultural Properties Review Committee (on which he had previously served) employs in its examinations of historic buildings. Among them are design (and Watson said the Lobato House's character "has been significantly altered"), setting ("It has changed radically, for example by the addition of traffic signals and the house's gardens"), materials (new *vigas*, plasters, doors, and brick coping), workmanship ("It was back then all done with your friends and relatives, but now the house boasts a level of workmanship that's extraordinary"), and feeling ("The entry experience is very different, and the sense of privacy now is very different because of the three-car garage and guest house").

Watson concluded that the Lobato House "has been significantly altered, even since Morley's work."

"Many of those points also pertain to other historic houses in Santa Fe, for example water-heavy landscaping and new stucco," Wilson said in his closing statement. "If Lobato isn't historically eligible for x and y reasons, then what about the others?"

*"The architecture of the Santa Fe Railyard should reflect the warehouse, industrial and commercial history of the site and the concept of an arts and cultural district."*

**— 2001 Santa Fe Railyard Master Plan**

# Chapter 5
# SANTA FE RAILYARD; ADAPTIVE RE-USE

ONE OF SANTA FE'S BIGGEST and most ambitious development plans came to fruit between 2007 and 2009 in the city's old railyard district. The $144 million endeavor included a new building for the Warehouse 21 teen center, an appropriately voluminous structure for the Santa Fe Farmers Market, and the large Market Station building (anchored by REI), all sited around a new plaza, plus many substantial improvements to the 10-acre property now known as Railyard Park.

The revitalization was the result of more than two decades of democratic planning. Before that got started, the city had declared the old railroad area as "blighted," then a plan surfaced that would have meant tearing up all of the rails for the development of a mall, a hotel, and other commerical uses.

In 1995, with help from the Trust for Public Land, the City of Santa Fe purchased the property. The following year, architect Gayla Bechtol suggested a R/UDAT process, in which the American Institute of Architects brings in experts to work with the local community. The Santa Fe AIA chapter, led by Bechtol and Lisette Ellis, with Suby Bowden as a team member, started the ball rolling for the three-week Regional/Urban Design Assistance Team program.

Other key planners included architects Wayne Lloyd and Steven Robinson, landscape architect Faith Okuma, and the Land Use Resource Center. Their work was guided by input from thousands of Santa Fe residents offered during nearly two dozen public meetings.

The redevelopment of the newly christened Santa Fe Railyard began in 2006. The growth of this area a half-mile southwest of the Santa Fe Plaza roughly corresponded with another revitalization. In December 2008, after almost eight decades, passenger rail service at Santa Fe resumed with the arrival of a new commuter train, the New Mexico Rail Runner Express. Multiple runs each day connect the capital city with Kewa Pueblo, Bernalillo, Albuquerque (which is also a station stop for the Amtrak line between Chicago and Los Angeles), and Belen.

Santa Fe's storied railroad history began in 1880. During the preceding decade, railway lines were expanded into the western United States. The anticipated arrival of trains in Santa Fe caused great excitement; the town's leaders planned to build many new houses and a special conveyance to connect the train stop with the Plaza.

The railroad developers instead chose Lamy as the station stop before the rails headed south to Albuquerque. Santa Feans quickly approved a bond issue that facilitated the construction of a spur line to Santa Fe. The first locomotive of the Atchison, Topeka & Santa Fe Railway arrived in the capital on Feb. 9, 1880.

Railway service hastened the demise of the Santa Fe Trail. Trains not only offered faster delivery, but the size, weight, and fragility of merchandise were no longer issues as they had been with wagon freight.

Santa Fe was a railroad town for the next half century — for most of those years served by not one but three railroads. In 1887, the AT&SF was joined by the Texas, Santa Fe & Northern Railway from Antonito, Colorado. This narrow-gauge line was later taken over by the Denver & Rio Grande Railroad — the "Chili Line." Then in 1904 came the "Bean Line" or Santa Fe Central, which became the New Mexico Central Railway after merging with the Albuquerque Eastern. The nicknames of the D&RG and the NMC testify to the regional importance of agriculture in former times. One line hauled highy valued New Mexico chile northward and the other transported pinto beans from farms in the Estancia Basin to El Paso and Santa Fe.

In its heyday as a railroad town, Santa Fe was fully equipped to handle passenger and freight trains, and to service steam locomotives. The rail yards had depots with loading docks and platforms, a 70-foot turntable that was used to rotate rail engines into a service roundhouse, an engine-repair building with a series of sandstone-lined trenches for working underneath locomotives, and a well and a massive water tower with sandstone-block foundations that were likely cut by French and Italian masons who had recently erected the St. Francis Cathedral and Loretto Chapel.

THE ATCHISON, TOPEKA & SANTA FE built its first depot in 1880. It was replaced in 1909 with a station designed in the Mission Revival style with

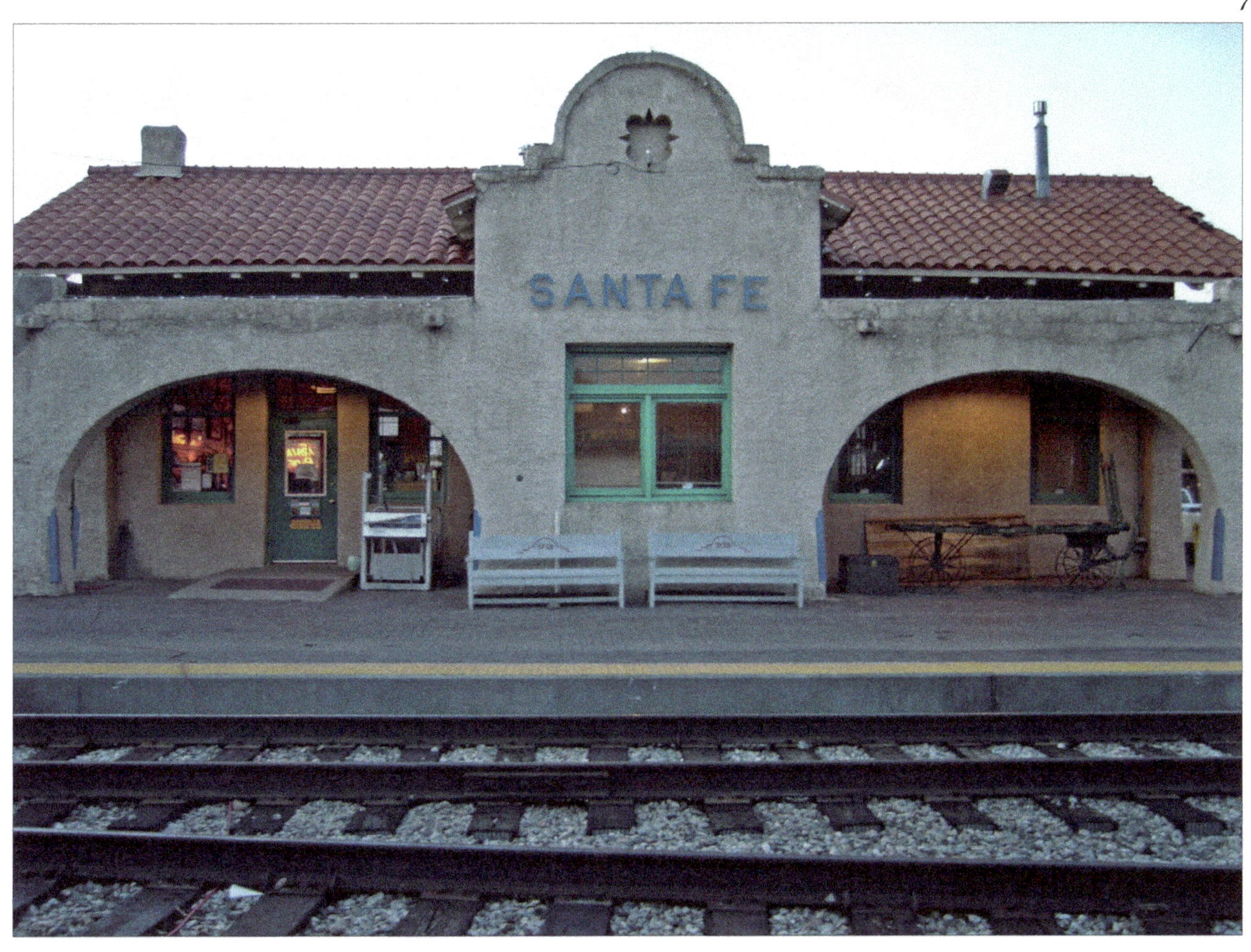


Santa Fe Depot, trackside

curvilinear parapets, walls of pentile and structural steel, and a red-tile roof: this is the Santa Fe Depot that is still in use and is a city historic landmark. The Denver & Rio Grande had its first station about a thousand yards north of what came to be known as Santa Fe's railyards, near today's intersection of Jefferson and Catron streets. The D&RG built its red-brick Union Depot (now Tomasita's Restaurant) in 1903 and the station soon also served the New Mexico Central.

In the late 1920s, the New Mexico Central lines were abandoned and bought by the Atchison, Topeka & Santa Fe Railway. The Chili Line tracks were empty after 1941. Passenger service to and from Santa Fe was canceled by the AT&SF in 1929. (A limited number of people still found a ride in the caboose, but that practice ended in 1961.)

During the remainder of the 20th century, the railyard area gradually declined and the various parcels were developed as needed, with little reference to railroading history. In June 1987, the Santa Fe City Council approved that "blighted area" resolution and eight years later, the city purchased the

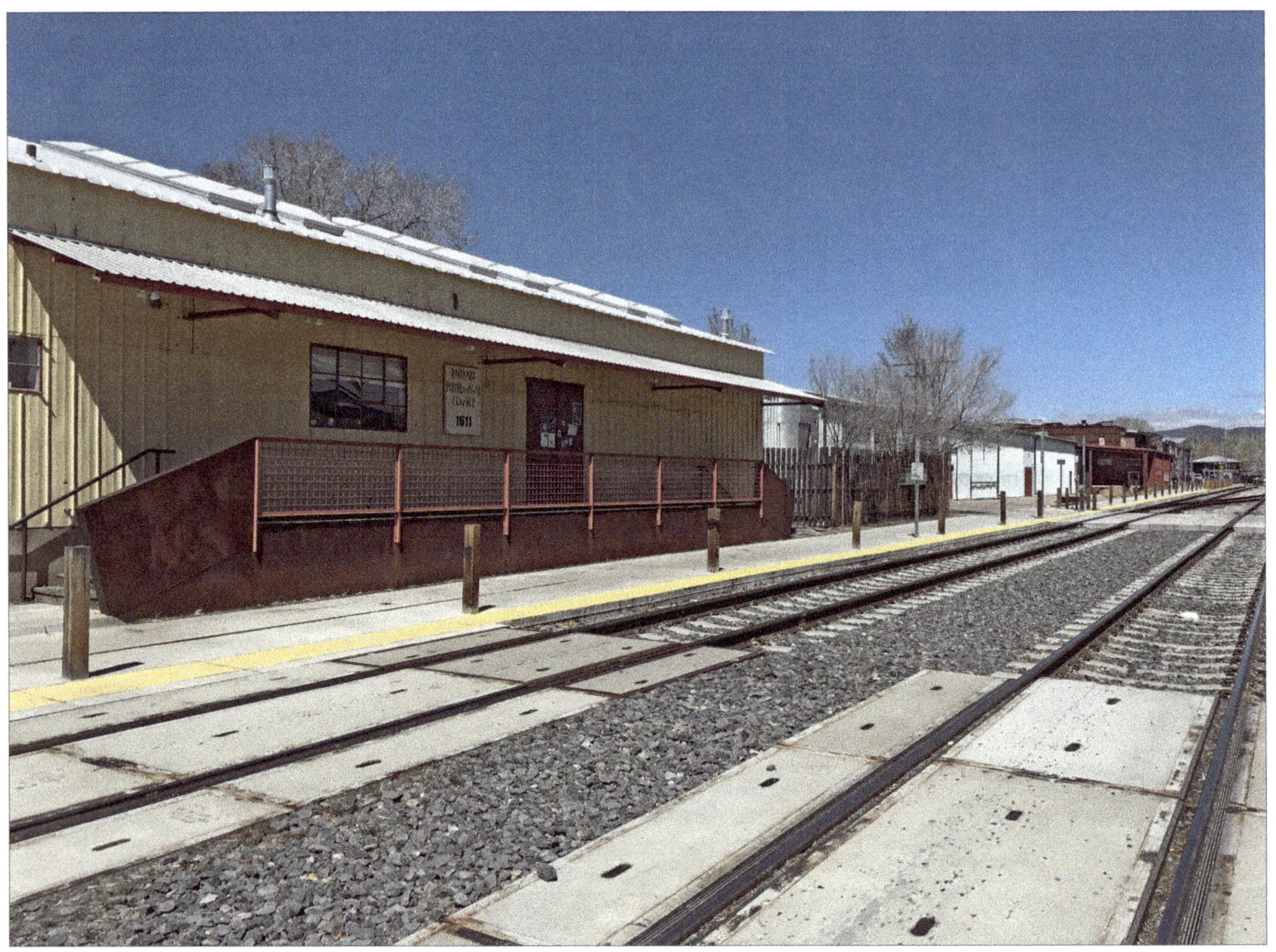

Railyard Performance Center and railroad tracks

50-acre tract. In 2002, Santa Fe's vision for an energized district took a leap with its adoption of the Railyard Master Plan shaped by a Design Workshop Inc. team that included Suby Bowden + Associates and Lloyd & Tryk Architects.

The master plan honors the site's history by embracing its "rugged, gritty" look, and it calls for new buildings to be designed with the simple massing that reflects what used to be there. Among the oldest businesses were the Capital Coal Yard, the D.L. Miller and Co. Cracker Factory, the Lemp Brewing Company, the Schnepple Storehouse, and the Hondo Pine Lumber Yard and Planing Mill. Most of the warehouses in the rail yards were built right up against the tracks, for easy loading and unloading of materials and merchandise from rail cars.

This is a part of town within which architects who love contemporary design have more freedom than in the central historic district, although there are still rules about appearance and uses. For one thing, the master plan dictates that the 1909 Santa Fe Depot and the 1913 Gross Kelly & Co. Warehouse will remain architecturally unique; their architectural styles — Mission Revival and Spanish-Pueblo Revival, respectively — may not be used in today's Santa Fe Railyard. Instead, architects have been challenged to work with the basic, boxy form that is exemplified by El Museo Cultural de Santa Fe, the Railyard Performance Center, and the James Kelly Contemporary Gallery (now Tai Modern).

Large windows are okay in the Santa Fe Railyard, because they remind us that trains transformed the town's business district with large glass panes beginning in the 1880s. Walls can be stucco, brick, or profiled metal. About that last one, it used to be called "corrugated metal" and had one undulating profile, which you can see in the old Butler Building at the south end of the Gross Kelly Warehouse. Modern versions of the material come in a variety of profiles and have often been employed by architects in the Santa Fe Railyard; two examples are Warehouse 21 (built on a design that originated with Mazria Odems Dzurec and was completed by Alexander Dzurec's Autotroph) and Railyard Galleries (Devendra Contractor and Deirdre Harris), which alternated buildings clad in metal and red stucco.

The long *portales* you see in many Santa Fe Style buildings are not allowed in the Railyard, but hanging canopies are, and they have been widely used, including on the Market Station and Railyard Galleries buildings, for their decorative value and to provide a modicum of shading.

**Adaptive re-use**

The Contractor-Harris remodel of James Kelly Contemporary was an early success story in the Railyard revitalization, and it won a New Mexico Heritage Preservation Award in 2008. It was also a good example of what architects call adaptive re-use.

Adaptive re-use is more than simply remodeling for a new tenant, bringing an old building up to code, and increasing its sustainability quotient. It's also a form of preservation, as the work is undertaken with a secondary motive: retaining the building's important, historic architectural features. In the gallery project, Contractor's firm incorporated glass and steel to contemporize what was originally a Sears & Roebuck Co. warehouse, built in the 1950s by Hansen Lumber. But he also preserved its heavy wood posts and ceiling joists, and just as importantly preserved their visibility in the new space. (But gallerists can be oblivious to such historic qualities: the last time I was there, I had to search to get a glimpse of the joists.)

If the application of adaptive re-use hinges on a building's historic character, it is prudent that only buildings that are undeniably historically important are chosen for this strategy. When Drury Hotels decided to convert the

1954 St. Vincent Hospital building into one of its fanciest offerings, the fact that the building is in Santa Fe's Downtown and Eastside Historic District and that it was designed by John Gaw Meem assured its preservation.

In October 2007, Drury bought the property for more than $20 million and with architect Mark Hogan began planning the substantial project, which resulted in a 182-room hotel that opened in the summer of 2014. In this case, the historic elements worthy of preservation were on the exterior: the fenestration pattern, architectural features that include balustraded balconies and areas of ornamental brickwork, and the general form of the structure.

During construction, virtually all of the interior walls were removed, leaving vast halls of cement columns on each floor. The insulation factor in the new rooms, hallways, and other spaces was substantially upgraded. On the south side of the old hospital, ICF blocks were used to build an adjoining, four-story addition. Its brick veneer syncs stylistically with the brick of the original building, as does the Territorial Revival-style brick coping along the rooflines and the white-painted pedimented lintels on some windows — Meem's response to what was obviously a limited budget was ingenious, as he strategically added such architectural adornments at aesthetically opportune places on the building.

The development of Drury Plaza Hotel was an excellent example of sustainable building, as well as of adaptive re-use. Rehabbing the existing building conserved the natural resources that would have been necessary for demolition and ground-up new construction, and it conserved the energy that would have been required to extract, process, and transport those building materials. It also helped strengthen the community's social fabric by replacing an eyesore of limited use but historic substance — hundreds of Santa Feans were born there — with a handsome, vital building.

*I would like for our work to belong in Santa Fe, but also to belong in the 21st century.*
**— architect and builder Gabriel Browne**

# Chapter 6
# SANTA FE STYLE IN THE 21st CENTURY

**ABOUT SANTA FE STYLE** in the 21st century, there are at least two topics upon which critical conversations hinge. One has to do with the design limitations for local architects, both in remodel work and new construction. A common comeback to their complaints is that clients and architects who enjoy more contemporary design ideas have freedom to stretch outside Santa Fe's central, historic district, which they should leave alone.

Another interesting realm of debate has to do with materials. Some critics say that Santa Fe has devolved into a "Disneyland" of fake-adobe buildings. After World War II, building quality declined; one example was the use of "viga ends" that appear to project through the wall as on historic buildings, but were only log stubs attached to the outer surface as a Santa Fe Style decoration. And then there was the proliferation of non-adobe materials that were assigned to masquerade as adobe. And no matter: whether adobe brick, hollow clay tile, kiln-baked brick, concrete block, or more recent materials, in all cases the resultant appearance should be that of adobe.

Then, as now (the argument goes), the appearance is the thing. With respect to changes made in the wake of the 1912 decisions, it actually may be that the town's architectural palette would be richer if most of the 19th-century Victorians that survived fires had not been obliterated in Territorial Revival re-dos. The trajectory of Santa Fe Style as the town's all-encompassing architectural signature could arguably have proceeded without subtracting so much of what was.

In an interesting tangent, also bearing on the issue of appearance, the owners of some buildings transformed their exterior finish in line with the fashion of the day. This was the case, for example, on two 19th-century buildings downtown. The Catron Block's red brick, and its mascarons and other ornamentation, are camouflaged under layers of brown paint so that it looks (at least from a distance) more like adobe. And in the 1970s, the adobe Oliver P. Hovey House was stenciled (painted to look like brick) after research indicated that such a "false finish" was historic and had at some point been stuccoed over.

Santa Fe Style first surfaced in the grand, early (1913-1940) gestures by Isaac Rapp and John Gaw Meem, but long ago, in the minds of some, it had been ersatz'd to death with endless knockoffs both in adobe-look (and sometimes grotesquely large) commercial and institutional buildings and in the standardized house plans by production builders. But just try to suggest that the style rules could be relaxed. In 2007, writing about the 50th anniversary of the city's 1957 historic-styles ordinance in my architecture/design column "The Art of Space" (in the *Santa Fe New Mexican's* weekly arts magazine, Pasatiempo), I recalled one sentence from the city code that says each of Santa Fe's buildings should "be recognized as a physical record of its time, place, and use," and I commented, "It's funny that we value this kind of honesty in historic structures but suspend it in regard to new structures." For that observation, more than one letter-writer took me to task.

Capitalizing on the charming adobe theme was the solution after the railroad bypassed Santa Fe in 1880, and it was still an incentive in 1957, when merchants were among the strongest supporters of the ordinance. It can be argued that a citywide affection for the traditional adobe look is paramount, but economics remains a force behind the continuing ban on contemporary architecture in the historic district, an overlay of a little more than six square miles centered (at least philosophically) on the Plaza.

Again, a contingent of architects has held the opinion that the codified Santa Fe Style has had a stultifying effect on the face and soul of the town. Two of those voices from the past were George Anselevicius, former dean of the School of Architecture and Planning at the University of New Mexico, who termed the historic style "memory wallpaper" and downgraded it to the "superficial and cosmetic"; and Santa Fe architect Philippe Register, who, according to his friend Paul Stevenson Oles, once said "everything is batter-dipped in Santa Fe: you make a house and then you dip it in batter, like a corn dog."

And yet the preponderance of critics also love the Spanish-Pueblo Revival and Territorial Revival styles. Even though so many buildings only *look* like adobe, that's what makes Santa Fe what it is.

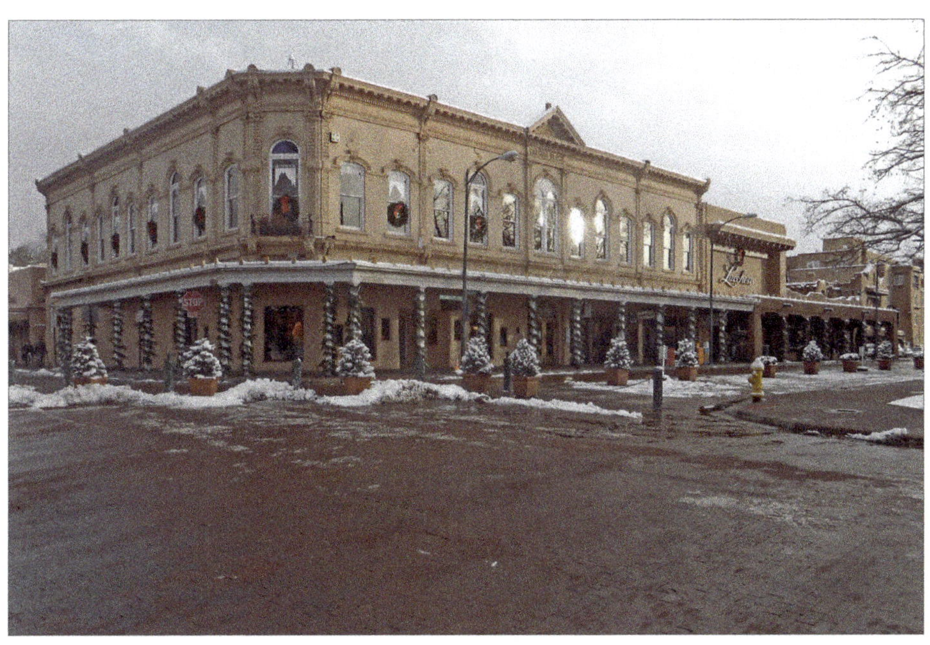

The Catron Block wrapped for Christmas. This brick building was long ago painted brown for a more Santa Fe Style personality.

**IT MAY BE CLAIMED** that these building styles are old-fashioned, and this is certainly true, but they are not merely anachronistic; they are based on rural precedents. Santa Fe Style homes — even many of the new, contemporized versions with harder edges, steel accents, and quite a bit of glass — look pastoral and organic, look like part of the landscape, compared to most other American house types.

Regarded from another angle, the "Santa Fe Style" reference is a bit silly. It doesn't admit into its warm fold many of the natural vernacular homes in Santa Fe, which must surely also be "Santa Fe-style" houses. A good example is the large Westside Guadalupe neighborhood, which (like much of Santa Fe) was farming country before the 20th century. The houses here sport all kinds of architectural and decorative personalizations. As Chris Wilson discusses in *The Myth of Santa Fe* (1997), these are owner-built houses with vivid colors, textured stucco, ornamental stone veneers, polychromatic brickwork, and wrought iron. He suggests that this "vibrant Baroque aesthetic" offers a significant counterpoint to the "muted Arts and Crafts palette of earth tones that predominate on the wealthy Anglo east side."

The city enforces adherence to its 1957 Historic Styles Ordinance by means of a committee whose members meet twice a month to rule on new construction and on building owners' proposed changes. Deciding what shapes, contexts, colors, and materials conform and do not conform to Santa Fe Style is a continuing challenge for the members of the H-Board. And to the extent that they allow for some degree of evolution of the style — as they are urged by progressive-minded applicants — their review objectives can sometimes seem like a moving target.

If the rules are relaxed in certain cases for good reasons, another problem arises: bad contemporary design can easily be more egregious than simply another faux-adobe building. Good design is key. But even then caution is wisdom. After all, architectural changes to a neighborhood are relatively permanent; in the argot of historic preservation, such changes can seriously compromise the historic fabric.

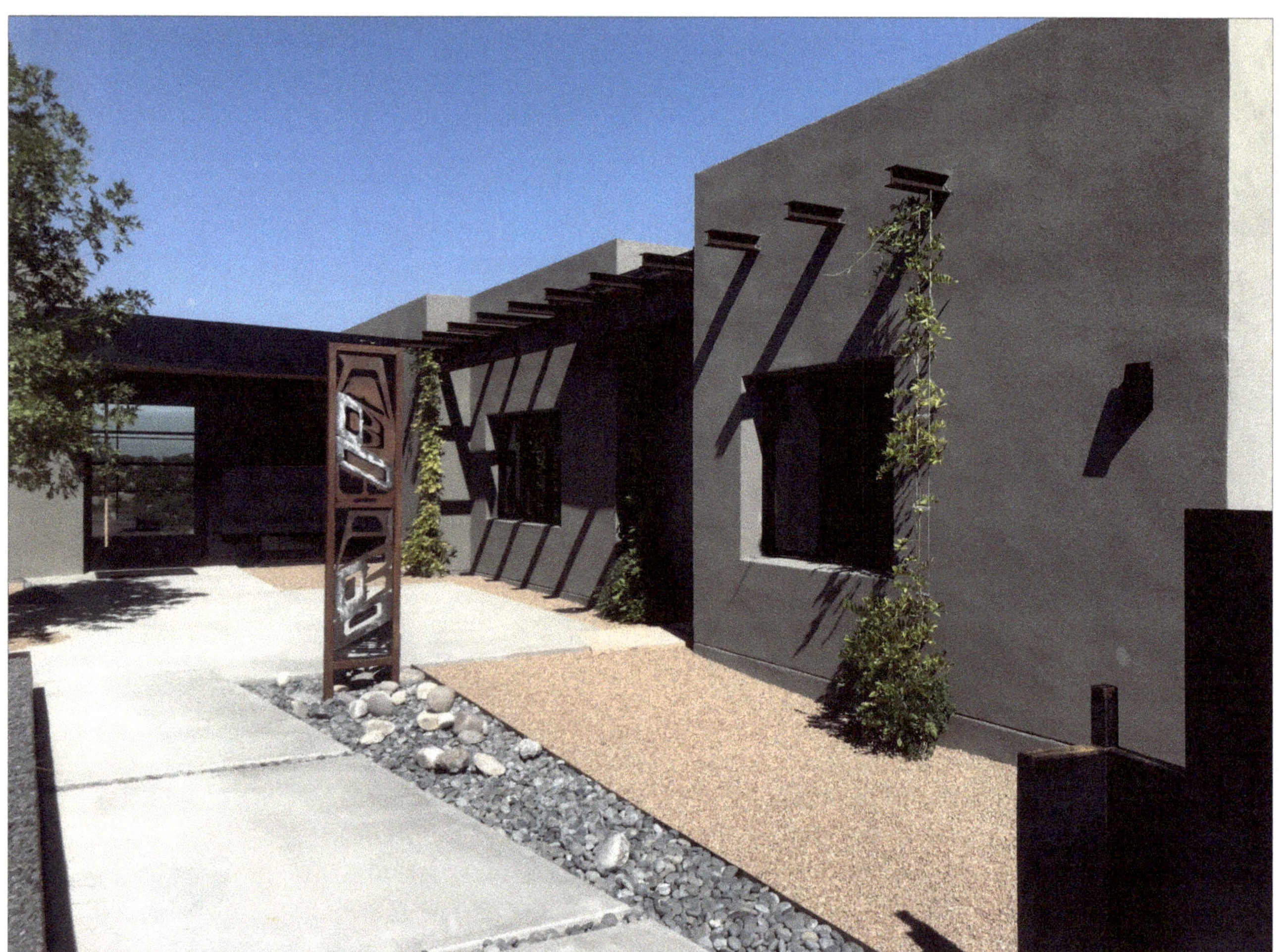

2019 house by Gabriel Browne, Praxis Design/Build, with entry-courtyard sculpture by Clayton Peshlakai

SO GOES THE CONVERSATION about the dominant paradigm, Santa Fe Style, in the capital city of New Mexico. In another Pasatiempo column, again arguing for a possible relaxing of The Ordinance in well-considered cases, I invoked the 1989 I.M. Pei pyramid at the Louvre and a more recent example of contemporary design juxtaposed with tradition: Moshe Safdie's 2006 Jepson Center for the Arts in Savannah, Georgia. It's easy to say we don't want a Gehry or Hadid or Koolhaas building in Santa Fe, yet any one of today's "starchitects" might contribute something wonderful if, rather than asserting a design that was aggressively "iconic," one might fashion a more modest beauty that's at least abstractly inspired by the local scene and traditional forms and materials.

The Santa Fe Community Convention Center, completed in 2008 three blocks from the Plaza, was considered by some to be an opportunity for a more modern building design. Beverley Spears, the project's local architect (working with Fentress Architects, Denver), had this response (also published in an "Art of Space" column) when that was suggested: "We have the heritage of Spanish Colonial architecture, but most of it's been destroyed. Most of what we have are not the authentic buildings; they're the revival buildings, like the New Mexico Museum of Art. Some of our best buildings are fake adobes. The Pueblo Revival style is a hundred years old, so it has an integrity in its own right, and, frankly, people love it and they expect it…

"Our downtown historic area is so small and fragmented that we need to support it rather than play off of it," Spears said. "Also this is a big, big building. A building of this scale, had it been contemporary, would have overpowered everything around it."

This project was one of the last possibilities for something intriguingly different in the downtown area. And yet the convention center, which is monumental but boasts soft lines, reads well at the pedestrian level and holds eminently functional spaces. It is, after all, a compliment to the city's famous stylebook and a tribute to the vision of the architects.

When the debate is focused on residential architecture, tweaks to the dominant paradigm may be more easily considered. In a 2007 interview, Sharon Woods, one of Santa Fe's builders of high-end homes and a longtime chairwoman of the Historic Districts Review Board, said, "People are paying a lot of money for lots; they want the views, and they want something reminiscent of traditional architecture, but there's almost a new style emerging that's neat. It's about the balance of mass and glass. What used to happen in traditional architecture is you'd have mostly mass and a little bit of glass. Now it's very thick walls and thick mass but a larger proportion of glass."

Deborah Auten was one of the first architects I spoke with about Santa Fe Style, back in 2000. "We have all these wonderful elements: the idea of the courtyard, the idea of sculptural massing, the ability to do a flat roof on a residential building," she said in a Pasatiempo interview. "That's almost unheard-of anywhere else, which means you get to do these buildings that look like a piece of sculpture on the land if you do it right."

In 1915, the *New York Evening Post* ran an editorial saying that Edgar Lee Hewett, Sylvanus Morley, "and all those who in one way or another were concerned in crystallizing this New Old Santa Fe style have accomplished something of lasting benefit not only to Santa Fe but to the entire country for the New Old Santa Fe style is beautiful and artistic and will become popular all over the country." On the contrary, and thankfully, Santa Fe for the most part retains its stylistic distinction.

Over the last century, Santa Fe Style has in many cases evolved significantly in form, and certainly has in materials: from adobe to concrete block and pentile to pumice-crete, strawbale, steel frame, and insulated concrete forms, all types usually finished not with mud plaster but with cement-based stucco or elastomeric (acrylic-based) stucco. However, the old crafts aspects of homebuilding is still alive and is another distinction for Northern New Mexico: finishing interior walls with the traditional three coats of plaster and incorporating *vigas*, posts, corbels, and *latillas* produced by local sawmills, as well as smaller-industry, traditionally made doors, *trasteros*, tables, chairs, and beds.

Regarding updates to Santa Fe Style, Meem himself was heading in directions away from the accepted norm. His idea for the 1943 Sanbusco commission for "A Santa Fe style House for Contemporary Living" was a modern, middle-class residence with a glass curtain wall along the south side that not only recalled Europe's International Style but offered solar gain; and instead of a parapet wall, he had a roof overhang to provide summertime shade from the sun.

Both ideas reappeared two years later in Meem's design of a prototype solar house for the Libby-Owens-Ford Glass Company. "I really wish those had been built," Nancy Meem Wirth said in a 2013 telephone interview. "My father was getting creative at that point, but was kind of pulled back by his clients saying, 'Hey, we want what you used to do.'"

In an October 2016 conversation, David Rasch, who was beginning his 14th year as Santa Fe's historic preservation officer, discussed an article titled "Spanish-Pueblo Architecture in Permanant Materials" written by Meem in 1975. "Look at these photos of Taos Pueblo and Zimmerman Library. One is erodable material, mud plaster, and wood, and the other is concrete masonry unit, concrete stucco, and asphalt roofing." Then Rasch showed me a photograph of a Greek temple. "Look at the triglyph in the frieze," he said. "The prototype was wood and in marble it's just decorative. That article by one of the authors of our historic-design ordinance opened my eyes. Now I get it: old Santa Fe Style is erodable and recent Santa Fe Style is permanent. But you have to keep the same vocabulary."

In 1953, Meem addressed an American Institute of Architects group in Santa Fe. On his topic, titled "The Regional New Mexican Architecture," he talked about the modern client requiring a low-maintenance building. People had used brick, concrete, tile, and "stabilized" adobes, but Meem said Native American structures hinted at "an even more direct solution" to the problem. "In many of the Pueblos, notably Santo Domingo, large numbers of houses have at least one adobe wall protected by an extension of the roof cantilevered on the ceiling beams or vigas. Why not devise a system of cantilevering the flat roof over all sides, thus protecting all of the walls..."

The architectural designer said eaves wouldn't represent a more radical change to the basic style than had the Spaniards' additions of windows, doors, and porches to the Pueblo style. "It is this very quality of adaptability that makes the style so exciting and alive and leaves one convinced that the Pueblo style through its various modifications can meet the demands of modern twentieth century criticism."

**IN CONCLUSION**, there is in the capital city today no easy solution to the Santa Fe Style "quandary," that is, the preservation and thoughtful extension of old Santa Fe versus a set of protocols that some would paint as backward-thinking protectionism and an obstacle to American property rights — but new owners claiming such an obstacle should not legally be able to claim ignorance of regulations that are anything but hidden. The city's budget depends on its historic-style reputation, and most residents and virtually all of the city's tourists love the look and feel of the old Plaza and the surrounding neighborhoods. It is probably true that sexy contemporary architectural statements would add to the city's overall vibrancy, but it's also true that the more offbeat projects of that type should probably be restricted to the areas outside of the historic district.

There remain many ways that the district itself may be dissipated if the city permits too many exceptions to the historic-style rules. The agendas of the Historic Districts Review Board have been getting longer, and it is possible — especially if future mayors and city councils are dumber about the importance of local historic preservation — that the board may be overwhelmed with proposals, and overwhelmed by smart architects arguing their clients' cases. The H-Board members must be equally smart, and tenacious, in their duty as guards of the historic fabric of the downtown. And we look forward to brilliant examples of contemporary architecture in other parts of the city.

# Santa Fe
## A CHRONOLOGICAL SAMPLER

A section of photographs made with a 1954 Rolleiflex film camera

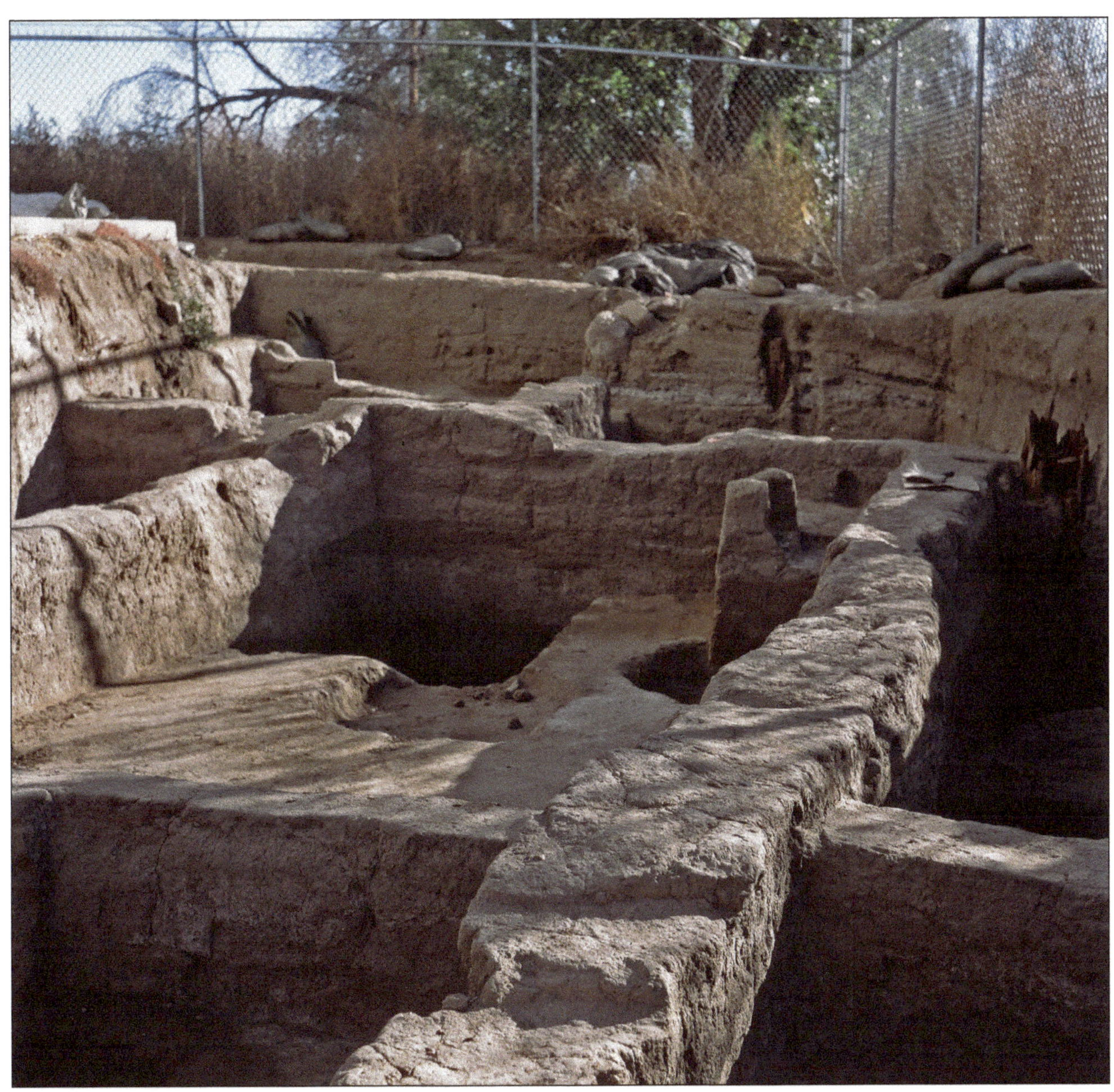

**Agua Fria Schoolhouse Pueblo**, located on land that is now in Agua Fria Village (about six miles downriver from central Santa Fe) was occupied by hundreds and perhaps thousands of Native people from the mid-1200s to the early 1400s. Cherie Scheick, Southwest Archaeological Consultants, led a series of digs on this 10-acre site beginning in 1988. The sections of rooms in this photograph were the most recent to be excavated, recorded, and reburied, in December 2015. To build one of the "coursed adobe" walls, the people laid down a long course made up of globs, or basketfuls, of damp clay. When that was dry, another level was added on top, and on up. When complete, wet earth was plastered on as a smooth "mud wash" interior wall finish. The roof material was also earthen, packed thickly on a cross-laid structure of poles and brush. Various types of recesses in the floors were likely hearths and pits for processing food or mixing mud plasters. In her long work on this site, Scheick has seen that later residents built rooms on top of older rooms that had been filled in and abandoned. "It's like a jigsaw puzzle, trying to figure out where the parts fit when you don't have all the parts," she said in 2017. "And if you consider that the site is probably spread over ten acres, we probably tested or excavated less than 1 percent of it." This pueblo and another named Pindi apparently co-existed on either side of the Santa Fe River. This may be an example of a dual-site pattern that existed in this area during the Coalition Period (A.D. 1200-1325).

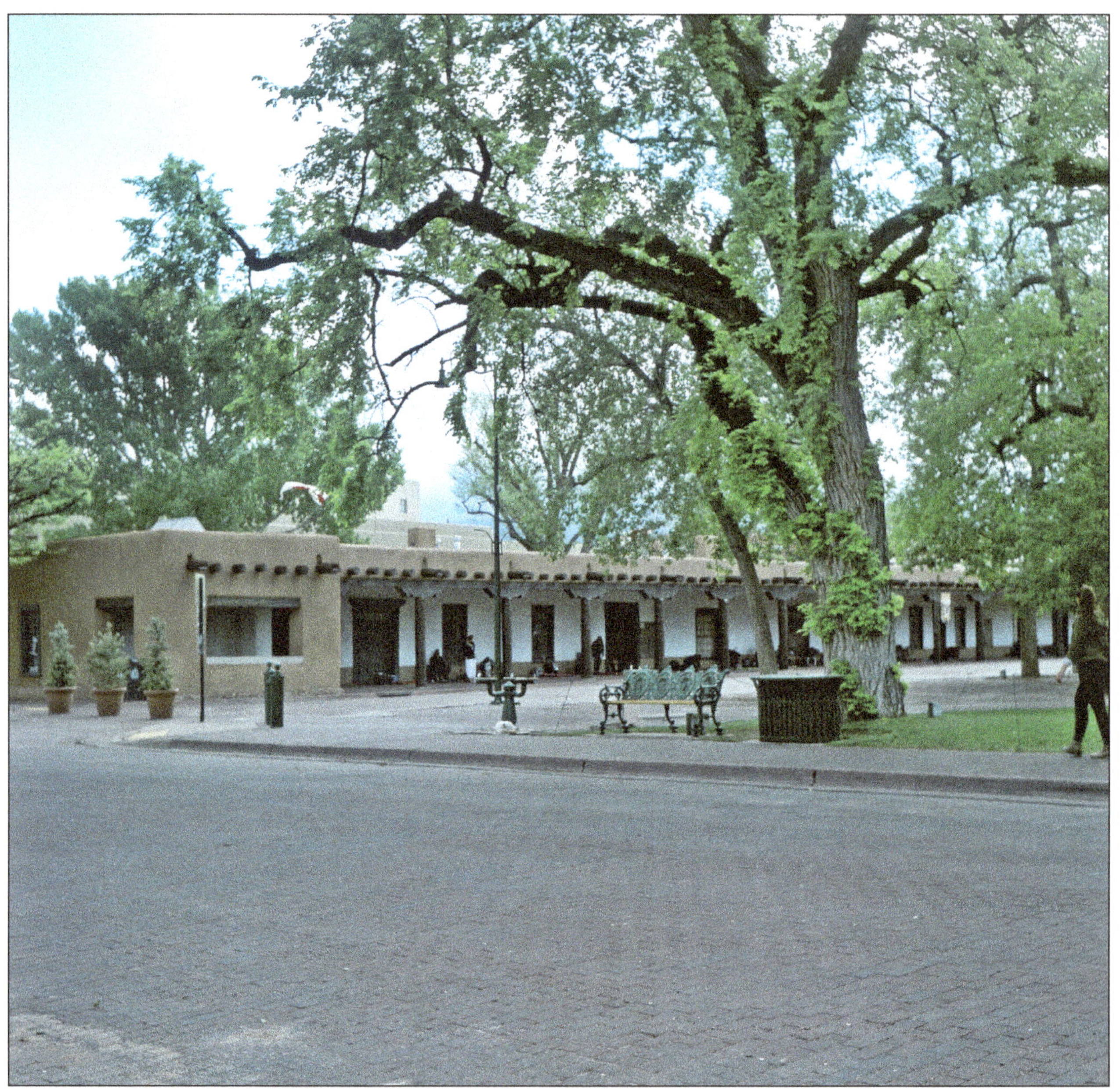

**The Palace of the Governors** is a bustling place virtually every day of the year, and it is also the most venerable, continuously used public building in the United States. The construction of what the Spanish called the *casas reales* was certainly a top priority at the founding of the town in, or just before, 1610, but the completion date was probably closer to 1620. After all, a great amount of earth had to be dug, mixed with water, formed into bricks, dried, and laid into walls; then many, many logs had to be laboriously harvested in the mountains and hauled down into the villa.

Whatever the exact year, the Palace has been old for a long time. The Sept. 24, 1883, issue of the *Santa Fe New Mexican* said tourists "will find pleasant seats beneath luxuriant shade trees in the plaza or public square, and having surrounding of interest in the old government palace on the north side, the U.S. military headquarters on the northwest, and the old Santa Fe trading houses surrounding three sides of the plaza." During the Pueblo Revolt years (1680-1693), the *casas reales* were altered to serve as Indian housing, perhaps four stories tall in places. When the Spanish returned, the changes were reversed and its role as the northern house of the government of New Spain resumed. The building presumably accommodated the various functions, and yet there is a report from just 20 years later that much of it was in poor condition,

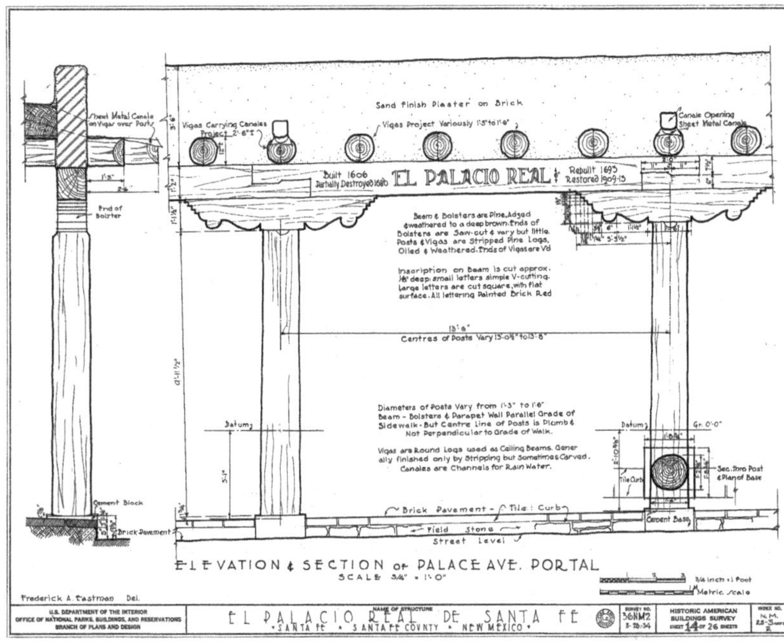


Measured drawing of the Old Palace made for the National Park Service's Historic American Buildings Survey in 1934; courtesy Library of Congress

and another made at the time of the 1846 occupation by the U.S. Army said the same thing.

Cordelia Snow, an archaeologist with the New Mexico Historic Preservation Division, commented during a November 2015 interview on the old problem of the Palace's upkeep. "Throughout the colonial period every governor had a *residencia* [a judicial review of an official's acts at the conclusion of his service] in which he defended his actions during his term of office, and although we don't have the *residencias* for all the governors, the majority of those we have say in essence, 'If it hadn't been for me and the repairs I paid for out of my own pocket, the Palace would have fallen.'"

Nevertheless, from the time it was built, the Palace was home to 59 Spanish royal governors and their families. For a quarter century beginning with Mexico's 1821 independence, it housed Mexican governors, then it served as a U.S. territorial capitol after 1846.

Its function as the seat of government ended with the construction of a new capitol building in 1886. That was the first of several new capitols, but the story is rather convoluted. In the early 1850s, work began on a stone territorial capitol 400 yards north of the Plaza. Designed by Joab Houghton, it wasn't finished until 1889, and after all that time it instead became Santa Fe's U.S. Courthouse — because, three years earlier, a yellow sandstone, double-domed capitol designed by E.S. Jenison of Chicago was completed on the south side of the Santa Fe River. "Messrs. Donoghue, Cavanaugh & Monier are putting in some hard licks on the new capitol these days," reported the *Santa Fe New Mexican* on Sept. 8, 1885. "Eight additional stone cutters were placed at work yesterday; the brick is all ready for delivery; three gangs are engaged in the quarries, and two car loads of stone daily are sent up from Lamy. Donoghue and his compadres are hummers." (That's humdingers to us modern folk.)

The Jenison building burned down just six years later. On the same site was built Isaac Rapp's single-domed capitol, which opened for business in 1900. In the early 1950s, Willard Kruger remodeled the Rapp capitol to conform to the Territorial Revival architectural mode favored at the time for state-government buildings. Then in 1966 the ribbon was cut on the current capitol building, the Roundhouse, which was also a Kruger design. The old Rapp building was renamed the Bataan Memorial Building and houses various state offices.

Through the years the Palace was used by five entitites — Spain, the Pueblo Revolt collective, Mexico, the Confederate States of America (for two weeks or so in 1862), and the United States of America — but it was never the state capitol building, because by the time statehood was granted in 1912, the government headquarters had been in the Rapp building for a dozen years. After the government departed the Old Palace, it provided space at different times for the U.S. Post Office, a territorial library, a jail, and the New Mexico Historical Society before it became home to the Museum of New Mexico starting in 1909.

Another story dates to the late 19th century, when Territorial governor Lew Wallace worked on the final sections of his novel *Ben-Hur* in the Palace.

The original *casas reales* may have been built by governors Pedro de Peralta or Juan de Eulate or perhaps by Alonso Peinado or Juan Chamiso. Cordelia Snow has "very decided opinions about the original Palace, not

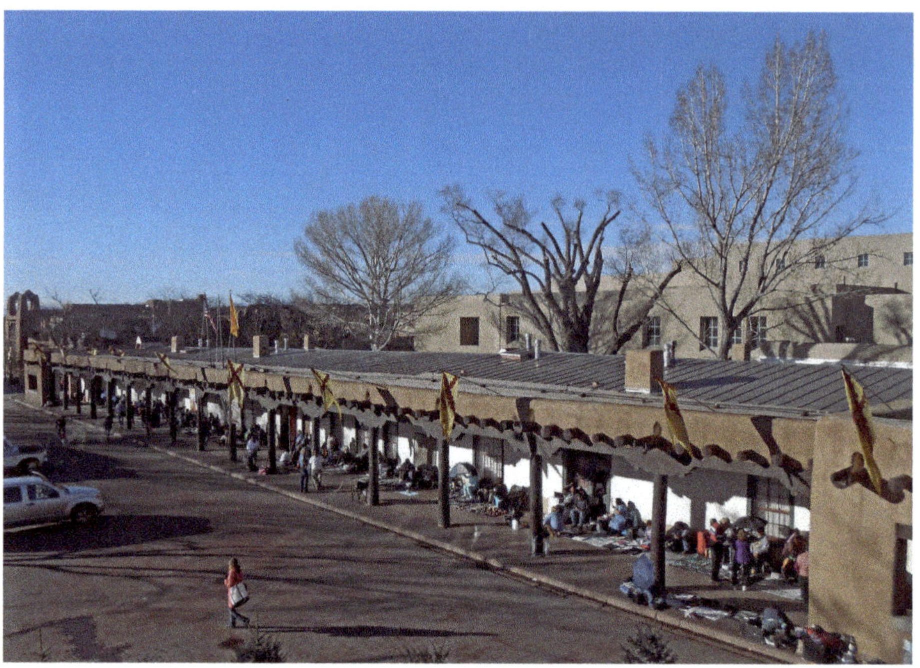

The Palace, with its Native American Vendors Program under the long *portal* and its many interesting interior exhibits (including excavation windows in the floor that provide glimpses into the building's remote history) is a thriving center of Santa Fe.

the least of which is that during the 17th and 18th centuries the building was two stories in height and was built around a large interior patio," she said, emphasizing that the early settlers of the Villa de Santa Fe "recreated insofar as possible the architecture and structures they had been familiar with in Mexico and Spain. Juan de Oñate and Pedro de Peralta and all the Spanish colonists who settled Nuevo Mexico brought their culture with them."

When speaking about the history of the Palace of the Governors, Snow gives special credit to Chamiso, a master mason who was "one of the least known of the 17th-century settlers in Santa Fe." She described him as "an Indian from the Valley of Mexico who was responsible for a number of improvements at the Palace during the early 1660s, during the time Bernardo Lopez de Mendizabal was governor." Snow believes the central patio was surrounded by a two-story colonnaded adobe arcade built by Chamiso. "In addition to his work on the Palace, Chamiso also acted as an advocate on behalf of local Puebloan laborers to ensure they would be paid for their work."

A lack of fair pay was just the tip of the iceberg for many Indians in the Santa Fe area in early colonial times. If you read accounts of their treatment by the Spanish soldiers and priests, a reaction like the Pueblo Revolt seems inevitable. And immediately after the 1693 resettlement, the Spaniards designated Santa Fe as a presidio, although it wasn't until the end of the 18th century that they began putting up defensive adobe walls. These walls enclosed a large area north of the Plaza, and the Palace was within them.

"In 1846, the presidio was remodeled, new dwellings for U.S. officers and enlisted men were built, and in 1859 the military compound was renamed Fort Marcy," says a 2002 report by archaeologists Stephen S. Post and Yvonne R. Oakes. "By 1895, the United States Army ceased operations on the Palace grounds at Fort Marcy and the fort was no longer in use." The Old Palace underwent major renovations in the mid-1850s and again in 1868-1878, when it was dolled-up with a Victorian balustrade across the front parapet. By the early 20th century, that feature was deemed nonhistoric and it was nixed during a major renovation. The work was led by Jesse Nusbaum, the first member of Museum of New Mexico founder and director Edgar Lee Hewett's staff at the Palace. Nusbaum's goal was to restore the building to an appearance more like what it was in the 17th century, and he was aided by a plan found in an old map in the British Museum.

The project took four years, ending in 1913. It involved the updating of electrical, plumbing, and heating systems; the repair of walls, woodwork, and fireplaces; and the excavation and removal of more than 2,000 wagonloads of trash and manure from the back property (the future *placita*), where livestock had long been stabled. But the most obvious change was to the front facade. That fancy balustrade was taken down, the parapet was beefed up, and new, heavier posts, *zapatas*, and *canales* were installed.

Today the Palace building is about 225 feet across, but it was once perhaps 350 feet wide facing the Plaza, with towers at both ends. The *torreon* on the east included the *ermita* de Nuestra Señora de la Luz and later a post office; that on the west was used for a *calabozo* (jail) and for gunpowder storage. Today 15 big posts support the long *portal* that runs between the open, roomlike masses at each end of the Palace fronting on the Santa Fe Plaza. Under the *portal* are 11 windows and five sets of doors, most of these openings surmounted by pedimented-lintel trim.

After nearly 30 generations of use and abuse, additions, destruction, and repairs, we're not far off the mark if we think of the old Adobe Palace as somewhat of a patchwork. There is some puddled-adobe construction remaining from the Revolt years. And when cement stucco was removed from the exterior of the courtyard walls during recent reconstruction work, adobe wasn't the only material found underneath. Pentile, the hollow clay tile produced at the former state penitentiary from the 19-teens into the 1940s, showed up, and pentile also was used to build a library addition on the Palace's eastern end in 1930; this space, built by the Federal Emergency Relief Administration, is now the museum gift shop. Also, not all of the *portal* dates back to the Nusbaum job. In 1995, it was substantially rebuilt after a driver crashed into it, and to make matters worse dry rot was discovered in the wooden members.

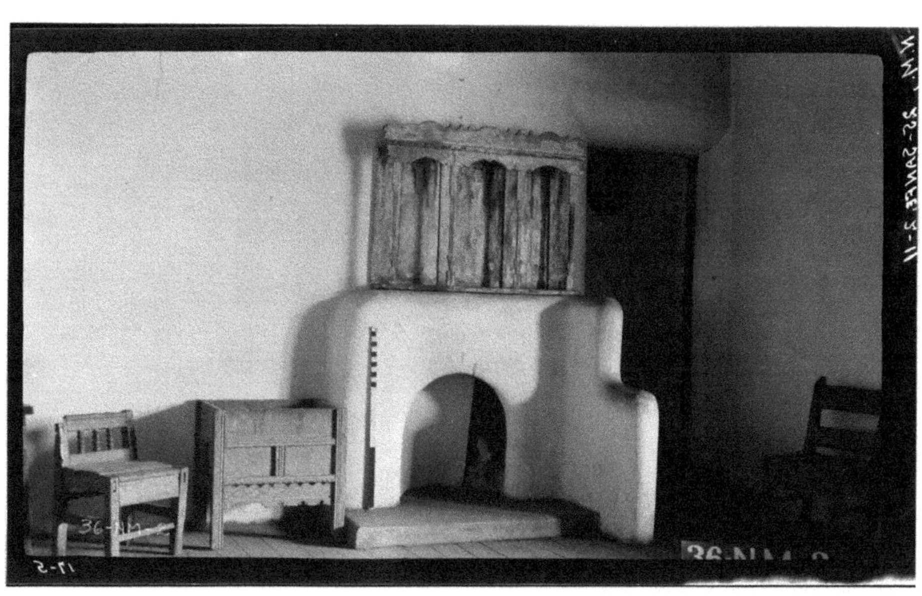

El Palacio Real (Palace of the Governors) fireplace photographed in 1934 by M. James Slack for the Historic American Buildings Survey; courtesy Library of Congress

Every day at the Palace, visitors buy jewelry and other works of art and craft from dozens of Native American artists who spread their wares on blankets under the long *portal*. Inside, you can view period rooms and exhibits featuring Indian, Spanish, and Anglo artifacts from more than four centuries of life in Santa Fe. You can also see portions of the building's cobble foundations dating to the first half of the 17th century in glass-topped pits that were left in the floor from the 1974-1975 archaeological digs by Cordelia Snow.

Some of the earliest excavations were made under Nusbaum, who worked in several rooms in 1909-1910. One of the latest digs was in 1987, when the Museum of New Mexico's Office of Archaeological Studies excavated a 1- by 1-meter pit in the Palace courtyard. Carried out in advance of a tree-planting ceremony in honor of the visiting King of Spain, the pit yielded 664 sherds of Pueblo-made pottery, 817 pieces of animal bone, and 68 lithic artifacts.

The oldest evidence of the Palace to be found by visitors today is in Room 5, in the southernmost of the two hatchways, Post said in 2019. "It has the diagonal adobe-brick floor, a course or two of adobe and some foundation, and I'd say that's from the mid-17th century. We know it's pre-Revolt because the people from Galisteo Pueblo built on top of the Spanish floors and inside the Spanish foundations within that room; we have evidence of that. We have the Pueblo Revolt walls and floors sitting on top of Spanish, so pre-1680."

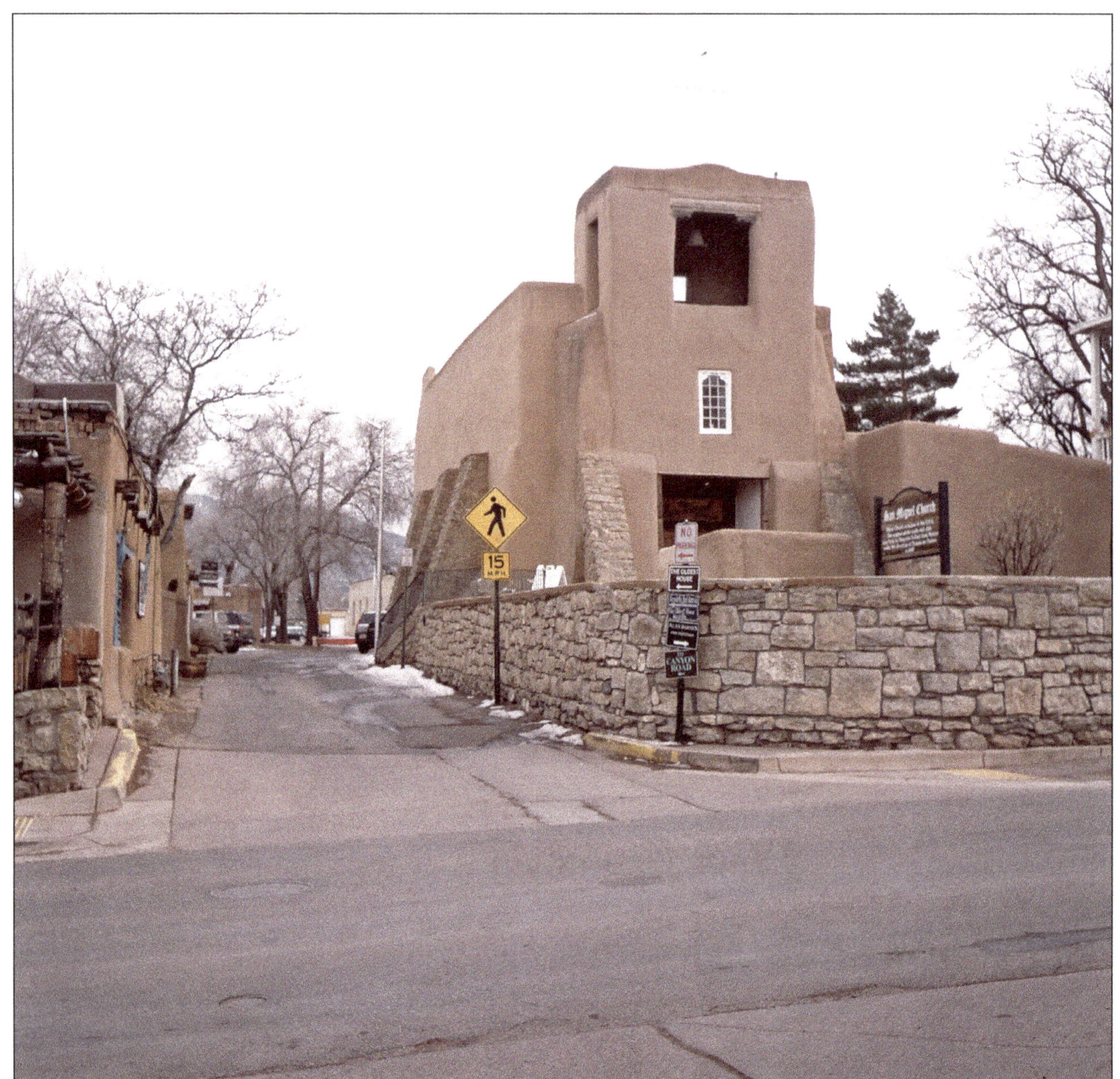


**San Miguel Chapel**, 401 Old Santa Fe Trail. The bones of this building go back four centuries, although most of what you see today dates to 1710, and to a 1955 remodel. Located in the Barrio de Analco, this is considered to be the oldest church in the United States. The first mention of San Miguel, according to Mark Treib's *Sanctuaries of Spanish New Mexico*, appeared in a July 28, 1628, document recounting that Governor Felipe de Sotelo Ossorio was charged with "impious conduct during the mass." It has long been thought to have been built by Tlaxcalan Indians from Mexico who aided the Spanish, although some Santa Fe archaeologists have reservations about that conventional wisdom. Severely damaged during the 1680 Pueblo Revolt, the structure was partially rebuilt in 1710 following the Spanish reconquest of Santa Fe. We do not know how it originally looked, and even since 1710 the chapel's appearance has been modified again and again. At various times it had a fortress-like crenellated roofline and a triple-tiered and triple-balconied tower. After a late-1880s remodel, the facade was a simple tall rectangle flanked by neat stone buttresses and with a high pair of arched windows under a shallow hip roof. The roof was removed and the upper windows replaced by a large *espadaña* opening for today's appearance.

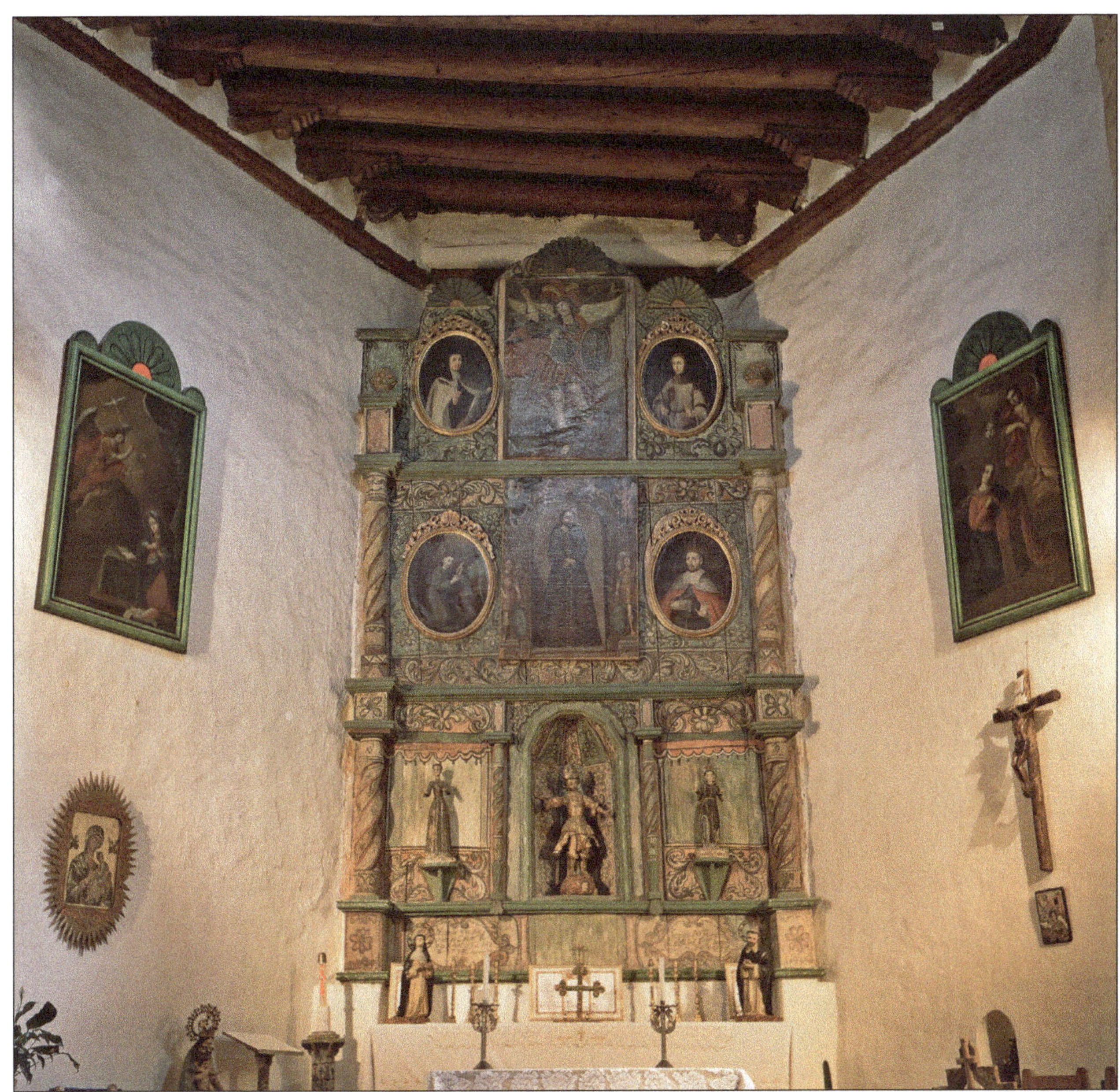

**San Miguel Chapel interior**. It is often said that, while the church exterior has had radically different appearances over the centuries, the interior is fairly intact. That may well be true of the walls and floor, but the altar screen was reportedly restored in the 1950s by E. Boyd and Alan Vedder, longtime curators of historic Spanish Colonial materials for the Museum of New Mexico, and the collection of 18th-century statues and painted figures on the altar screen is significantly changed from what is visible in a 1909 Library of Congress photograph. Today, a statue of San Miguel (St. Michael) is in the niche at bottom center. Above him are paintings of St. Francis of Assisi, Christ the Nazarene, and St. Louis IX of France; above them are St. Teresa of Avila, St. Michael the Archangel, and St. Clare of Assisi.

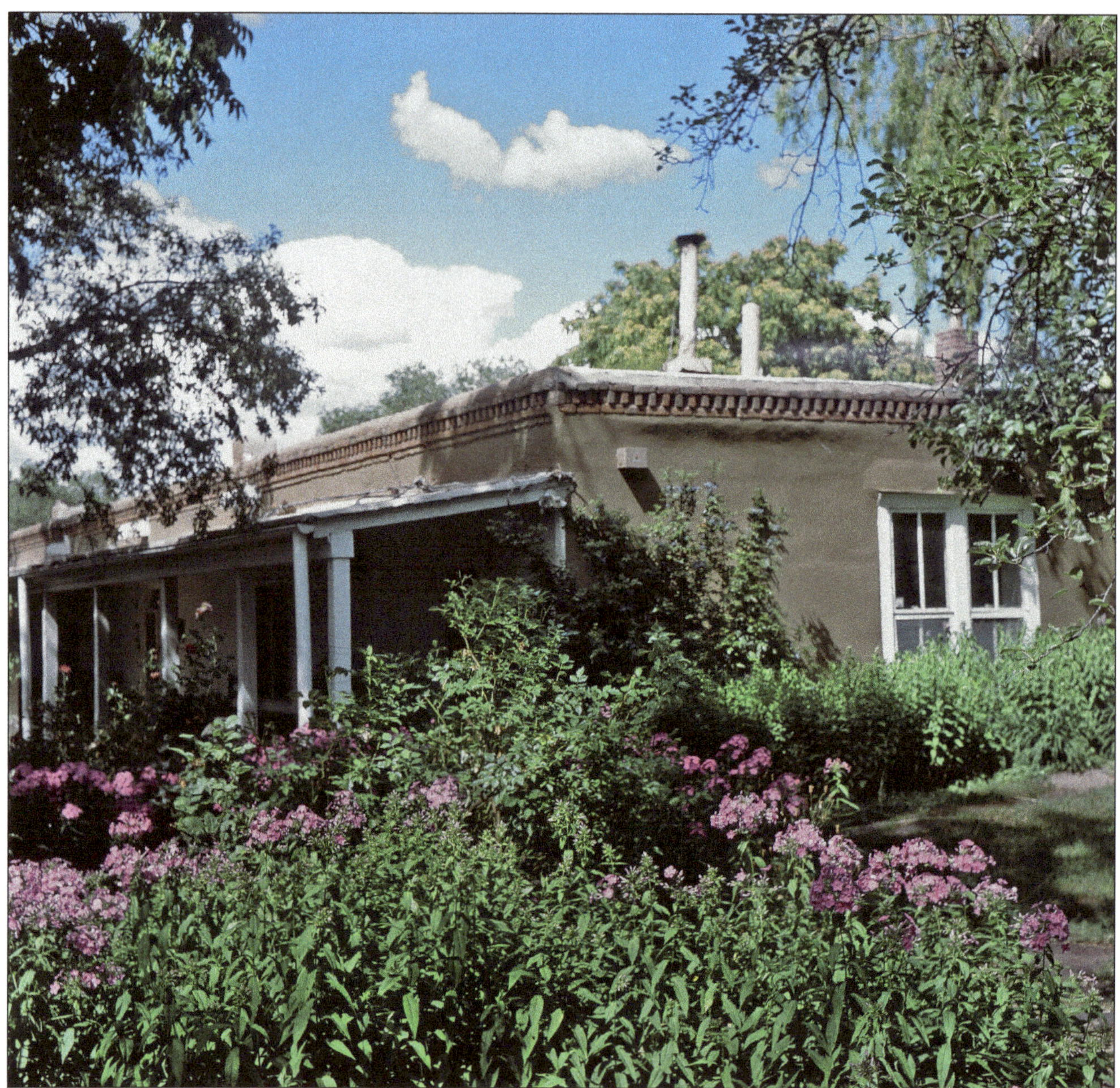

**Gregorio Crespín House**, 132 E. De Vargas Street, may date to as early as 1710, according to analyses of *viga* samples by the Laboratory of Tree Ring Research at the University of Arizona — so it is likely even older than the Arthur Boyle House, which is quite probably older than Santa Fe's "Oldest House." (Dating is not precise, because tree-ring analysis indicates only when the tree died. If it was cut for *vigas*, they may have been used for the building in which we find them today, or they may have been recycled from building to building over the centuries.) This land was part of a grant by General de Vargas to Juan de León Brito, who is thought to have been a Tlaxcalan Indian who participated in the 1693 Reconquest. It is recorded that Juan and his brother, Diego Brito, contributed 1,500 adobe bricks for the 1710 rebuilding of San Miguel Chapel. Gregorio Crespín was one of the later owners; so were Bartolomé Marquez, Blas Roibal, and Anastacio Sandoval. In the 19th century, the Territorial trim was added to this house, which has been in the Mayer family since about 1904.

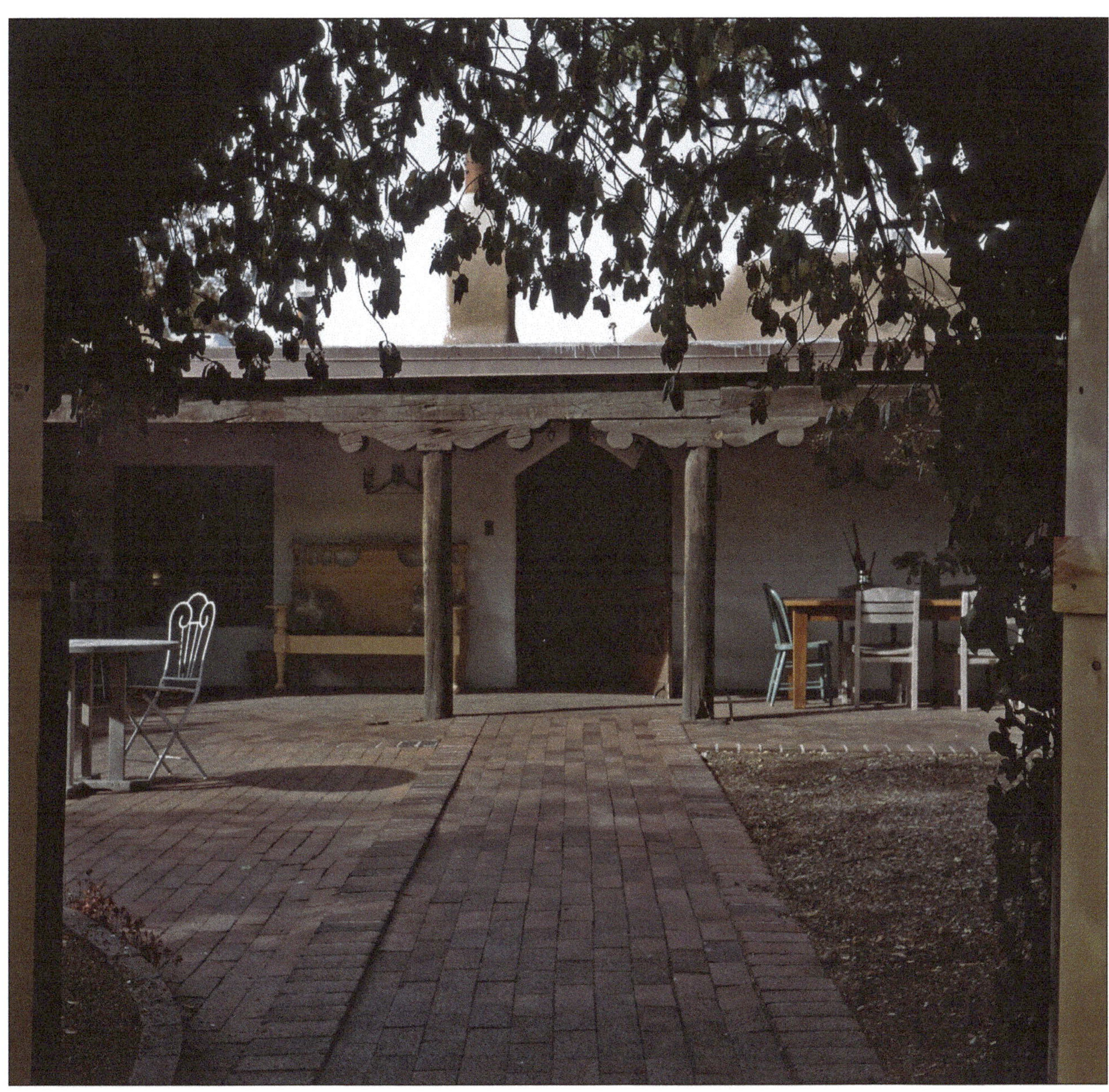

**Arthur Boyle House**, 327 E. De Vargas Street, probably dates to the late 1720s. Owners included Salvador Martín in the early 1800s, the Very Rev. Peter Eguillon (who brought the Christian Brothers to Santa Fe from France and helped found St. Michael's College) in the 1860s, and, from 1881, Arthur Boyle, who previously was a sheepman in Australia and then served as secretary to Sir Charles Brooke, second white rajah of Sarawak! In Santa Fe, Boyle and his wife, Blanche Blackmore, started Clarendon Gardens. The business and its successors (the last was Stuppy-May Flowers) furnished Santa Fe with beautiful blooms from 1887 to the 1950s. The *portal* that shades the east facade — in approximately the center of which is a distinctive, pointed door — was built for the 1912 *New-Old Santa Fe* exhibition at the Palace of the Governors and was afterwards taken apart and rebuilt as a shade-bestowing addition to this house. Among the changes to the house over the years were a circa 1895 room addition on the north and a few Santa Fe Style alterations by Kate Chapman in about 1915.

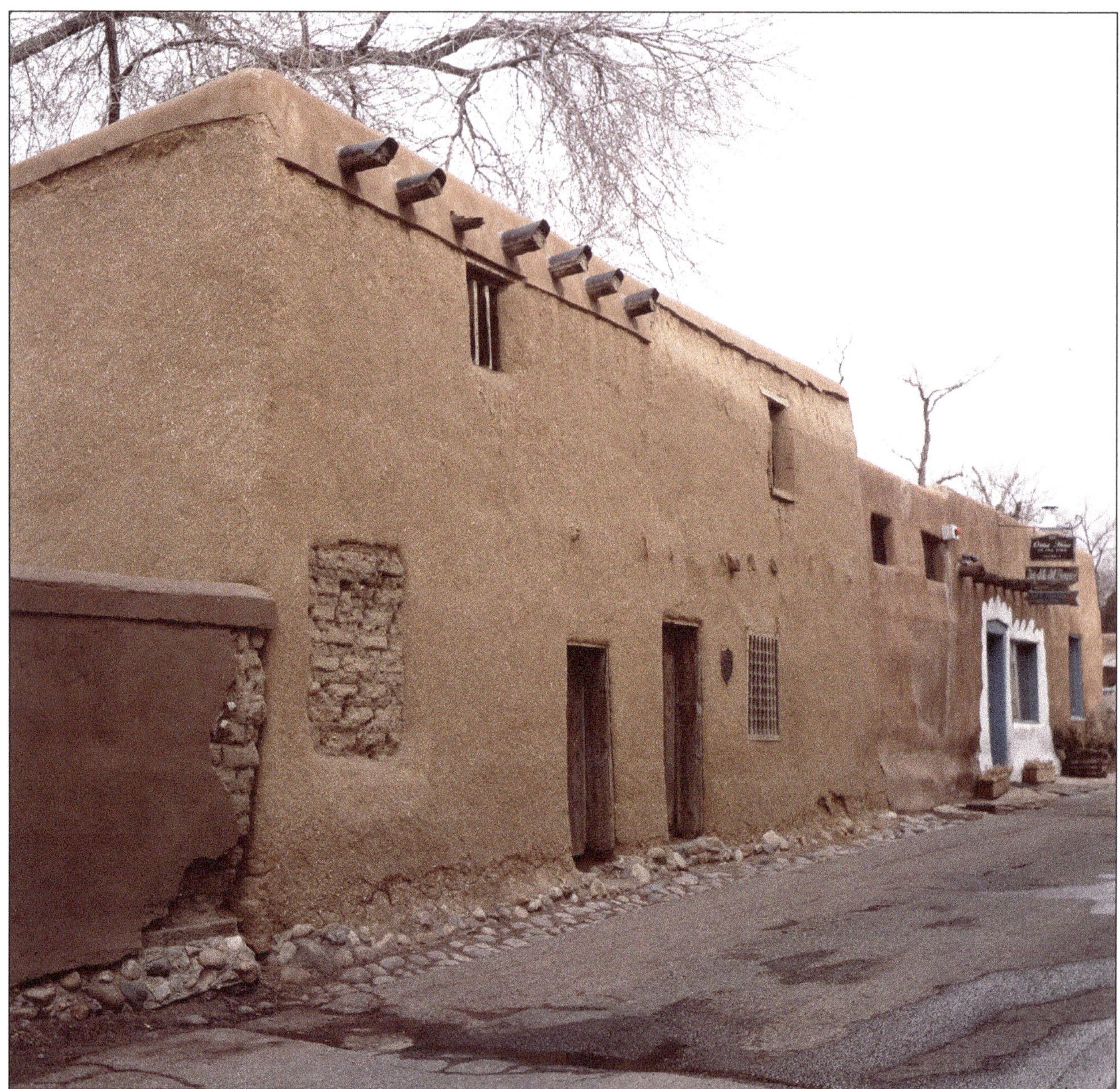

**The "Oldest House"** at 209-215 E. De Vargas Street. In spite of the common name, nobody knows the age of this house. Legend has it that it was built over a centuries-old Indian abode. Dendrochronology testing of vigas in the "Oldest House," and the fact that there was a house in this location on the 1766 map drawn by José de Urrutia, suggest that it was built in about the 1750s. In 1879 (eight years before the St. Francis Cathedral was finished), *Harper's Weekly* called it "the oldest inhabited home in the U.S." Was it a Tlaxcalan Indian family that built the house? The common wisdom is that this neighborhood on the south side of the Santa Fe River — the Barrio de Analco — was settled by Tlaxcalan (or Tlaxcaltecan) Indians from Mexico. However, the presence of any Tlaxcalans in Santa Fe's early years is questioned by archaeologists including Cordelia Snow and Elizabeth Oster. *Berger's Tourists' Guide to New Mexico* (1883) said half of the "Old Pueblo House" belonged to the family of Manuela Armenta and the other half to that of Ularia Ensiñas. The dwelling had a second story in the 19th century, then it was gone, then it was built up again. The house's antiquity is told by the fact that it's built right at the street and has no *portal*. Although its precise origin is nothing but an enigma, it is inarguably one of Santa Fe's oldest tourist attractions.

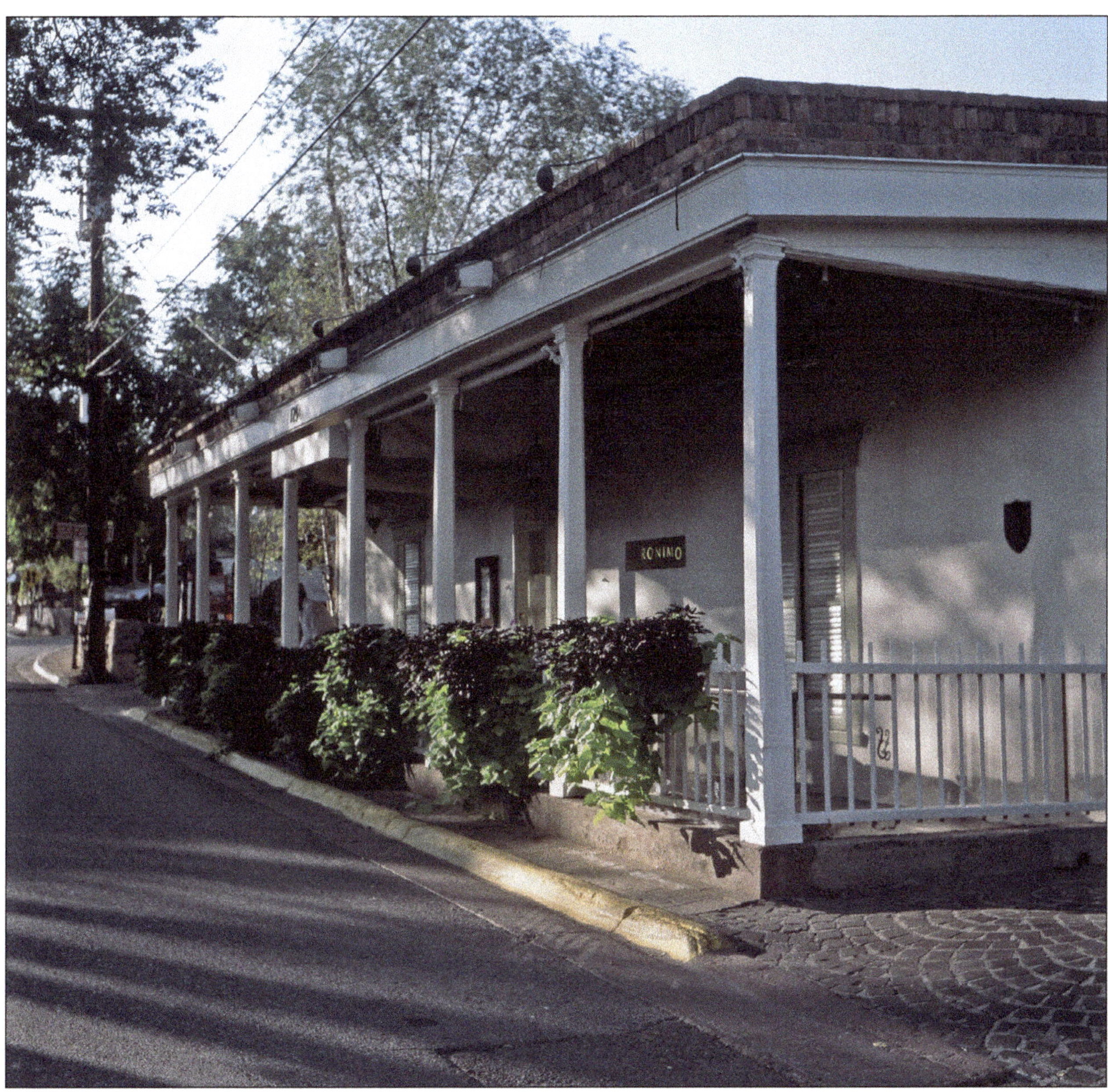


Parts of the **Rafael Borrego House**, 724 Canyon Road, may date to the late 1700s, but the characteristic Territorial front *portal* and *sala* were probably added in the mid-19th century by Rafael Borrego. In 1928, Margretta Dietrich bought the house and won a Cyrus McCormick Prize for her restoration work, which was performed by Kate Chapman. The building's uses during the past five or six decades include the Three Cities of Spain coffee house and Geronimo restaurant; today the latter establishment stands out amid more than 50 art galleries along less than a mile of Canyon Road's main commercial stretch (which was mostly populated by cornfields and burros and here and there a few artists like Hal West and Georgia O'Keeffe when my wife was a kid walking around this neighborhood in the early 1960s). The Borrego House is one of the few Santa Fe buildings that was studied as part of the Historic American Buildings Survey. The HABS collection at the Library of Congress boasts eight photographs and five measured drawings made in 1940.

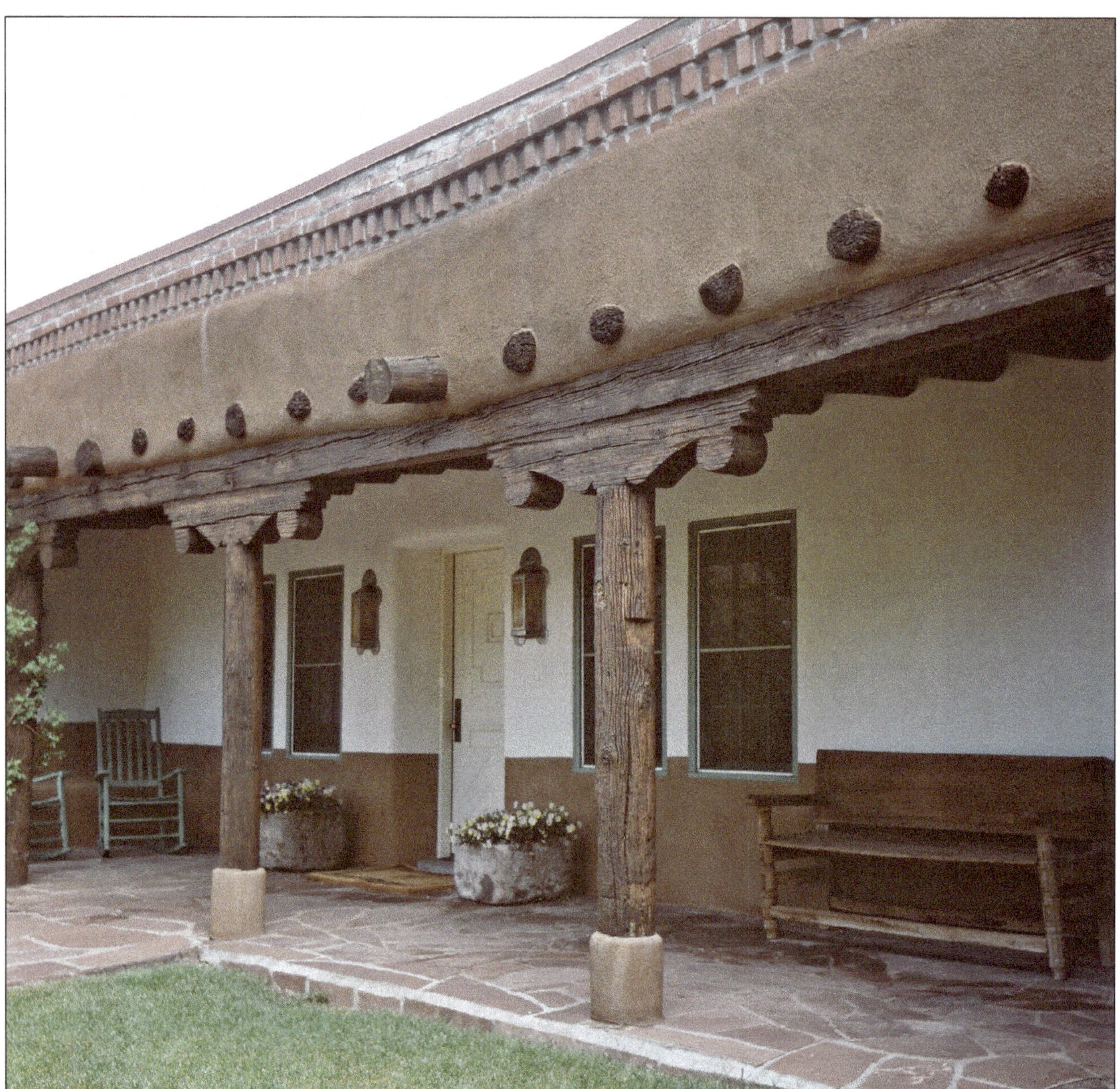

**Roque Lobato House**, 311 Washington Avenue. The core of this residence dates to 1785. Lobato was a soldier and armorer to the Royal Spanish Garrison of Santa Fe. In 1910, the house was purchased, renovated, and expanded by Museum of New Mexico archaeologist Sylvanus G. Morley. That simply adds a second "period of significance" to its historic profile. However, changes by other owners in the 1960s and 1970s — including the addition of brick coping on the parapet and an abbreviation of the front *portal* (which used to be 16 feet deep) in order to create an interior hallway — resulted in the City of Santa Fe removing the house's historic status. Karl and Susan Horn bought the house in 2004 and after a few years engaged architect Craig Hoopes to help them with a restoration that was guided by the Arts and Crafts aesthetic of Morley's work a century earlier.

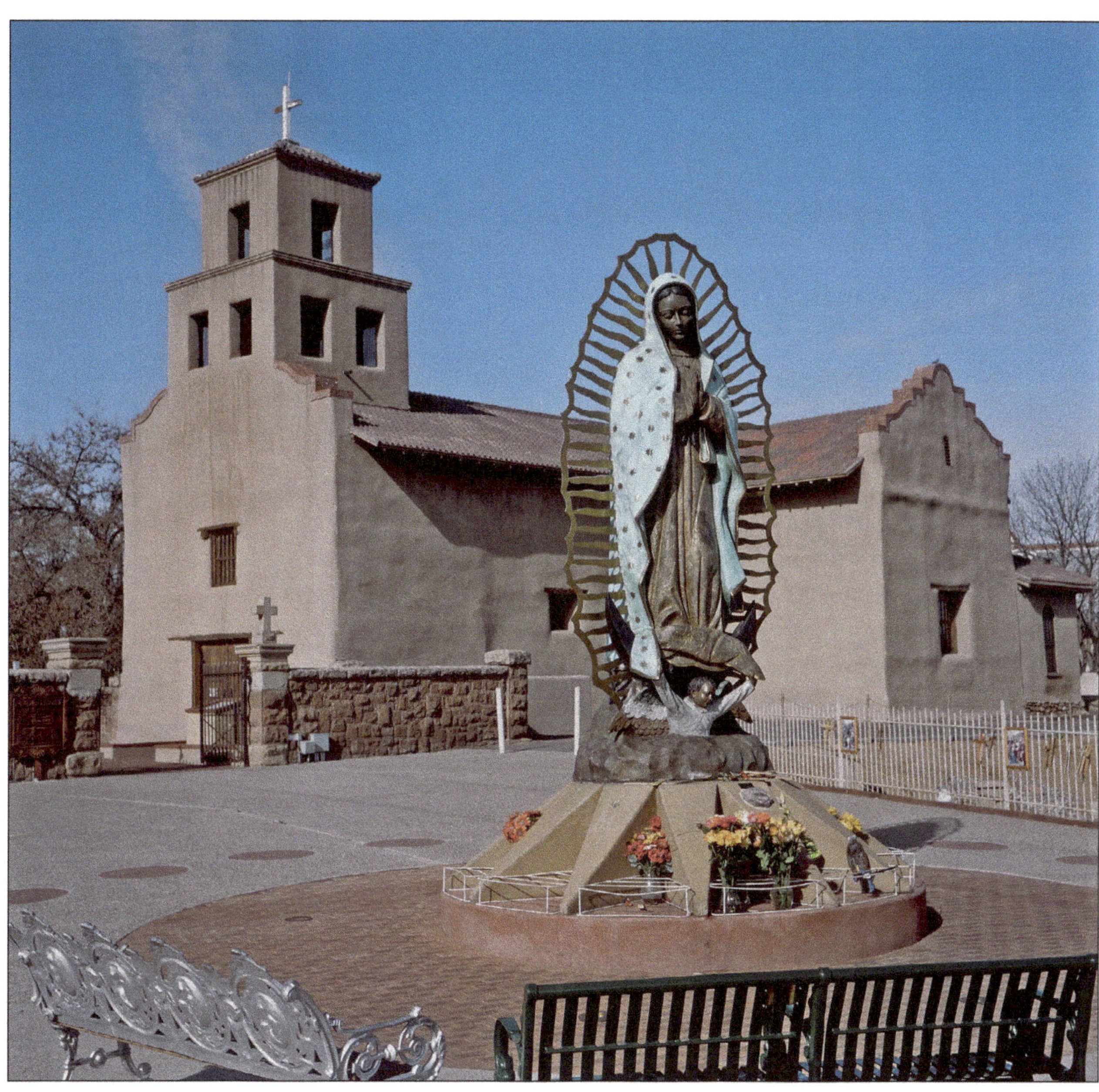

**Santuario de Guadalupe**, 100 Guadalupe Street. The adobe church, also known as Nuestra Senora de Guadalupe, was built as a mission church at the end of the Camino Real. It houses a singular painting of Our Lady of Guadalupe, standing in the center of four images that tell the story of her "origin" — of the sightings of this unique Marian apparition by Mexican Indian Juan Gabriel in 1531. The painting was signed by José de Alcibar in 1783. The church is the country's oldest shrine to Our Lady of Guadalupe in continuous use. There is a record of its construction license issued in 1795, and the building was probably completed within the next decade or two. By the time the first trains came to Santa Fe in the early 1880s, the church was decrepit. It was rebuilt with a pitched roof and a tall steeple, which burned away in a 1922 blaze. The next remodeling was done using elements of the popular California Mission style, but also with a *campanario* more akin to the old New Mexico mission churches. When the congregation outgrew the premises, a new church was built next door (the first mass held in 1961) and Santuario (with architects Victor Johnson and Robert Nestor consulting) was renovated as a museum. In 2006, it was resanctified; mass is now held daily. The 12-foot bronze statue of Our Lady of Guadalupe that is installed outside the church was commissoned from Mexican artist Georgina Farías and transported from Mexico City in 2008.

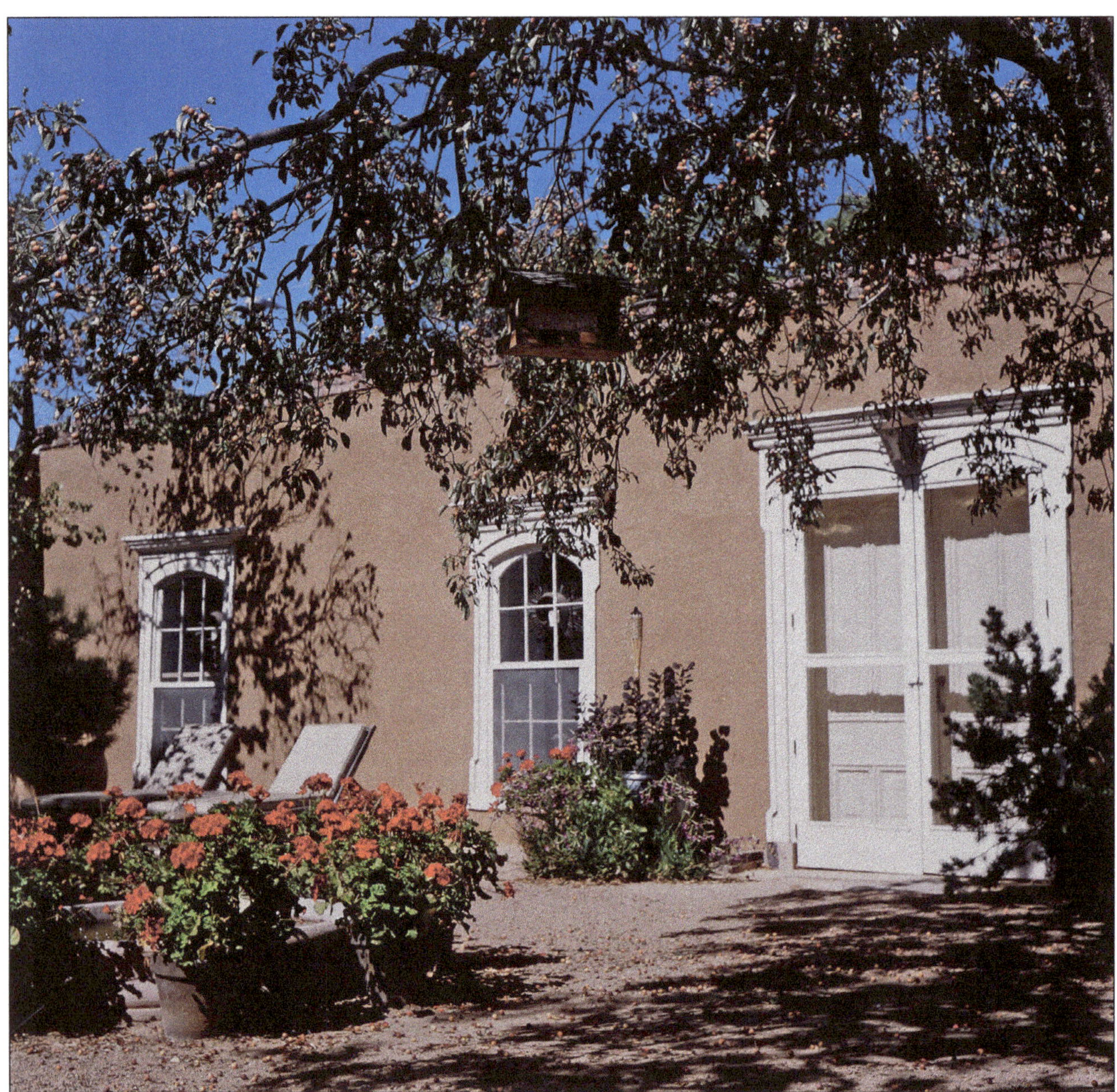

**Donaciano Vigil House**, 518 Alto Street, has a facade finished with mud plaster, once customary in Santa Fe but a rarity today. In 1832 this house was the residence of city official Juan Cristobal Vigil and his family, according to the Historic Santa Fe Foundation, which owned the house for many years. Vigil's son, Donaciano, was military secretary to Governor Manuel Armijo during Mexican rule (1821-1846) and went on to serve as secretary of the territory under American occupation. Architect/artist William Lumpkins bought the home in 1946. Among his improvements was transplanting five windows and a door from the old Loretto Academy — a few are visible in this courtyard photo. The property was purchased by Charlotte White and Boris Gilbertson in 1958. Their improvements were influenced by their trips to Mexico. One was the massive wooden gate, with a human-size door cut into it, that Gilbertson placed at the entrance to the *zaguan*. In their work on the residence, the couple made use of hundreds of adobes produced by the neighbor boys and thousands of kiln-baked bricks from the recently decommissioned New Mexico Territorial Penitentiary, according to *Within Adobe Walls, a Santa Fe Journal: Selections from the Charlotte White Journals*. In May of 1961, two women from Cañones mud-plastered the exterior walls. Their final coat was fine-sifted earth added to tortilla-flour paste. "It fits in all the cracks and looks gorgeous," White wrote.

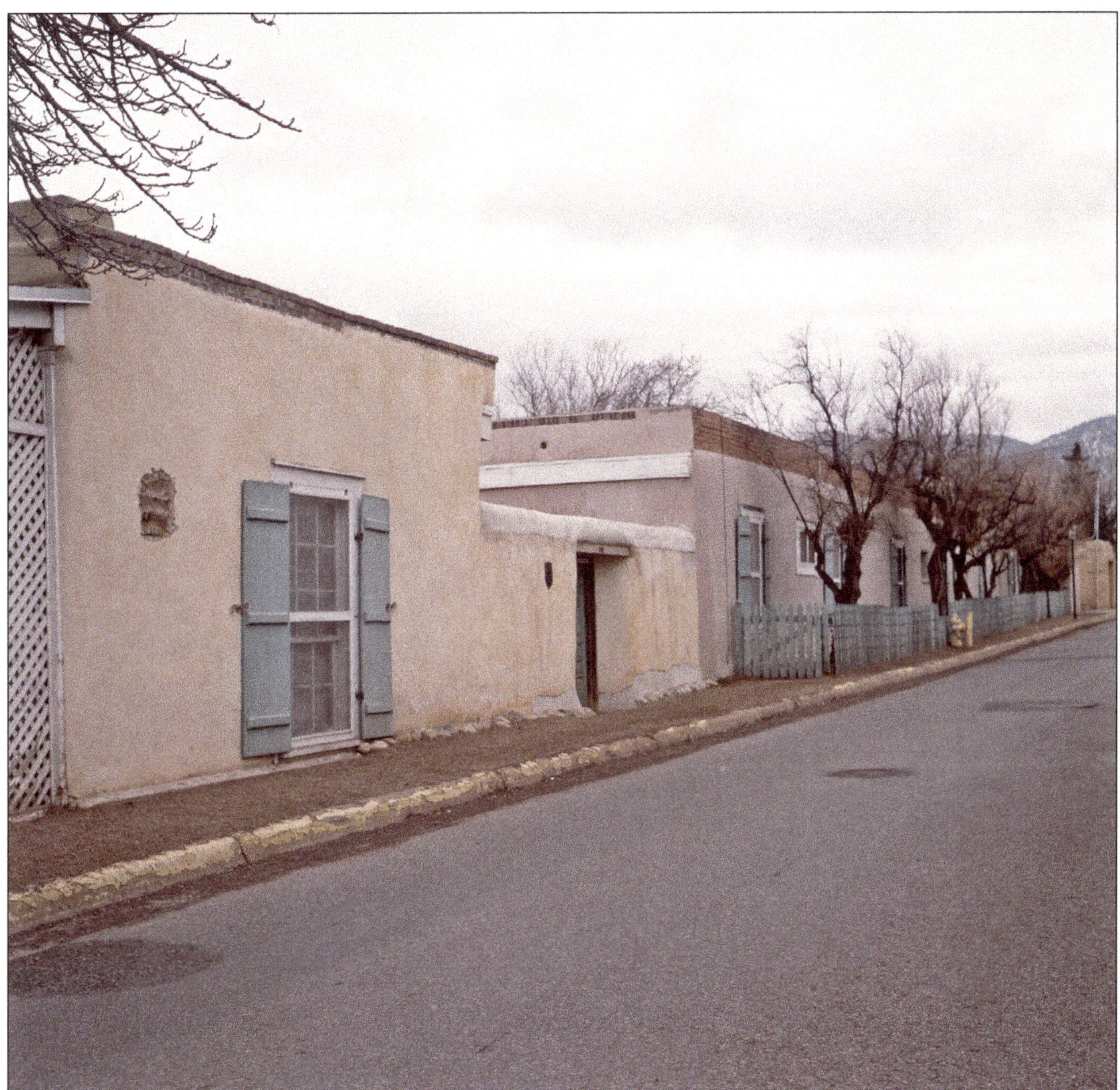

**El Zaguan**, 545 Canyon Road, is the modern name for the old James L. Johnson house. A successful Santa Fe Trail merchant, Johnson bought the property in 1854. He and his wife, María Jesús Montóya, raised seven children here. "On the lower terrace behind the houses were orchards, a cornfield, and large corrals where freighters on the Santa Fe Trail kept their horses and oxen before making the return trip," says *Old Santa Fe Today*. The house was purchased in 1927 by Margretta S. Dietrich, a Nebraska suffragette who went on to help establish the Indian Arts Fund and the Spanish Colonial Arts Society. Today it is the headquarters of the Historic Santa Fe Foundation, which has owned it since 1979. More than 180 feet long on the street and adjoining a beloved old garden, the house has Territorial-style brick parapets. The arched opening leads into a little courtyard and then to the *zaguan*, a long corridor along which are doors to the HSFF office and several apartments traditionally rented to artists. The little "truth window" visible on a wall in this photo not only reveals the adobe-brick structure, but *rajuelar*: a system (little known in Santa Fe) in which small, flat stones were added to the mortar to anchor the lime-plaster finish.

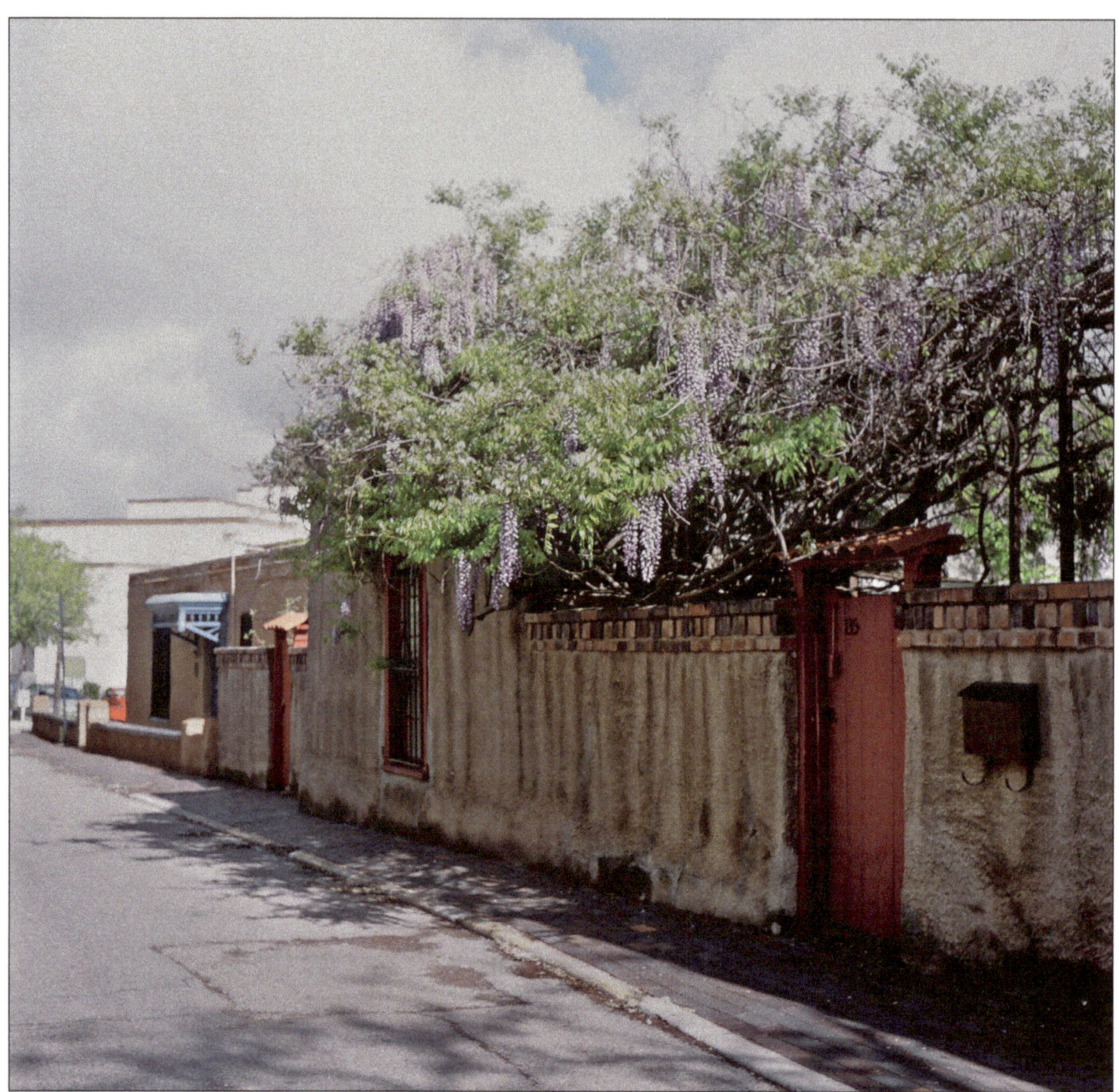


**Roque Tudesqui House**, 135 East De Vargas Street, is in the old Santa Fe neighborhood historically called the Barrio de Analco. The house is mostly hidden from the street, but its presence is told by a glorious old wisteria spilling over a wall. Tudesqui, an Italian-born Santa Fe Trail merchant, bought the house in 1839. Architectural historian Bainbridge Bunting wrote in *New Mexico Architecture* in 1970, "Many of its adobe walls are more than three feet thick, and at least one of them was built partially of puddled adobe, suggesting Indian construction."

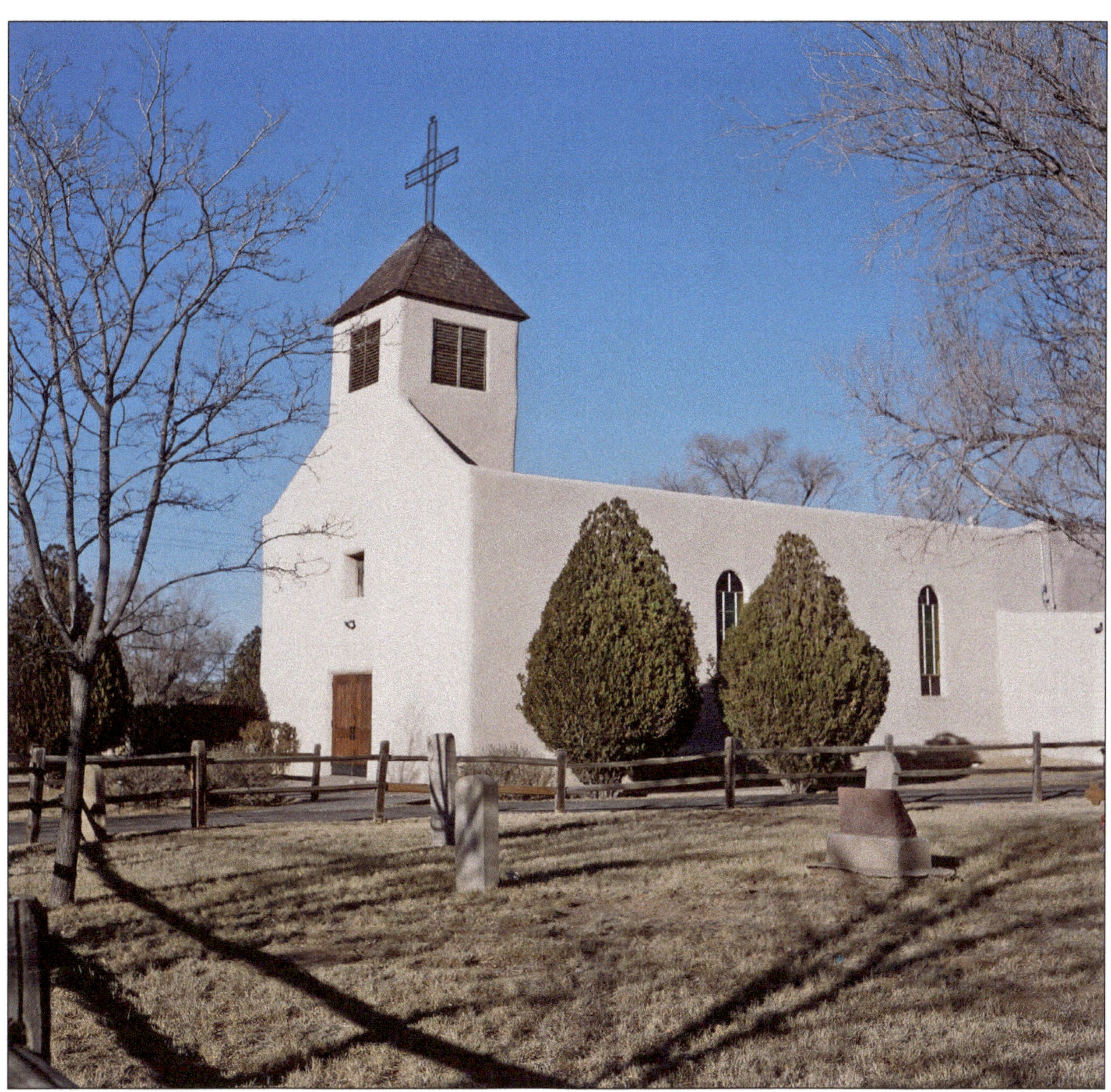

**San Isidro Catholic Church**, 3552 Agua Fria Street. A State Highway Department marker says this adobe church is dedicated to San Isidro, ploughman, patron saint of farmers and protector of crops. Christian tradition maintains that in order to allow San Isidro time for his daily prayers, an angel plowed his fields. In order to attend mass in the early 1800s, residents from the Agua Fria Village had to travel all the way into Santa Fe — to Our Lady of Guadalupe or the St. Francis Cathedral —which, with necessary chores and then horse-and-wagon preparations, could take most of a day. "If it was your turn to water from the acequia on Sunday, you would just have to forego going to church," Agua Fria historian William Henry Mee has written. "In the winter it was hard to keep the fire going in the house, and someone might be elected to stay home." A positive solution began when José Jacinto Gallegos told his neighbors that he would donate land for a local church. Where exactly should it be sited? He threw up his hat, and it landed on this site. People in the village built the church in 1835 using hand-made adobes. The women expertly applied the earthen plaster on walls and the major families in the village built the roof of *vigas* supported by corbels.

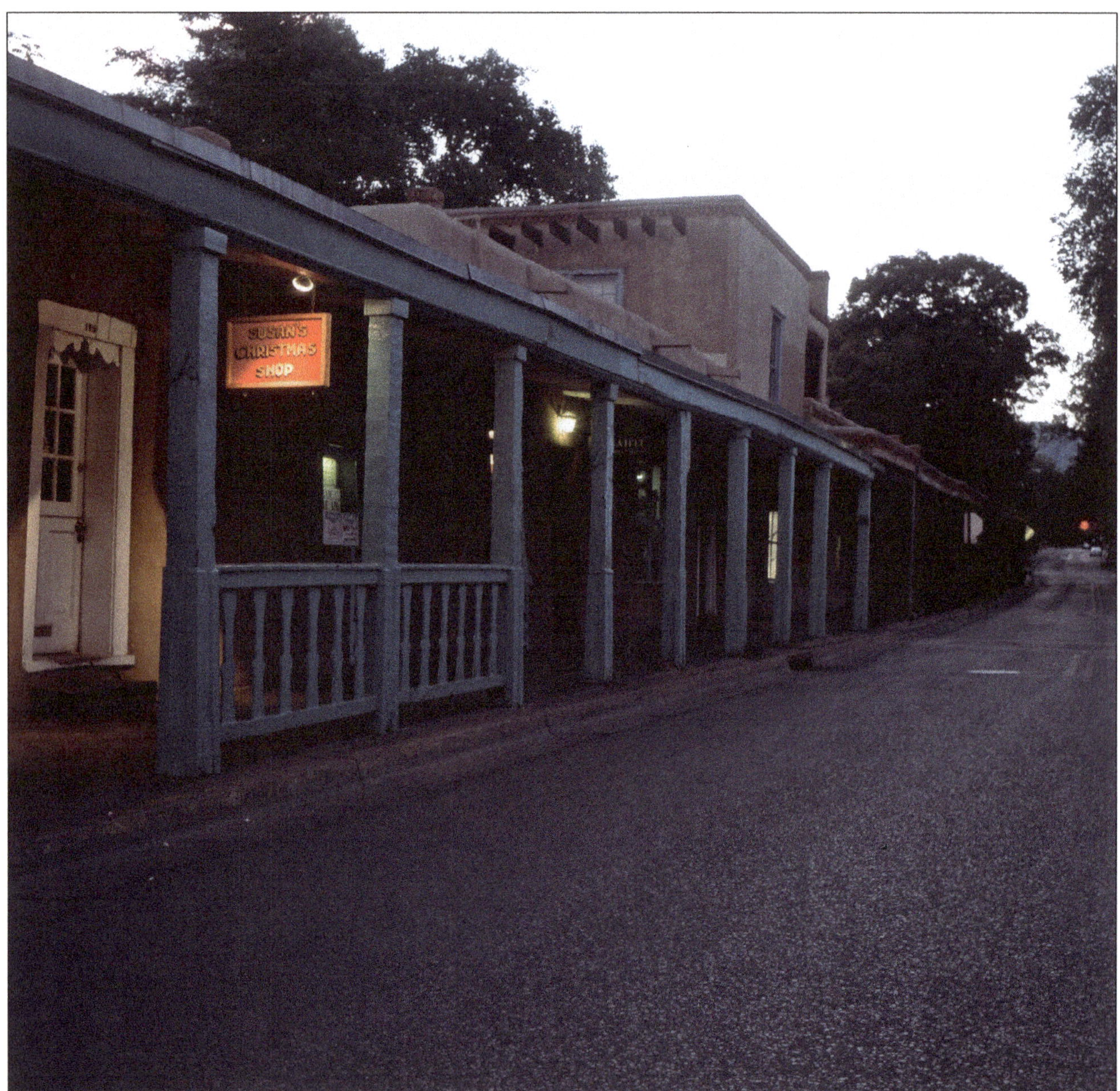


**Arias de Quiros Site**, 107-137 E. Palace, is a connected strip of buildings just east of the Palace of the Governors and fronted by about 380 feet of *portales*. Some foundations may date back to the 17th century, but the complex is based on the later Prince, Trujillo, and Sena houses. Among their early owners were L. Bradford Prince, a Territorial Supreme Court justice and later territorial governor (and great-grandfather of architect Bart Prince), and María de la Cruz Carmen "Carmel" Benavides and her husband, Antoine Robidoux, who served as guide for the U.S. Army general, Stephen Watts Kearny, who led the 1846 American takeover of the New Mexico Territory. Dorothy McKibben staffed the Atomic Energy Commission's Manhattan Project office in Trujillo Plaza during World War II. Old photographs show no *portales*; these were often added to historic buildings during the early 20th century for their aesthetic value and the shade they provide.

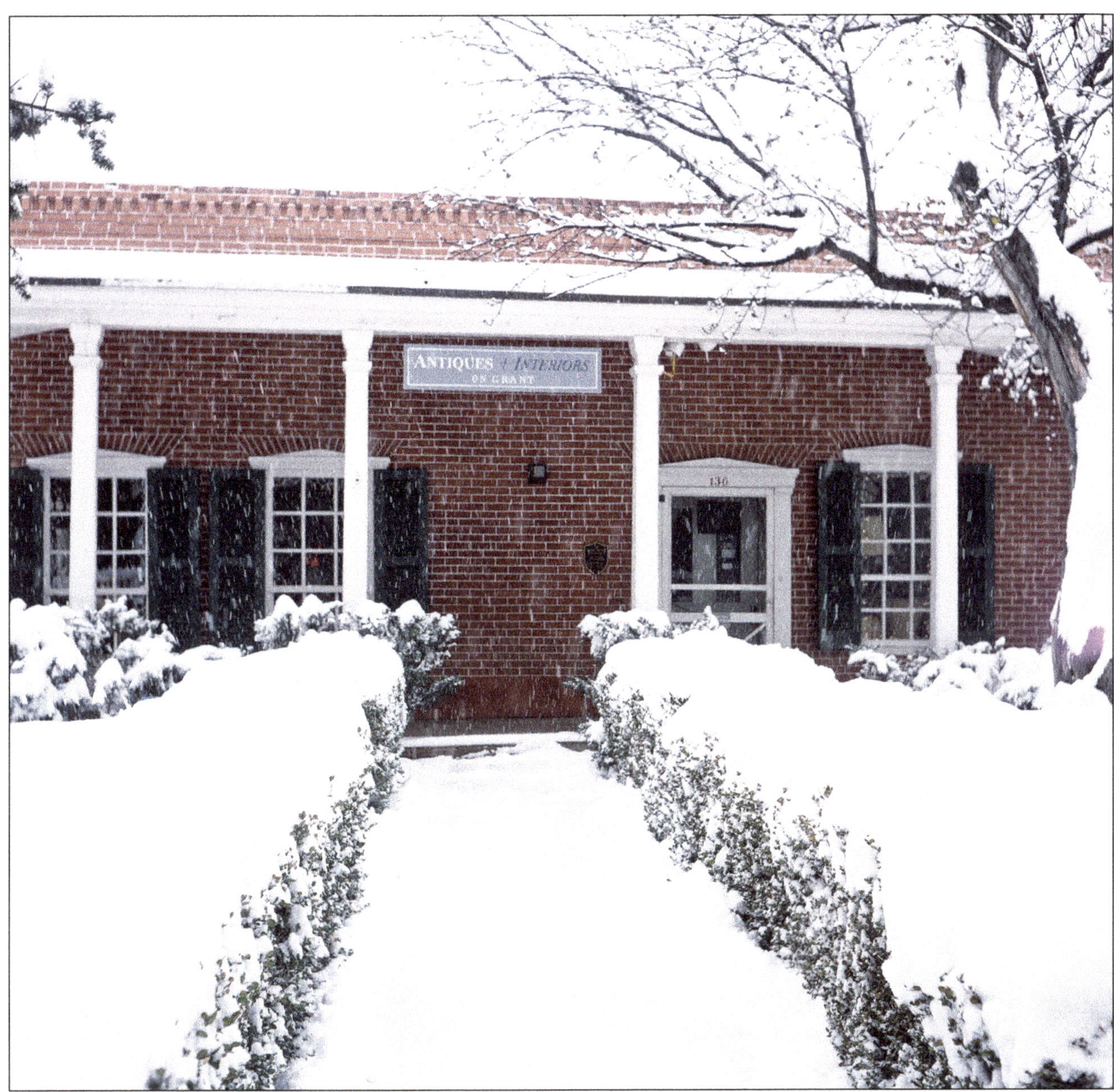


**Oliver P. Hovey House**, 136 Grant Avenue, has a distinction not noticeable without a close look: the adobe walls are painted to imitate brick. The 1851 house was expanded in the 1880s with the addition of a tenth room with bay window on the south side. It is described as a "Territorial example with the exterior surviving as originally built" in Virginia Savage McAlester's *A Field Guide to American Houses*. In 1976, when it was purchased by the Historic Santa Fe Foundation, the walls were covered in stucco — but an early photograph shows a faux-brick surface. The foundation discovered fragments of such decoration under the stucco and proceeded to restore the "stenciling." Oliver Hovey was a publisher and editor of the *Santa Fe Republican* newspaper. Other owners of the house over the years included Pinckney R. Tully, trader; William Pelham, the first U.S. Surveyor General for New Mexico; Henry L. Waldo, supreme court justice; and Rufus J. Palen and Levi A. Hughes, who were both presidents of the First National Bank of Santa Fe.

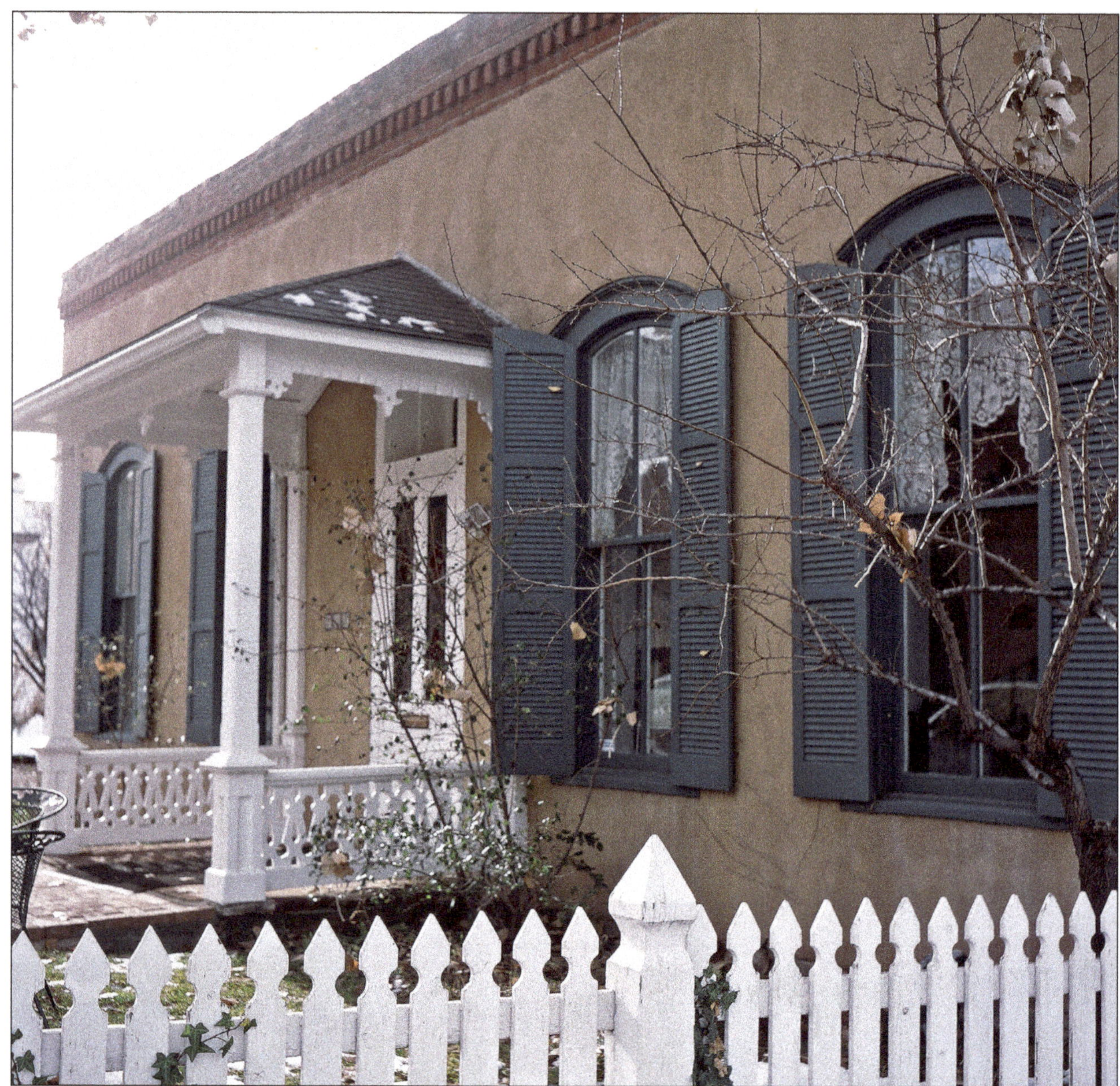

**Surveyor General's Quarters**, 208 Griffin Street. This Territorial-era adobe building exists with a simple grace (and quite anonymously) in the Staab-McKenzie neighborhood a quarter-mile northwest of The Plaza; it is one of the few buildings here that predates 1885. One of the plaques on its front tells us the house is a Registered Cultural Property in the State of New Mexico. Here's the history: after the 1846 U.S. takeover of the territory from Mexico, the Treaty of Guadalupe Hidalgo guaranteed that properties held by Mexican residents would be respected. The Office of the Surveyor General was created eight years later with the mandate to validate these land claims. The program was largely unsuccessful, and in 1891 the office was replaced with the Court of Private Land Claims. This house was also once used by the U.S. Indian Agency. It is listed on the National Register of Historic Places, but only as part of the context of the Santa Fe Historic District, which was listed on the National Register in 1973.

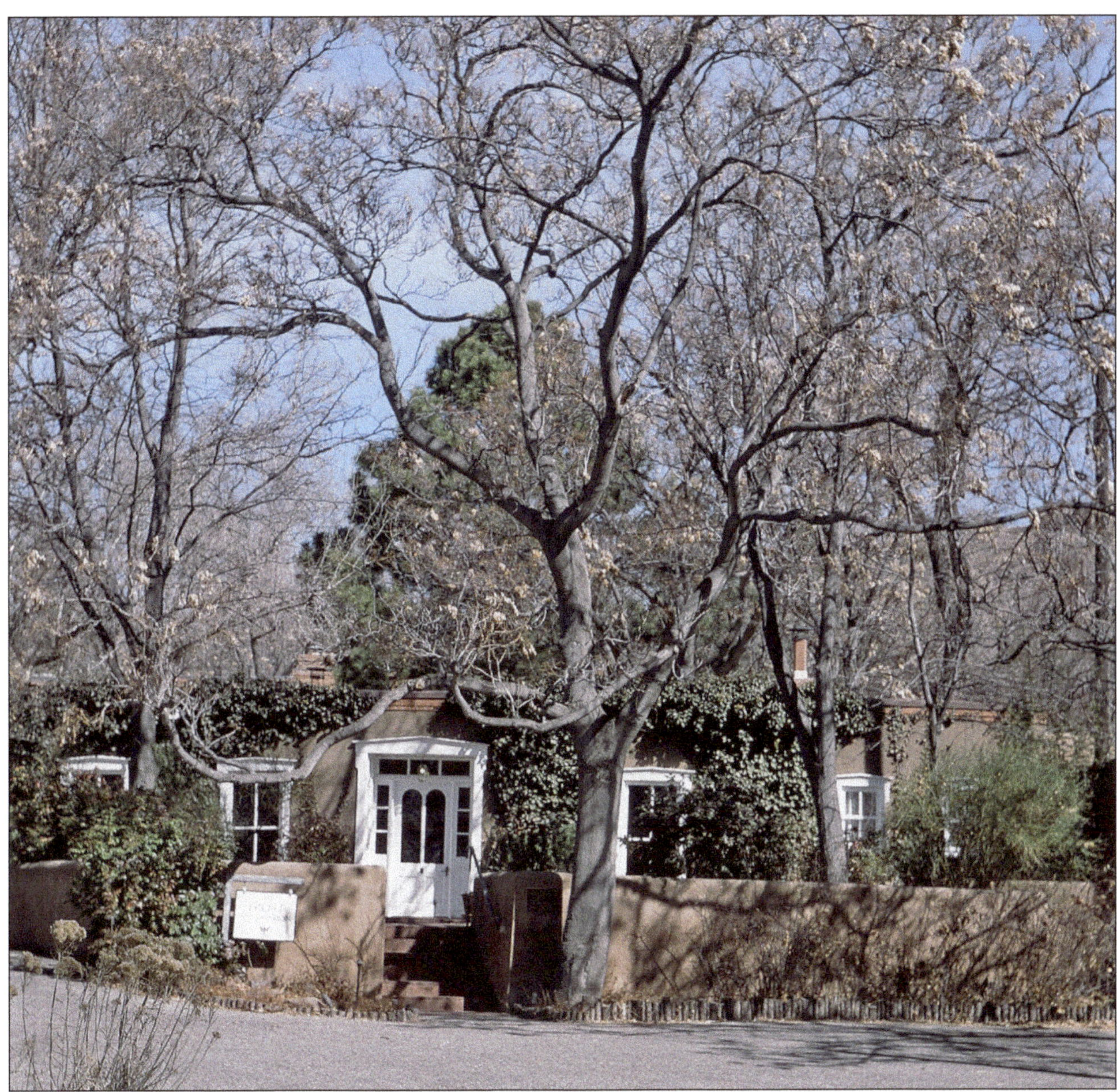

**Professor J.A. Wood House**, 511 Armijo Street, is named after the man who served as superintendent of the Santa Fe City Schools from 1899 to 1912. Wood was a Baptist who was known for his derby and bicycling to work as well as for planning the district's first high school building. The known property record for 511 Armijo goes back to 1860. An 1879 sale to Abelerio Nuañez and Victoria Sanches de Nuañez described a four-room house — the rooms arranged in a cluster rather than in a line, denoting a Territorial rather than Spanish Colonial plan — with 42 *vigas*, according to *Old Santa Fe Today*. In the next decade or so, "the adobe received a fashionable sprucing up with new Territorial entrance and front window treatments, including a 'store-bought' front door with arched panes over panels, sidelights with paneled bases, and a transom." Wood purchased the house in 1899. (This was probably a different person from the Col. J.A. Wood who in 1917 was manager of the Santa Fe Gold Dredging Co. and president of the Southwest Mission Hotel Co. that proposed to build a hotel at the Old Fonda site — on which another company built La Fonda seven years later.)

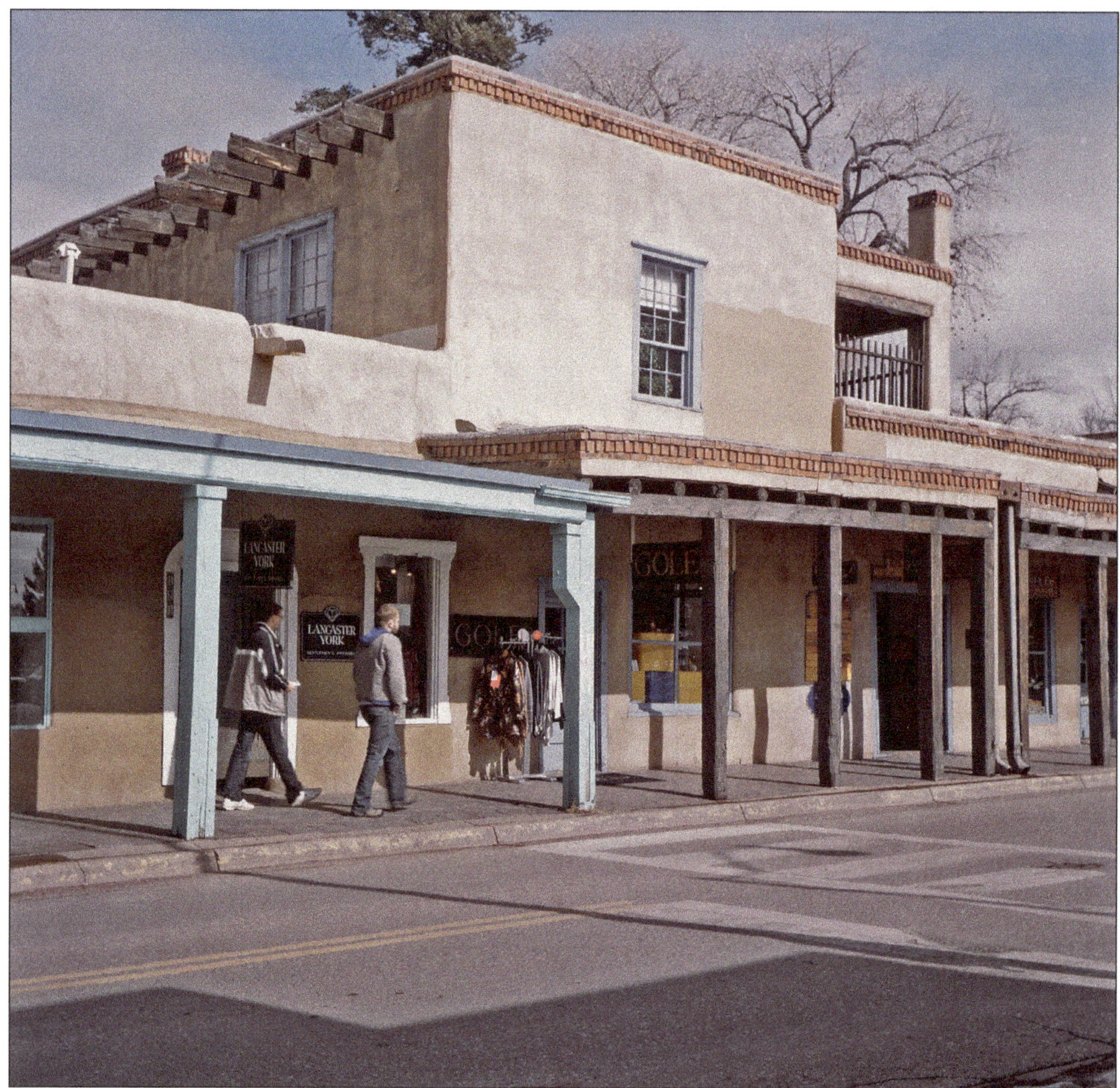


**Sena House**, 125 E. Palace Avenue, was formerly the easternmost residence in what is now known as the Arias de Quiros Site; the land was granted to a captain of that name by General Diego de Vargas in 1697. The Sena house — a small adobe that was expanded to 33 rooms — is named for José D. Sena, an owner who served as a U.S. Army major in the Civil War. His family lived around three sides of the large *placita* while the north-side buildings were reserved for servants, chickens, and storage. The dominant second story on the west side, an early addition, passed to Dr. Frank Mera (of Sunmount Sanitarium fame). The rest of the house was deeded to Senator Bronson Cutting and Amelia and Martha White in 1927, at which time the illustrious artist and builder William Penhallow Henderson was hired to supervise the construction of a second story on the north and east sections. "It is a classic example of how a historic building can be restored and reconstructed to adapt to modern business requirements while keeping the integrity of the original," according to the book *Old Santa Fe Today*. (The darker area in the stucco next to the second-floor street window is a painted graffiti patch, a new addition to the Santa Fe Style vocabulary.)

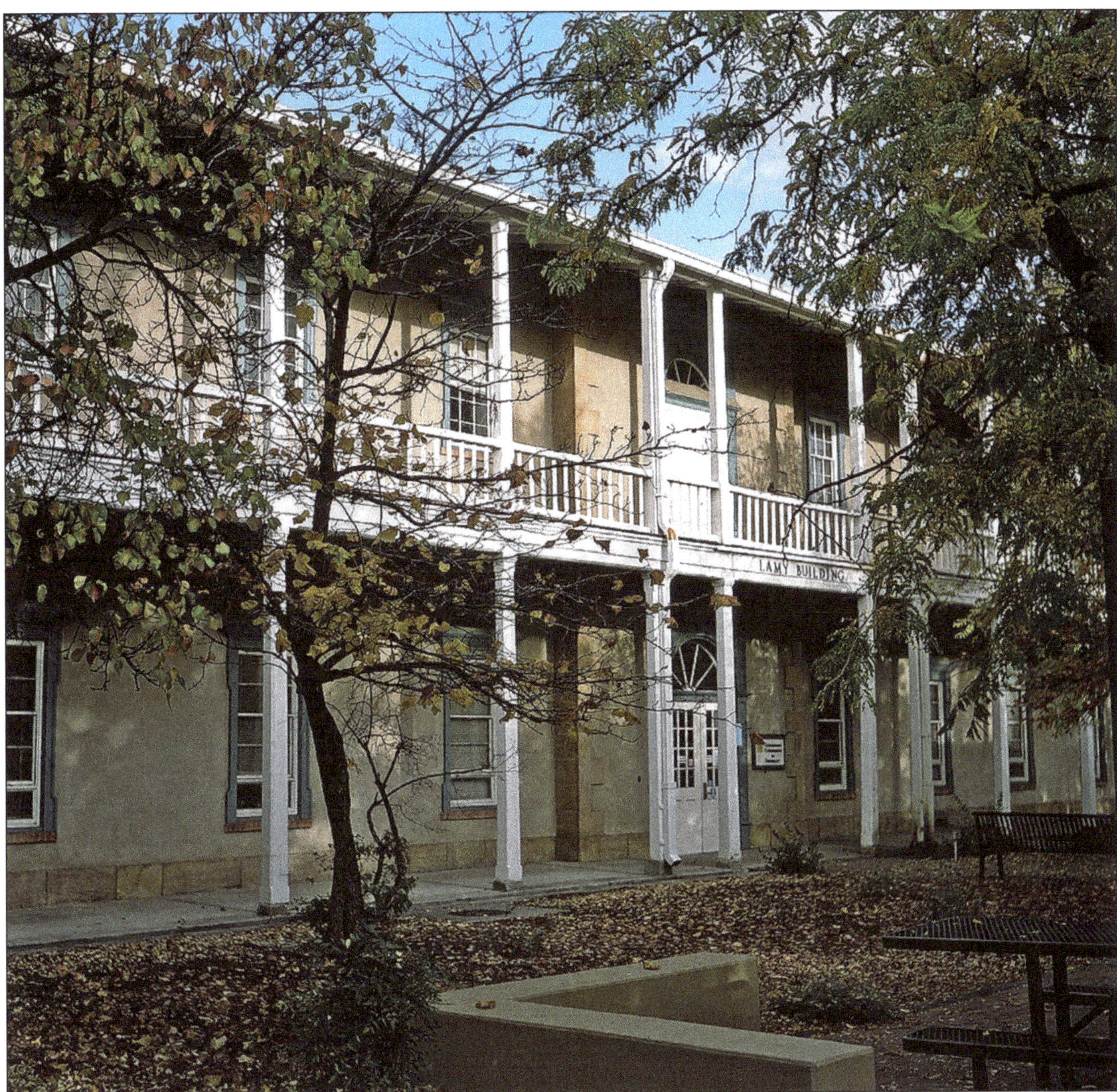


**Lamy Building**, 491 Old Santa Fe Trail. "We were yesterday shown by Brothers Botulph and Baldwin a well-drawn plan of the new college building which it is proposed to erect on the spacious grounds of St. Michael's College ... The plan is drawn in the Elizabethan style of architecture, with double verandas surrounding the four sides of the building, dormer windows in the attic roof, and ornate cupola rising from the centre..." This report in the *Santa Fe New Mexican* of March 14, 1877, described the school structure built by the Christian Brothers right next to old San Miguel Chapel, and completed the next year. A 1926 fire destroyed the ornate, mansard-roofed third floor and tower, but the remaining adobe structure survives, providing office space for New Mexico state agencies. It sports a 1950s Territorial Revival coping along the roofline but retains the original stone quoins and bi-level front doors with fanlights in a shallow central bay. Second-floor balconies once circled the building; those survive only on the rear (shown here) and the north side. In 2005, Spears Architects completed a restoration, which included rebuilding the *espadaña* that was added to the front facade in the Fifties remodel.

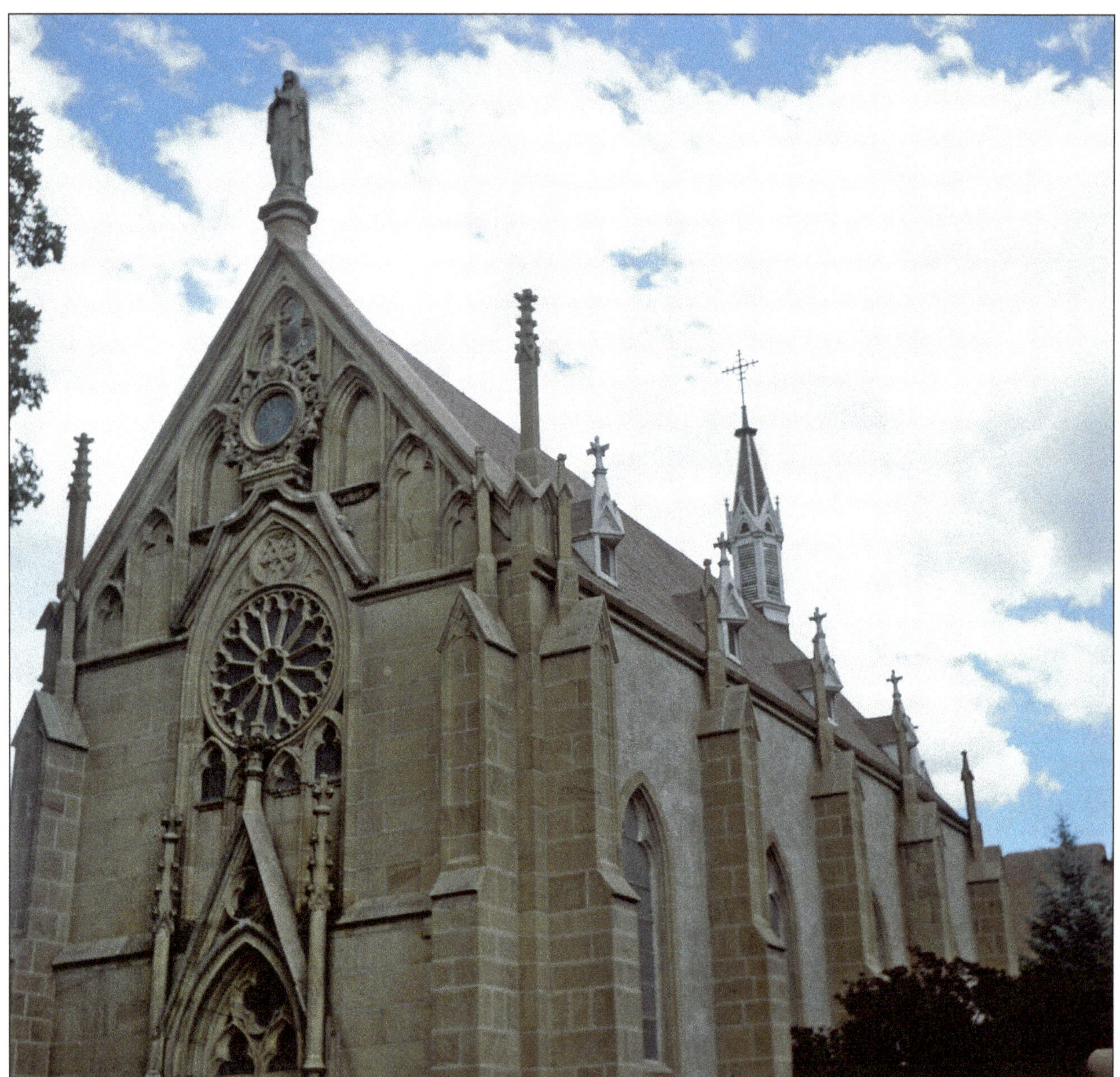

**The Loretto Chapel**, 219 Old Santa Fe Trail, is a Gothic Revival jewel that was completed in 1878 for a contingent of the Kentucky-based Sisters of Loretto. The sisters opened the Academy of Our Lady of Light in Santa Fe in 1853. Once flanked by the Loretto Academy and convent, the chapel is the only building remaining. It was designed by Antoine and Projectus Mouly based on King Louis IX's Sainte-Chapelle in Paris. This chapel's stained glass was purchased in 1876 from the DuBois Studio in Paris and came to Santa Fe by ship, paddleboat, and covered wagon, according to the chapel history. Its "miraculous" spiral staircase, in local legend constructed by a mysterious visitor after an access to the choir loft was forgotten, makes more than two complete 360-degree turns and has no center support, its parts fastened only with wooden pegs. The chapel today is a private museum and performance space.

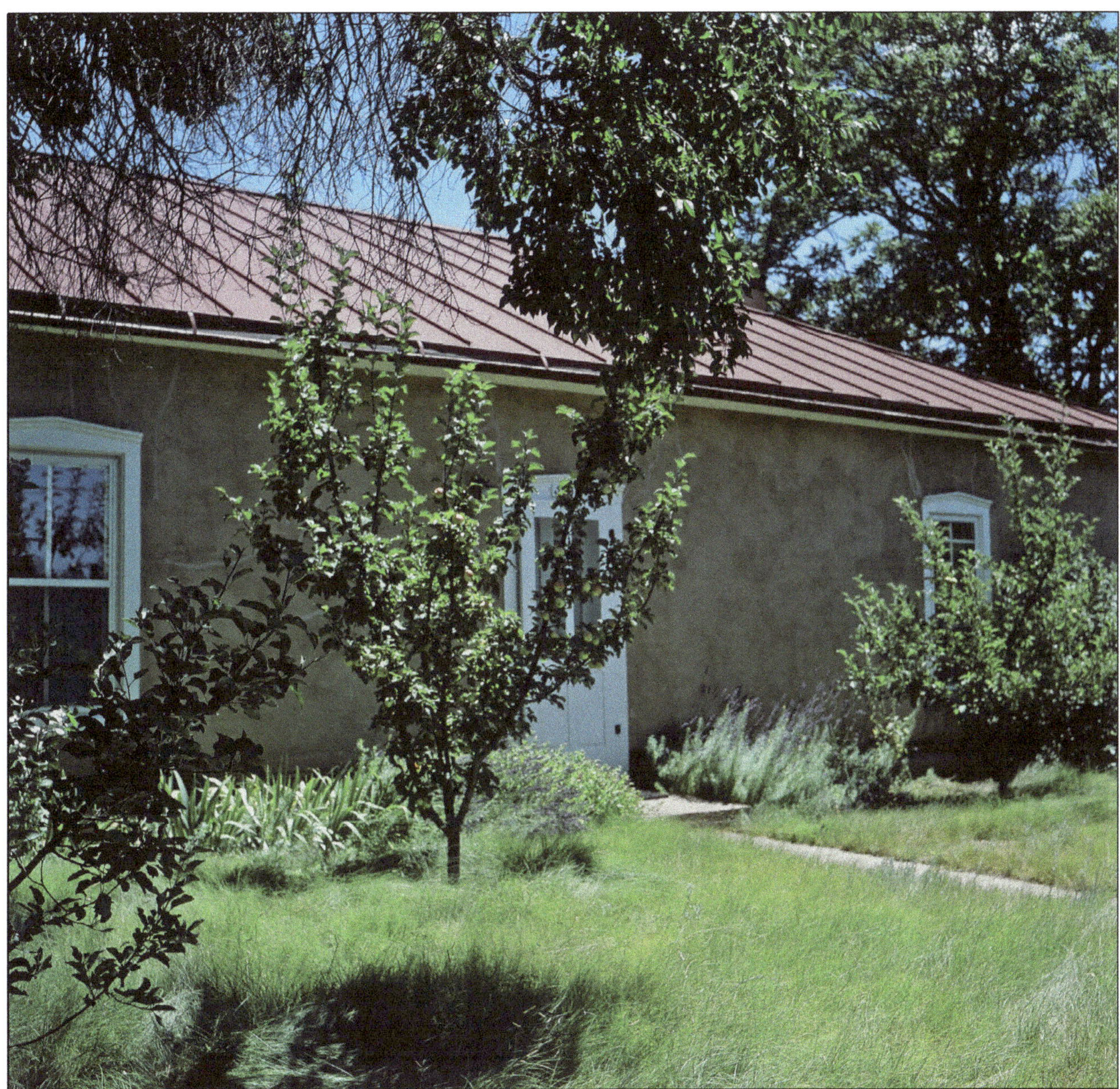

**José Dolores García House**, 533 Garcia Street, is the oldest house on what was known as El Camino de los Garcías back in the days when the neighborhood was mostly cornfields and when children rode burros and played in the *acequias*. This was the home of José Dolores García, who was killed by lightning while on horseback tending his sheep in the Valle Grande, according to his grandson, Pete García. "The story is that there was a child on the horse, too, and the lightning killed my grandfather and the horse but not the child," he said in a 2003 interview for *The New Mexican*. García also said that the material for the house's first metal roof came to Santa Fe on the new Atchison, Topeka & Santa Fe Railway lines in 1880 or so. The García family had the house until the 1960s. It is now owned by Armin Rembe, whose family has the beautiful Los Poblanos Inn and lavender farm on Rio Grande Boulevard in Albuquerque.

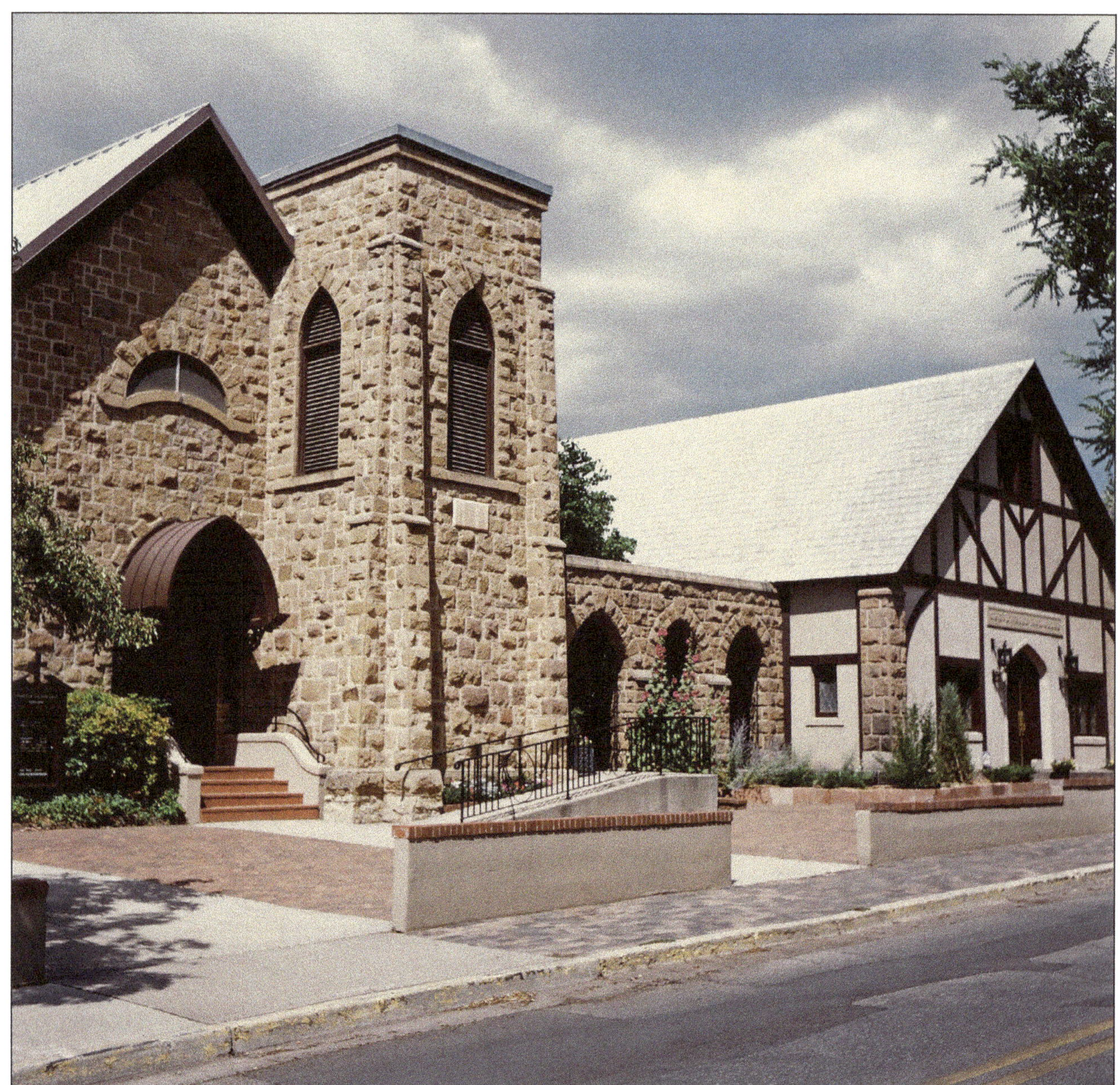

**The Church of the Holy Faith**, 311 E. Palace Avenue, is one of Santa Fe's wonderful stone buildings and also an example of the few pre-1912 institutional buildings downtown that was not given a Santa Fe Style remodel. Episcopal bishop George Kelly Dunlop laid the cornerstone in September 1881 and the church was completed the following year. Levi Ackroyd, an immigrant from England, was responsible for the stonework. Additions over the years included an 1893 rectory, 1925's Palen Hall — a sometimes contentious collaboration between John Gaw Meem and builder Antonio Windsor — at right in this picture, and Conkey House in 1966.

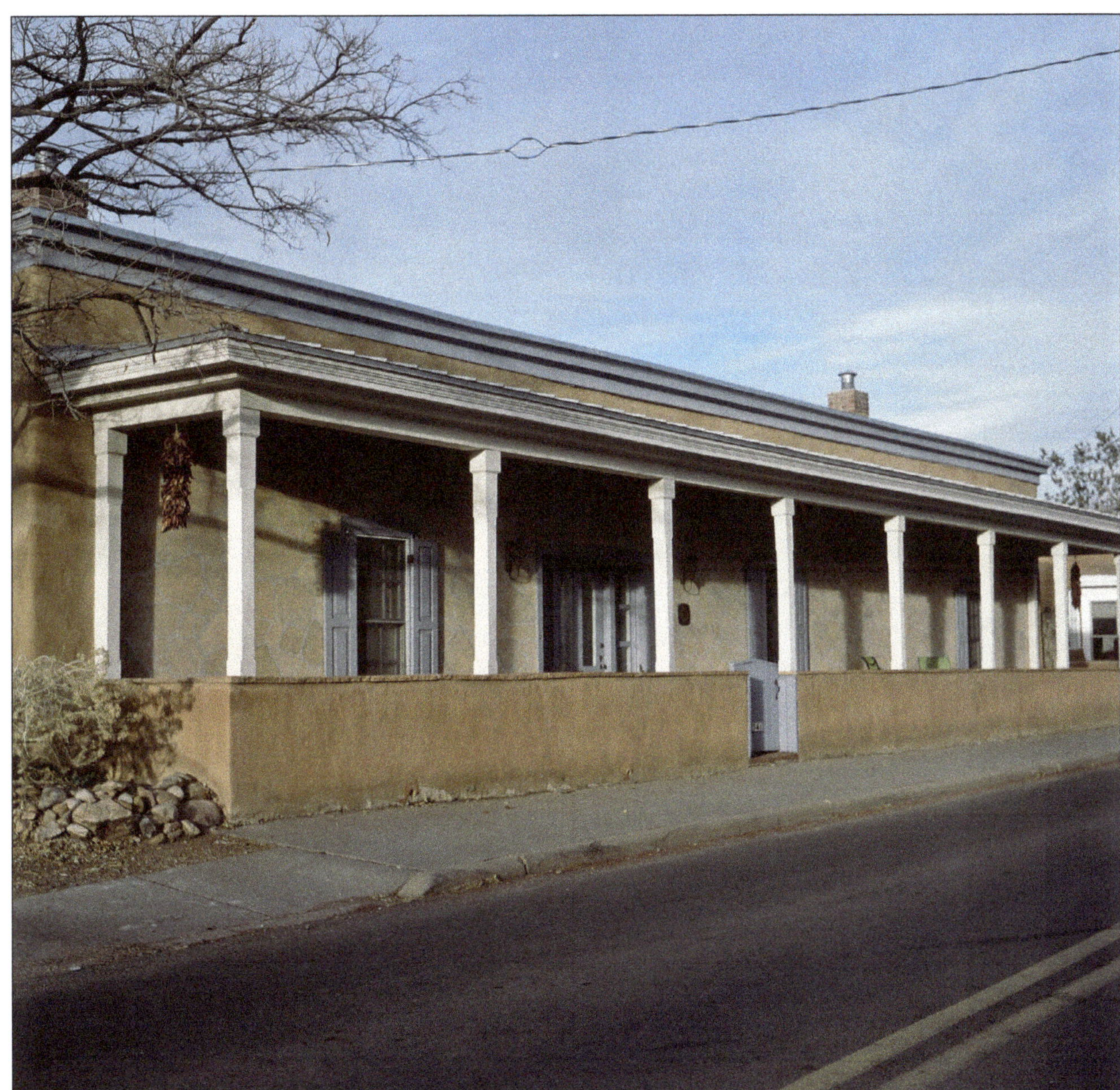

**José Rafael Roybal House**, 541 Agua Fria Street. The entire street facade of this home was painted to resemble ashlar. This simulated-stone faux finish is not unlike the "brick" stenciling on the Oliver P. Hovey House. The Roybal is a one-story Territorial-era dwelling, with a low-pitch shed roof, that was built directly along the street line. The original section, built before 1883, has three rectilinear rooms with adobe walls up to two feet thick. The rooms have brick floors and *viga* ceilings. A full-front, white-painted *portal* is anchored inside a low street wall. Roybal purchased the original section of this dwelling in the early 1880s, according to a historic building inventory. It is reported that his granddaughter, Theresa Quintana Perry, said he was for many years caretaker at the Normal School in Silver City and would live in the house when he was on vacation, then he moved here permanently after retirement. Roybal died at 82; his *Santa Fe New Mexican* obituary on Oct. 15, 1925, referred to him as a "well-known and highly esteemed citizen." The house remained in the family until it was sold by Mrs. Perry in 1984.

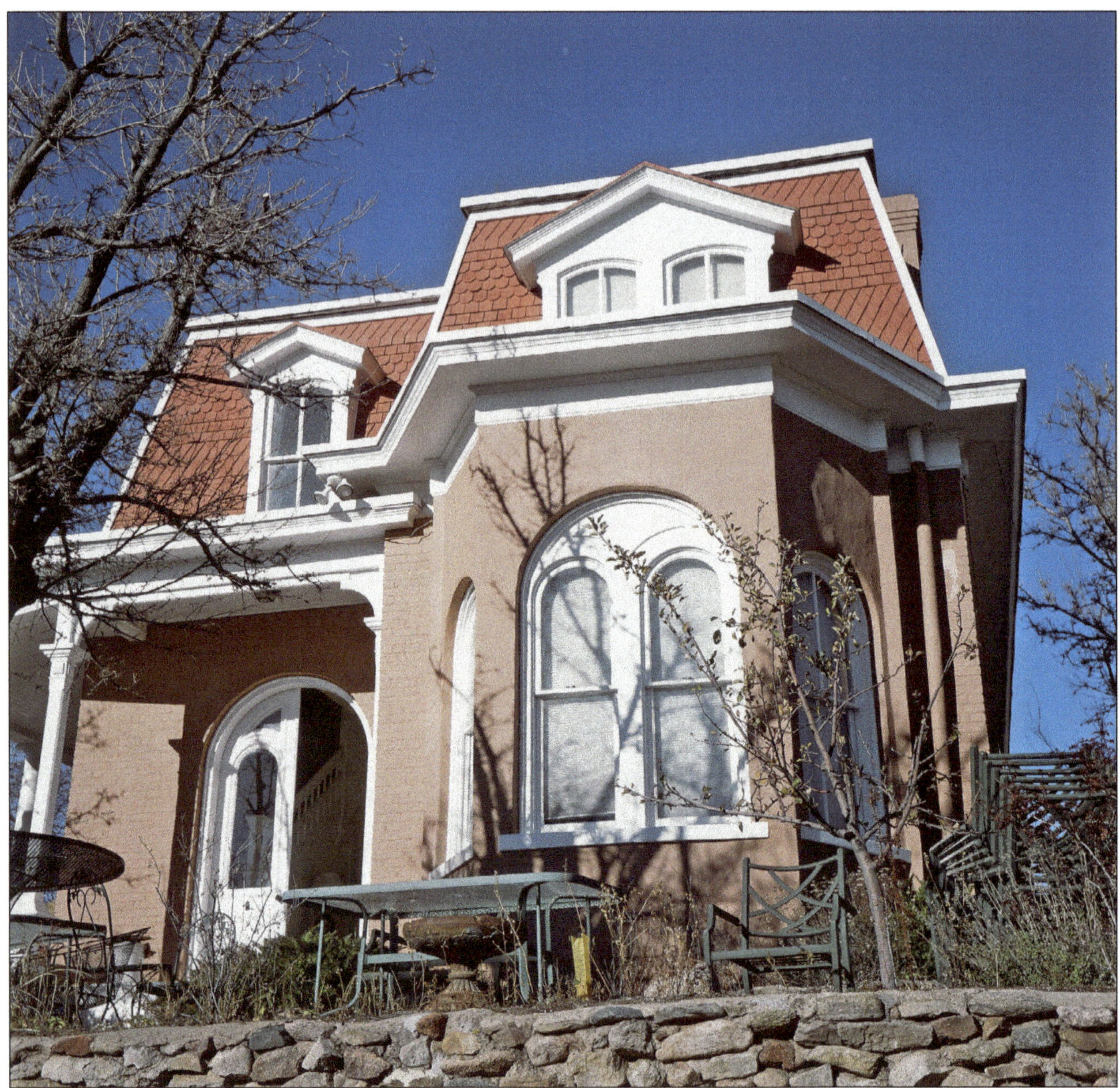

**Hayt-Wientge Mansion**, 620 Paseo de la Cuma, is one of the state's best extant Victorian buildings, designed in a style that was fairly common in Santa Fe in the 19th century. The mansard-roofed house was built in 1882 by merchant Walter Hayt, who sold it six years later to Christina and Frederick Wientge. Its brick came from nearby. "They had an *horno* down on Rosario Boulevard and they harvested clay and baked the bricks right there," said Santa Fe contractor Burke Denman, who owned the house from 2004 until his death in 2016. On a tour of the wonderful interior, he pointed out the fireplaces made of slate and faux-finished to resemble marble and black walnut. In the 1920s, the front porch was extended along the west side; Wientge family tradition has the porch coming from the old De Vargas Hotel on Water Street. Also in the early 20th century, jeweler Frederick Wientge's adobe workshop was incorporated into the main building. For nearly 140 years this house has enjoyed an elevated perspective looking south on the growth of Santa Fe.

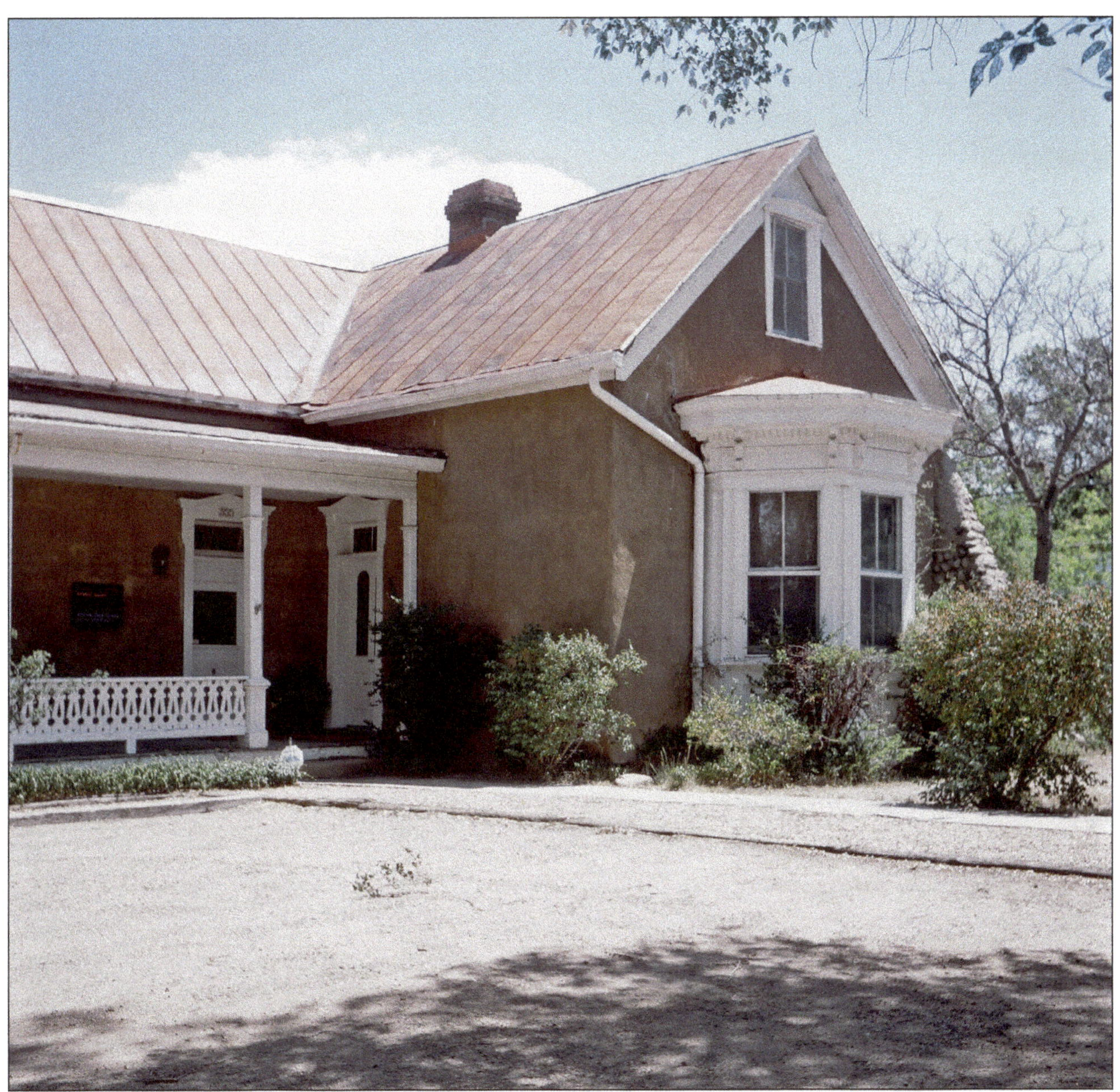

**Francisca Hinojos House**, 355 E. Palace Avenue, was built by French artisans that Archbishop Jean-Baptiste Lamy summoned from New Orleans to erect his Cathedral of St. Francis of Asissi. The late-19th-century adobe structure was enlivened by white-painted Greek Revival pediments, balustrades, and modillion cornices — including on the lovely bay-window element — as well as a terneplate roof. The house is named for the daughter of Blas Hinojos, who was a commandante principal of the New Mexico Territory. Doña Hinojos bequeathed it to her son, Alfredo Hinojos, a man who served as organist at the cathedral for nearly a half century. This photograph of the beloved old house was taken before it was seriously damaged by a fire — and sections of the adobes unavoidably damaged by firefighters' hoses — in February 2013. Santa Fe homebuilder John Wolf bought the house and (quite faithfully) restored it 2015-2017 as his family's personal residence.

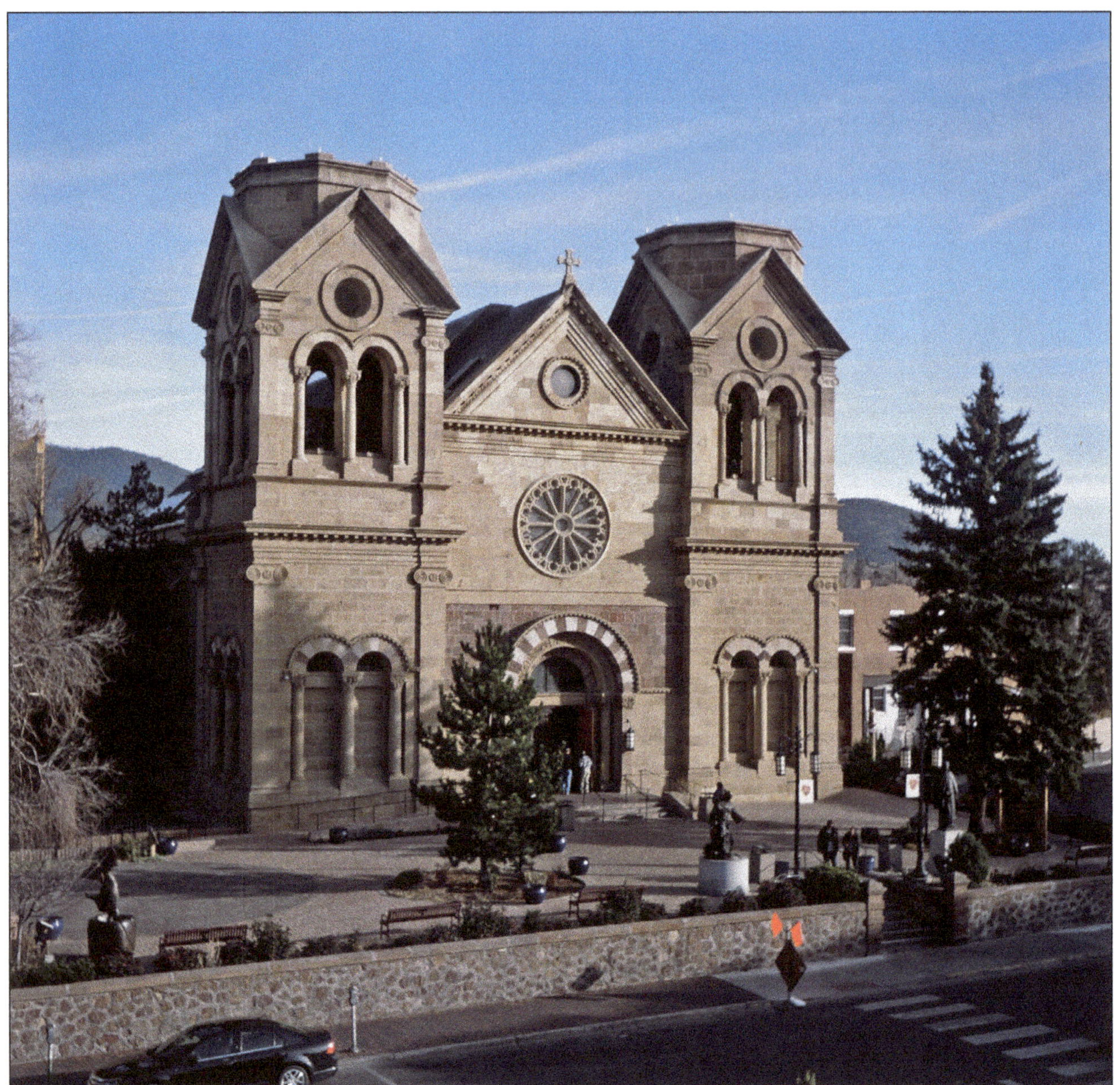

**Cathedral Basilica of St. Francis of Assisi**. This photograph was made in November 2012. The perspective, from a roof of the Museum of Contemporary Native Arts across the street, frames the 19th-century, French-inspired building with a mountainous background — enjoying the views of distant mountains has been a treasured dimension of old Santa Fe, and this quality has been invoked over the years when such views have been threatened by tall development proposals in the historic district.

**ONE OF THE INTERESTING SUBJECTS IN SANTA FE'S ARCHITECTURAL AND CULTURAL HISTORY IS ITS CHURCHES**, especially those developed within a few stone's throws of the Plaza during the villa's first three centuries. The earliest in the series of European religious structures was built in the second decade of the 17th century just east of the Plaza, which originally extended all the way to what is today Cathedral Park. It was a temporary building made of mud-plastered poles, or *jacal* construction. Fray Alonso de Peinado replaced it with another structure that also did not last very long.

In line with their missionary program, the Spanish priests and soldiers put a priority on constructing churches for Native peoples, including the Mexican Indians who had served them on their frontier campaign north. **San Miguel Chapel**, located on the south side of the river in Santa Fe, may have been the first, but

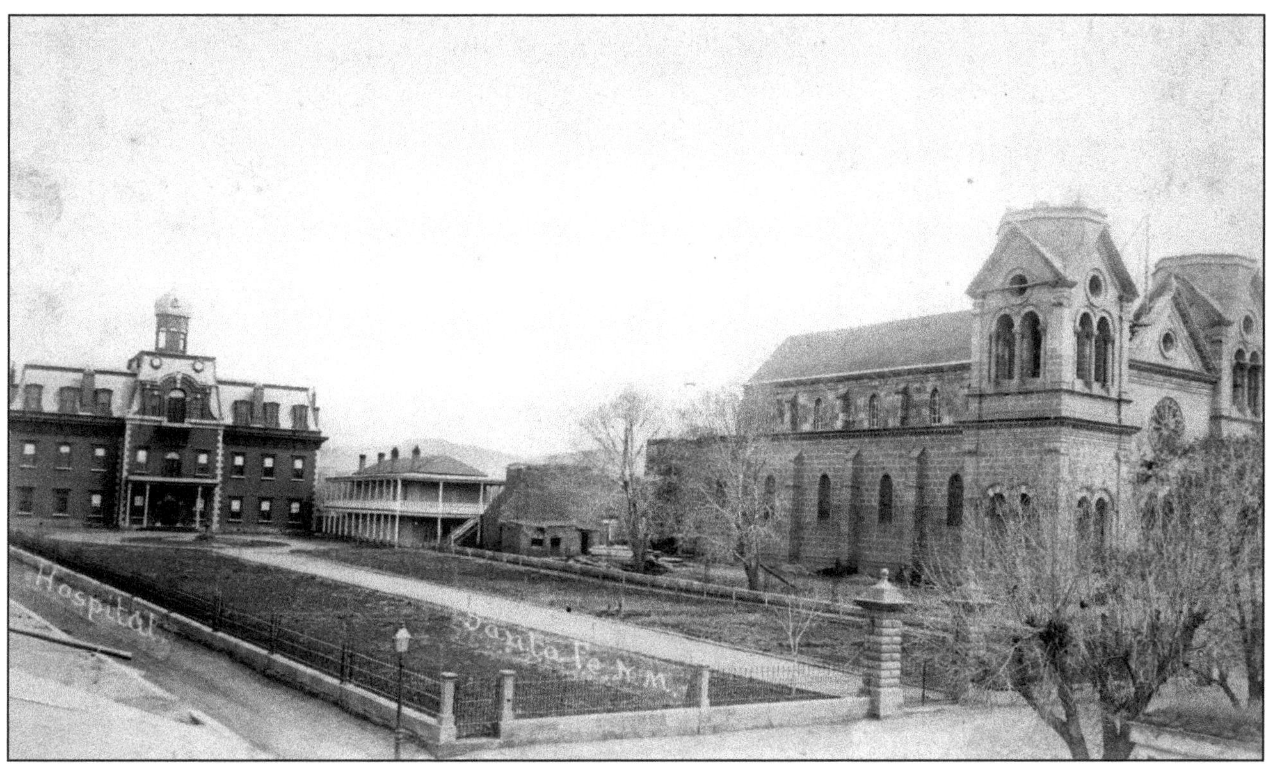


St. Vincent Sanatorium and St. Francis Cathedral, Santa Fe, New Mexico, 1888

Negative No. 105949 courtesy Palace of the Governors Photo Archives (NMHM/DCA)

during colonial times the Franciscans built more than four dozen beautiful adobe churches at the Indian pueblos. "The material is the soil itself piled high and thick, pierced by few windows, with a roof line that recalls the deck levels of ships at sea upon the desert," writes George Kubler in his 1940 tome *The Religious Architecture of New Mexico in the Colonial Period and Since the American Occupation*. "The scale of these buildings dominates the urban profile; where the town buildings hug the landscape in low files, the churches stand forth in a scale that is neither human nor canonical, but military and hieratic."

San Miguel was never massive — never anything like the San Esteven del Rey mission church at the Pueblo of Acoma — but it was one of the four substantial construction efforts undertaken during the town's earliest years. The others were the Palace of the Governors, the *plaza mayor*, and the *acequia madre* or mother ditch.

San Miguel Chapel, built in about 1628, was partially destroyed during the Pueblo Revolt years (1680-1693) and was rebuilt in 1710. The church has been remodeled a number of times over the centuries, each time resulting in a quite different appearance. A proper **parish church (*parroquia*)** east of the Plaza was probably under construction at the same time as San Miguel, with Fray Alonso de Benavides in charge of construction. This church endured but six decades and was also demolished during the revolt. In about 1717, the Spanish completed a **second *parroquia***, a large, two-towered structure erected a few yards south of the first, so that it faced directly on the *calle real de San Francisco*.

There was also a small chapel, **Nuestra Señora de la Luz**, at the east end of the Old Palace that was used for worship by the garrison's soldiers. It likely also served as the temporary home of La Conquistadora, the small Marian statue that was first brought to Santa Fe in 1626 by Fr. Benavides. La Conquistadora was secreted out with the routed Spanish at the onset of the revolt, spent a dozen years with them in El Paso, and was brought back in 1693 — the annual Fiesta de Santa Fe was begun by the Hispanic leaders to give thanks for her assistance in the resettlement.

The Palace chapel was demolished in 1714 and within five years a military chapel was built on the south side of the Plaza and was given the same name. The Chapel of Our Lady of Light, also known as **La Cas-**

**trense**, was an imposing adobe building with a transept. At the front of the flat roof was an arched bell-tower flanked by two smaller arches. The most important feature of the interior was a *reredos*, carved from stone in 1760, that dominated the rear wall.

La Castrense was razed in 1859 after Archbishop Jean Baptiste Lamy sold it to help fund a huge construction project: the building of a cathedral. Work began in 1869 on the structure (now the Cathedral Basilica of St. Francis of Assisi). It was actually built around the old *parroquia*; workers took advantage of the adobe structure's flat roof, using it as a platform for erecting the cathedral's vaults. Lamy brought architects Antoine and Projectus Mouly from Paris to supervise. (Mid-project, architect François Mallet replaced Antoine Mouly, who returned, blind, to France in 1874.) The Romanesque-style cathedral was built of light volcanic stone, quarried from the Arroyo Sais just east of downtown, and limestone brought from the Cerro Colorado in Lamy.

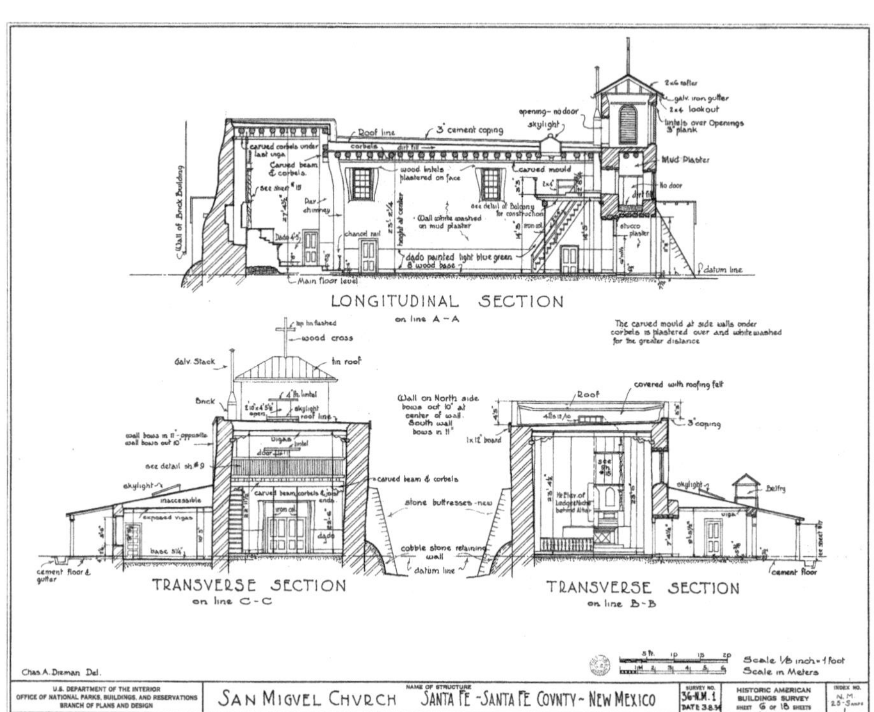


Measured drawings of San Miguel Chapel, Historic American Buildings Survey, 1934; courtesy Library of Congress

For their model, the Moulys referenced another cathedral being built in Marseille. Construction of the Santa Fe building ceased in 1887 — and most Santa Feans who love this building consider it fortunate that Lamy ran out of money: to complete his design, 75-foot spires would have been added on top of the facade's twin towers.

Today's Conquistadora Chapel, adjoining the cathedral and functioning as its north transept, is an adobe remnant of the second *parroquia*, preserved during the cathedral construction. The rest of the old parish church was demolished as the cathedral took shape around it, and the adobe rubble was used by citizens to stabilize the banks of the Santa Fe River.

Some detail on the cathedral's roof was provided by Santa Fe resident Bill Layden. "My dad had a sheet-metal shop when I was in my 20s and I worked for him putting on a new roof for the cathedral in the 1960s," he said in a July 2011 conversation. "My wife and I got married there and we did this job after that. The remodel was designed by Urban Weidner, architect. It took us nine months or more. It was all copper and we'd have to go to work early and get off of the roof by 10 in the morning because it got so hot you couldn't touch it."

Why copper? "It's a lifetime roof," Layden said. "We used 20- and 16-gauge copper in four-foot pieces. When it was new it was bright copper color and you could see it shining from La Bajada when you came up from Albuquerque."

– – – – 30 – – – –

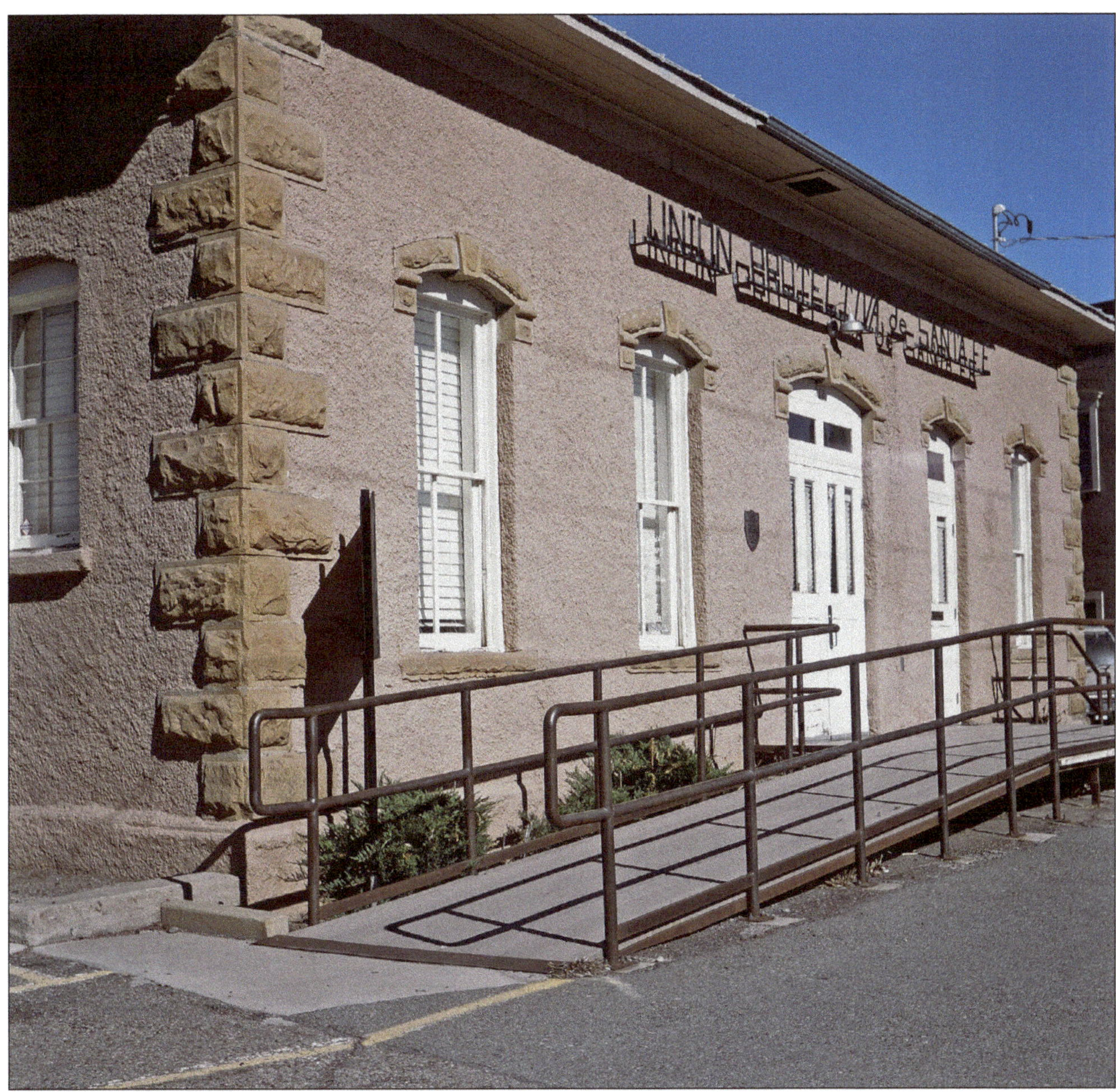

**Second Ward School**, 312 Sandoval Street. This was Santa Fe's first purpose-built schoolhouse, probably constructed by brick manufacturer and contractor Florence Donoghue, who was also busy in 1886 with the territorial capitol building. The exterior surface dates to 1900, when Donaciano Urioste won a $200 contract to add a pebble-cement finish onto the brick walls. The Second Ward School closed after Alvord School was built in 1932 on Hickox Street. Four years later, the building was purchased by the burial society La Union Protectiva de Santa Fe. An updating project by Sunil Sakhalkar of Suby Bowden & Associates won a 2009 city historic preservation award. About those distinctive sandstone quoins and eyebrow hoods over the front door and windows, preservationist Alan "Mac" Watson said, "I'm almost dead certain that the stone came from Cerro Colorado, which is across the mighty Galisteo River from Lamy and is the same stone found at the Cathedral, Loretto Chapel and several other buildings in town."

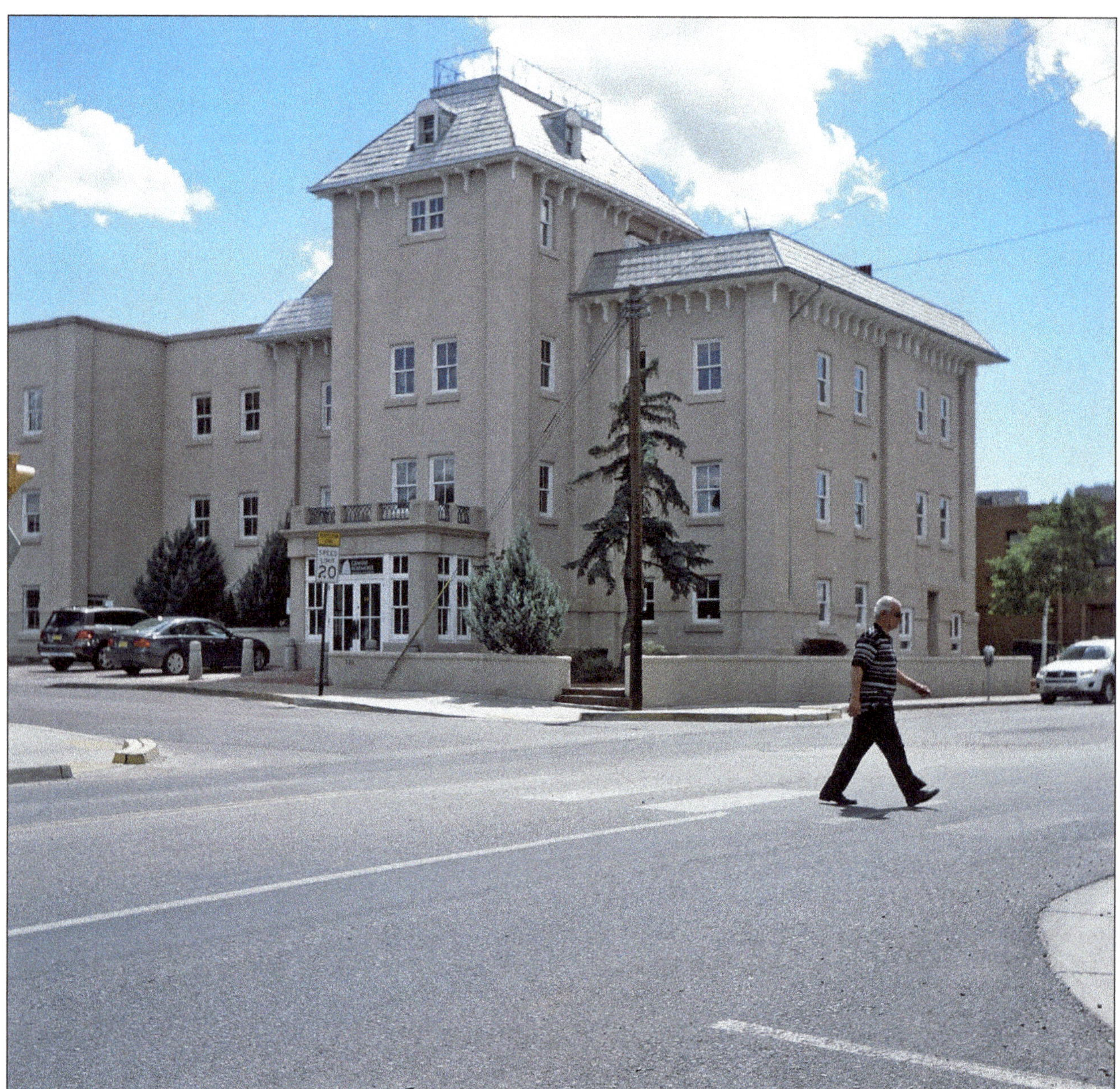


**Whitin Hall**, 330 Garfield, was built for the first University of New Mexico, established in 1881 by Congregational minister Horatio O. Ladd. The first president of the college's board of trustees was territorial supreme-court justice L. Bradford Prince. The cornerstone for Whitin Hall (named for a benefactor from Massachusetts) was laid on Oct. 21, 1882. The brick and stone structure by M. Berardinelli & Co. was not completed until 1887 and the school only lasted another year. Apparently not adequately popular with the public, it closed its doors in 1888. (The second and current University of New Mexico was founded in Albuquerque the following year.) Whitin Hall housed the New West Academy for five years, then was rented by the New West Education Commission to the local board of education for high-school classes. In 1928, the building became the Franciscan Hotel. Five years later, it was converted by Archbishop Rudolph Aloysius Gerken for the missionary sisters of Our Lady of Guadalupe and the Franciscan Sisters of Posta, Colombia. It operated as St. Mary's Convent until the late 1940s and was later the Garfield Apartments. Today the building provides quarters for the Santa Fe office of Gemini Rosemont Commercial Real Estate.

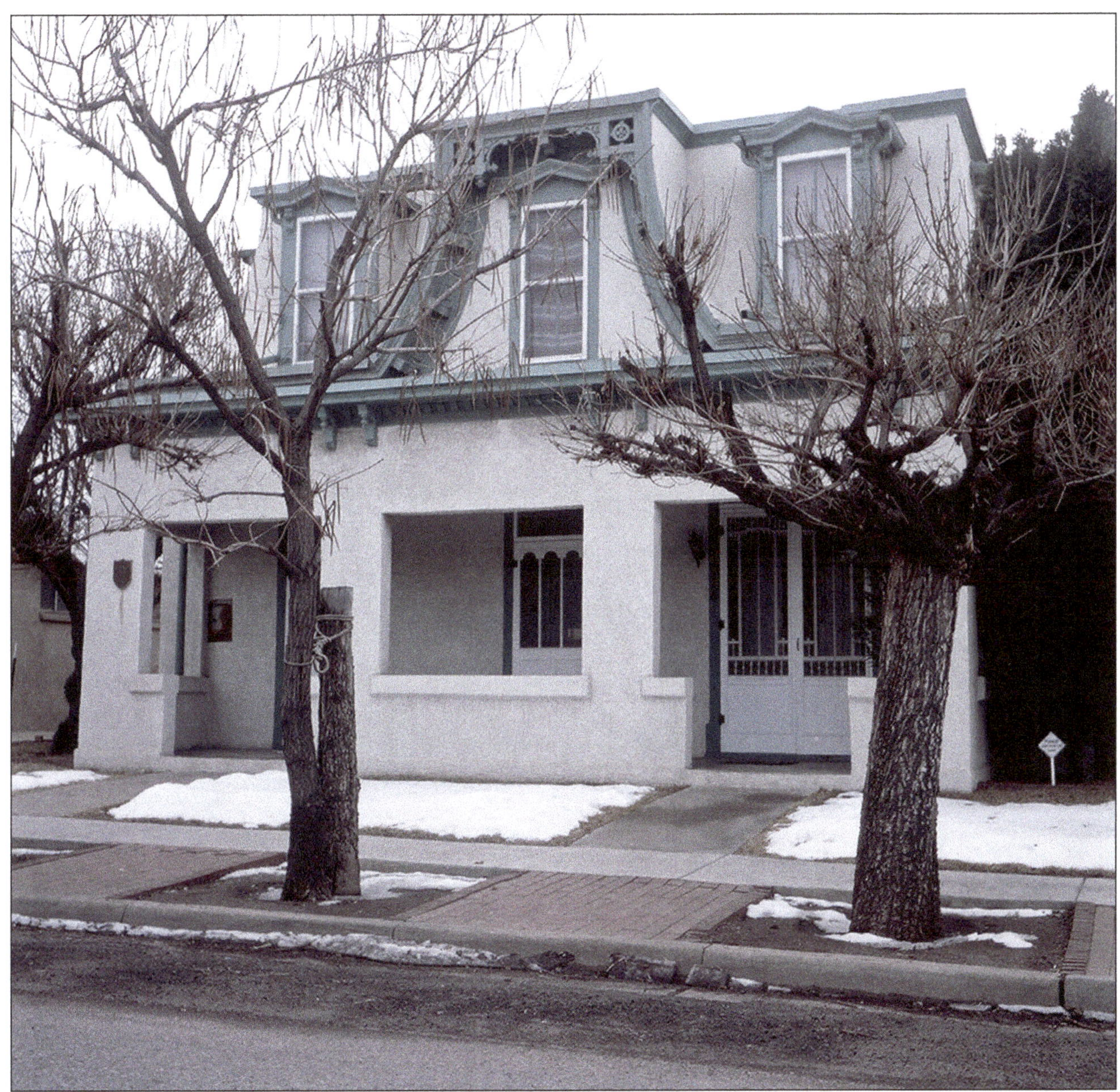

**Philip Hesch House**, 324 Read Street, is immediately distinctive for its roof and exterior woodwork. It was built in 1888 by Hesch, a Canadian-born master carpenter. "Characterized by an imposing mansard roof and 'carpenter style' exterior ornament, it is one of the few remaining late-19th-century structures in the city influenced by contemporary European architectural details," says *Old Santa Fe Today*. The wood-frame house is stuccoed, although the second story was originally shingled. Hesch is known for another house at what is now 1411 Paseo de Peralta. Nestora Lucero de Kirchner commissioned him to build that hip-roofed house in 1890 — and in the 20th century it was the home of the famed sculptor Eugenie Shonnard. The adobe house was named to the National Register of Historic Places in 1975.

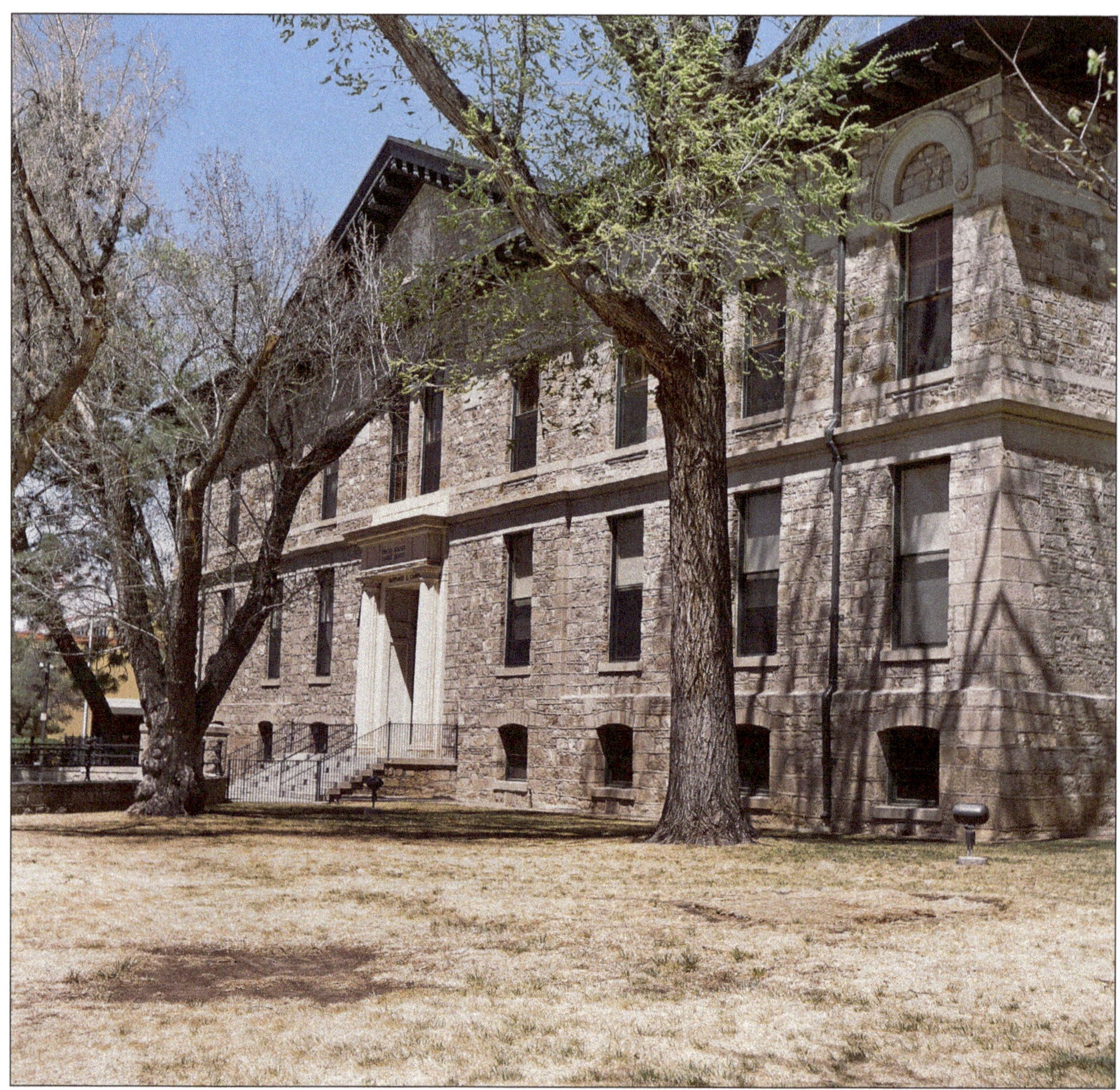

**United States Courthouse**, 100 S. Federal Place. This building has an interesting history. It was originally going to be the first territorial capitol building. Construction started in 1853, but because of financing problems, the building designed by Joab Houghton was not completed until 36 years later. It did not have a roof for decades — and it is shown that way on the wonderful 1882 illustrated map "Bird's Eye View of the City of Santa Fé, N.M." by J.J. Stoner. By the time the building was finished, there was already a new capitol building, so this was designated the U.S. Courthouse. Stone for the Neo-Classical Revival structure was quarried near Gonzales Road and in Los Cerrillos. A substantial wing was added at the north side in 1930. Eight years later, the building interior was beautified with a series of artworks by William Penhallow Henderson. The painting of *Taos Mountain*, *Cabezon*, *Old Cuba Road on the Espiritu Santo Grant*, and four other huge murals exhibiting what the artist called the "best country" was sponsored by the Treasury Relief Art Project.

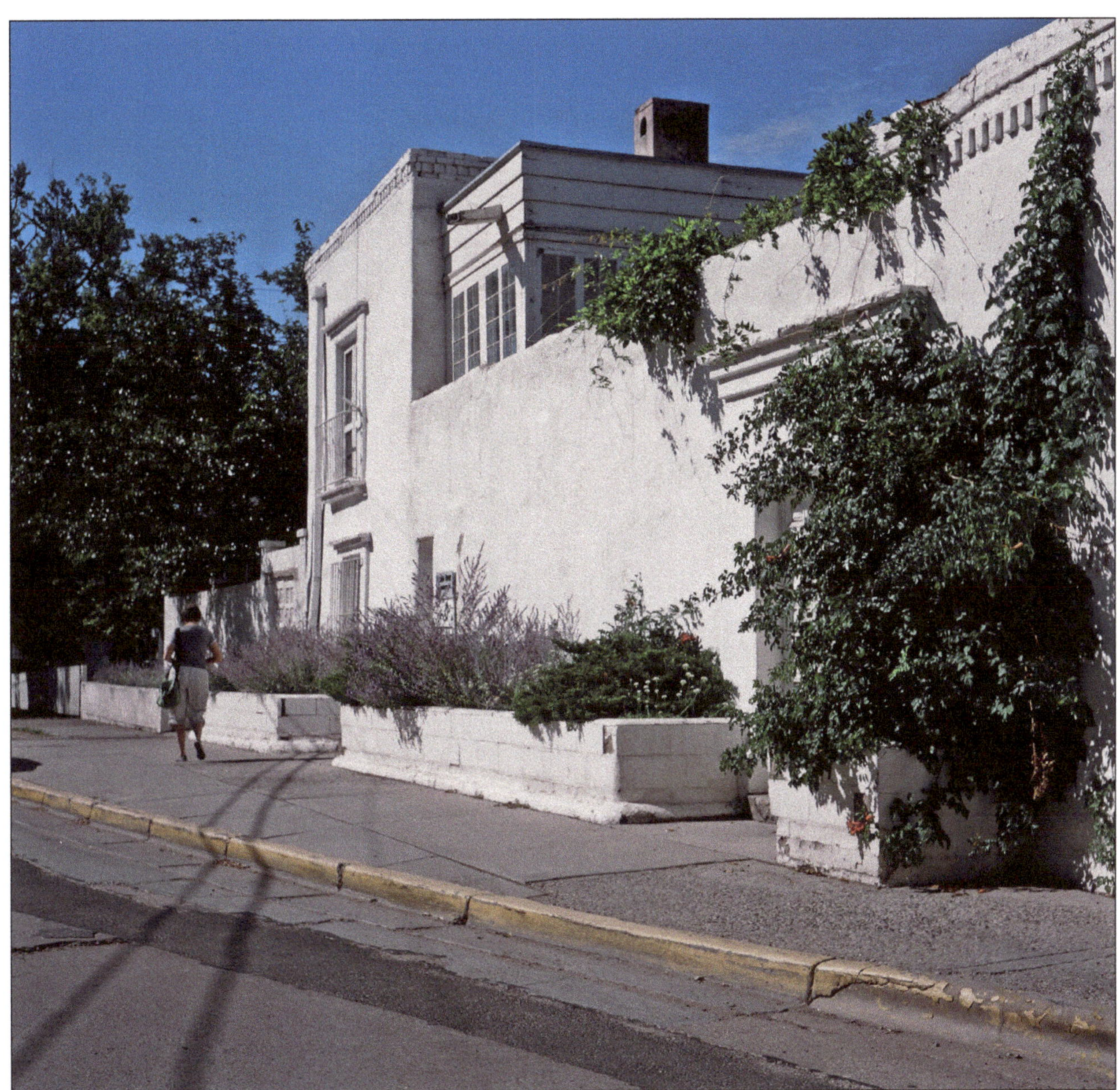

**Escudero House**, 206 McKenzie Street. The original part of the big, white building was built in about 1885. It has been known as the Escudero property, but that name is not explained. Cleofas Jaramillo, founder of the Sociedad Folklorico de Santa Fe, was resident for most of the years between 1922 and 1943. Jaramillo's daughter, 18-year-old Angelina, was sexually assaulted and murdered in this house in 1931. Thomas Johnson, a local African-American auto mechanic with a history of property crimes, was arrested and convicted — it is Santa Fe's real-life version of a novel written three decades later: *To Kill a Mockingbird*. Cleofas Jaramillo authored several books, among them *New Mexico Tasty Recipes* (1942) and *Romance of a Little Village Girl* (1955). In 1934-1937, it was home to artist Hazel Hyde, who added a second story and a studio. Edna Ballard, founder of the I Am spiritual group, resided in this house until 1953. While the original section is adobe, later additions are concrete block, wood frame, brick, and pentile.

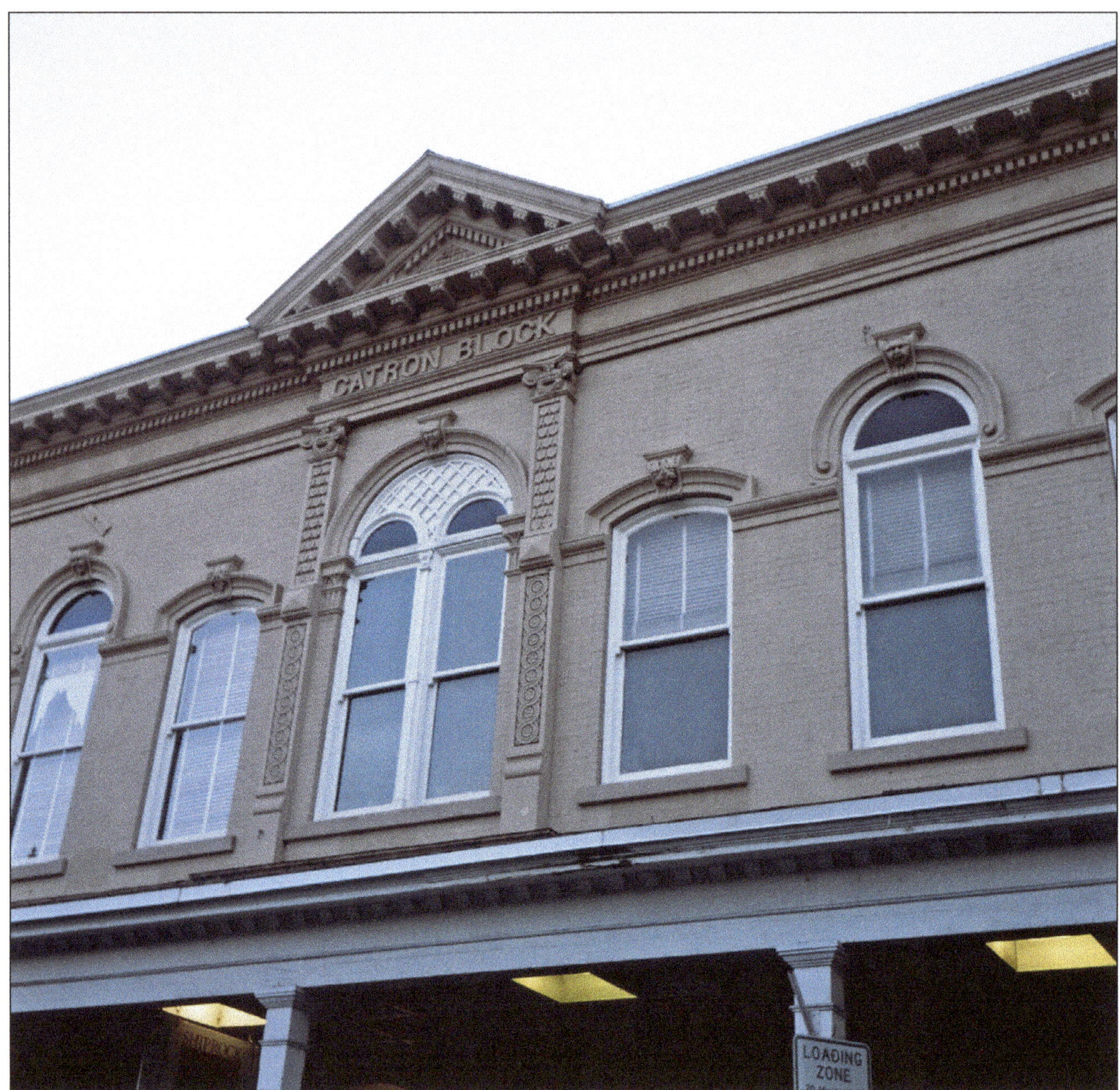


**Catron Block**, 53 Old Santa Fe Trail, was built in 1891 by Berardinelli & Palladino, who came to Santa Fe a decade or two earlier to work on the cathedral and then formed a partnership, specializing in brick and stone buildings. As construction commenced, the local newspaper reported the arrival of a carload of galvanized cornice of "beautiful designs" and an order of 40,000 pressed bricks from the territorial penitentiary. The Catron Block sports an Italianate design, as did many structures on the Plaza in the late 19th century. Among the prominent features are arched windows with heavy hoods and keystones bearing carved acanthi and mascarons, decoratively carved pilasters, and an overhanging modillion cornice topped in the center by a small pediment. The Catron Block (aka Blatt Building) was the home of The Guarantee department store from 1912 to 1988. In the second half of the 20th century, the old-fashioned display windows on the street were modernized, a Territorial-style *portal* was added, and the building was painted "Santa Fe brown."

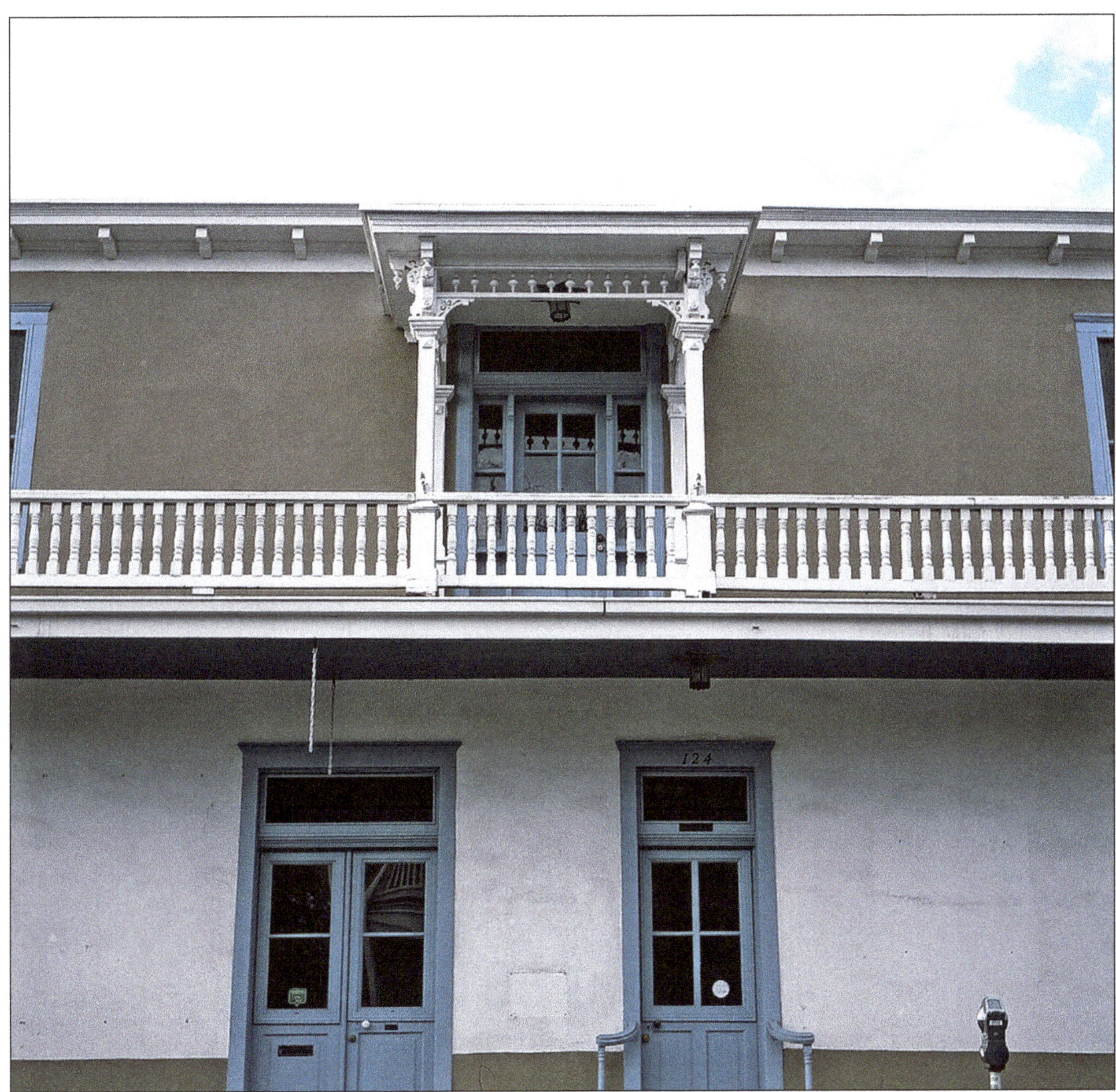


**Felipe B. Delgado House**, 124 West Palace Avenue, was built in 1890 by Delgado, a prominent local merchant. It was apparently first a one-story adobe home, but a second story had been added by 1900. The main distinctive elements of this lovely late Territorial Period house are the hipped roof and that second floor with an Italianate cornice, a cantilevered balcony with spindled balustrade, and a central porch full of fancy, white-painted woodwork. The builders may have been the same French or Italian fellows who constructed the Francisca Hinojos House and the main building at St. Catherine Indian School. Quintien ("Cassian") Monier, of Monier & Colloudon (St. Michael's College and Loretto Chapel), was quite possibly the designer. In the 1970s, John Gaw Meem purchased and renovated the house, then donated it to the Historic Santa Fe Foundation. The original roof, made of durable and fire-proof terneplate, was replaced by the foundation in 2011 with new terne — however, the steel plates were dipped in a tin/zinc alloy rather than in lead/zinc like the originals.

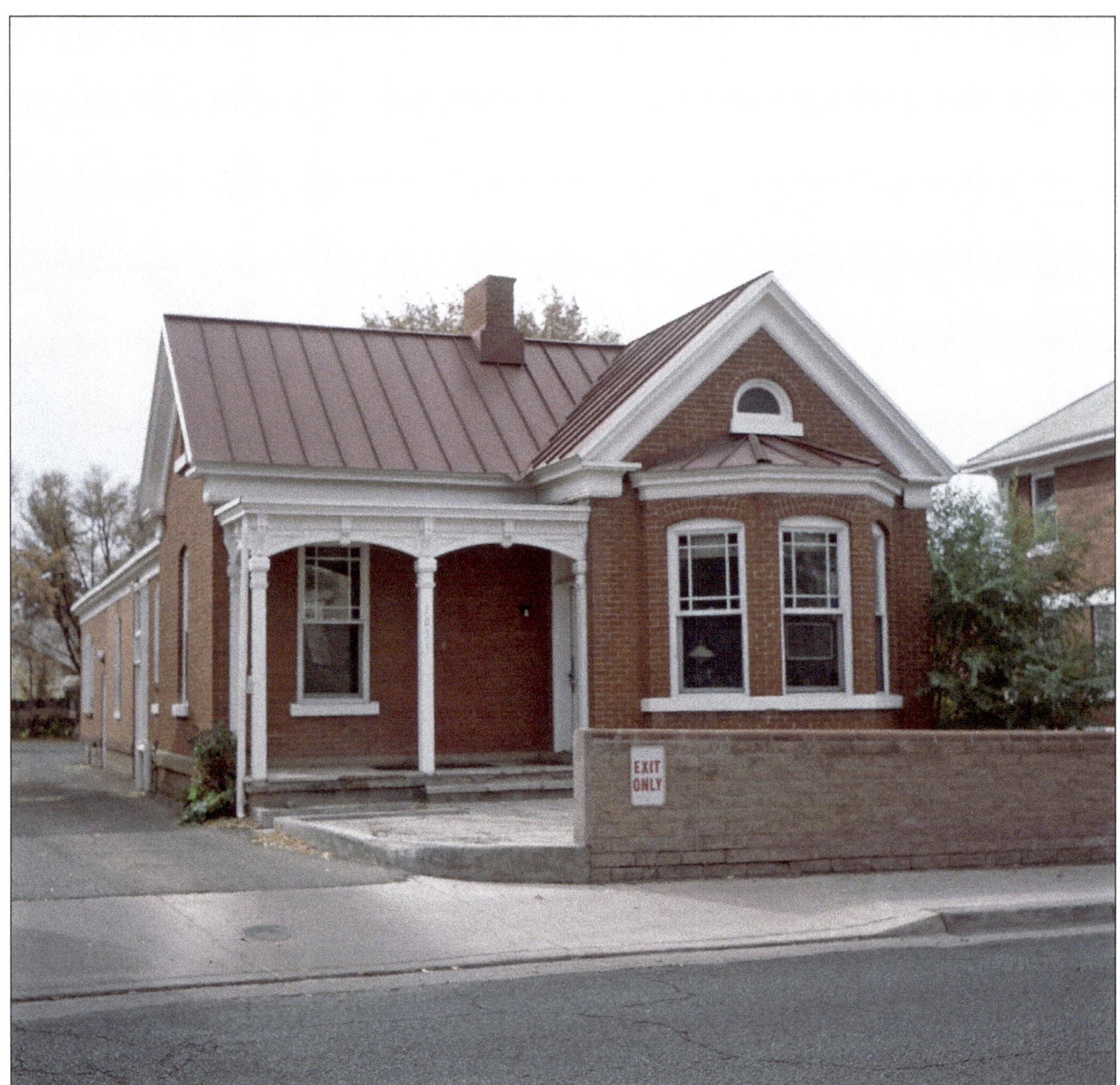


**Digneo-Valdes House**, 1231 Paseo de Peralta, was built by Carlo Digneo on a section of Manhattan Street that was absorbed by the 1960s development of the Paseo loop. Digneo came to Santa Fe in 1880 and was one of the stoneworkers on the cathedral project. At the end of that decade, he built his house on a foundation of sandstone. It originally had corbeled brick chimneys on the cross-gabled roof. Today the house is directly south of the Roundhouse. Its red-brick walls and bay window contrast handsomely with the white-painted Prairie-style windows and fan-light gable windows, doors, deep gable fascias, and the porch with its carved and bracketed entablature.

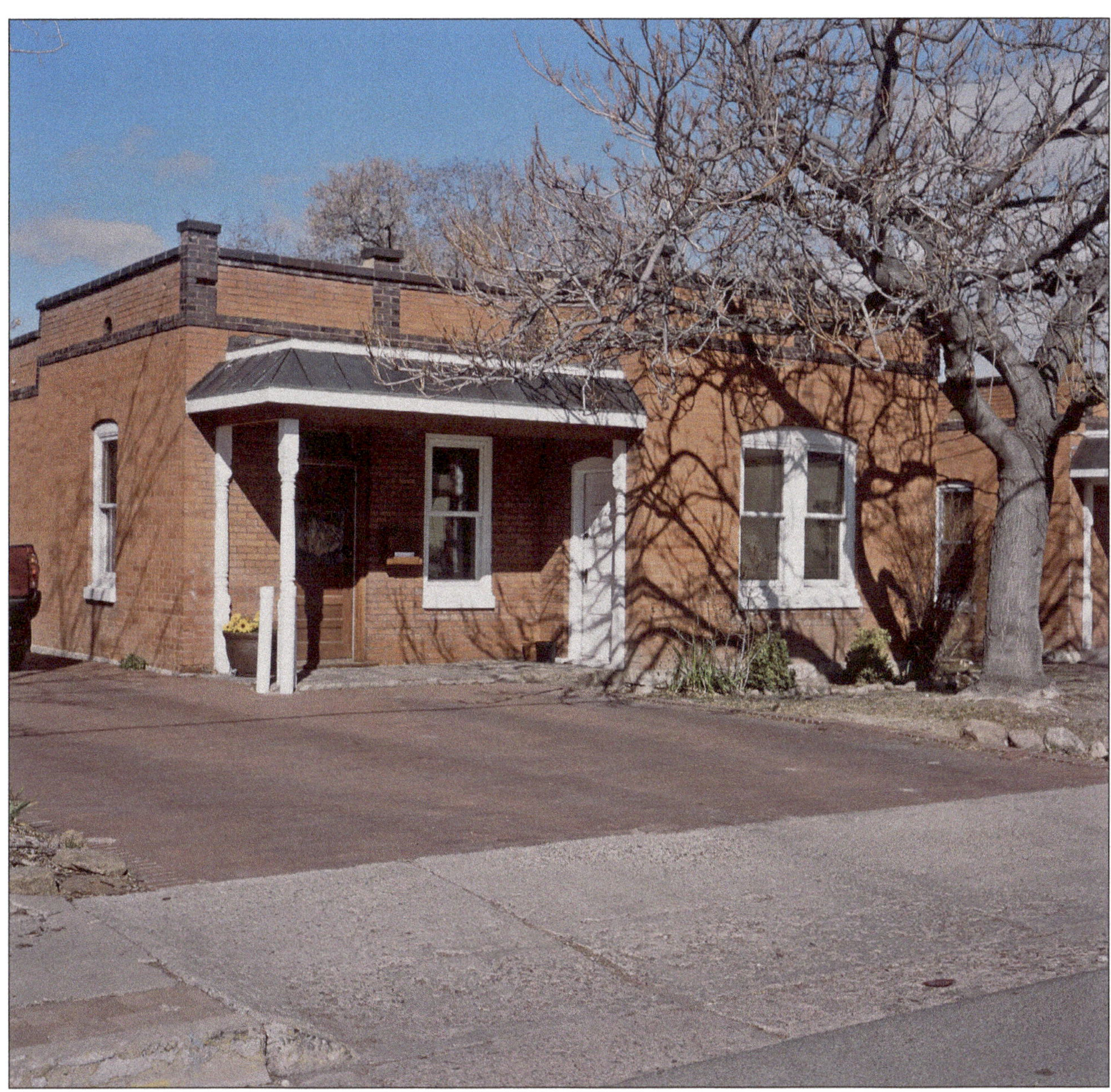

**Frederick Muller House**, 506 Galisteo Street. This distinctive residence, built in the late 19th century or early 20th century, is a member of one of Santa Fe's several twin- or trio-house "sets." 506 Galisteo is flanked by two other identical houses, obviously built (for some reason) as a group. All are described in the city's architectural survey database as characterized by "decorative brick." Built on a stone foundation, the Muller House has brick-lined parapets and pilasters with tile caps above a high string course, all of these elements made with a darker brick to stand out from the red-brick walls. The porch has a sloped metal roof and the windows are topped by brick segmental arches. Frederick Muller was a German immigrant who fought Apache Indians for the U.S. Army and later moved to Santa Fe. He was a grocer and also served as Santa Fe County treasurer and a commissioner of public lands.

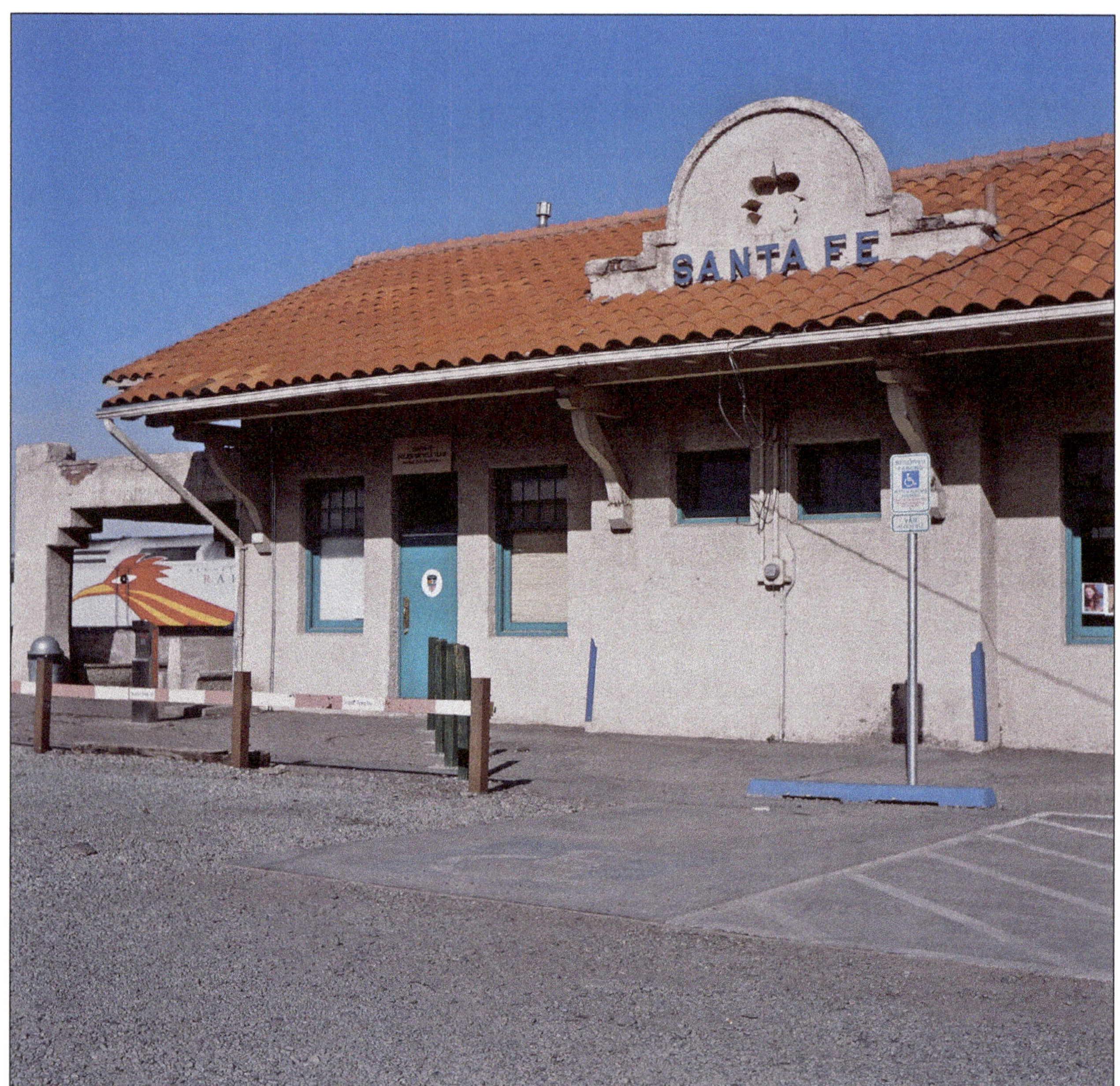


**Santa Fe Depot**, 410 Guadalupe Street, was built by the Atchison, Topeka & Santa Fe Railroad, which had served Santa Fe since 1880, at the terminus of an 18-mile spur line from Lamy. In a 1992 *Bulletin* written for the Historic Santa Fe Foundation, historian Corinne Sze calls the California Mission Revival-style depot and the Gross Kelly Warehouse "the most significant unaltered buildings remaining in the railroad yard." The depot has a tile roof over walls constructed of penitentiary brick, stuccoed over and pebble-dashed. The building has "Landmark" status in the city's historic district — and it exemplifies the fact that historic status does not guarantee proper maintenance. Here it's not just a matter of cosmetics; there are several instances of obvious structural deterioration challenging the city. In 2009, the New Mexico Rail Runner Express initiated regular passenger runs to and from Santa Fe, nearly 70 years after the AT&SF ceased providing this service. In this photo, the new train's roadrunner logo can be seen on the rail engine through the depot's outside waiting area.

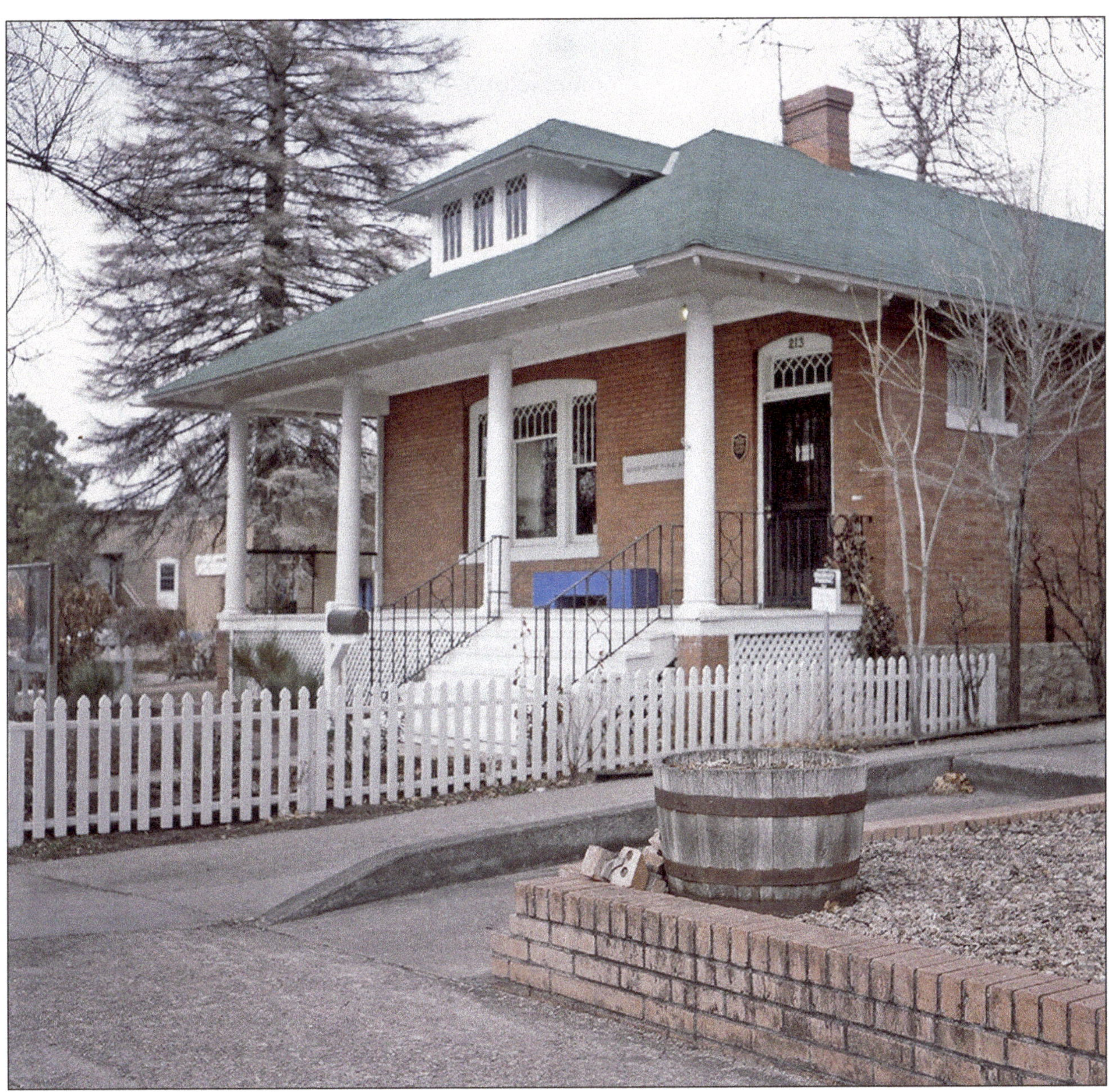


**Elizabeth and Henry Berchtold House**, 213 E. Marcy Street, is a red-brick bungalow with a hip roof and prominent dormer and a deep porch. It was built in about 1912, when such houses were seen as a modern alternative to adobe — but that sentiment would soon be considered as somewhat subversive after city leaders put new priority on "Santa Fe Style." One of the Berchtolds' children, Clara, was presented with the Pro Ecclesia et Pontifice Medal from Pope Pius XII for her church service. Her husband in later life was former governor Thomas J. Mabry. Clara died in Santa Fe in 1999 at the age of 101.

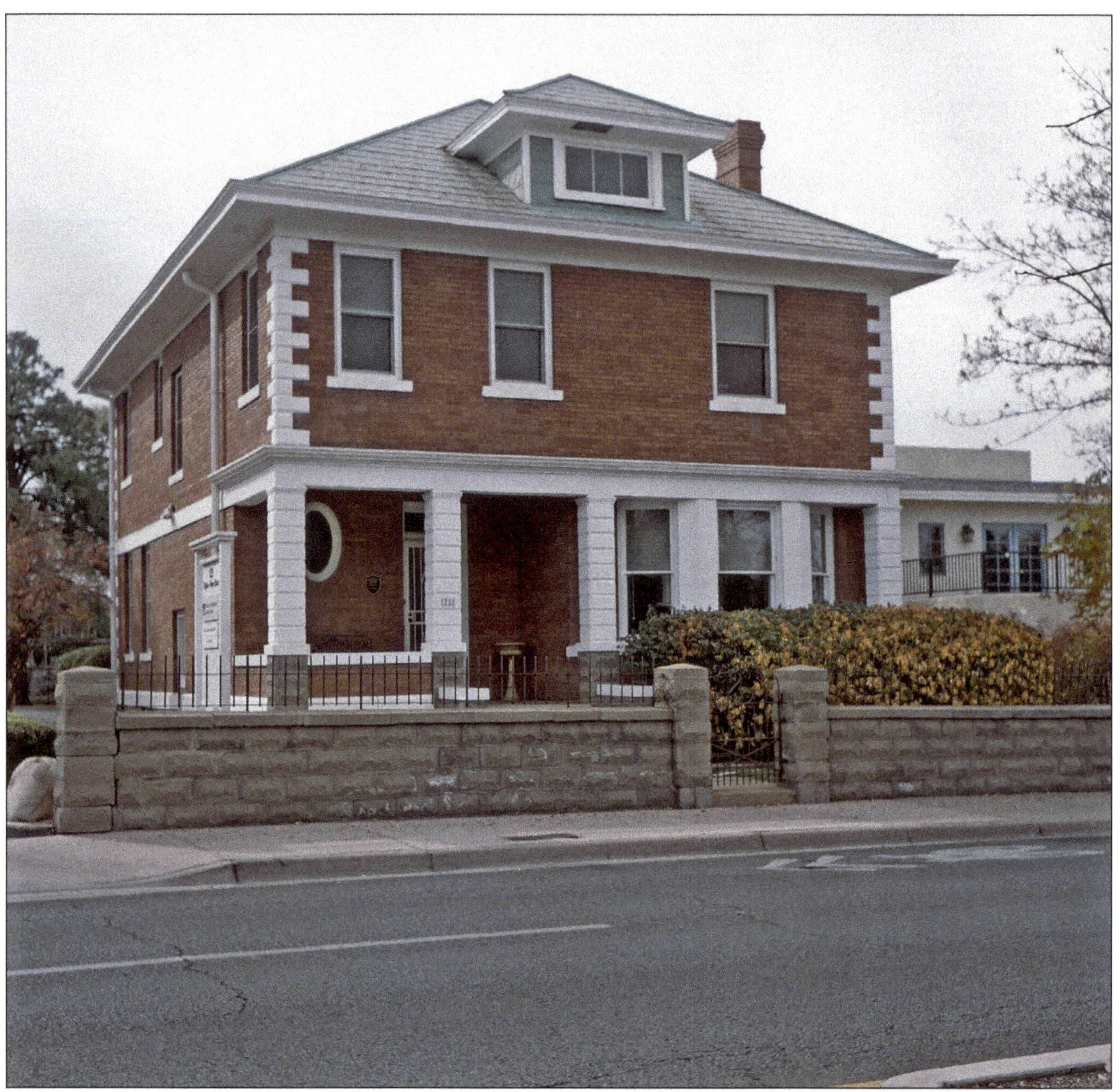

**Digneo-Moore House**, 1233 Paseo de Peralta. Carlo Digneo built his second house right next to his first home in 1911, nine years after the death of his first wife, Angela Damiani. His new bride, Magdalena Delgado, was a daughter of merchant Felipe B. Delgado. The brick dwelling has a similar ground-floor layout with left porch and right bay-window element, but 1233 has a second story with white-painted granite quoins and a pressed-metal hip roof with central dormer. Digneo also is known as builder of the 1906 First Ward School (now Ventana Fine Art) on Canyon Road. The Digneo-Moore House is currently in use as a showroom for the Reside Home design/furnishings business.

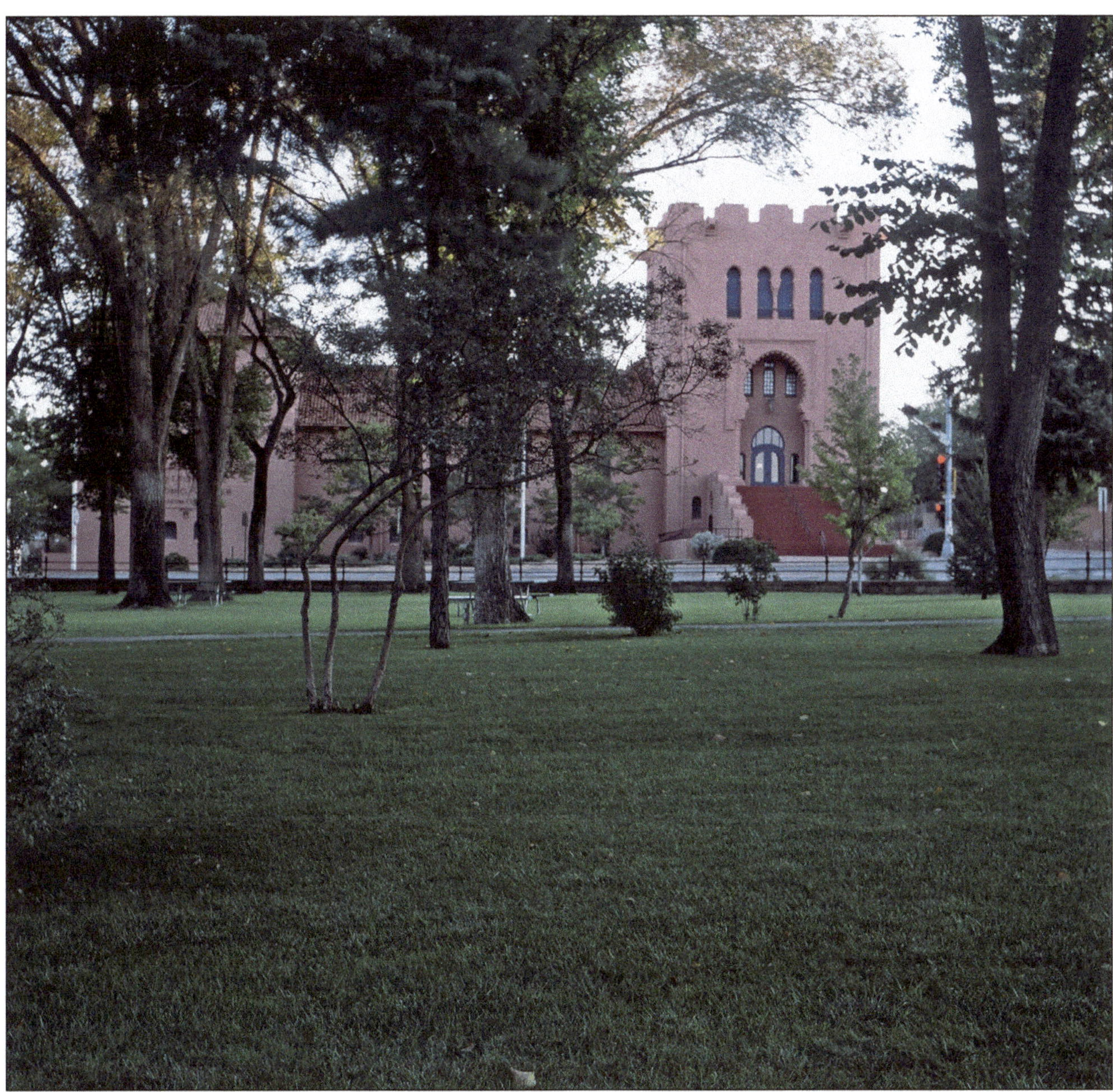

**Scottish Rite Center**, 463 Paseo de Peralta, was dedicated in November 1912. Inspired by the 13th-century Spanish Alhambra, the structure was built by Antonio Windsor and designed by Los Angeles architects Sumner Hunt and Silas Reese Burns. It is obvious that the central theme was repeated in Hunt & Burns' 1914 Southwest Museum of the American Indian in Los Angeles: each exhibits rows of arched windows along a long midsection, flanked by two towers — the right one tall with a stepped (SWAI) or crenellated (Scottish Rite) parapet, and the left tower lower with a hip roof. Interestingly, the L.A. museum was cofounded by Charles F. Lummis, a 19th-century journalist, expeditionist, and archaeologist who once spent eight days in Santa Fe on a 20-week walk from Ohio to Los Angeles and was a founding board member of the School of American Archaeology in Santa Fe. The detailing inside Scottish Rite bears renditions of the star, square, compass, and other symbols used in freemasonry. The dimensions of architectural arches were determined with reference to the Fibonacci sequence and the golden mean. The building boasts the original pipe organ, the Frank Adam Control System for Lighting, and nearly a hundred hand-painted scenery backdrops used by the Masons in a sequence of 29 "degrees" or morality plays.

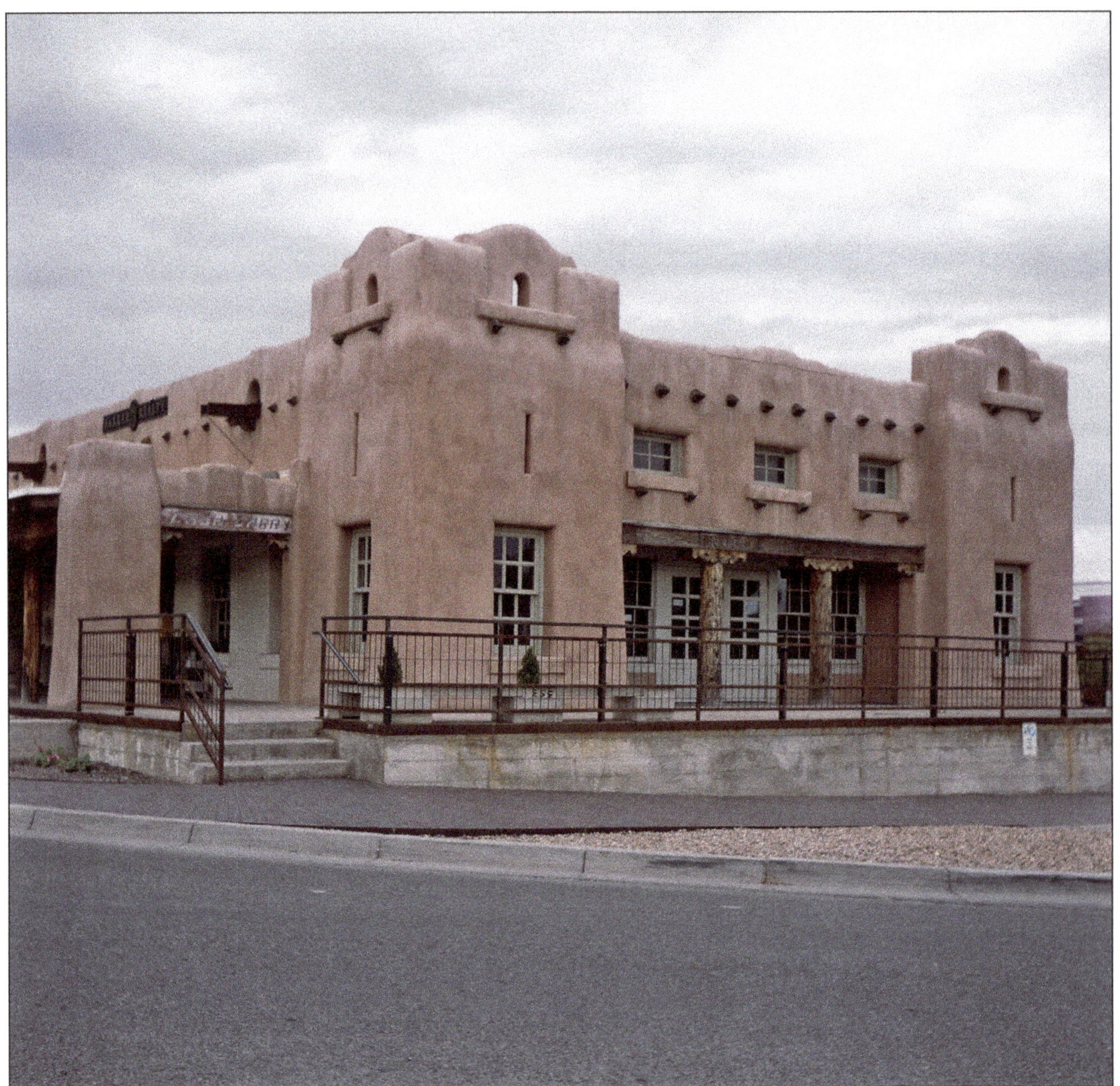

**Gross Kelly Warehouse**, 530 S. Guadalupe Street, is a city landmark building designed by Isaac Rapp for Gross, Kelly and Co., a purveyor of groceries, patent medicines, and hardware. Completed in 1913, it was one of the state's first commercial buildings in the Spanish-Pueblo Revival style. "Rapp based the overall form and design of the warehouse, a long rectangular building with flat roof, battered walls and corner towers, on the mission churches that the Spanish Colonial friars convinced the Pueblo Indians to build," says *Old Santa Fe Today*. "However, instead of traditional adobe, prison brick was used and rounded contours were created with concrete." The "viga ends" protruding from three sides are merely decorative, but the building certainly has a muscular defensive solidity, even including balistrariae (shooting slits). Covered loading docks on both long sides facilitated the transfer of goods from trains on adjacent railroad tracks. Mark Hogan was the architect on a splendid 2002 interior remodel for Barker Realty.

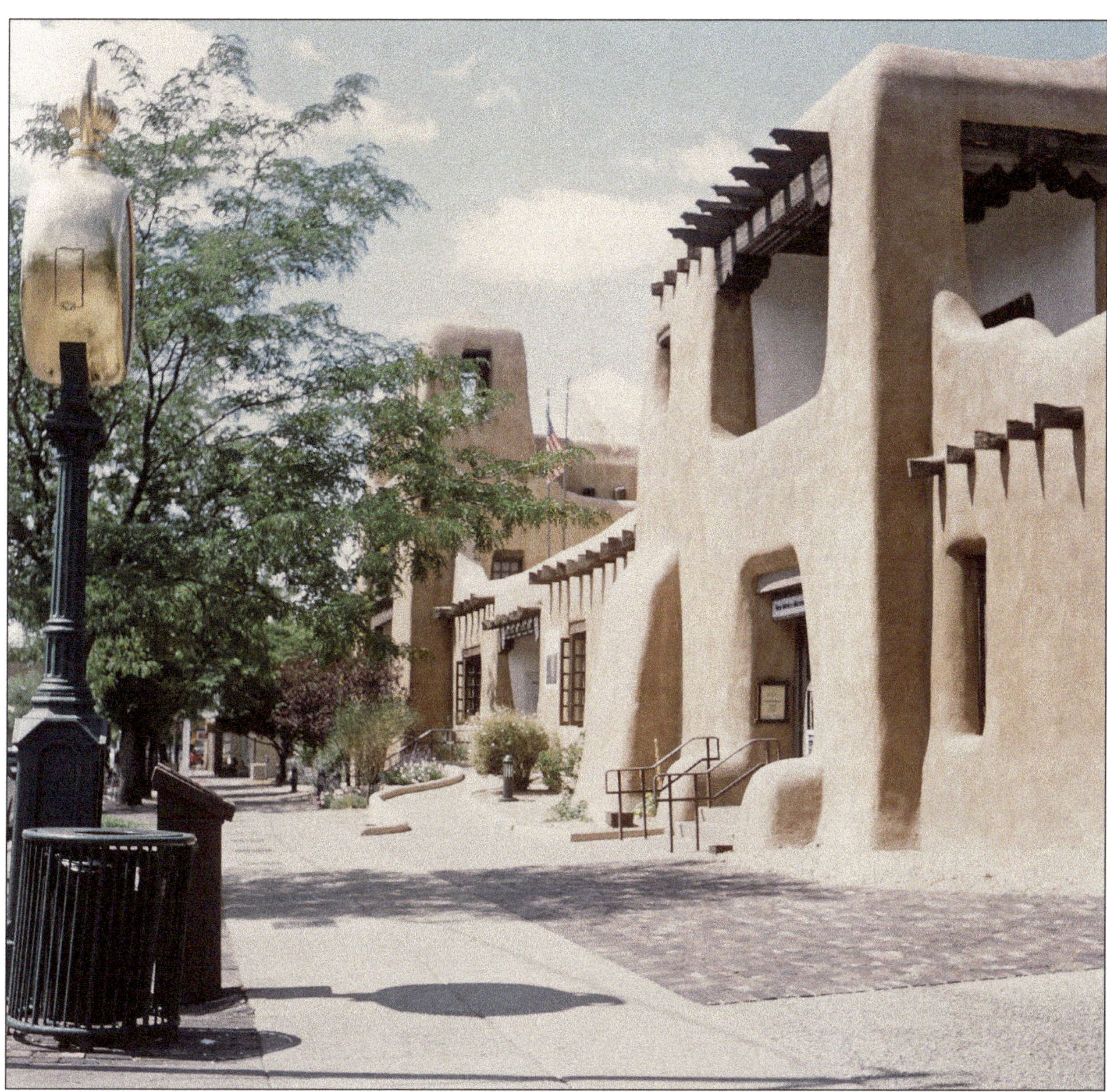

**New Mexico Museum of Art**, 107 W. Palace Avenue. Formerly known as the Museum of Fine Arts, this is a beautiful example of respectful mimicry. Rapp & Rapp based it on the New Mexico Pavilion they designed for the 1915 Panama-California Exposition in San Diego, and that was modeled after the 1642 San Esteban del Rey mission church at Acoma Pueblo. For the new museum, the architects also built in references to other regional churches, most prominently San Felipe on the Lincoln Avenue elevation. The museum was built on the site of the Old Barracks building from Fort Marcy days. After its demolition, Jesse Nusbaum directed excavations that yielded 50 pounds of pottery, nearly two dozen human skeletons, and other remains of a prehistoric Native American settlement. Other excavated materials were transported 600 feet north to enlarge the high school (today's City Hall). The state penitentiary furnished 750,000 bricks to build the museum that offered splendid exhibition spaces for the 8-year-old Museum of New Mexico — and for years also provided studio space for local artists. The museum's stately St. Francis Auditorium boasts six murals of the saint (begun by Don Beauregard and finished by Carlos Vierra) under a ceiling that *The New Mexican* in February 1917 described as "heavy wooden beams and 'herring-bone' thatching of seasoned spruce sticks brought from the 'burns' on the Sangre de Cristo."

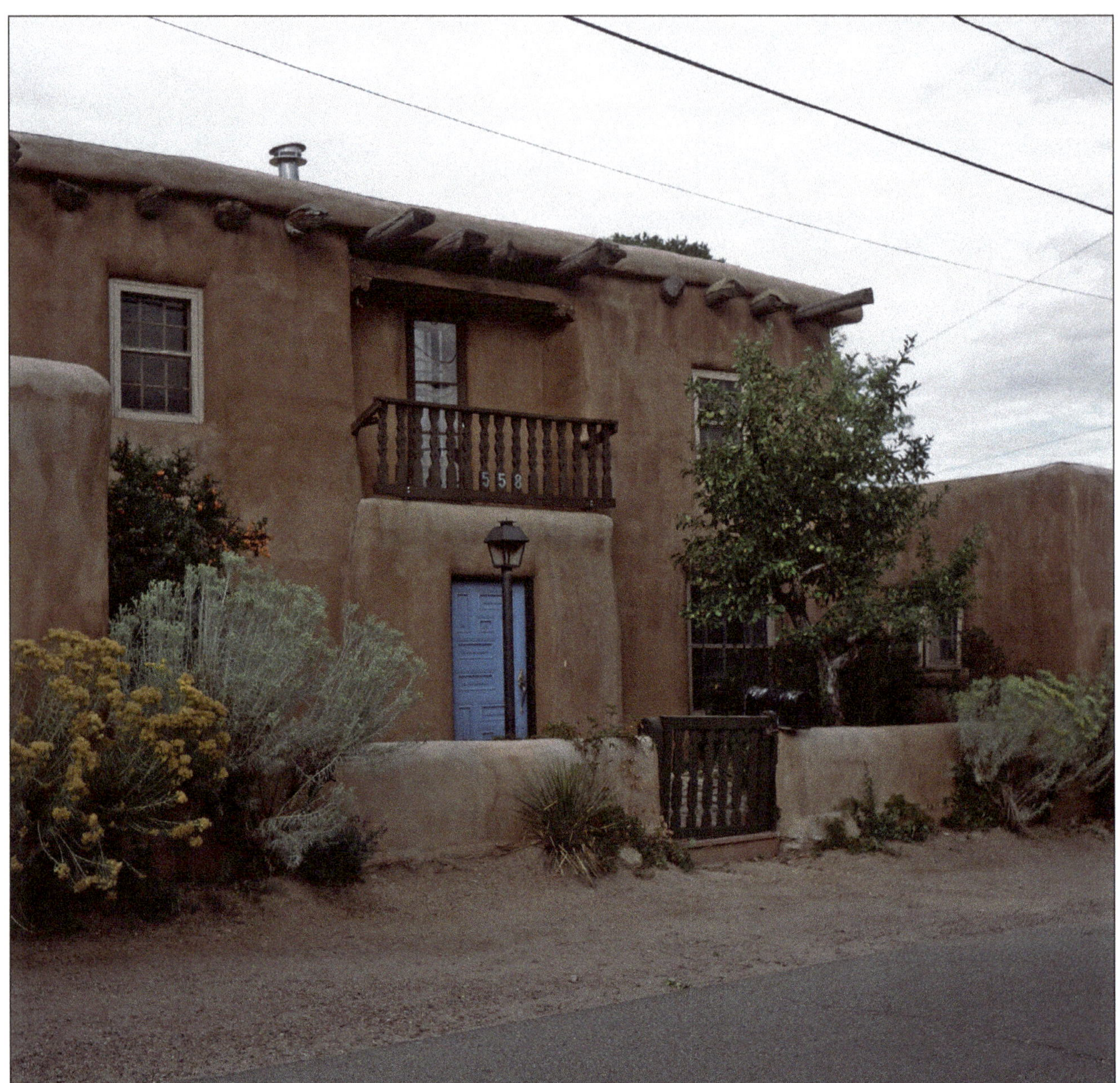


**Frank Applegate House**, 558 Camino del Monte Sol. Applegate, a native of Illinois, built this two-story adobe in 1921, the year he moved to Santa Fe. In the next decade, he designed and built adobe houses in the neighborhood for writer Mary Austin and for four of the five artists - Jozef Bakos, Fremont Ellis, Walter Mruk, Willard Nash, and Will Shuster — who were known as the *Cinco Pintores* (and in some circles as "the five nuts in mud huts"). He and Austin were among the founders of the organization today known as the Spanish Colonial Arts Society. William Lumpkins added a sunroom in 1978.

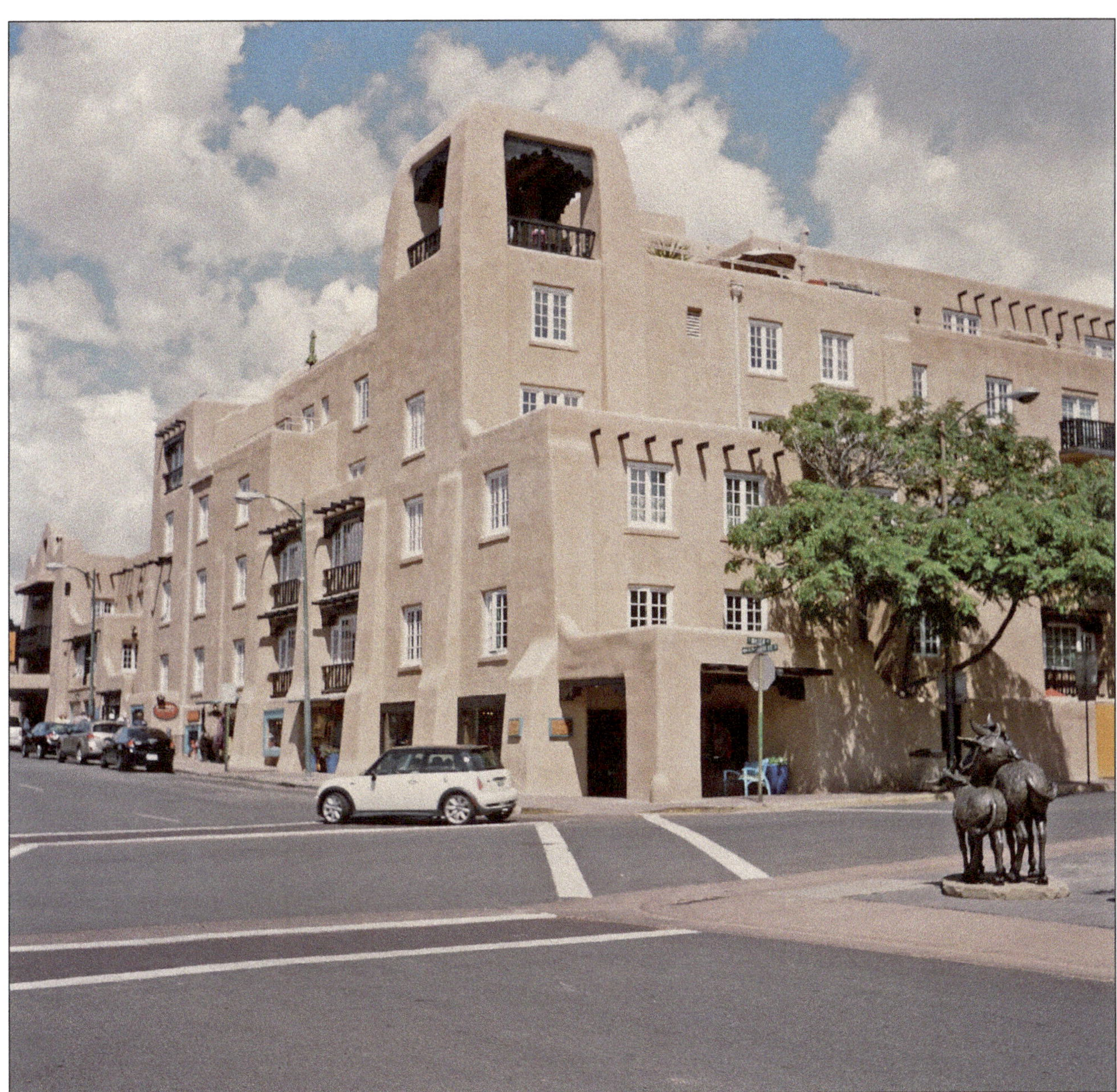

**La Fonda**, 100 E. San Francisco Street, is by far the oldest, and arguably the most "palatable" (in terms of historic fabric and scale) of the multi-level hotels in downtown Santa Fe. It was built on the site of the 19th-century Exchange Hotel and was completed in 1922 with design by Rapp, Rapp & Hendrickson. (The adobe Exchange was demolished by a World War I tank named the Mud Puppy — that was a festive but exceedingly dusty event.) La Fonda has seen several substantial changes. After purchase by the Atchison, Topeka & Santa Fe Railroad in 1925, it was run as a Harvey House for several decades. John Gaw Meem and Mary Jane Colter did a renovation and expansion in the late 1920s. Holabird & Root & Burgee, Chicago, was responsible for a 1949 addition on Water Street; the same year, Colter designed the La Cantinita lounge (now the French Pastry Shop). Architect William Lumpkins effected the 1976 conversion of the hotel's court-yard into La Plazuela restaurant. W.C. Kruger and Associates did the 1986 Carriage House parking-garage addition. And in 2009-2016, architect Barbara Felix led substantive renovation work. This photo favors the Meem tower on the hotel's southwest corner.

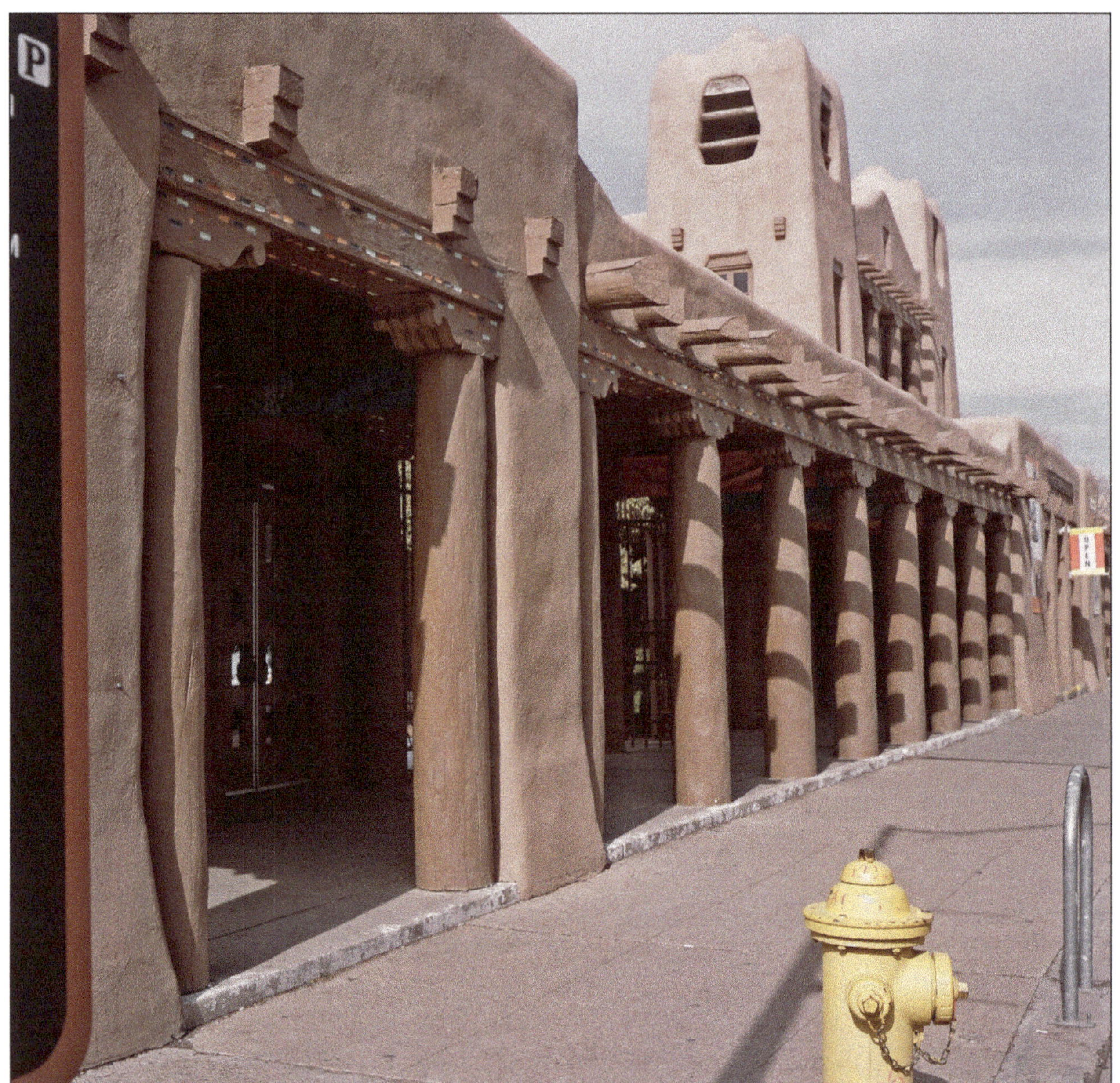


**Museum of Contemporary Native Art**, 108 Cathedral Place. This raked perspective was preferred because it de-emphasizes the rigid Beaux Arts symmetry of this building. The dominant central section holds twin towers flanking a peaked parapet, a grid of windows divided into three by wooden posts, and under that three door-shaped openings on the street. Each of the long *portales* extending north and south has precisely 22 projecting *vigas*, and eight posts and eight *zapatas* supporting the bullet-carved beams. The building looks like adobe, but it's actually a "concrete-frame building faced with brick and covered with stucco to simulate mud plaster," according to a historic-building inventory. A cornerstone has the date 1921 and the name of James A. Wetmore of the U.S. Office of the Supervising Architect, but it is more likely that this post office was designed by Louis A. Simon. The $300,000 federal building was constructed during a time when the city paved downtown streets, installed a sewer system, and put up ornamental street lights. The *Santa Fe New Mexican* of Nov. 22, 1919, called it a "Million Dollar City Improvement Campaign" and included a full page of photographs of buildings and the heading "Beautiful and Distinctive Architecture Makes Santa Fe 'City Different.'"

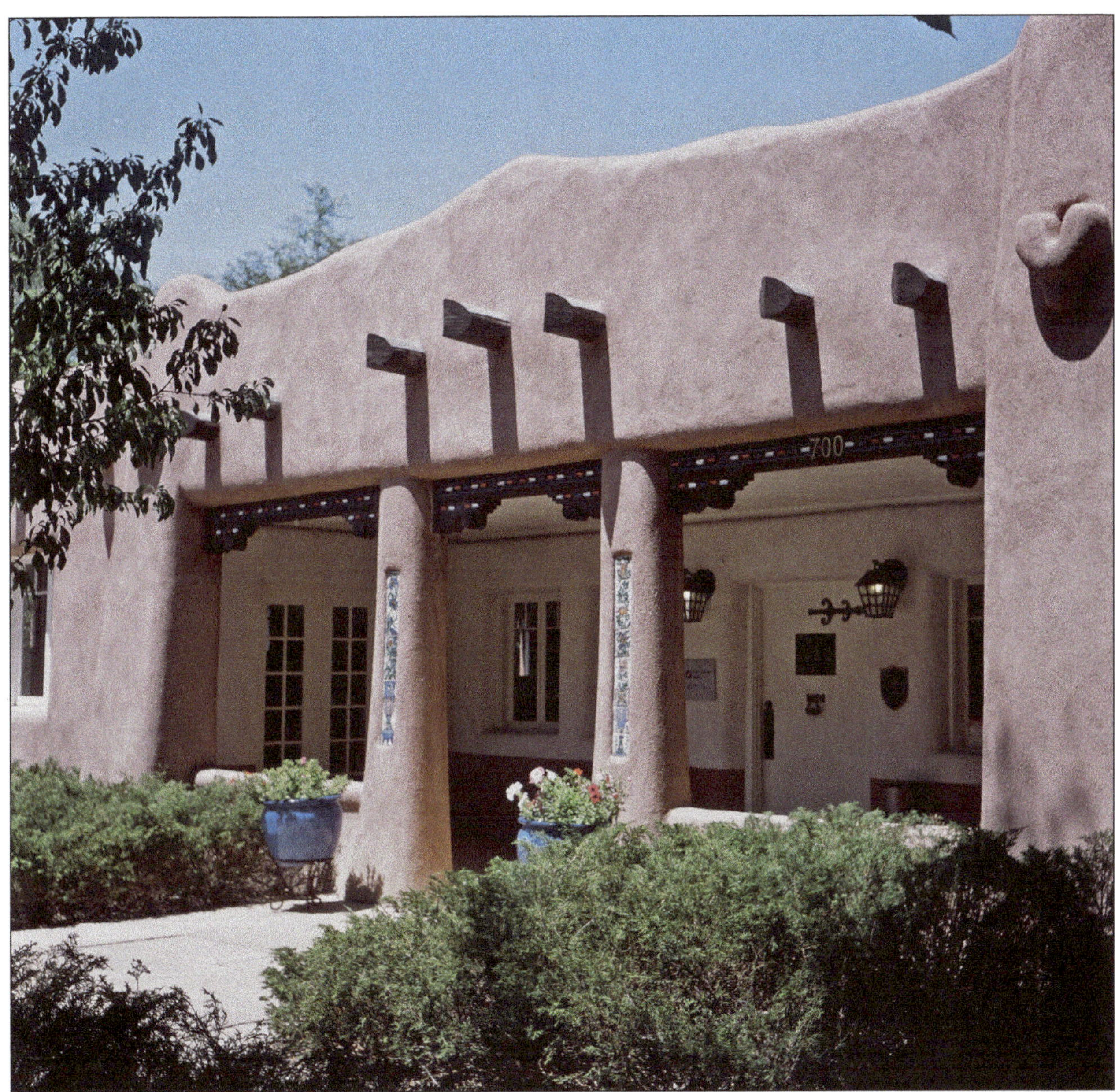


**Martin and Florence Spitz Gardesky House**, 700 Paseo de Peralta. This 1923 home for Martin Gardesky, the owner of the Capital Pharmacy, and his wife, the daughter of jeweler Solomon Spitz, boasts some unusual features. One is the porch columns — instead of the usual log posts, these are stuccoed and bear decorative tiles. There are also stuccoed, rather than wood, *canales*. The plane of the front elevation is interrupted by several decorative pilastered columns, or partial columns standing out in relief from the wall surface, and the curvilinear parapet brings to mind the California Mission Revival style, a reference that has usually been considered verboten in the historic district. In a 1998 report for the Historic Santa Fe Foundation, historian Corinne Sze wrote that the "strict symmetry" of the front "is the opposite of the irregularity of indigenous or Hispanic precedent. Such symmetry is an expression of the classical aesthetic that was expressed in Santa Fe by the Territorial style created by Anglo American immigrants after 1846." Sze also notes that the Spitz Gardesky House, which is accorded "Significant" status in the historic district, was built primarily with pentile.

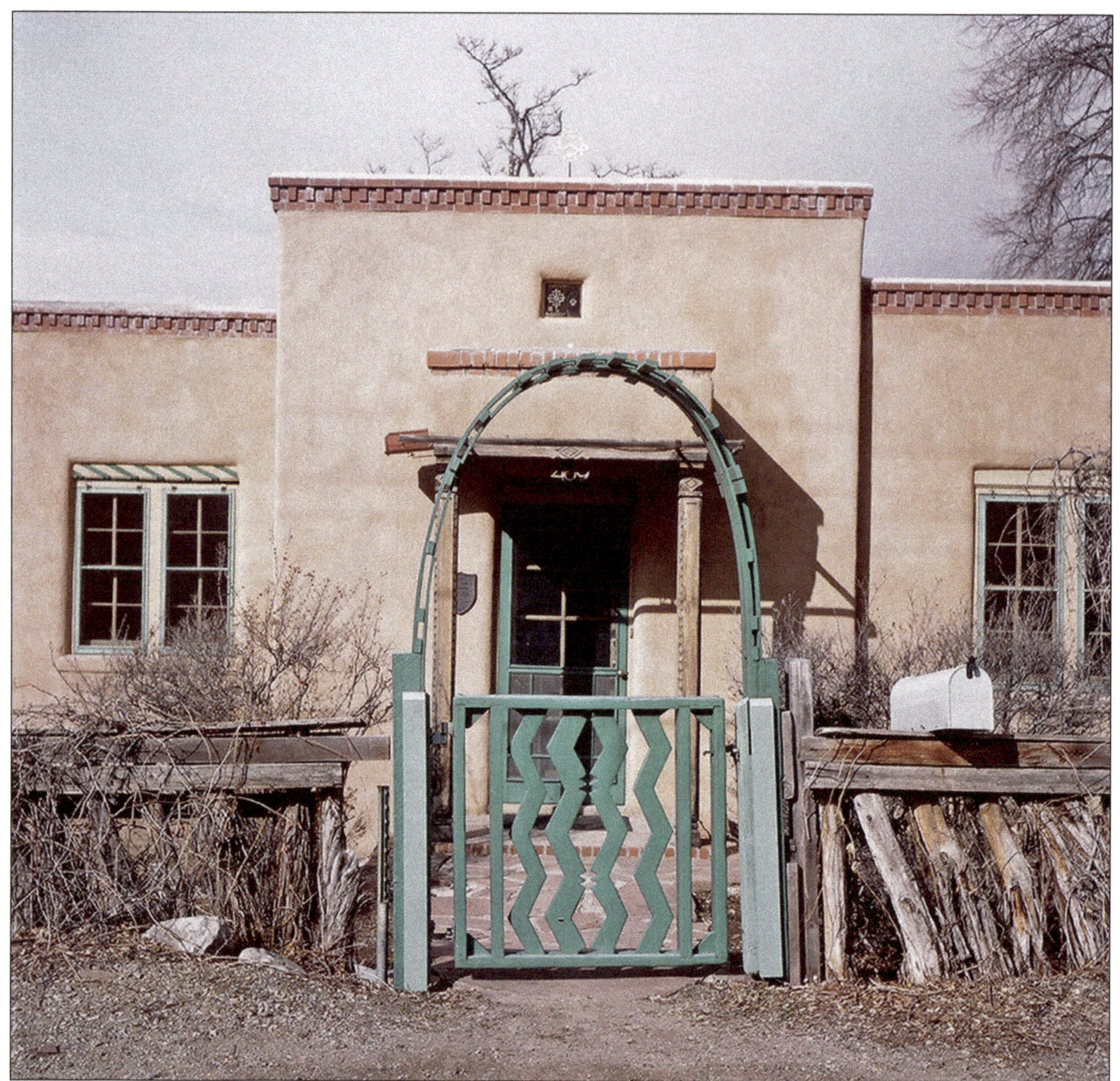

**Jane and Gustave Baumann House**, 409 Camino de las Animas. See that gate and the rope-carved lintel? In them you see evidence of the rampant creativity of this house's owner. Artist Gustave Baumann built it in 1923 and hired architect Tjalke Charles Gaastra to help carry out his design. There's a small front porch — definitely not Santa Fe Style — and a bright studio, a small kitchen, and an octagonal foyer with octagonal skylight to serve as a gallery to exhibit his prints for clients. In the center of the house is a fireproof room he used to store his woodblocks and prints. In the 2000s, the Historic Santa Fe Foundation purchased the house, did a sensitive renovation (preserving the artist's hand-painted and carved decorations on walls and woodwork), and sold it, with a historic preservation easement in place, to Nancy Meem Wirth.

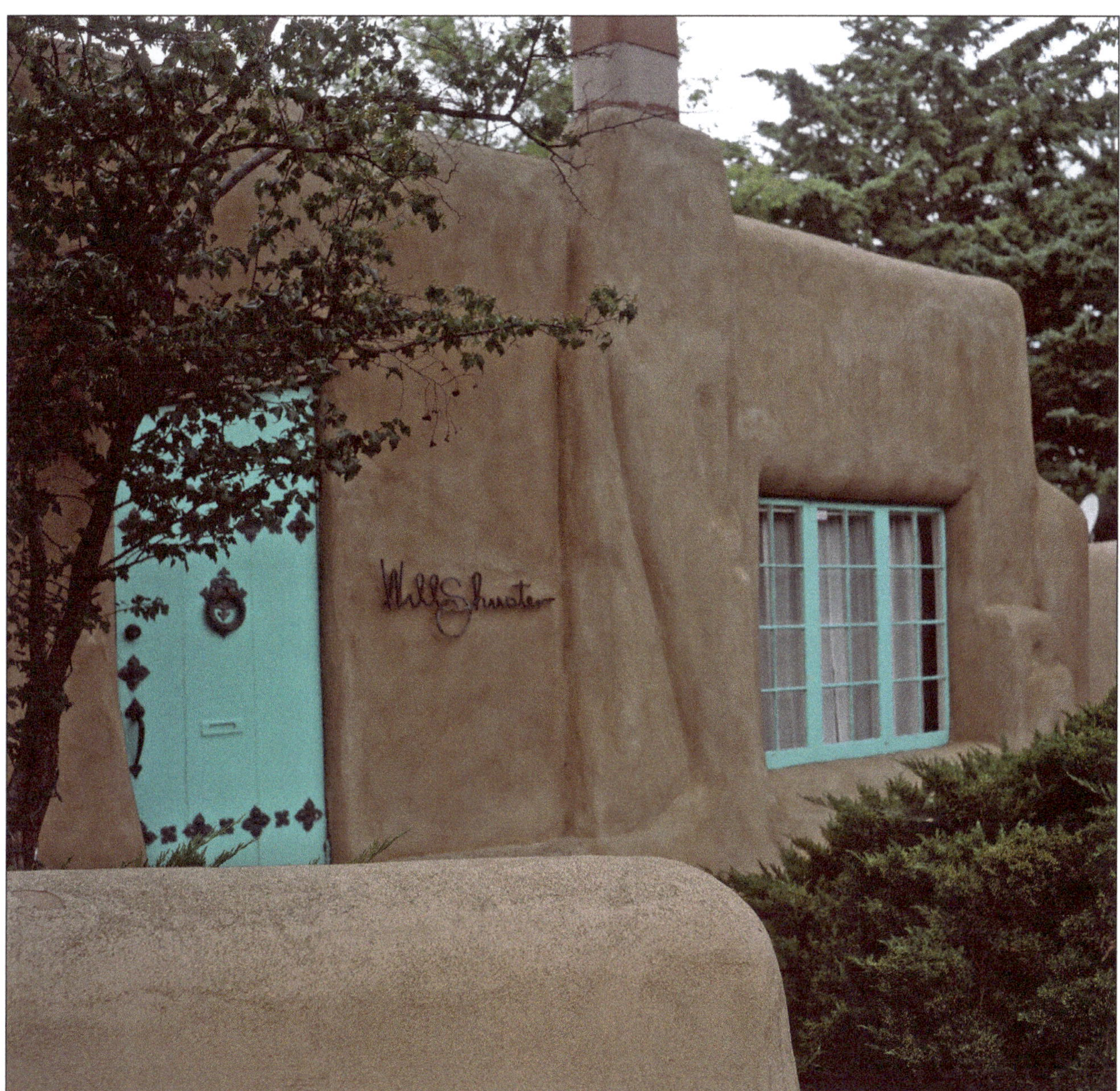


**Will Shuster House**, 550 Camino del Monte Sol. Shuster was a member of the famed Cinco Pintores group, five Santa Fe fine-art painters who were also enthusiastic about preserving the area's vernacular adobe architecture. Most of their homes along the Camino were built in the Spanish-Pueblo Revival style during the 1920s by ceramics artist Frank Applegate, who, unlike the Cinco Pintores, had construction experience. The Shuster house boasts pleasing buttresses, a singular painted-pine front door beneath a whimsically angled lintel (not visible in this photo), the wrought-iron "Will Shuster" next to the door, and a sculpted chimney that, according to *Frank Applegate of Santa Fe: Artist & Preservationist*, is reminiscent of the Cubism-inspired woodcarvings he was exhibiting in 1923 and 1924.

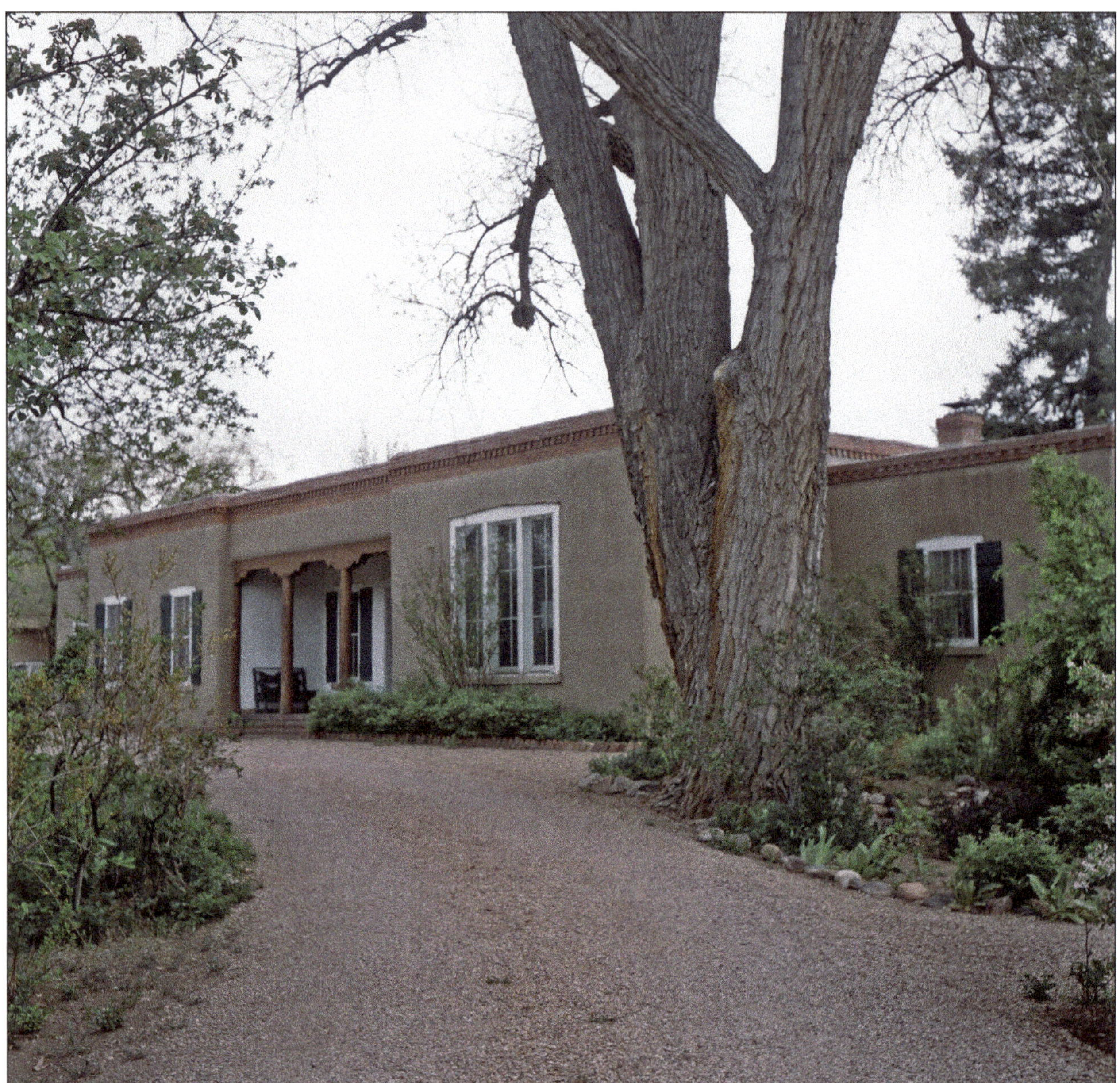

**Fényes Curtin Paloheimo House**, 614 Acequia Madre Street, was designed and built in 1926 by three remarkable women: Eva Scott Fényes (1849-1930) and her daughter and granddaughter, Leonora Scott Muse Curtin (1879-1972) and Leonora Frances Curtin Paloheimo (1903-1999). They are remembered for their achievements in the arts, science, business, and cultural preservation. The nonprofit Women's International Study Center was founded in 2013 in tribute to Eva and the Leonoras. The stately Territorial Revival-style house (with an alteration by architect Irving Parsons) is filled with antique furniture and artworks from the Southwest and Finland, as well as Depression-era tinwork, textiles, and furniture made for the Native Market cooperative that was subsidized by Leonora Paloheimo.

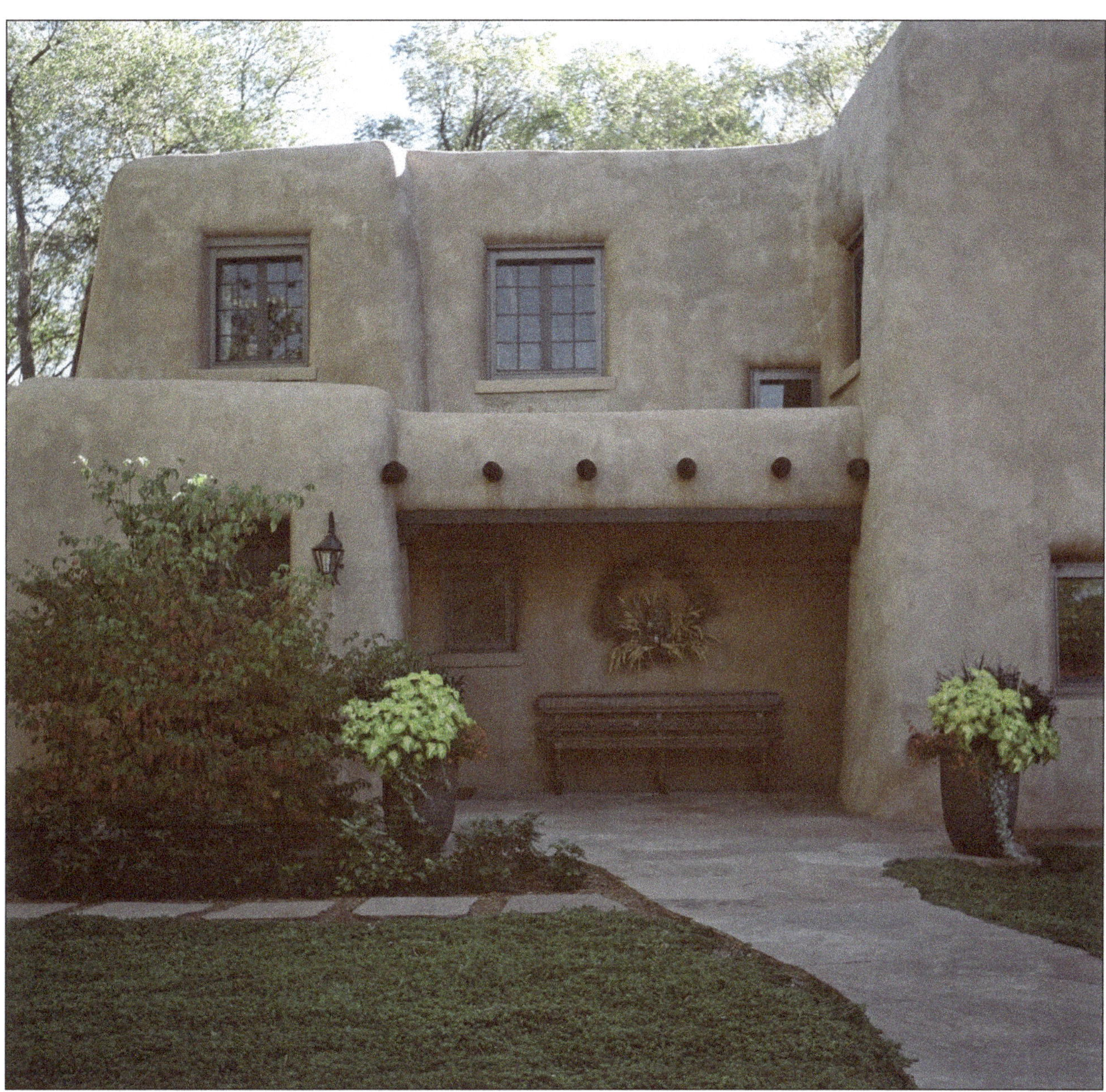

**Katherine Stinson-Otero House**, 438 Acequia Madre. Alabama-born Stinson was a pioneering woman pilot (billed as "The Flying Schoolgirl") whose daring aerobatics included looping and rolling at night with magnesium flares. The U.S. military refused her offers to fly in the hunt for Pancho Villa and to aid the country in World War I, because of her gender. She instead drove a Red Cross ambulance in Europe. After she contracted influenza and then tuberculosis, Stinson became a patient at Santa Fe's Sunmount Sanitarium — and there began a lifelong friendship with John Gaw Meem. In the mid-1920s, she embarked on a new career as a homebuilder. "Stinson Otero's approach to architectural design was highly unconventional," according to a University of New Mexico Center for Southwest Research biography. "She drew only informal design-level plans for the homes she created. Additionally, she walked around the construction site with her workmen, pointing out to them where she wanted the walls constructed as work progressed." In 1925, she bought land that became Plaza Chamisal; her houses in that compound include this one, which she built in 1927-1928 for herself and her husband, Miguel Otero Jr., the son of a former New Mexico governor. It won an award as the best example of a new residence costing between $8,000 and $10,000 in a 1930 city architectural competition. Stinson-Otero died in this house on July 8, 1977.

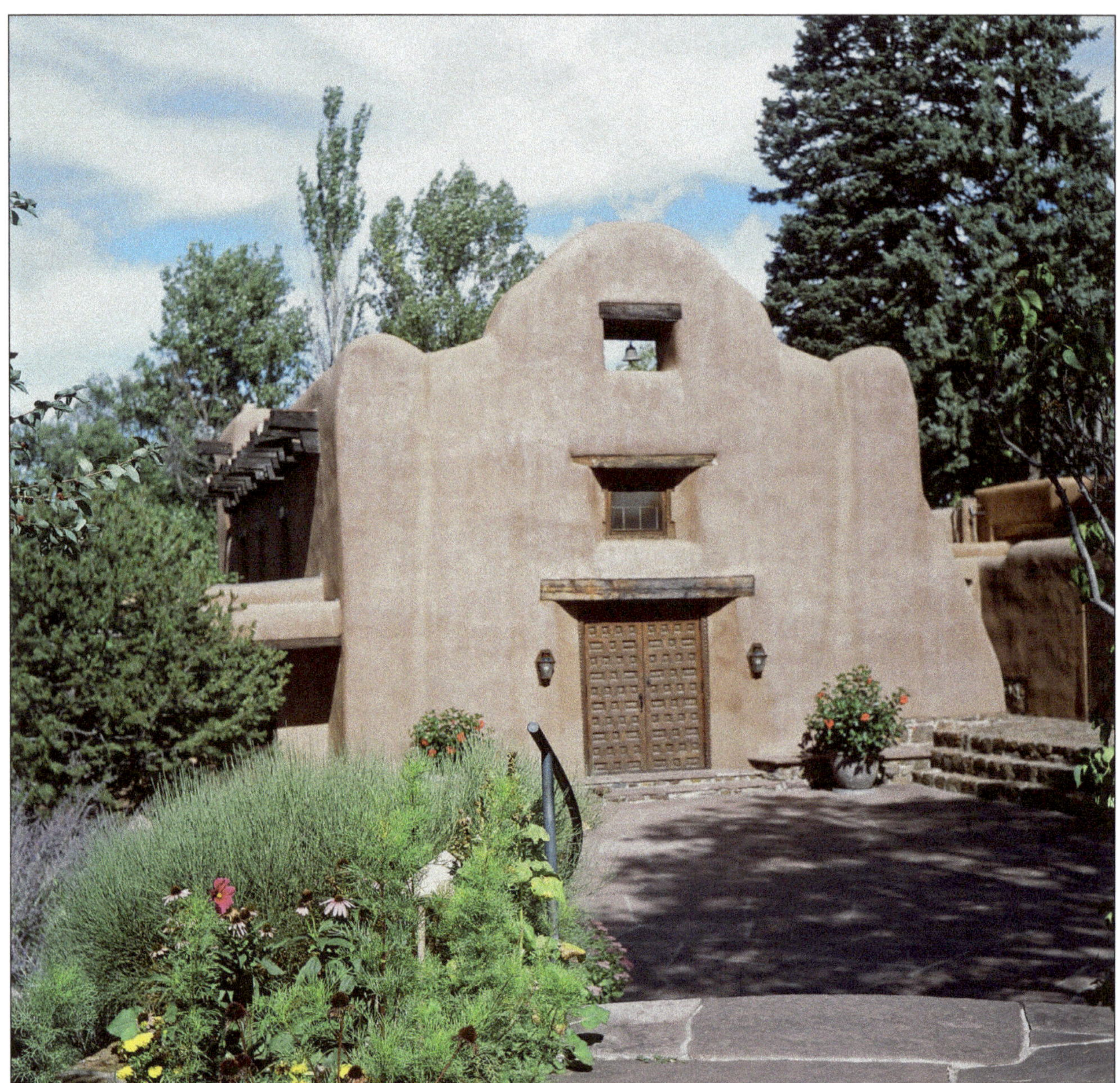

**School for Advanced Research**, 660 Garcia Street. This beauty, the SAR administration building, is the former home of Martha Root White and Amelia Elizabeth White, and they called it El Delirio. Like several other buildings on the campus, it was designed and built in the 1920s by artist William Penhallow Henderson. The White home boasts a churchlike facade, resembling the Laguna Pueblo mission church, with its curvilinear parapet flanked by hornlike projections. A long, enclosed *portal* leads to the SAR president's office (the former dining room). Its fireplace is set in an altar screen that Sylvanus Morley salvaged from an earthquake-damaged church in Guatemala; the Whites apparently didn't like the crucifixion scenes on the side panels and had Gustave Baumann replace them with lute-playing angels. At one end of the building's main room is a "choir loft" feature with a six-volume 1890 dictionary cleverly housed and anchored in an *alacena*. The campus' other lovely buildings include the Bandelier House, expanded from a 19th-century adobe; the 1920s Douglas W. Schwartz Seminar House; the 1978 Indian Arts Research Center; and SAR Press, which is the result of 1990s alterations to a former archaeology lab, which itself was remodeled in 1962 by John Gaw Meem from a kennels building that had been used by the Whites to breed Irish wolfhounds and Afghan hounds in the 1930s. Nearby is an old hound cemetery.

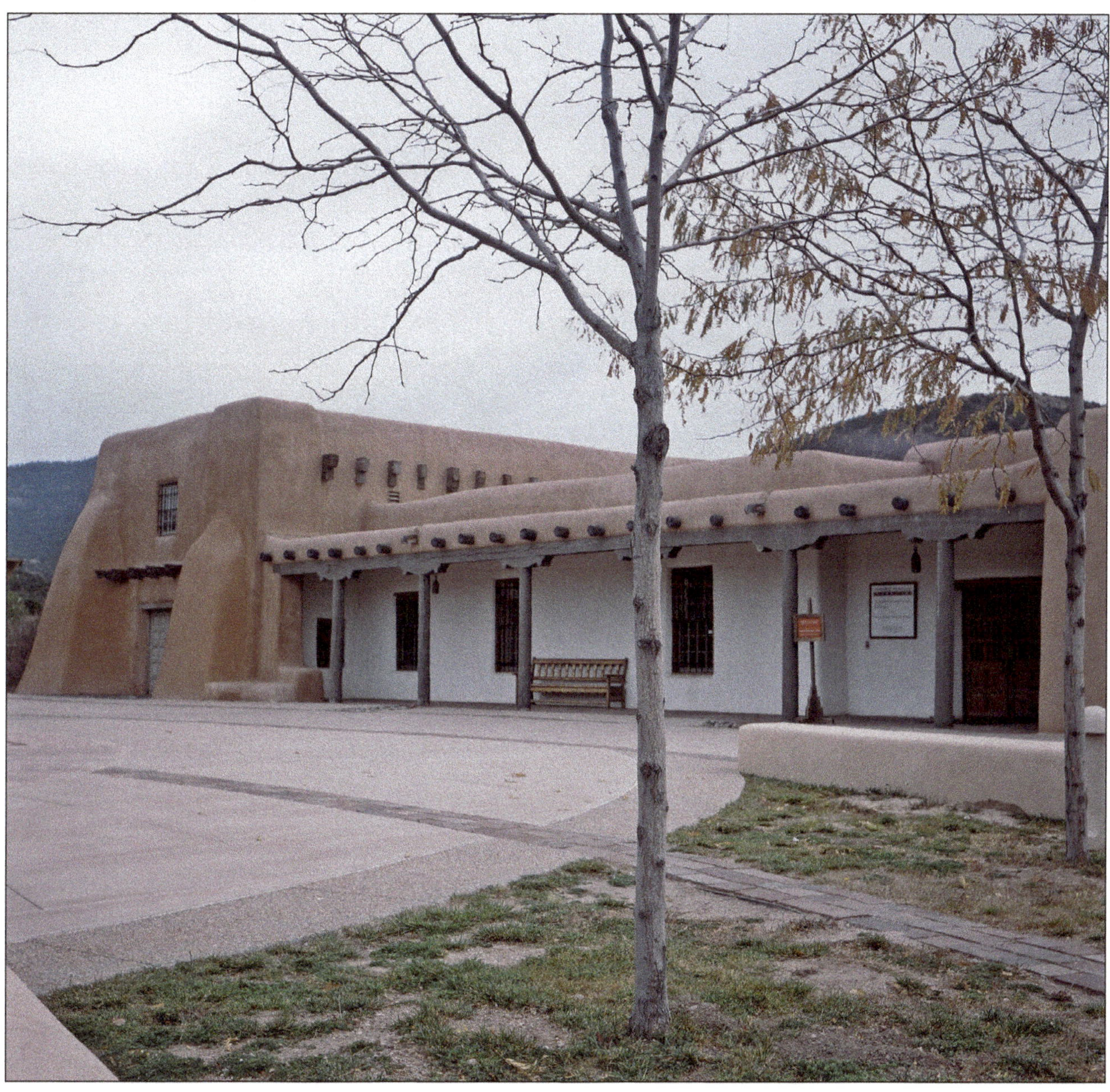

**Laboratory of Anthropology**, 710 Camino Lejo, is a wonderfully balanced (and obviously asymmetrical!) composition by John Gaw Meem. One interesting feature (but to the right of what was framed for this photo) is a set of double windows on a projecting bay of the right wing — "rare in Spanish-Pueblo architecture, but imagine the proportions of the central bay of this wing without it," Bainbridge Bunting wrote. The building's dominant feature is the two-story mass at far left, which has its own lovely irregularity in two bulky, hollow buttresses of different size and shape; plus the mass' top right corner includes a slight tower form — this is a subtle and masterful gesture by the artist Meem. The lab was founded by John D. Rockefeller in 1927 with a mission to study the indigenous cultures of the Southwest; its building opened on Sept. 1, 1931.

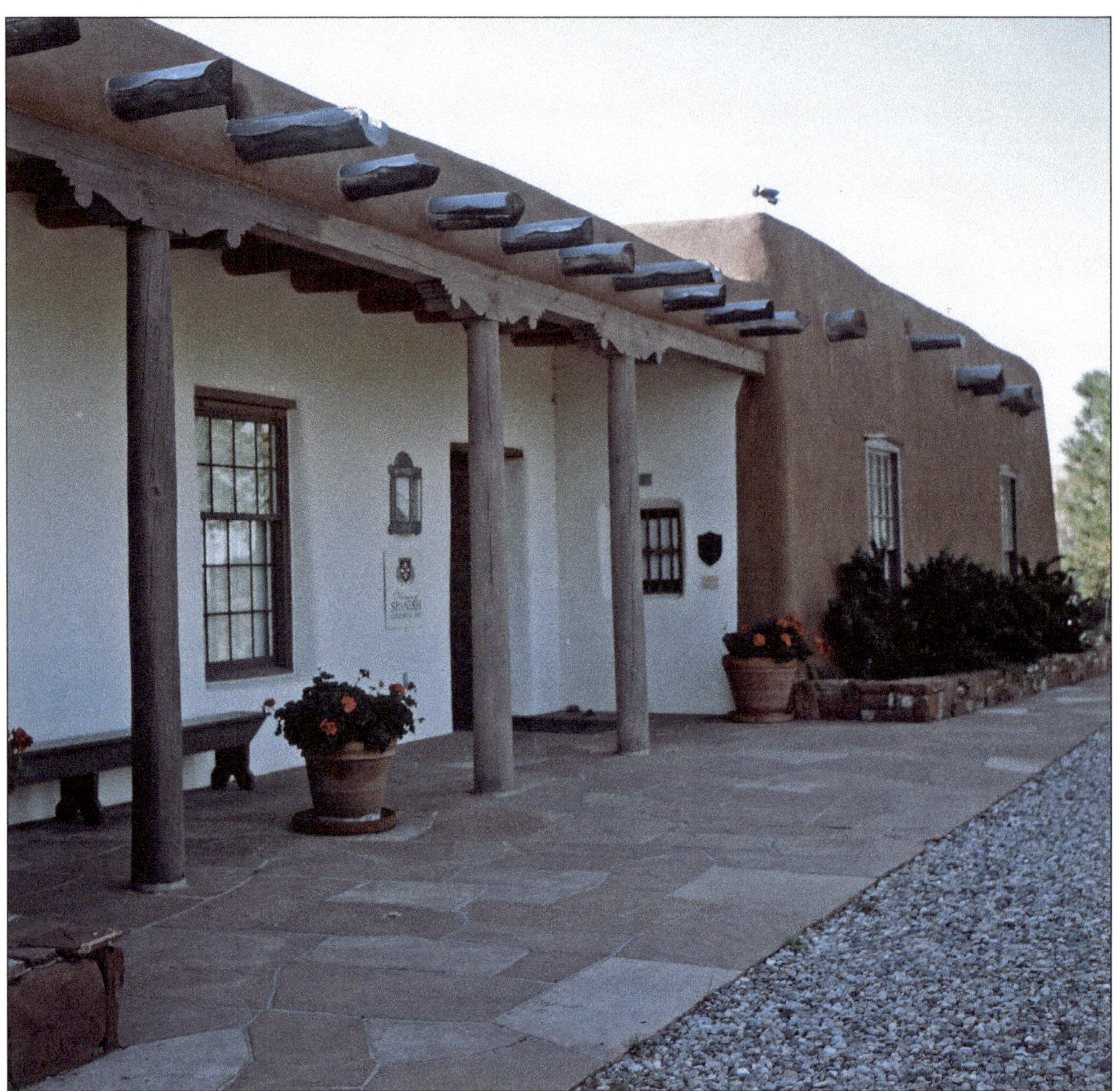

**Laboratory Director's Residence**, 750 Camino Lejo. Now known as the Museum of Spanish Colonial Art, this house was constructed to accommodate the director of the Laboratory of Anthropology — both are 1930 buildings by John Gaw Meem, and this is another of Meem's Spanish-Pueblo Revival compositions that are asymmetrical yet satisfyingly balanced. Features include a welcoming front *portal* with carved corbels and the style's characteristic protruding roof *vigas*. Inside are floors of tile, brick, or wide-plank wood; glowing, plastered walls with *nichos* for display and *alacenas* for storage; *trasteros*; deep window seats; and ceiling types including planks on *vigas*, planks on squared beams, and *latillas* on *vigas*. A 2001 remodel to transform the house into a museum housing the wonderful collection of the Spanish Colonial Arts Society was designed by architect Eric Enfield.

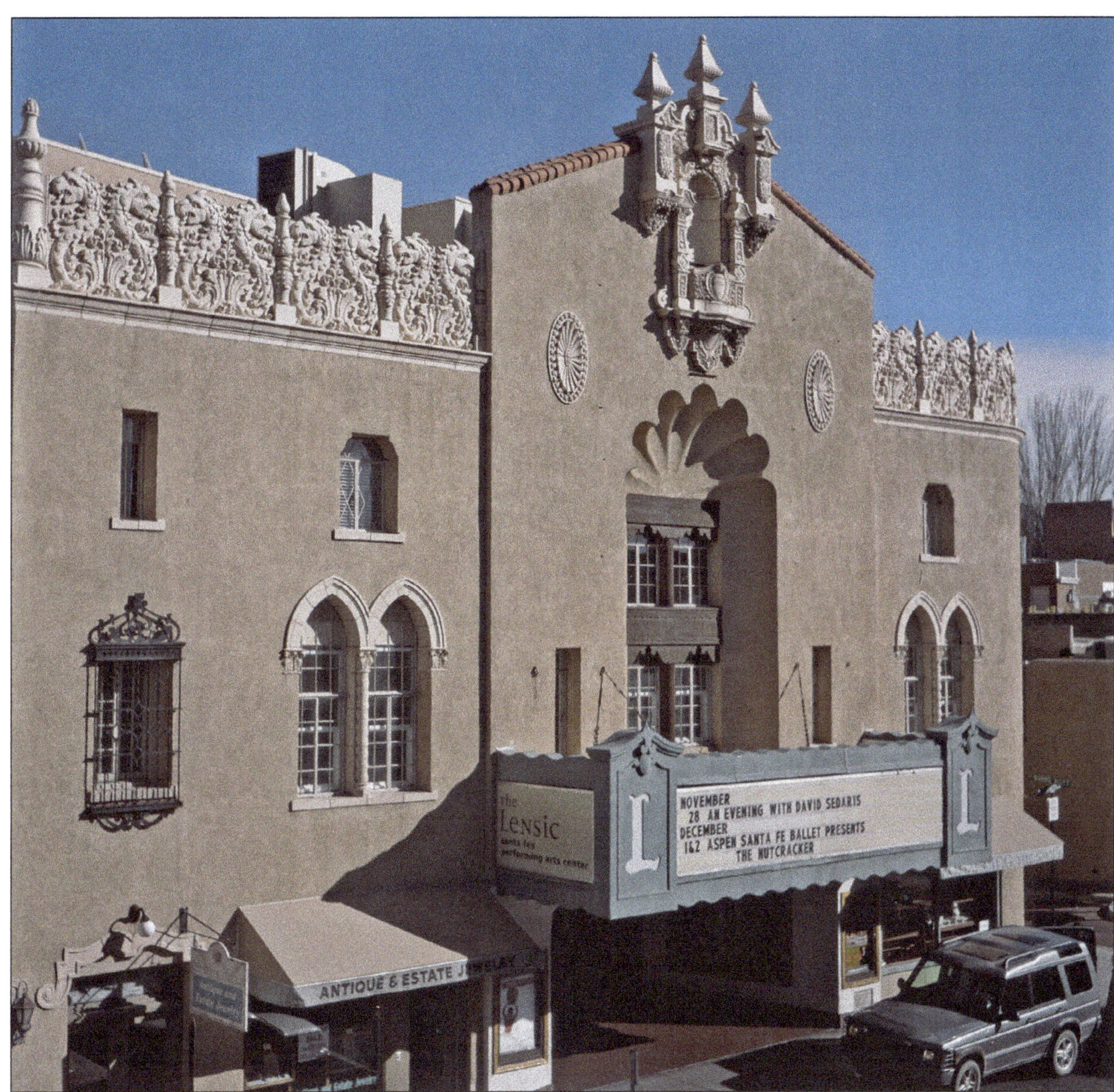


**Lensic Performing Arts Center**, 211 W. San Francisco Street, opened as a theater for vaudeville acts and movies on June 24, 1931, with a program featuring Chet Grass and his Frontier Knights Orchestra, Miss Mae Delle ("five foot two with eyes of blue") presenting a series of "snappy dances," and the film *Daddy Longlegs*. Hollywood stars who appeared at the Lensic in the coming years included Claudette Colbert (attending a premiere of *Cleopatra*), Judy Garland, Rudy Vallee, Rita Hayworth, and Roy Rogers. The Lensic was financed by merchant Nathan Salmon, an immigrant from Syria. His architect, Boller & Boller of Kansas City, topped the front facade of the pseudo-Moorish/Spanish Renaissance building (of brick-veneered pentile) with a triple-finialed superstructure flanked by rows of terracotta dragons. The original interior had chandeliers; murals; leather, upholstered rocking seats; carved-plaster wall ornamentations covered with metal leaf, shellac, and colored glazes; and a billowing, ceiling-anchored tapestry meant to give the feeling of an Arabian tent. After the theater's doors closed in 1999, Bill and Nancy Zeckendorf raised $9 million for a major restoration, with Craig Hoopes as project architect. The Zeckendorfs incorporated the new multipurpose performing-arts space as a nonprofit and, in April 2001, the magnificent building celebrated its second grand opening.

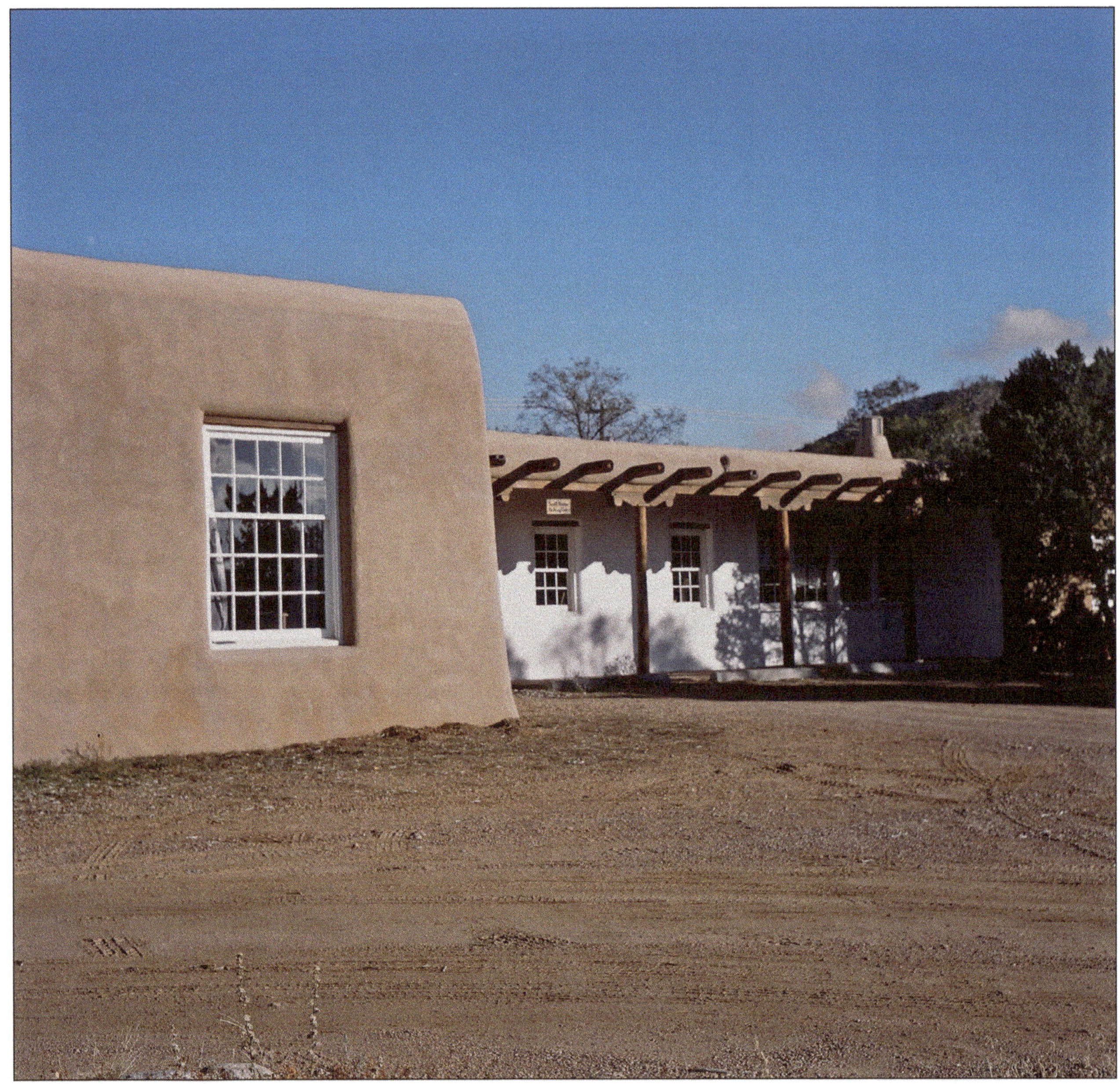

**John Gaw Meem Architects Office**, 785 Camino Del Monte Sol, was designed and built by John Gaw Meem as his architectural-design office and studio as well as living quarters for himself. Meem had been working in a tiny studio provided by Dr. Frank Mera at Sunmount Sanitarium. "In 1929 and 1930, Meem was plotting how he could have his own office and bachelor pad. He had no money then," said Alan "Mac" Watson, who supervised a restoration in 2013-2014. The original L-shaped 1931 building had walls of pentile (with no added insulation), strip-oak floors, carved-wood radiator covers, and fireplaces with beautiful iron damper handles. The long drafting room was brightened by a wall of tall windows with eight-lite hoppers at their tops. After his 1933 marriage to Faith Bemis, Meem added a living room (the projecting mass at left in this photo) and kitchen. Other additions were designed by Edward Holien (1951) and Victor Johnson (1991). The structure is now used as the Santa Fe Preparatory School art building.

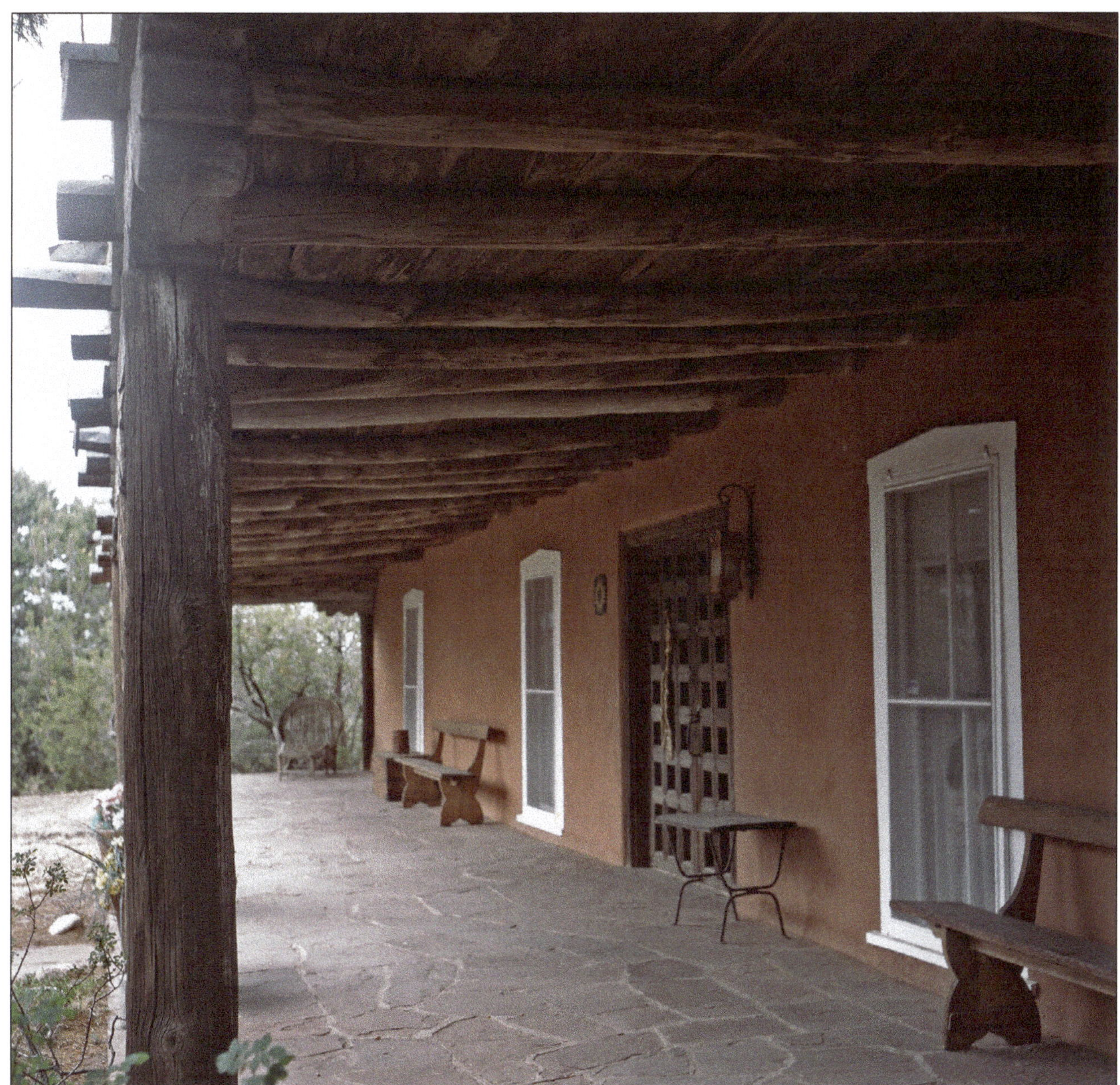

**Dorothy McKibbin House**, 1099 Old Santa Fe Trail, was designed and built by Katherine Stinson, who was a renowned stunt pilot in the second decade of the 20th century, before she moved to Santa Fe and took up homebuilding. She had no professional training in architecture, but was a hands-on, and award-winning, practitioner of the craft. Her client for this residence was Dorothy McKibbin, who was employed during World War II by the U.S. government as the "gatekeeper" for scientists headed to Los Alamos for the secret Manhattan Project; her office was 109 E. Palace Avenue in Trujillo Plaza. This house was built in the mid-1930s, according to a 1971 *Santa Fe New Mexican* story. "Long narrow rooms, thick adobe walls plus a 68-foot *portal* authentically furnished with Southwestern pieces and artifacts show what can be accomplished today," it said. Stinson-Otero used some materials, such as windows and *vigas*, that McKibben found in old houses that were being demolished. Another *New Mexican* article related that Project scientists would meet and relax in the McKibbin residence, and that 13 marriages were conducted here because there were no suitable buildings for weddings in Los Alamos during the war years.

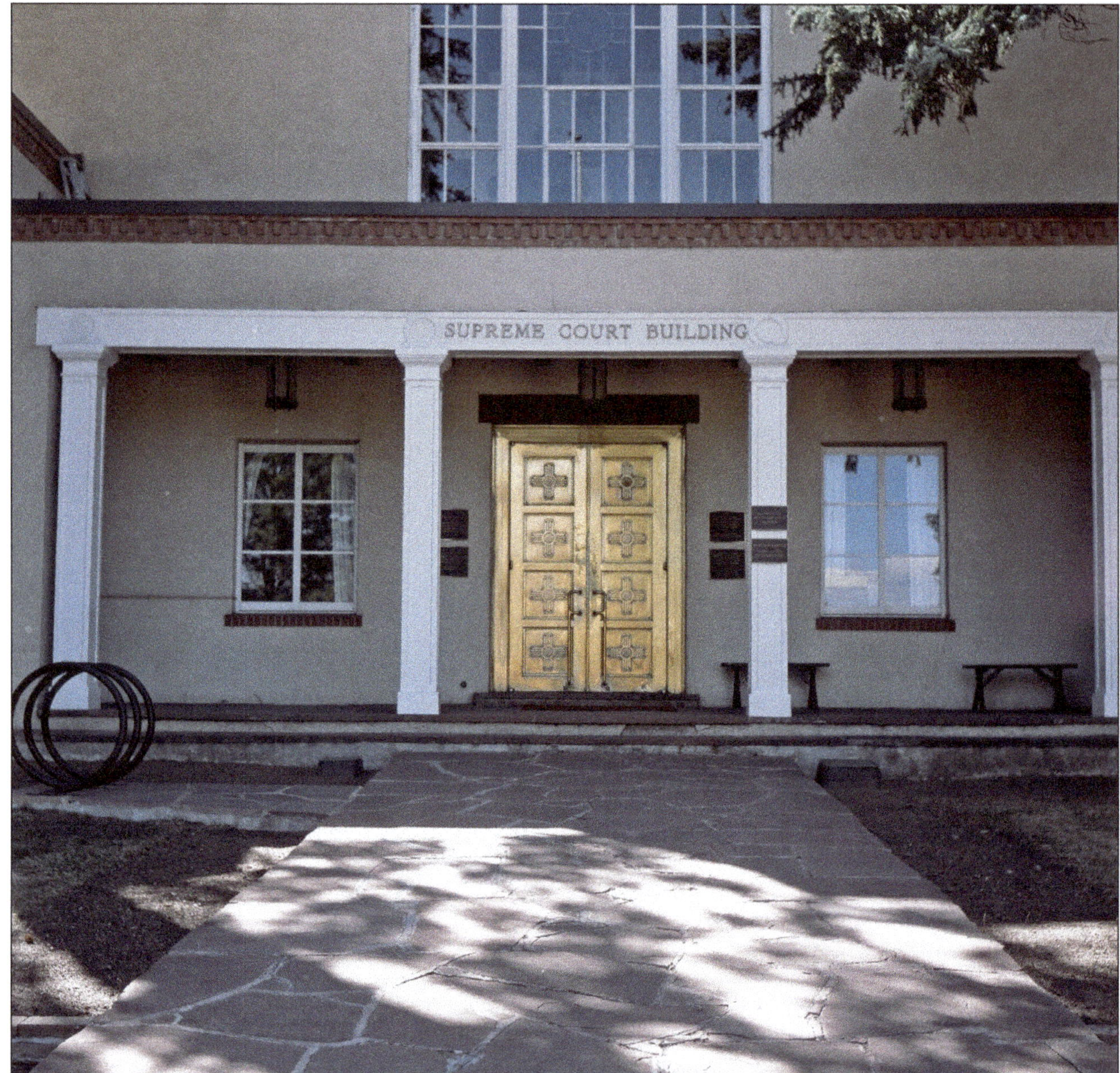


**New Mexico Supreme Court**, 237 Don Gaspar Avenue. This building, designed by Gordon Street and completed in 1937, is "perhaps the most important pre-World War II building" in the Territorial Revival style, according to John P. Conron and R. Patrick Christopher's "The Architecture of Santa Fe: A Survey of Styles" in the September-October 1978 issue of *New Mexico Architecture*. It was built for $307,000 by the New Deal-era Works Progress Administration. Artisans with the WPA were commissioned to create the unique chandeliers and windows in the courtroom, which also boasts the original cork floors and hand-carved woodwork. Multiple iterations of the Zia sun symbol appear, including on the courtroom's brass doorplates and windows and as decorative elements in the beautiful railings in the three-story law library. The city grades the Supreme Court building "Significant" in the historic district. In 1965, W.C. Kruger & Associates designed a large reinforced-concrete addition; the fact that this did not alter the grand front appearance — an embrace of twin, angled wings leading to a recessed portal with bright brass, Zia-emblazoned entrance doors — no doubt averted a downgrade in historic status, which usually happens with substantial remodels. Major renovations in the 1990s included new carpeting by Santa Fe interior designer Gene d'laurel Pattison.

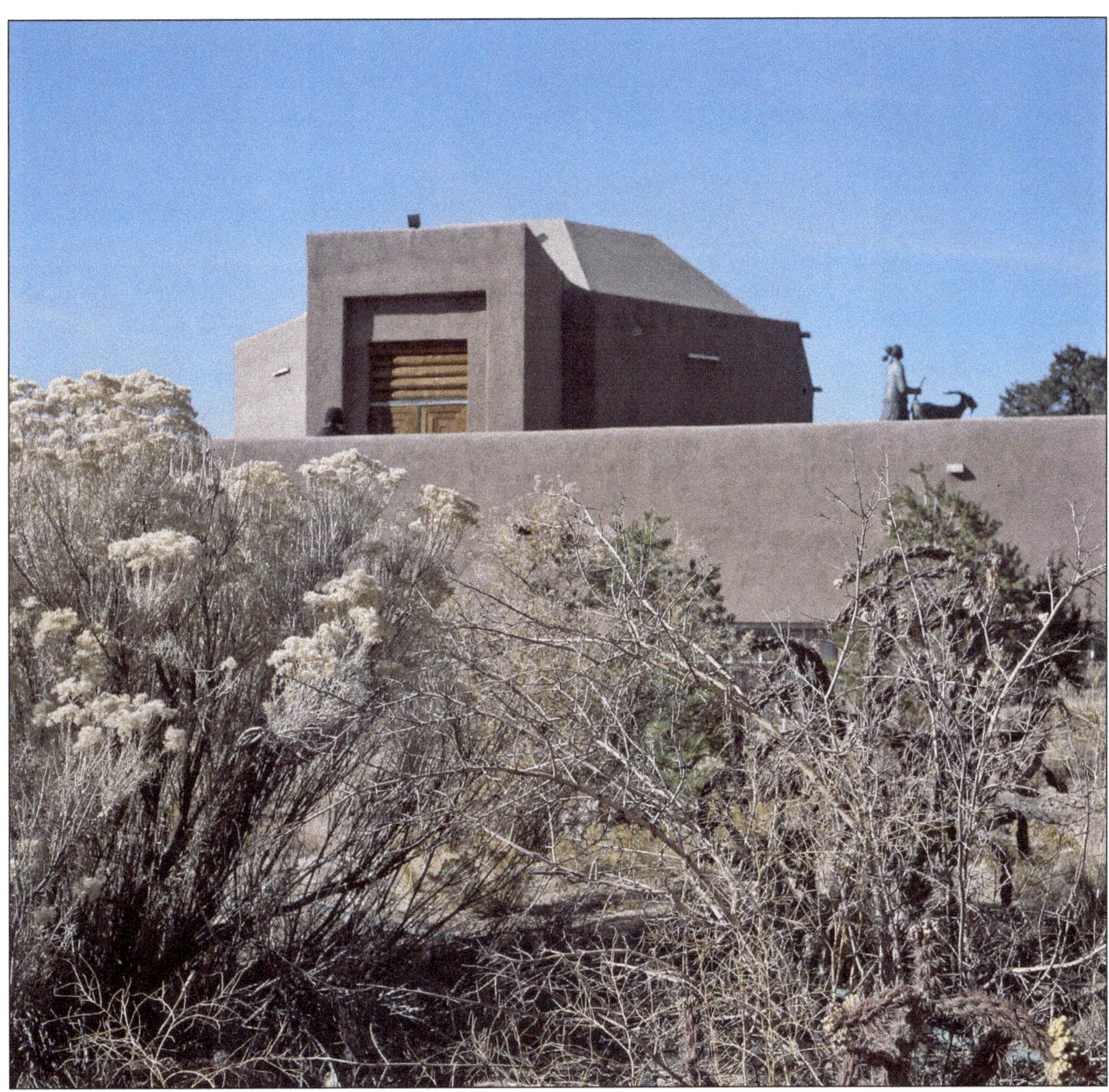

**Wheelwright Museum of the American Indian**, 704 Camino Lejo, began life in 1937 as the Museum of Navajo Ceremonial Art, founded by Bostonian Mary Cabot Wheelwright in collaboration with Hastiin Klah, a Diné (Navajo) singer or "medicine man." Its design is based on the hogan, the traditional Diné dwelling and ceremonial space. The museum "appears from the public approach as an elongated octagon with a truncated pyramidal roof with flat-roofed rectangular extensions projecting from the east and west sides," according to the successful National Register of Historic Places nomination. The building was designed by architect, painter, and furniture maker William Penhallow Henderson and was constructed using concrete, penitentiary tile, and Denison tile blocks, with a roof of native pine logs. The museum name was changed in 1977 after the institution repatriated medicine bundles and other cultural items to the Diné people. There have been several additions, including the 2000 library/curatorial center and the 2014 jewelry gallery, both designed by Jeffrey Seres of Studio Southwest Architects. Visible on the museum's entrance plaza in this photograph is Allan C. Houser's 1980 bronze *Heading Home*.

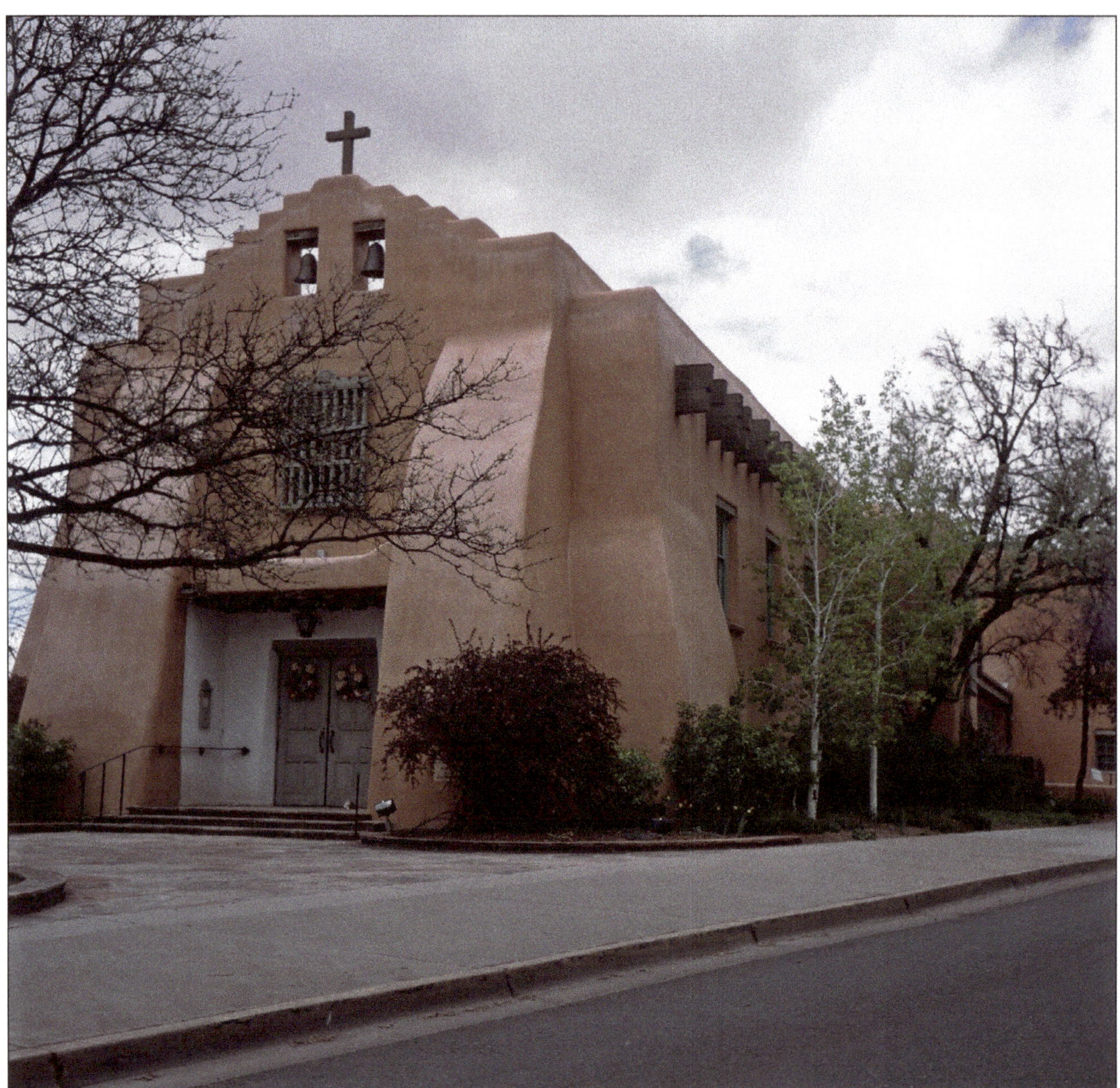

**First Presbyterian Church**, 208 Grant Avenue. The 1883 *Berger's Tourists' Guide to New Mexico* told visitors that the Presbyterian Church "is a tasteful brick edifice standing on a conspicuous triangle immediately west of the Military Quarter." The church had recently replaced the city's first Protestant sanctuary, a former adobe Baptist church. And in 1939, John Gaw Meem designed a new Presbyterian church, combining bricks from the older building with tile — presumably pentile — for the walls. The church boasts a stepped-*espadaña* (bell-cote) façade flanked by massive buttress forms, and long rows of beam-ends project at the tops of the exterior walls on both sides. Bunting wrote that the "excessive inclination and irregularity of the buttresses... are so exaggerated as to destabilize the visual equilibrium of the facade." But the now-venerable church is an undeniably distinctive presence on its triangular lot. In the early 2000s, architects Wayne Lloyd and Gayla Bechtol were hired to demolish related buildings (including a chapel designed by Philippe Register) and to improve acoustics, lighting, and HVAC systems in the main church.

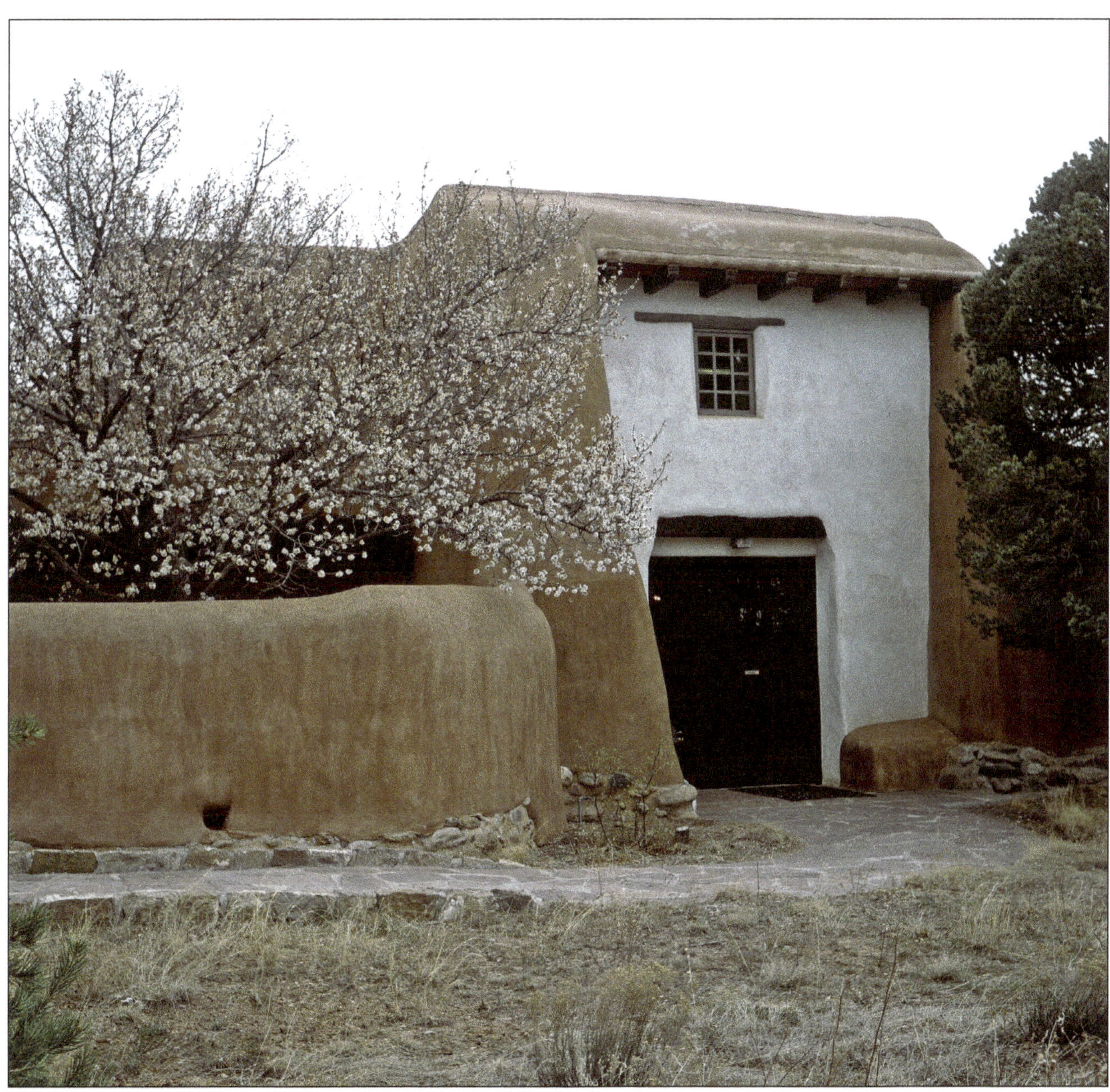

**National Park Service building**, 1100 Old Santa Fe Trail. The Park Service's 1939 Southwest Regional Office is the largest adobe office building in the country. The Spanish-Pueblo Revival building was designed by NPS architect Cecil Doty (who learned his craft from NPS architect Herbert Maier). It was the Great Depression, and local young men, supervised by Santa Fe Company 833 of the Civilian Conservation Corps, hand-made the approximately 280,000 adobe bricks for the walls that are up to 57 inches thick, and also crafted the building's tables and chairs. Everything exemplifies the rustic "parkitecture" design ethic delineated in *Park Structures and Facilities*, a Depression-era manual that encourages the use of local materials and local architectural traditions. Doty worked with Santa Fe artist Carlos Vierra, who served as construction foreman, and with landscape architect Harvey Cornell, designer of the spacious courtyard patio. At nearly 7,000 square feet, this *placita* is surrounded by deep portales — zapatas on ranks of tapered posts bracing adzed beams that support a continuous plank-on-viga ceiling. The WPA Federal Art Project complemented the rooms with pottery by Maria and Julian Martinez of San Ildefonso Pueblo, Lela Gutierrez and Eulogia Naranjo of Santa Clara Pueblo, and Agapita Quintana of Cochiti Pueblo; dozens of Navajo rugs; paintings by E. Boyd and Victor Higgins; etchings by Gene Kloss; and lithographs by B.J.O. Nordfeldt.

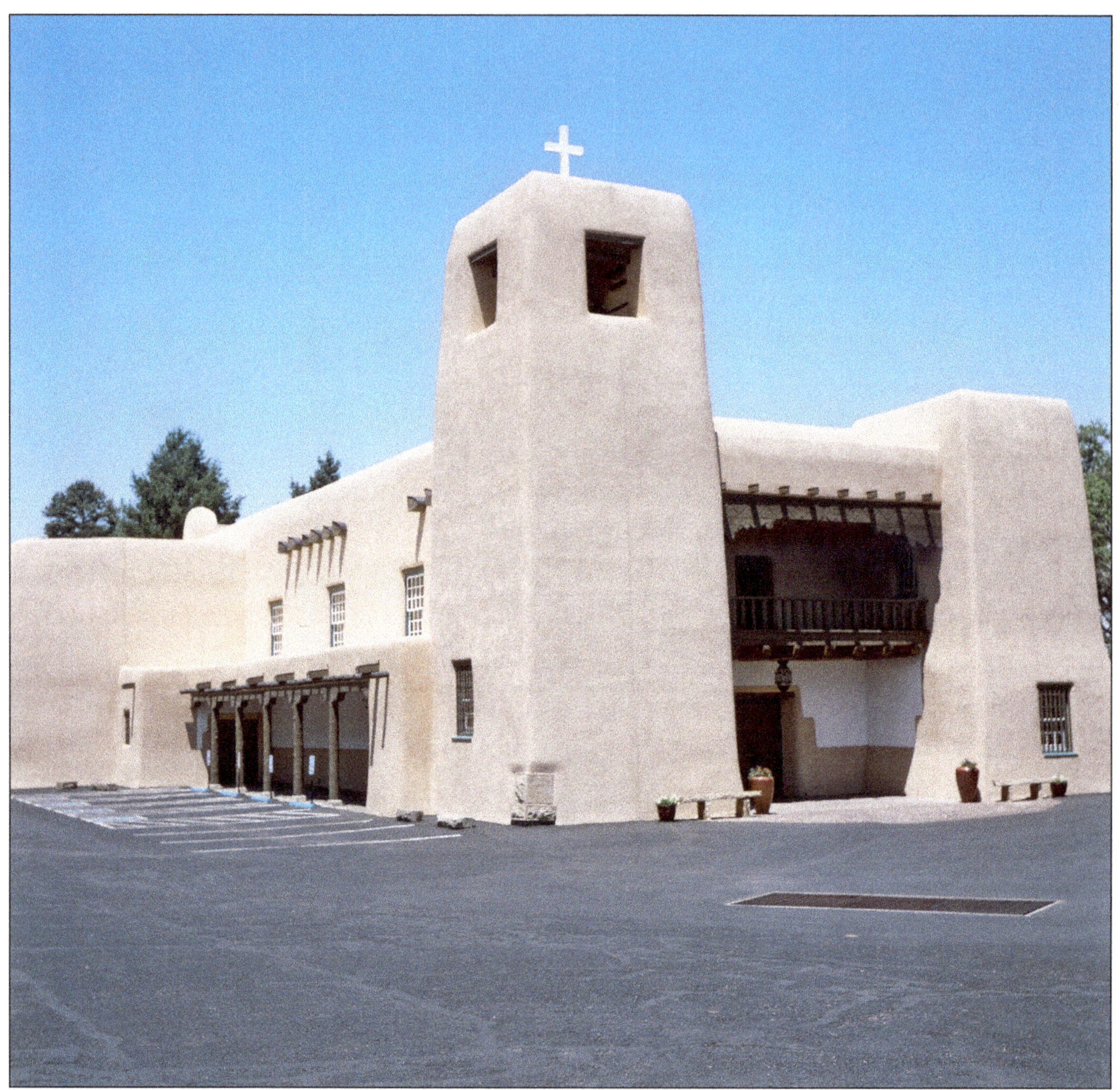

**Cristo Rey Church**, 1120 Canyon Road, is another wonderfully asymmetrical masterwork by John Gaw Meem, completed in 1940. His workmen used local earth to make 180,000 adobe bricks for the walls, which are bolstered by a few bands of steel-reinforced concrete. The roof of the 350-foot church has 222 ponderosa-pine vigas anchored by invisible steel girders. Cristo Rey "has the grand scale and at least one tower of Acoma, the balconied facade of Trampas, the transepts of the old *parroquia* of Santa Fe, and the effective transverse clerestory of Santa Ana," Bainbridge Bunting wrote. "It also has the long portal extending along one side of the nave, which John had used so frequently since he first sketched this feature at the outset of his career."

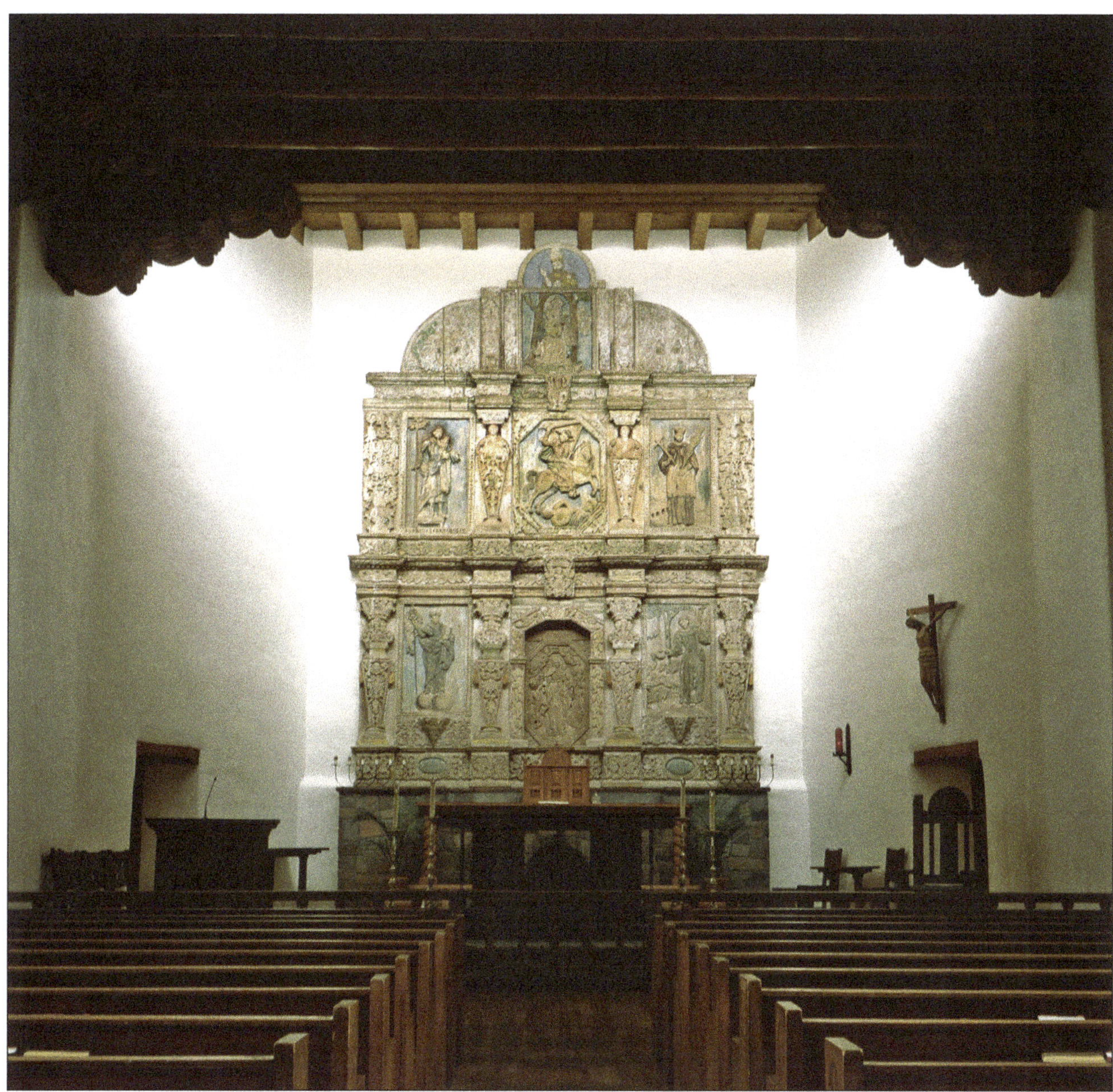

**Cristo Rey Church interior**. The stunning carved-stone *reredos* originally graced La Castrense, the soldiers' chapel that was built on the south side of the Santa Fe Plaza. It was in place from 1761 until Archbishop Lamy sold the chapel a century later to help pay for his cathedral project. In this building we witness the "magical" light thrown onto the altar via the *claraboya*; here it illuminates a splendor of carved figures on the decidedly Jesuit-themed *retablo*. They include Our Lady of Light (within the recess in the center of the first tier), St. James the Greater, St. Joseph, St. Ignatius, St. Francis Solano, St. John Nepomuk, Our Lady of Valvanera, and Our Lady of Light, all surmounted by God the Father.

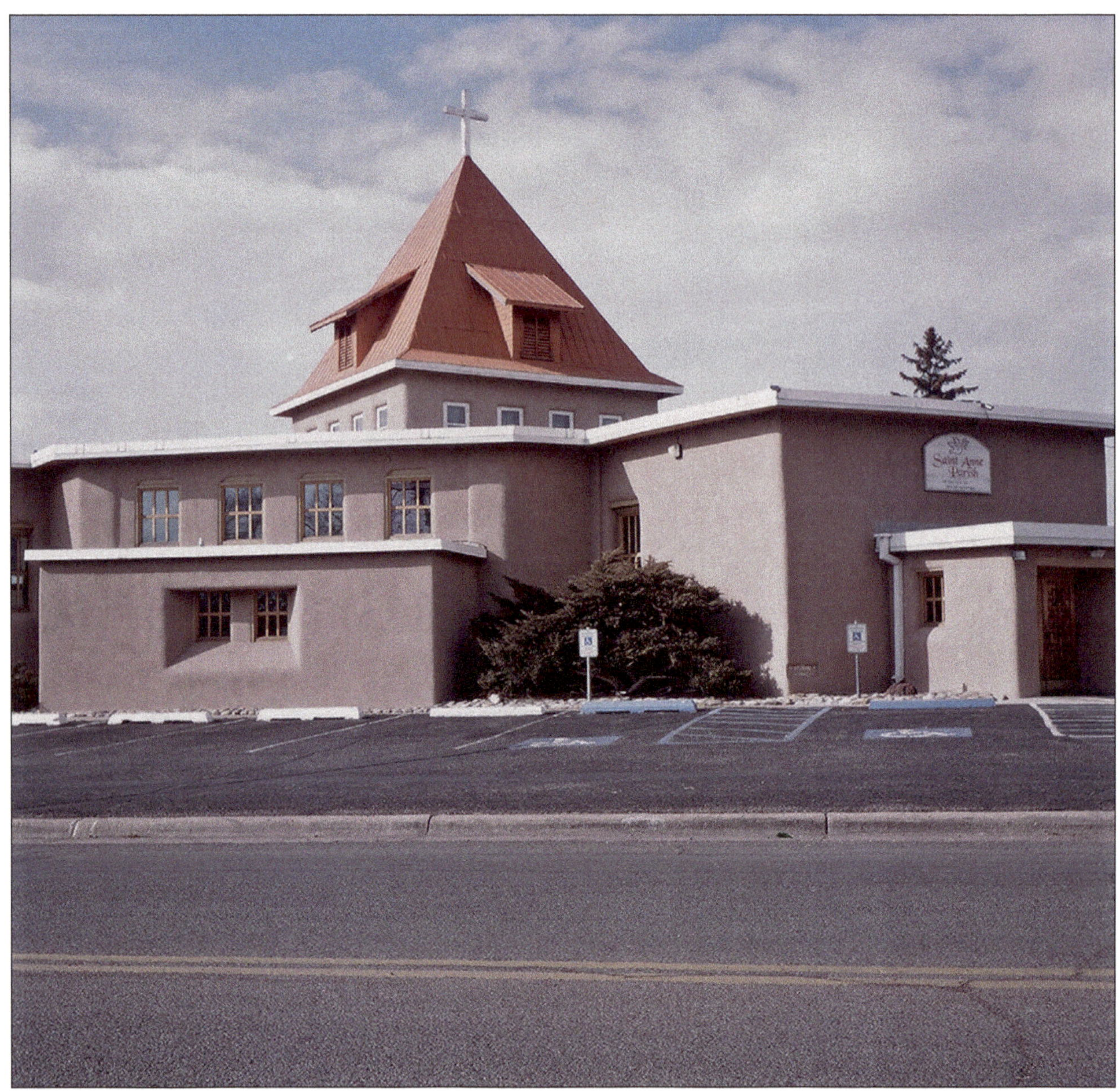

**St. Anne Catholic Church**, 511 Alicia Street, is a cruciform adobe building with a central short tower element with red peaked pyramid-hip roof and four dormers. The church, built in 1942, was an accomplishment of Rudolph Aloysius Gerken, archbishop of Santa Fe (1933-1943), under whose auspices were also established Cristo Rey Church, St. Mary's Convent, the St. Charles Borromeo Church in Albuquerque, and John Gaw Meem's Santo Tomás Church in Abiquiú. The architect of St. Anne's is unknown. According to a 1960 story in *The Santa Fe New Mexican*, steel was in short supply during World War II, so Gerken and contractor Fred Grill built it "in the form of a cross, with narrow corridors, using adobe and 'vigas' for supporting beams... To prevent a long corridor effect, the altar was built in the center of the cross." Meem was quoted as saying the church plan was "novel and quite an innovation at that time." Local residents donated labor, so the church cost was only $25,000. A July 22, 1943, announcement in the newspaper said St. Anne's parish "will give a baile at St. Michael's gymnasium Wednesday night to pay the cost of plastering the outside walls of the church. The work is being done by men of the parish working in the evening." Women from Tesuque Pueblo did the interior plastering.

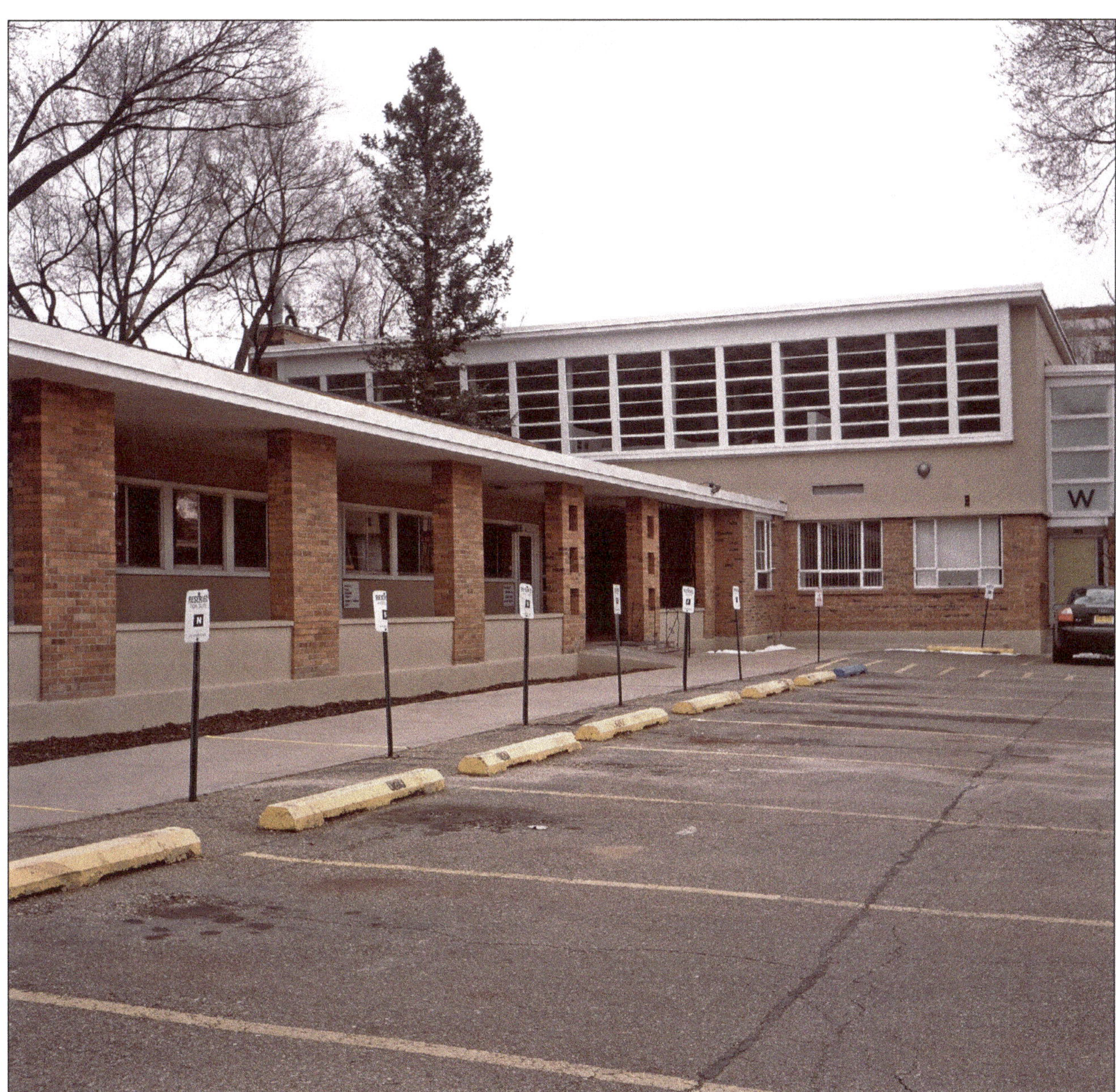


**Kruger Professional Building**, 227 E. Palace Avenue, is arguably splendid in its Mid-century Modern (anti-Santa Fe Style) posture. The vast, canted bank of north-facing windows on the second story admitted perfect light for the architectural studio of W.C. Kruger and Associates. Kruger designed the building, which opened in October 1950. Located across from the soon-to-open St. Vincent Hospital, it had a doctors' office and pharmacy on the first floor. Kruger's drafting office, paneled with milled Philippine mahogany, is today home to Trey Jordan Architecture and Radius Books.

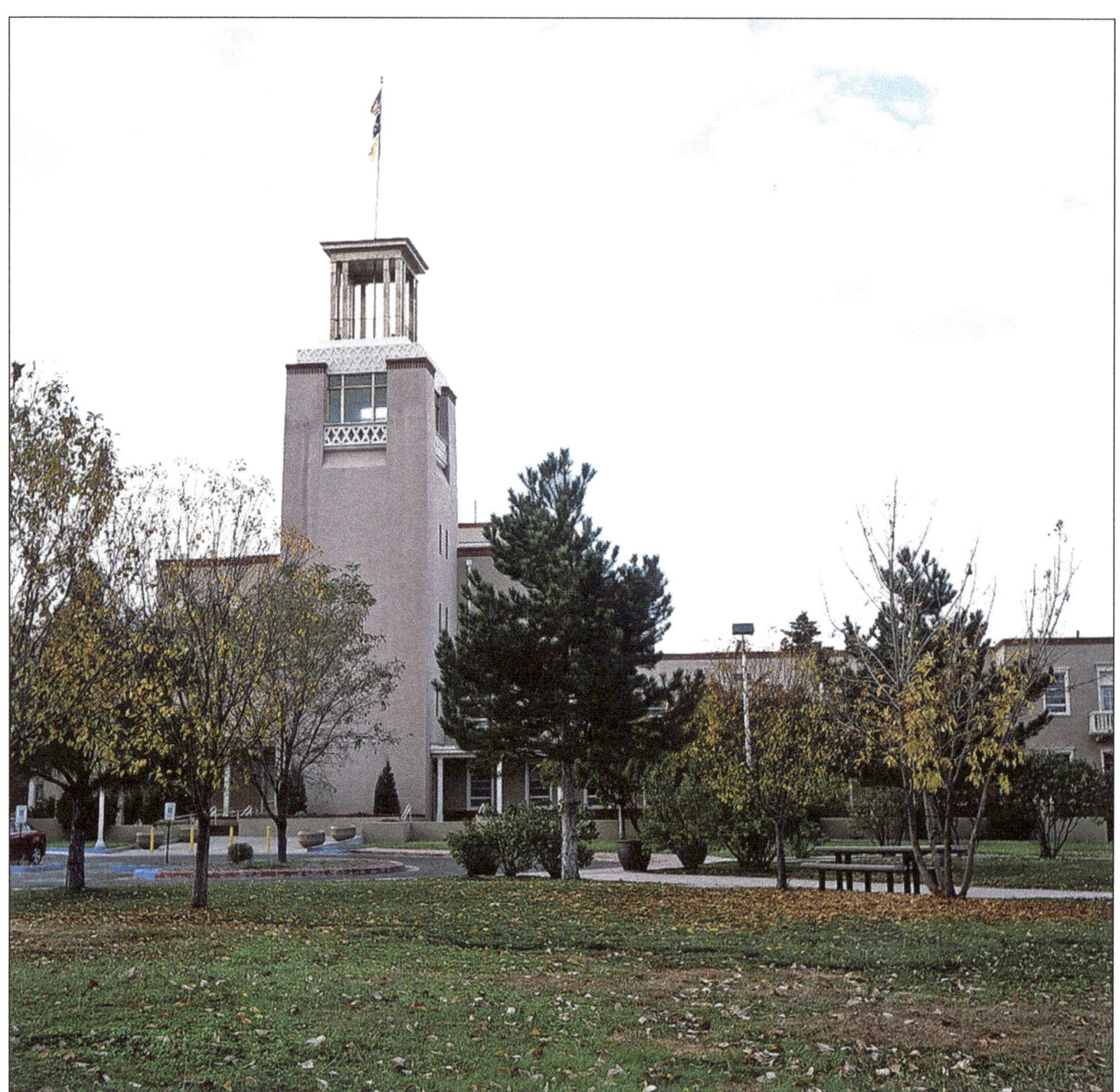

**Bataan Memorial Building**, 407 Galisteo, was originally the territory's new capitol building, completed in 1900. Designed by Isaac Rapp, it had a silvery dome and a grand pedimented portico. These features were removed, and a 105-foot tower added, during an early-1950s remodel to bring the structure in line with the Territorial Revival style. The responsible architect, W.C. Kruger, was also chosen to design its replacement, the Roundhouse. Former governor Bruce King, in his *Cowboy in the Roundhouse: A Political Life*, wrote that the old capitol was definitely showing its age: "One time we had about 75 children visit. Since we didn't have a gallery where citizens could observe the session, these school kids had to sit up front on the floor, and it starting cracking like it was about to crash down on the Senate below us." The building has housed various state offices ever since the capitol functions moved to the Roundhouse in 1966.

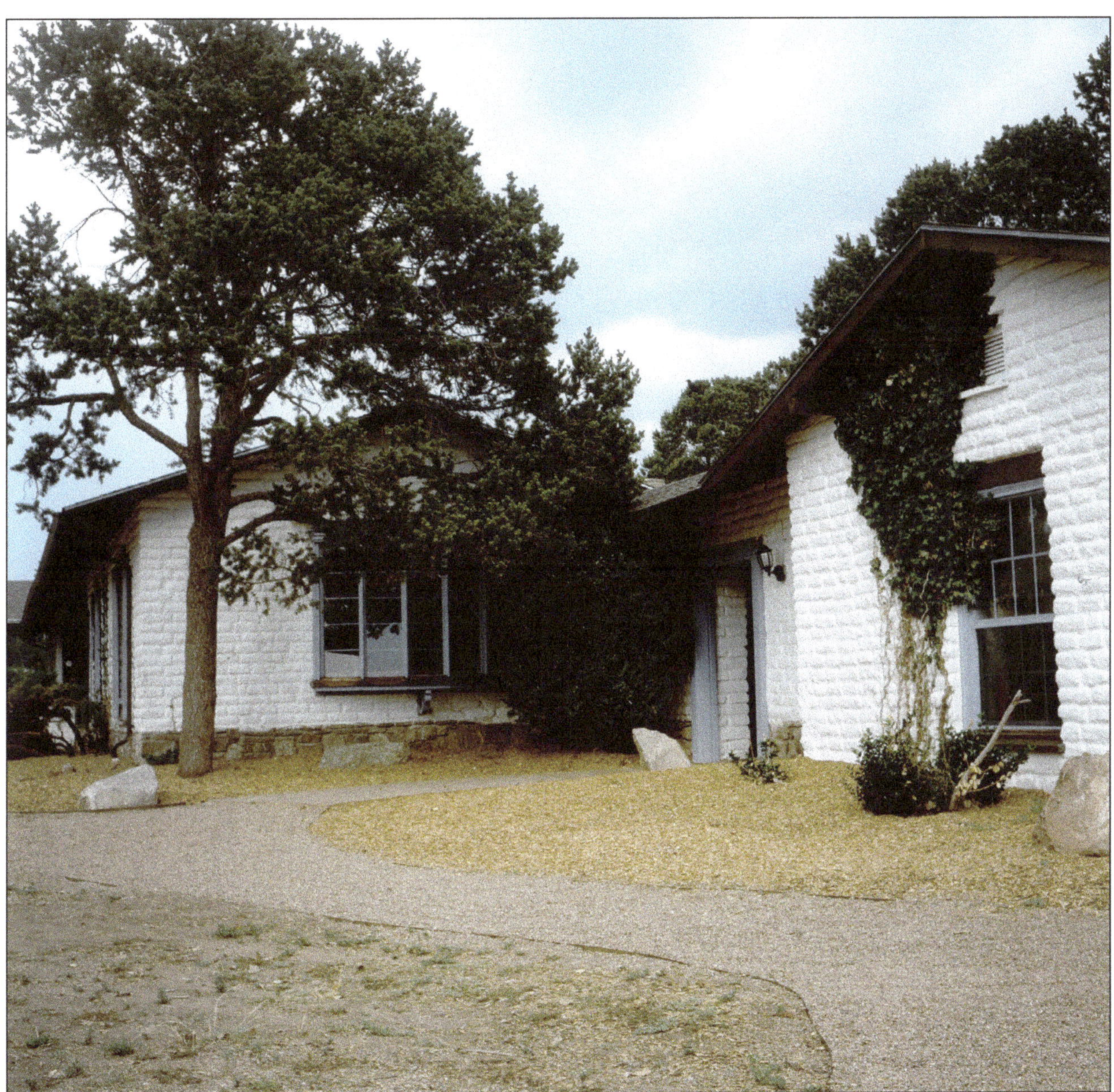

**Eldorado Community Center**, 1 Hacienda Loop. William Lumpkins designed this ranch-style house in 1953 for Frank and Carolyn Teal. Three years later, the Teals sold it, and the 27,000-acre ranch around it, to Alva and Annaliese Simpson, who sold it in 1969 to The American Realty and Petroleum Corporation (AMREP). A decade earlier, AMREP bought 55,000 acres some 50 miles to the southwest and began the development that today is Rio Rancho, the third largest city in New Mexico (Santa Fe is fourth). AMREP's similarly ambitious plans for Eldorado at Santa Fe were limited by Santa Fe County's diligence in regard to water supply — as a result, about 2,700 homesites were developed on about 6,000 acres, and more than 4,000 acres were maintained in an undeveloped state as the Eldorado Community Preserve. The old Lumpkins house is pretty unique, because it's an adobe and it's pure white: an unusual example of a white-painted adobe building.

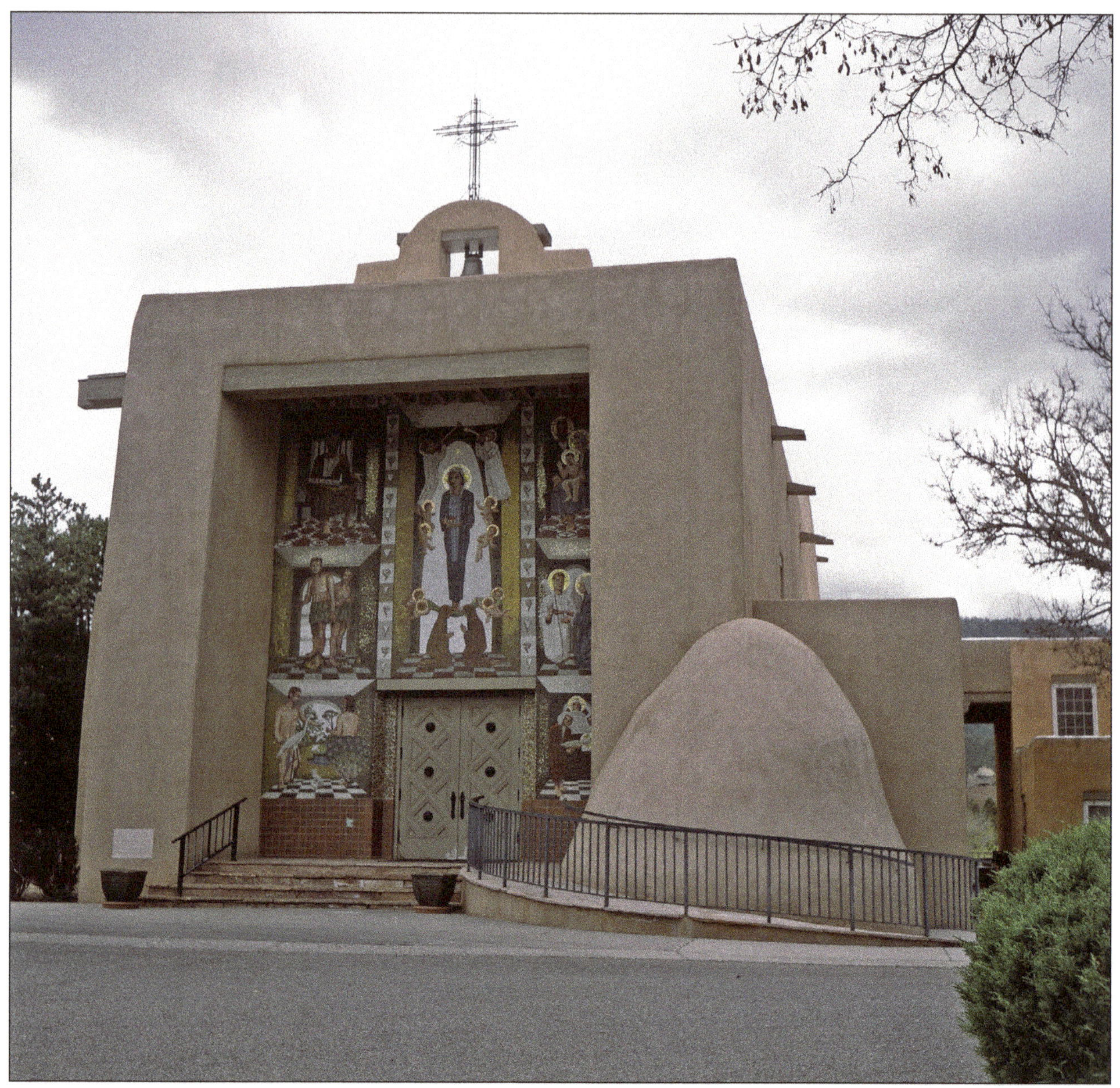

**Immaculate Heart of Mary Chapel**, Mount Carmel Road. McHugh & Hooker & Bradley P. Kidder & Associates designed this building for the Immaculate Heart of Mary Seminary. The front mosaic panel surmounted by the bell tower and flanked by an asymmetric buttress form adorn the Spanish-Pueblo Revival chapel. The building was part of a master plan by the architects that included remodeled existing buildings (many of them built for the old Sunmount Sanitarium) and putting in a system of roads to preserve "a pleasant village street atmosphere — rather than make a more conventional campus-type arrangement with formal landscaped quadrangles," according to a story headlined "Archbishop To Lay Chapel Cornerstone," in the *Santa Fe New Mexican* of Dec. 3, 1961. The chapel was completed in 1962. The following year, lead architect John W. McHugh, who worked on other such projects around the state and who was then president of the New Mexico chapter of the American Institute of Architects, presented a lecture at Highlands University on "Modern Religious Architecture."

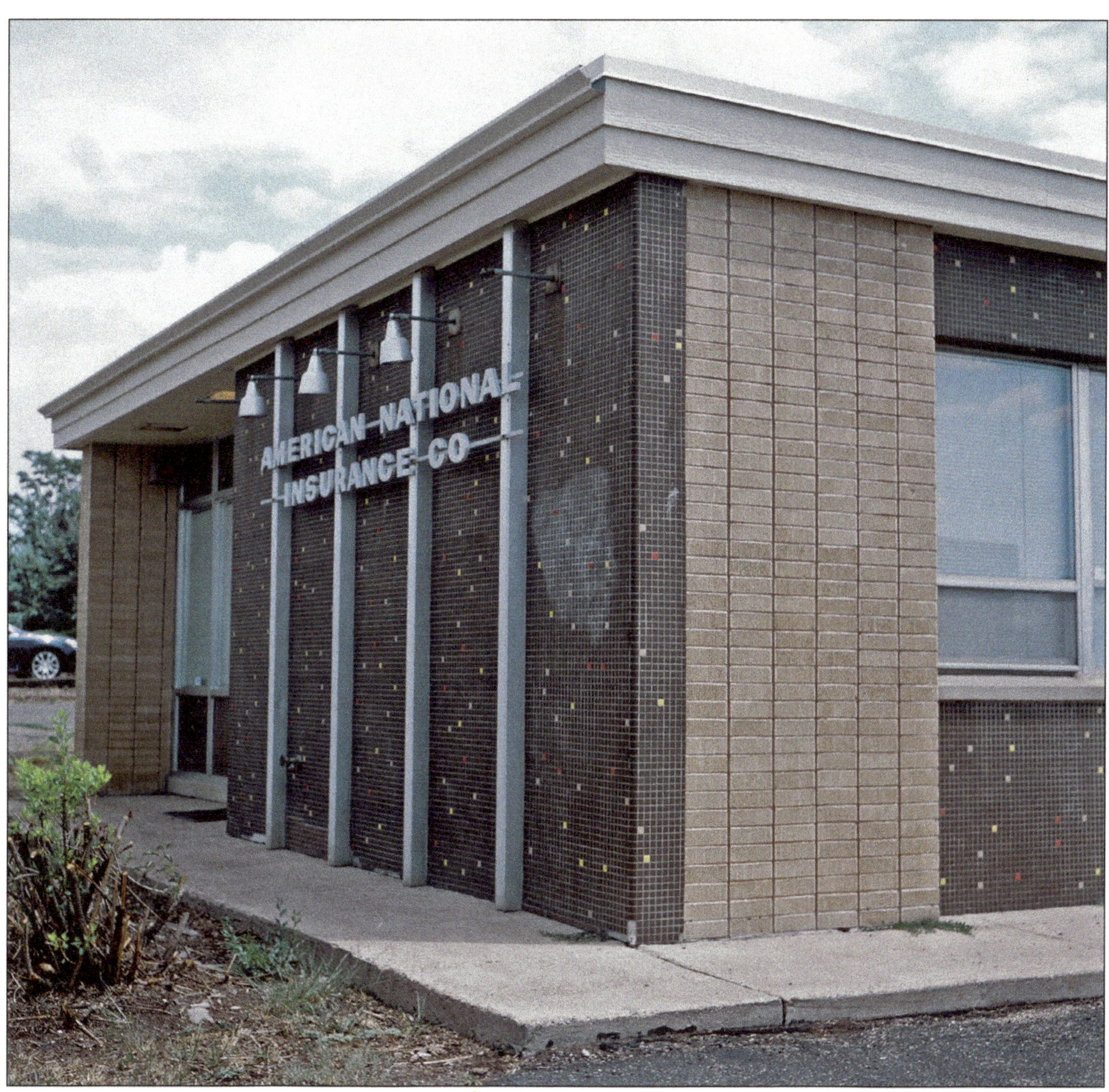


**American National Insurance Co.**, 432 Alta Vista Street, was built in about 1960 and has been owned by Dave Sorenson of Roswell since 1984. The architect is unknown, but apparently there were once many American National Insurance offices with buildings just like this one. The company was founded in 1905 by William L. Moody, Jr. and is headquartered in Galveston.

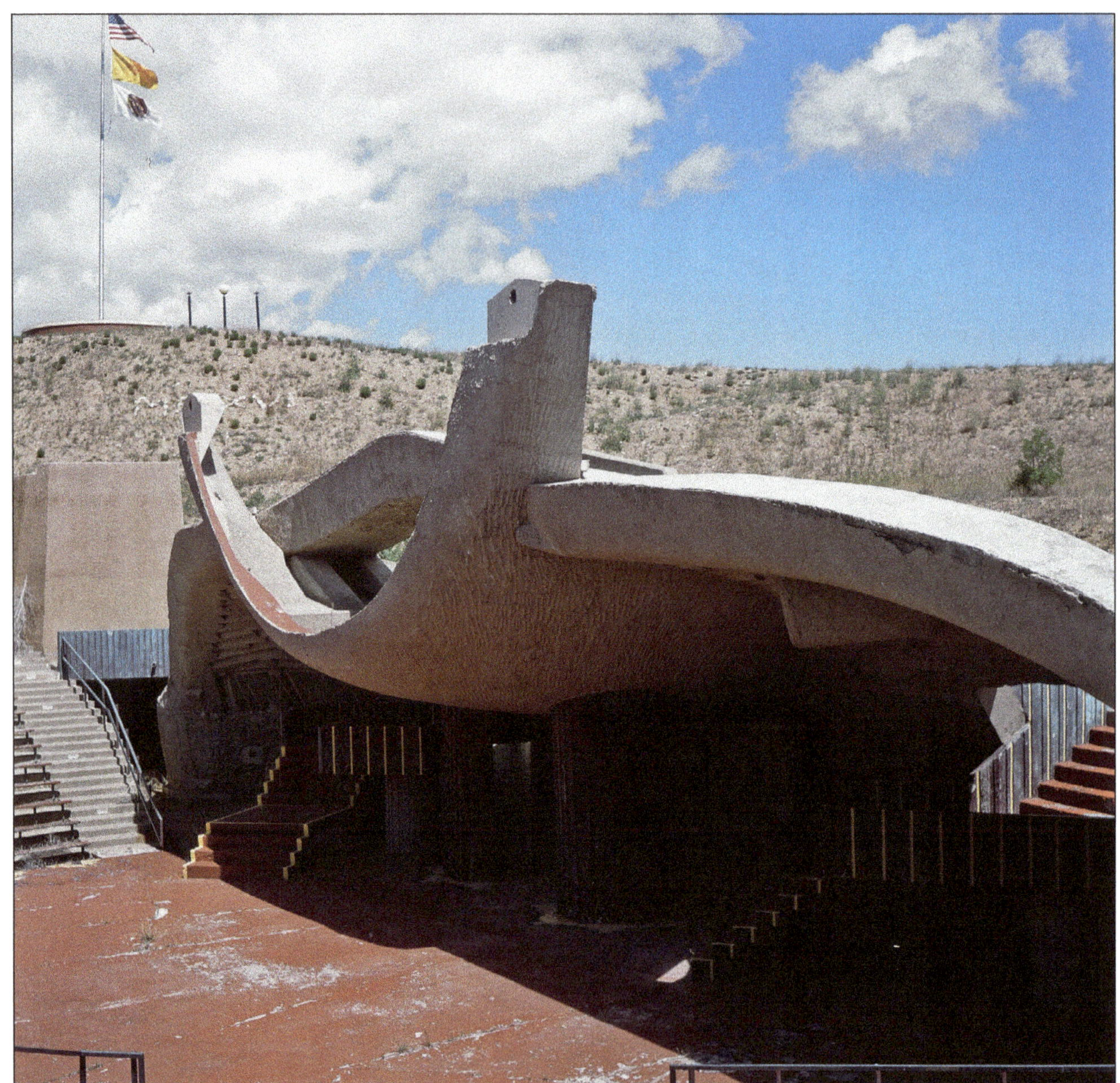

**Paolo Soleri Amphitheater**, Santa Fe Indian School, is one of Santa Fe's most unique (and today increasingly unknown) architectural masterworks. Designed for the Institute of American Indian Arts' performing arts program, it was completed in 1966 by Soleri, IAIA students, and the architect's apprentice assistants from his educational Cosanti Foundation in Arizona. They built with earth-cast, steel-reinforced concrete to create the unique theater with its dramatic arc over a semicircular thrust stage and its open-air bench seating for 2,000. In his wonderfully detailed description and analysis (at conradskinner.com), architect Conrad Skinner said the Soleri theater's components "synthesize abstractions of traditional tribal ceremonial spaces into an architecture for performance of secular indigenous drama." John Conron and Patrick Christopher wrote in *New Mexico Architecture* in 1978 that while the preponderance of the city's "folk expressionist" buildings did not comply with the rules developed for the central historic core, "it is just such self-expressionism which continues the vitality and uniqueness of the Santa Fe style of life and architecture." The theater, remembered fondly as the stage for concerts by k.d. lang, Santana, and many other performers, was closed to the public by the All Indian Pueblo Council in 2010.

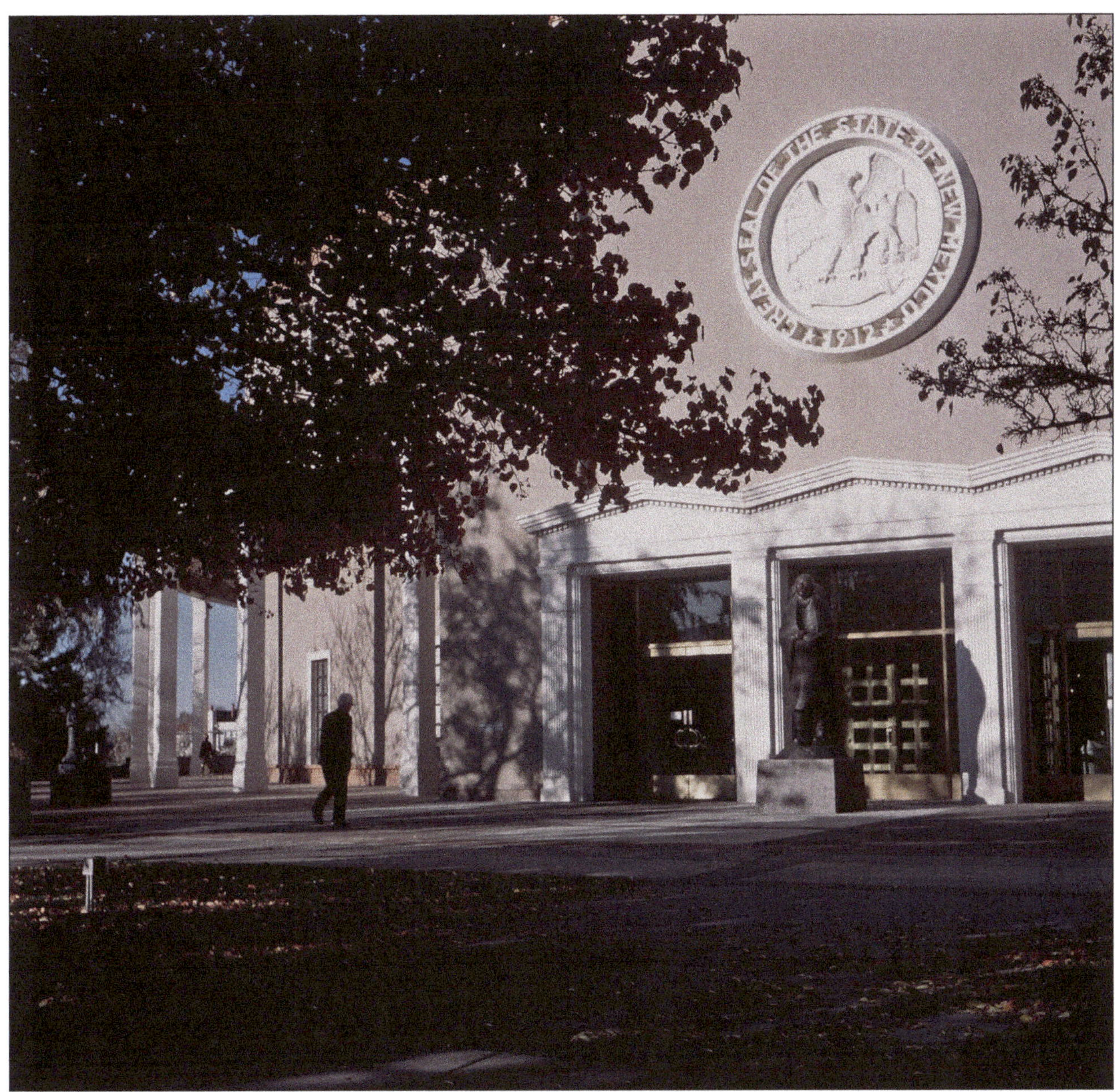


**The Roundhouse**, 400 Don Gaspar, is New Mexico's fifth capitol building and the only circular one in the country. For centuries, the capital function was served by the Palace of the Governors. The first of two territorial-era capitols was designed by Chicago architect E.S. Jenison and completed in 1886. The double-domed structure burned down six years later, then Isaac Rapp designed a new government headquarters, finished in 1900. Its stately, pedimented portico and silver dome were subtracted in an early-1950s remodel that brought the capitol in sync with the Territorial Revival style. (This is now known as the Bataan Memorial Building.) W.C. Kruger's first design for a new, circular capitol, which he referred to as "monumental pueblo architecture," was attacked by critics as "a damnable monstrosity" that resembled the Roman Coliseum. The final iteration looks a lot like the official state Zia sun symbol in plan view. Four squared pavilion entries near the cardinal points offset its perfect roundness. Inside, the floor of the rotunda bears the New Mexico state seal inlaid in brass and turquoise. During the 1966 dedication, a telegram from President Lyndon Johnson was read, proclaiming that the new capitol "demonstrates anew that your great state is also a land of progress."

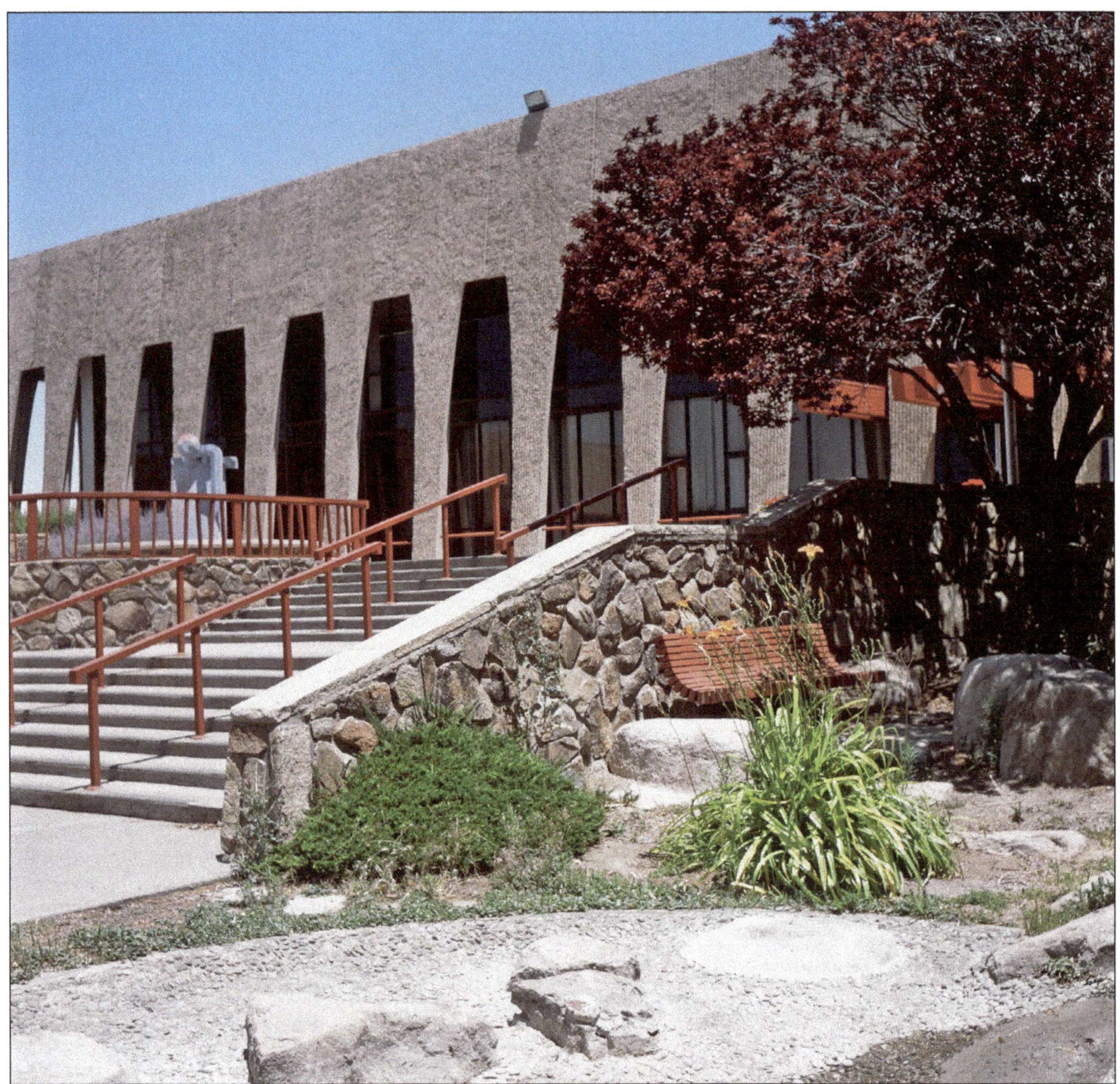

**College of Santa Fe**, 1600 St. Michael's Drive. The Fogelson Library Center, pictured here, is one of the significant buildings that Philippe Register designed for the College of Santa Fe in the 1960s and 1970s. The designs of the library and adjacent buildings relate to the ancient Indian pueblos at Chaco Canyon. The Greer Garson Theatre, a classroom building, a science building, a physical education building, and six dormitory buildings are also Register designs: quite a body of work in one spot, architect Gayla Bechtol commented in 2017, and added, "At the time, he was really trying to come up with a regional modernism." The institution, founded in 1859 as St. Michael's College, was originally located just south of the Santa Fe Plaza. After World War II, it moved to the large campus two miles to the south, first occupying the newly derelict buildings of the U.S. Army's Bruns General Hospital. The college (repurposed for most of its last decade as the for-profit Santa Fe University of Art & Design) closed in 2018.

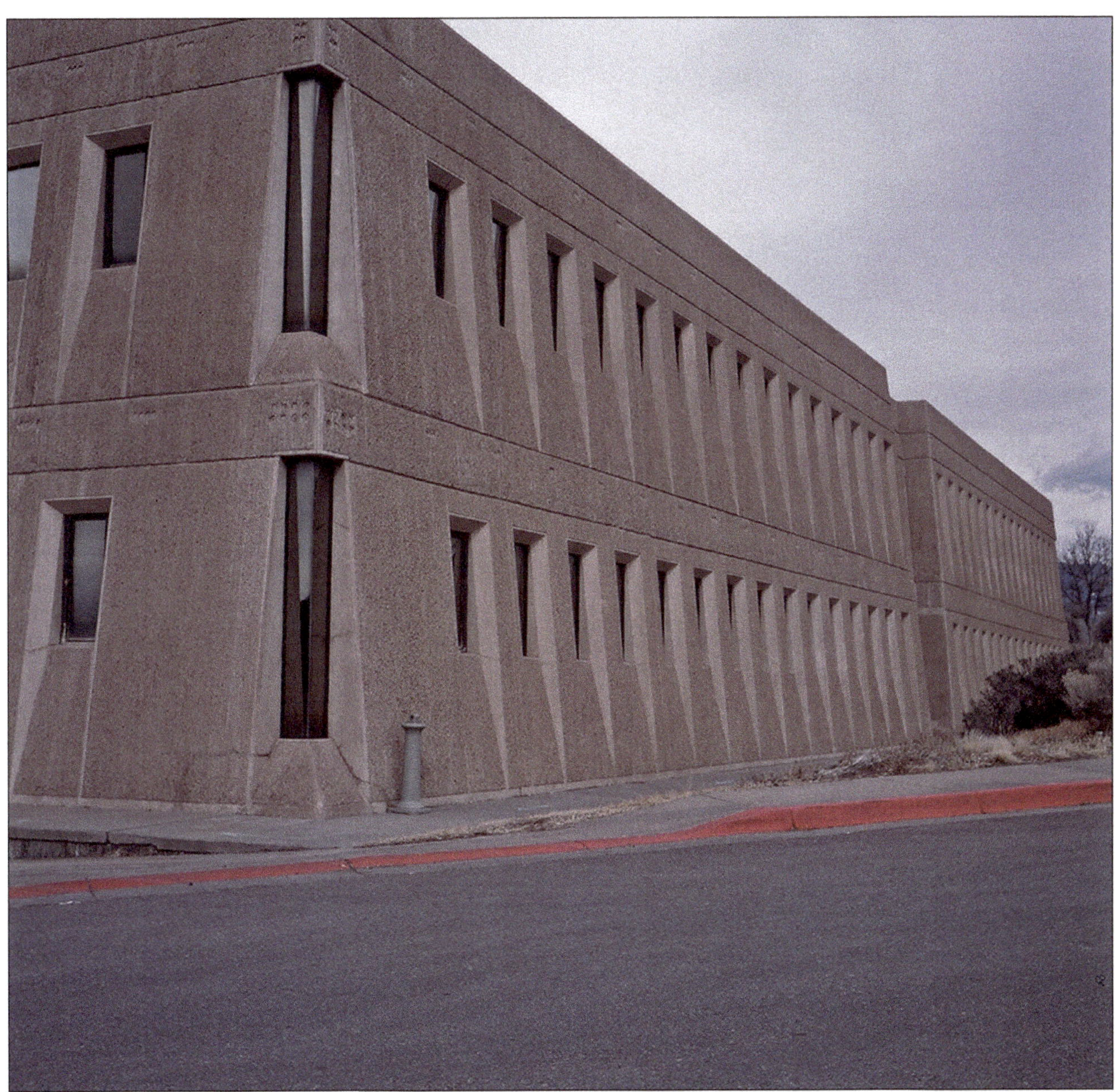

**Manuel Lujan Jr. Building**, 1200 St. Francis Drive. You can see from above that this building is square, and from the ground it looks a little like a truncated pyramid. Ted Luna, the architect who designed it, reportedly had returned from Central America and was influenced by ancient religious structures, likely including the pyramids of Yucatan. Luna said the state-government building (even though outside Santa Fe's central historic district) was designed to meet the specifications for such buildings and called it "a fine contemporary expression within that vernacular." So he specified that the outer walls were to be finished in warm-tone sand concrete mixed with native Santa Fe rock. The pyramid form is rigorously symmetrical, and Luna followed that idea with his windows: vertical scooped slits placed every five feet around the building perimeter at both the first- and second-floor levels. The 1974 Lujan Building is also notable for its fortress-like solidity. It was designed and constructed to serve as the state's data center and to accommodate the large mainframe computers used in the late 1960s. You can see dimples below each window in the stucco; these are the cable attachment-points for the post-tension building.

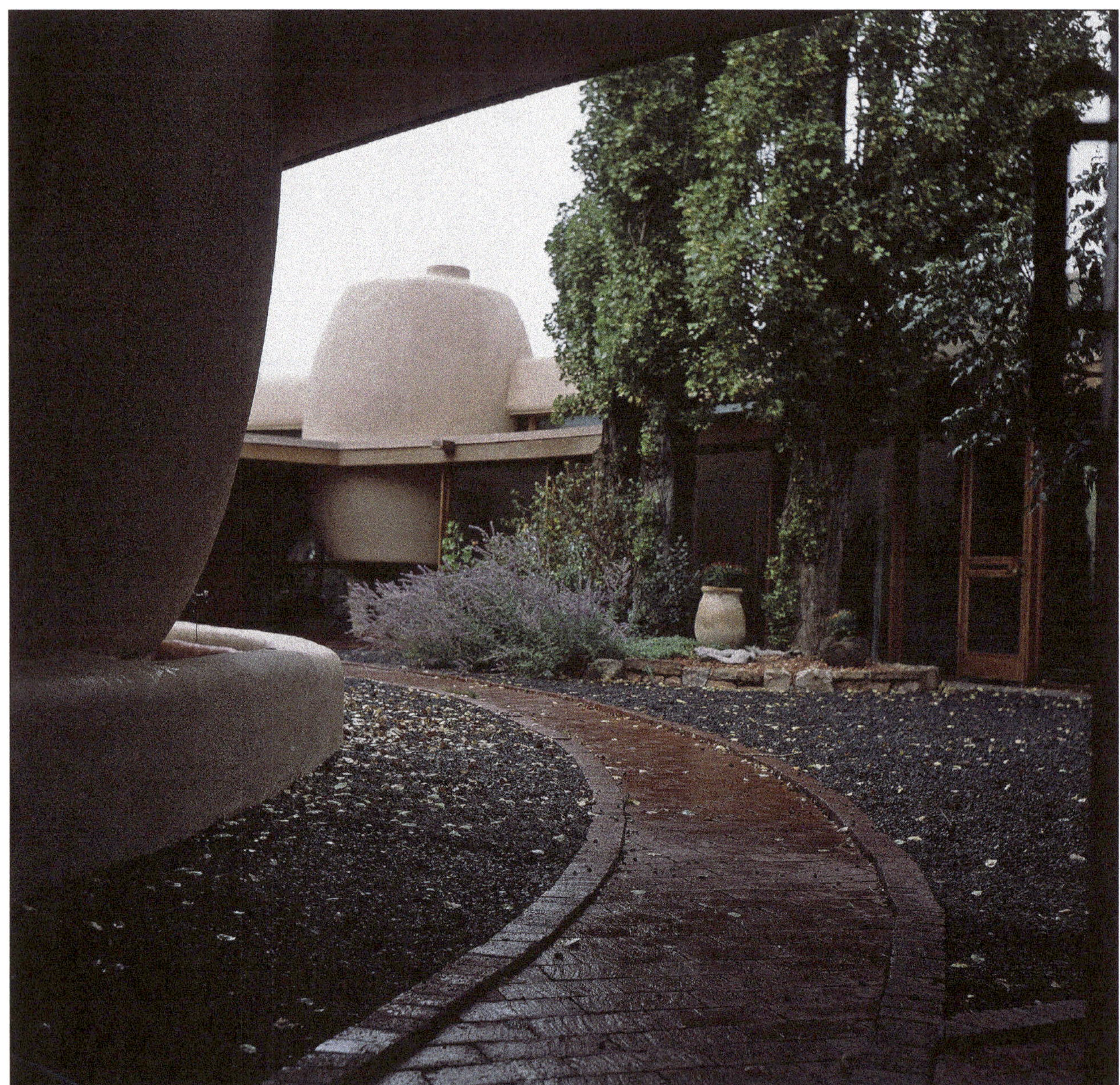

**Pottery House** on Cañada Ancha was adapted from a 1928 Frank Lloyd Wright design for a home in El Paso. For the Santa Fe site, Taliesin Associated Architects' Charles Montooth and Wesley Peters (who was Wright's structural engineer on the famous Fallingwater house and the Guggenheim Museum) nearly doubled the house's size. They also added an earth-bermed three-car garage and a swimming pool that features a narrowed swimming lane that goes right into the house. In plan view, the house resembles an eye, and that shape is repeated in feature windows and in the central courtyard. The house's walls incorporate pot-like forms, the largest showing in the big fireplace that opens both to the living room and the courtyard. Wright specified a double row of clay drainage tiles set high in the walls to provide light and ventilation. Montooth glazed them, since the new design was to be air-conditioned. Construction on what turned out to be the only adobe building designed by Wright (so far) was completed in 1984.

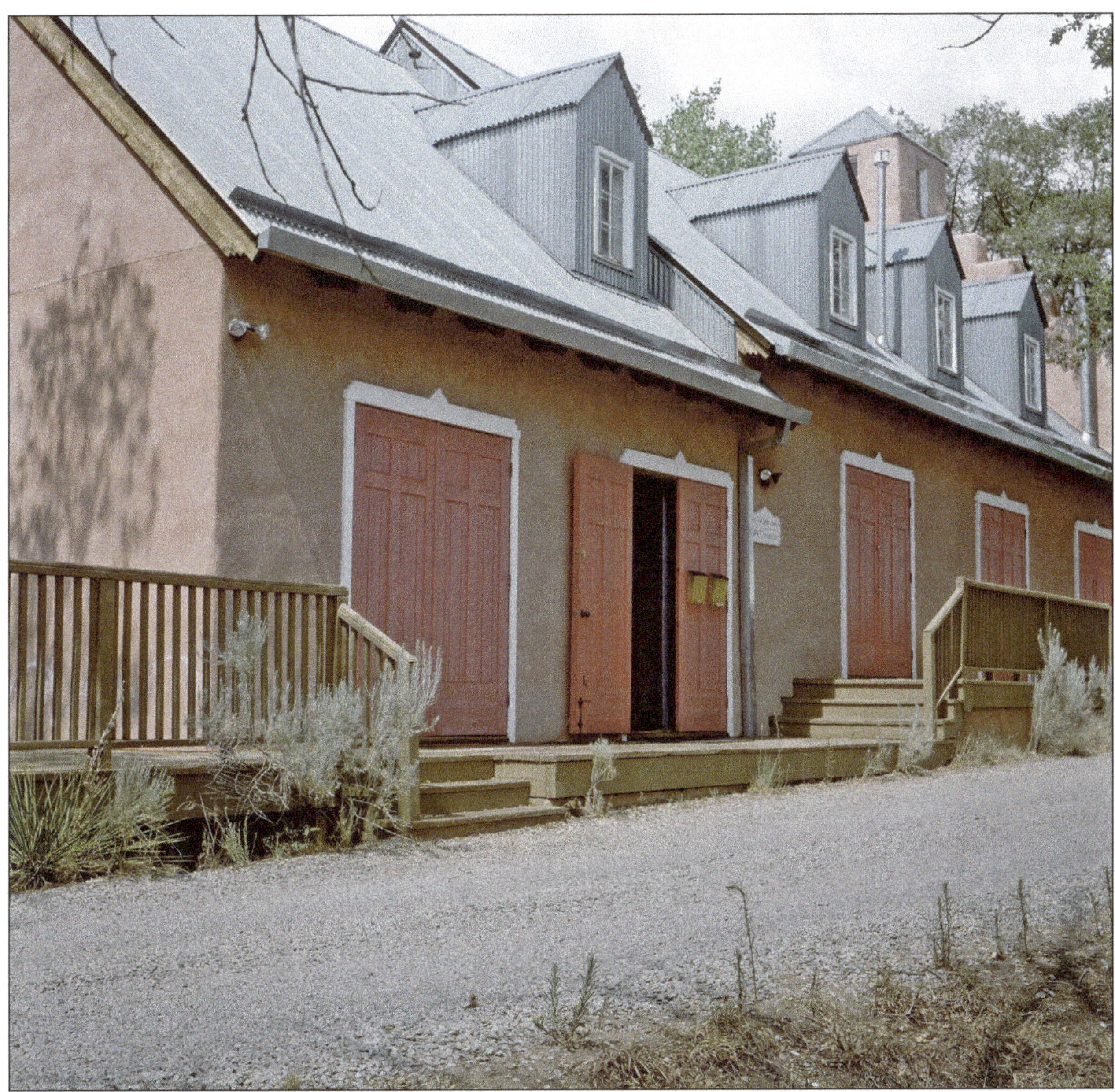

**Pink Church Art Center**, 1516 Pacheco Street, was the first of L.D. Burke's forays into architecture in Santa Fe. The Masschusetts native was a successful graphic designer in Chicago and San Francisco before moving to New Mexico's capital city in the early 1980s. A self-termed industrial designer as well as a writer and enthusiastic windsurfer, he may be more widely known for his elaborate mirrors, chairs, beds, and *trasteros*. The Pink Church, finished in about 1988, was in fact designed to house L.D. Burke Cowboy Furniture. His other buildings are The Nunnery, just behind the art center, the Fortaleza Coyote building, the four tall Granaries residential buildings (one each in tan, brown, red, and blue), the twin-towered building at Jackalope, and his home on Don Gaspar Avenue. In 2012, he told me (in an interview for the *Santa Fe New Mexican*), "The stuff I've done is sort of 'theme' architecture more than anything you'd see in *Architectural Digest*, or rather than doing a particular style over and over."

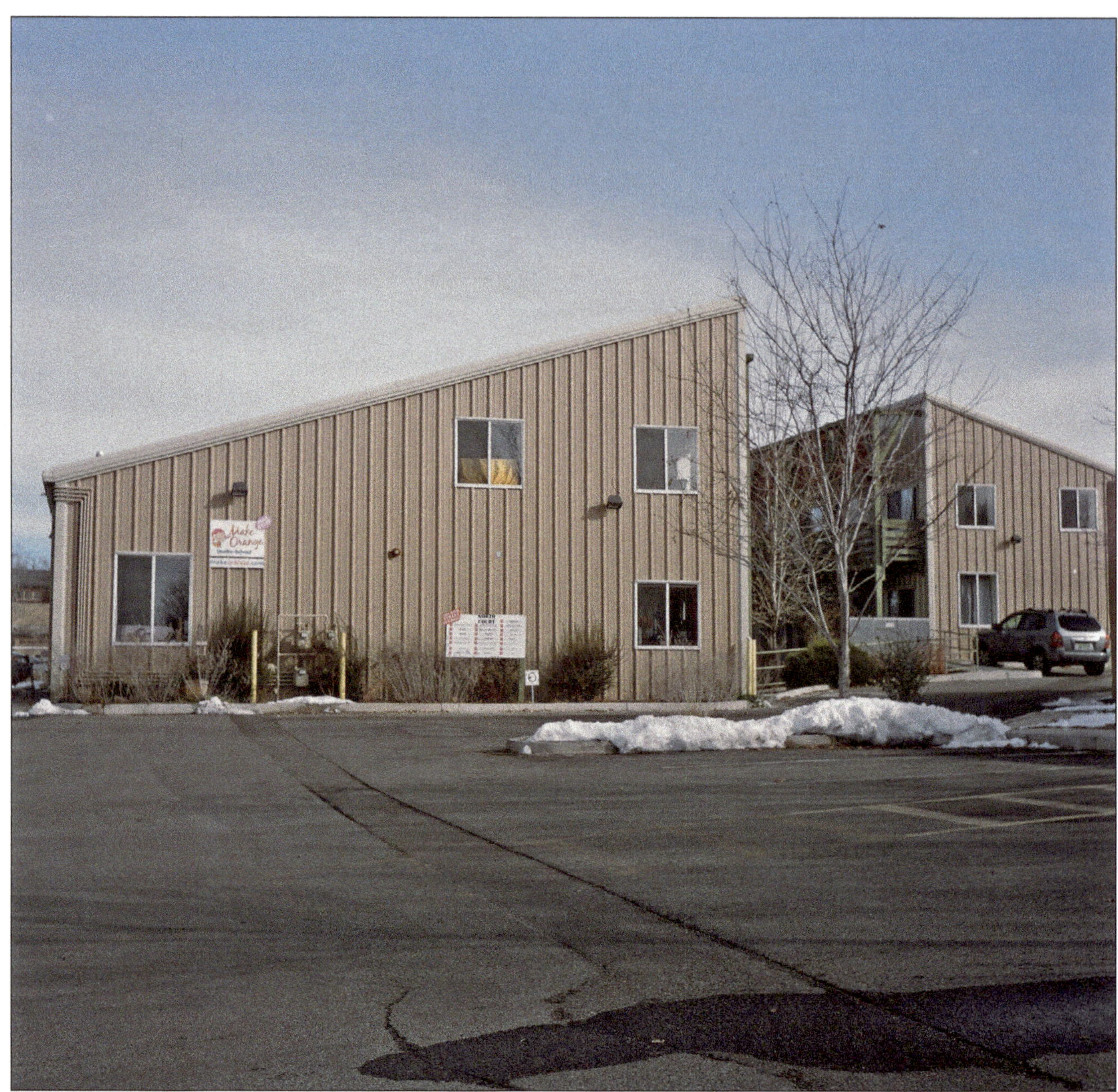

**Second Street Studios**, 1807 Second Street, was developed in the 1990s by Wayne and Susan Nichols. Robert Venturi was an inspiration for the live-work rental community, especially in the emphasis of interest on the front faces of the modest and affordable metal buildings that were designed by architect and urban planner Peter Calthorpe. The mixed-use community incorporates plenty of parking and landscaped courtyards, providing spaces for tenant gatherings and networking. The Nicholses own Communico, which has long specialized in passive-solar homes — in the 1980s, they worked with Edward Mazria and Douglas Balcomb to educate builders and architects about passive-solar design. Second Street Studios is composed of 13 buildings with nearly 100 tenants in spaces ranging from 600 to 2,280 square feet. There are art, design, and fitness studios, luthiers, seamstresses, acupuncturists, and caterers, as well as a 15-desk coworking space.

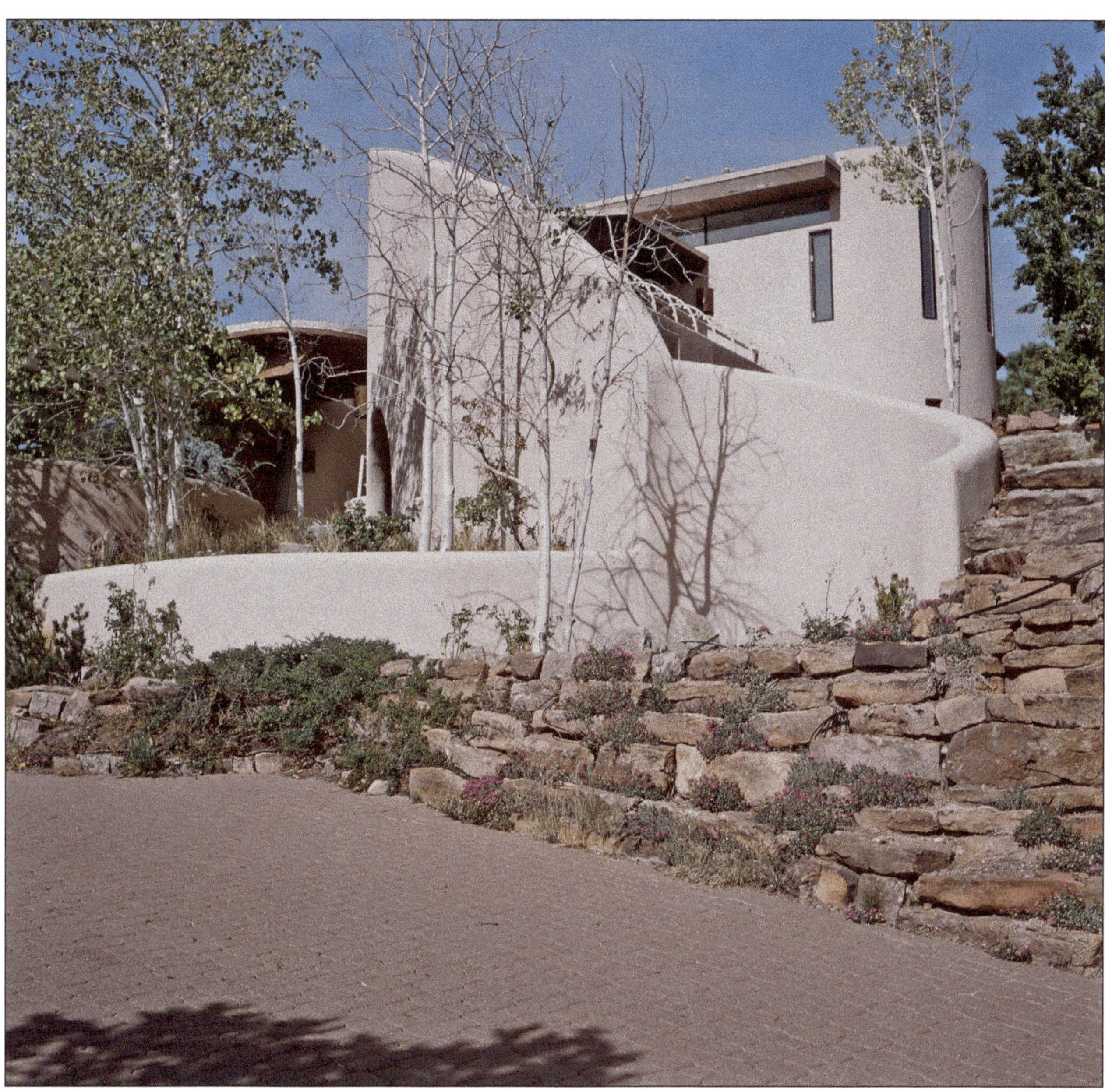

**Residence by Bart Prince** on N. Summit Drive. Architect Prince's 1993 house for Barbara and Jerry Ruther sports an adventurous design, as do all of his homes around the country. This one capitalizes on vistas with plenty of glass and terraces. The house, divided by an exterior stairway to the main entrance, features rounded and soaring forms. The living room, kitchen, and dining areas are within a massive, triangular, wedgelike section that "tears free of gravity to leap into space from its mountaintop," Christopher Curtis Mead wrote in his 1999 book about Prince's work. He adds that this and the house's other architectural gestures may be finished with earth-tone stucco, but they really suggest "how culturally pertinent but now largely missing qualities of magic and wonder might be restored to Santa Fe." Prince is the great-grandson of L. Bradford Prince, who was governor of New Mexico Territory 1889-1893. "I was born [in Santa Fe] so I have a great appreciation for Pueblo architecture and the vernacular, but not for most everything that's been done in Santa Fe, the roadrunner cartoon idea," Prince told *The New Mexican* in 2004. "That house has the massiveness and softness of the vernacular without having it be a literal quotation."

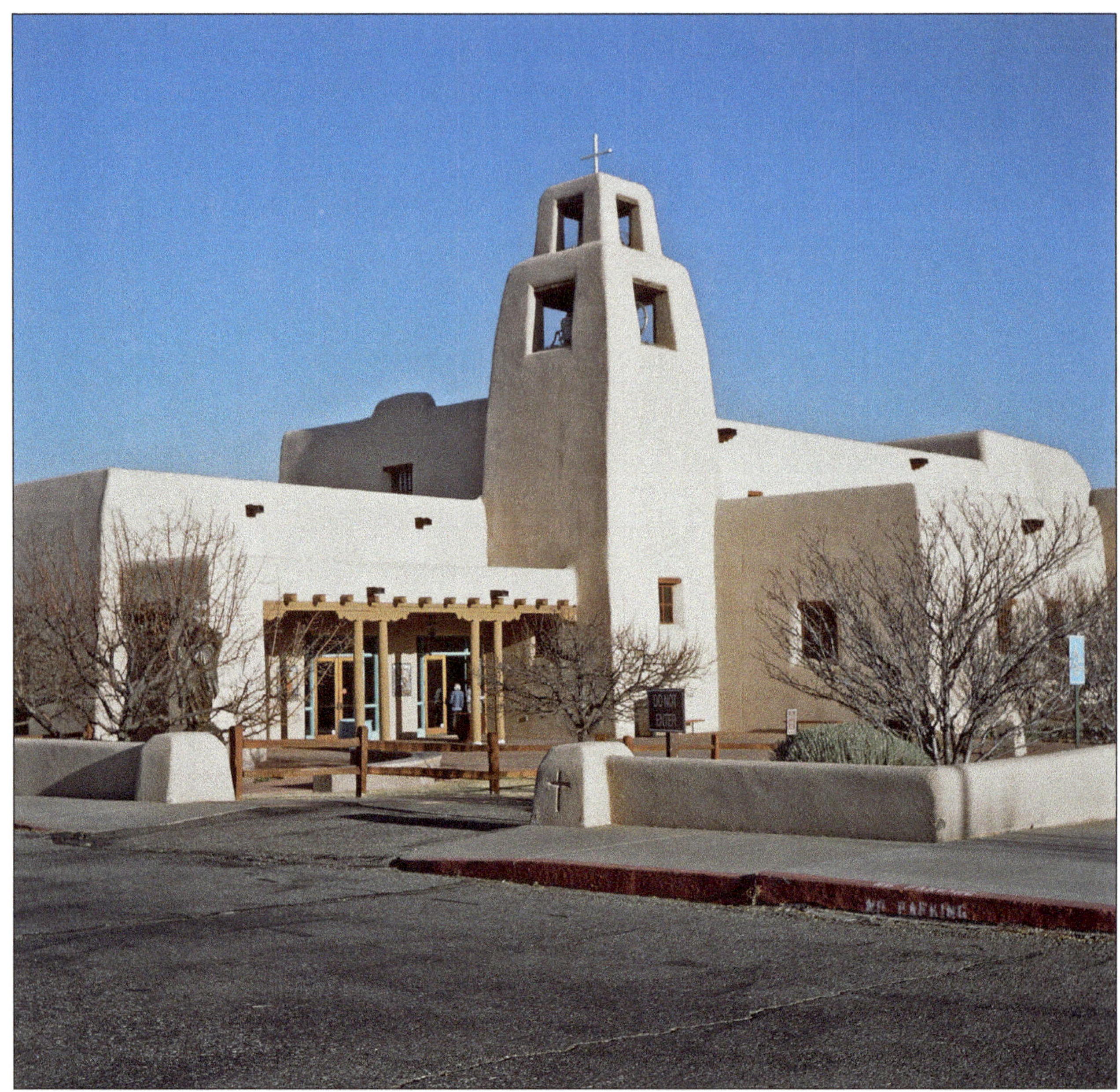


**Santa Maria de la Paz Catholic Church**, 11 College Avenue, won an award in the national Eugene Potente liturgical design competition. The judges admired the modern interior as well as the references to Northern New Mexico's Spanish Colonial mission church tradition — the hand-carved corbels and *vigas*, the artistic tinwork and *nichos* to hold works by prominent *santeros*, and the two-tiered belltower adjacent to the entry. The 10,000-square-foot building with seating for 900 was completed in 1994. It was designed by Johnson, Nestor, Mortier, Rodriguez & Purvis Architects. Victor Johnson served as partner-in-charge and project architect for the initial church that established the parish on the site and then for the religious education wing a few years later. Bernabe Romero, Antonio Ortega, and Jake Rodriguez were architects on the adjacent 2006 Santo Niño Regional Catholic School, whose functions replaced those of the old St. Francis of Assisi Cathedral School and Cristo Rey Catholic School in the downtown area, 6 1/2 miles north.

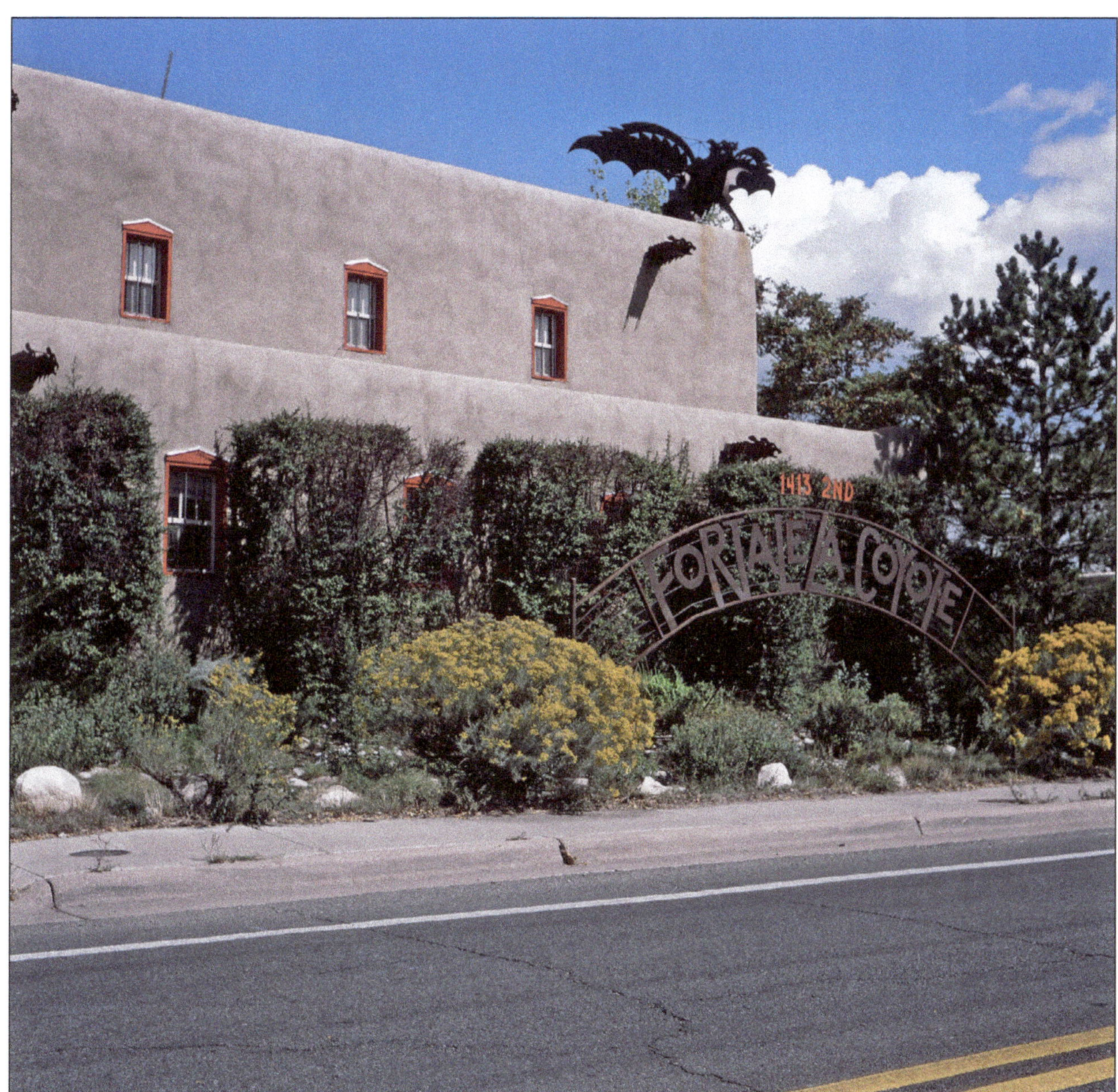


**Fortaleza Coyote**, 1413 Second Street, by L.D. Burke, is one of the so-called City Different's different buildings. The street facade of the L-shaped building has gargoyle *canales* and a large steel figure, Rusty the gargoyle, perched on the roof. Burke, a building-designer, furniture-maker, poet, and composer, designed Rusty, and it was fabricated by local blacksmith Jeff Smith. In 1996, Burke told a reporter that the windows of the Fortaleza Coyote building relate to ancient Chinese ideas about harmony and proportion, and that its design was inspired in part by Chicago's postmodernist 1991 Harold Washington Library Center by HBRA Architects.

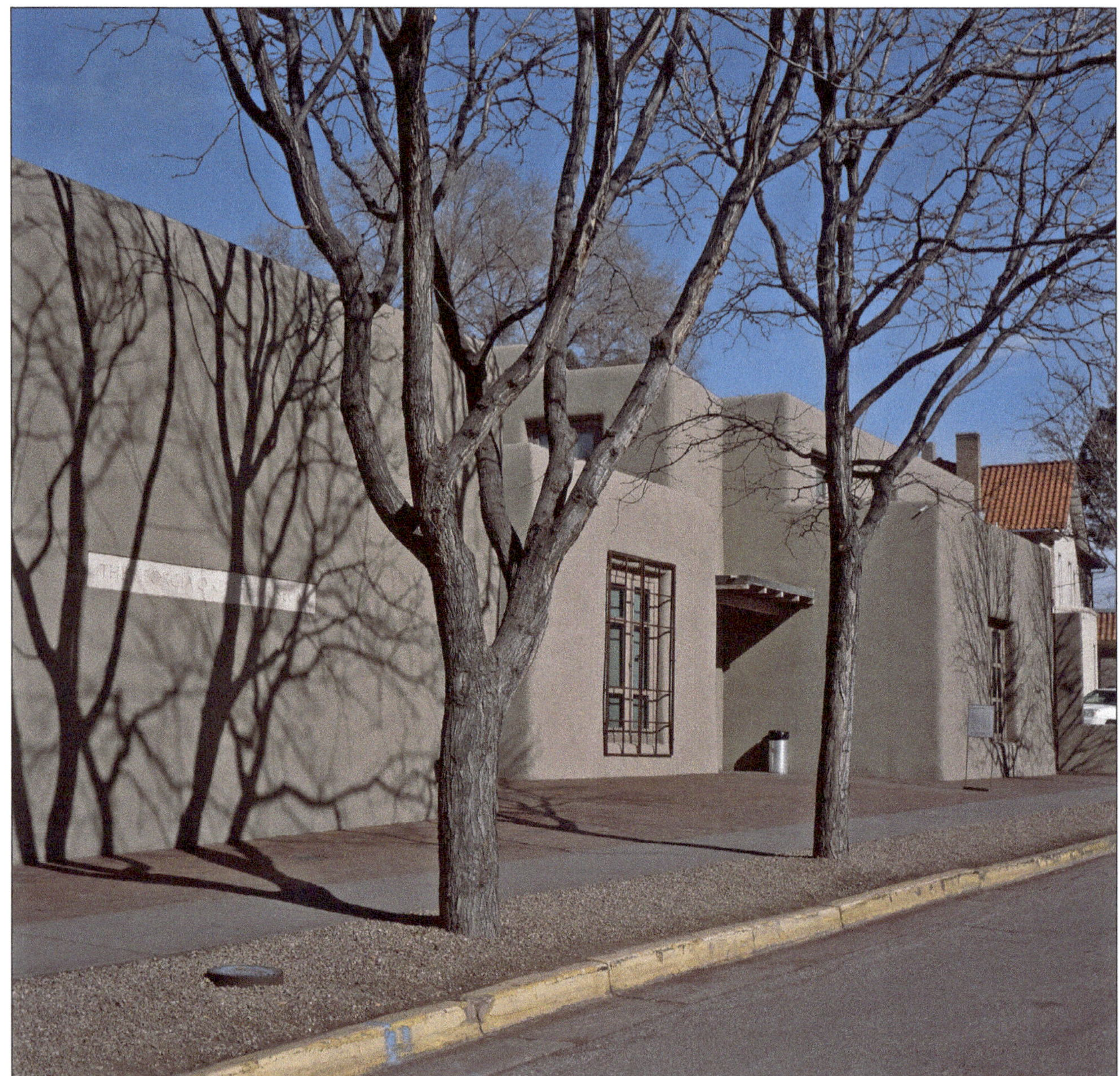

**Georgia O'Keeffe Museum**, 217 Johnson Street, is part of a street of commercial buildings adapted from houses built in the first two decades of the 20th century and is across from the 1939 John Gaw Meem-designed County Courthouse. The museum may have begun life as a church and was later remodeled for the New Mexico Repertory Theater, then again in 1990-1991 for the Allene Lapides Gallery; architect Ron Robles provided a sophisticated interior treatment and on the exterior he slightly canted the top top feet of the front walls, minimizing a looming impact on Johnson Street. In 1996, Greg Allegretti was selected as associate architect for the new Georgia O'Keeffe Museum, accompanying project architect Richard Gluckman & Associates. The museum opened ten months later.

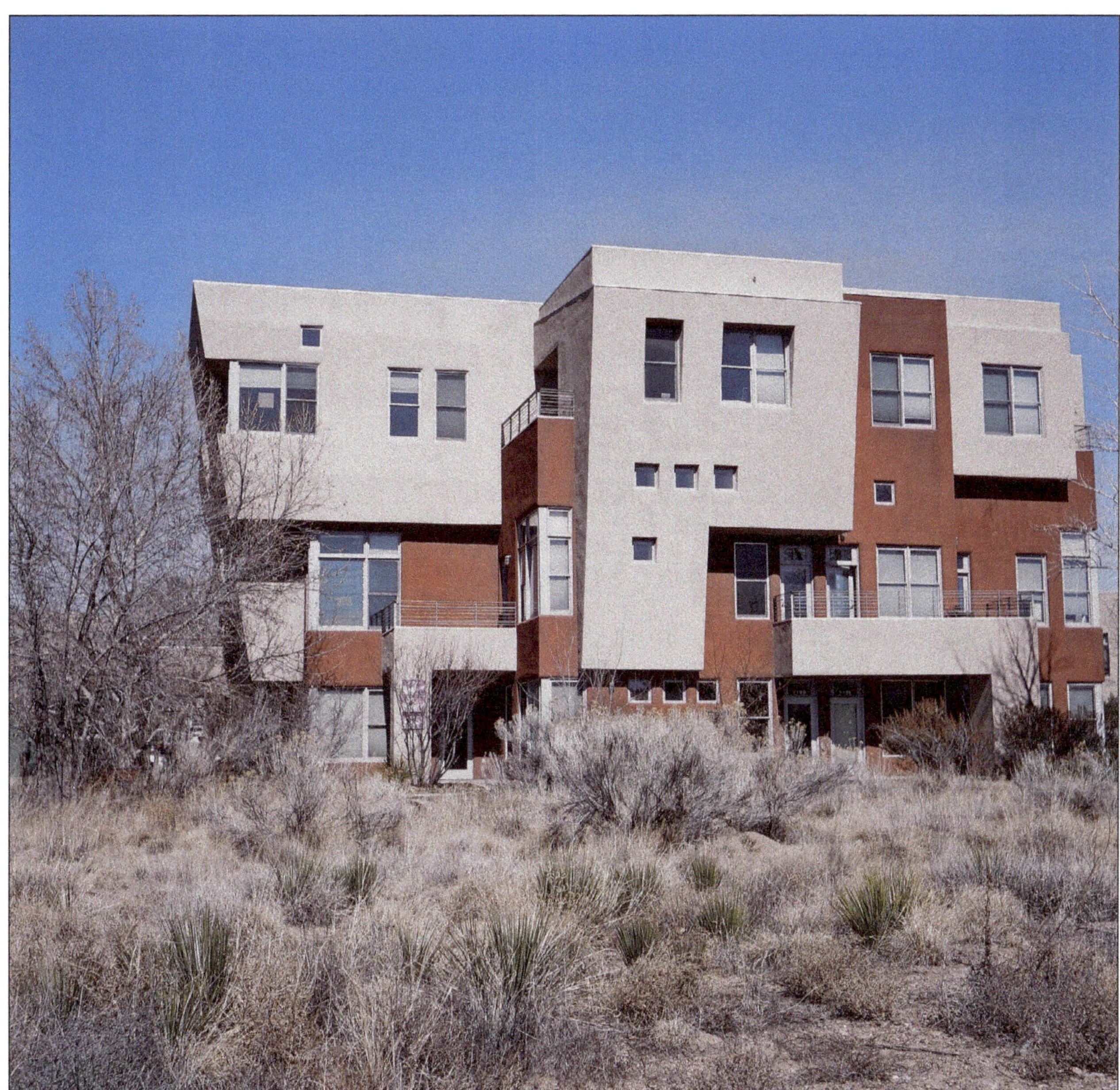

**The Lofts**, 3600 Cerrillos Road, is a live/work community developed beginning in the late 1990s behind the old Yucca Drive-In site. Owner/developer Don Wiviott made few concessions to the Santa Fe Style paradigm, and he didn't have to, since the site is well outside of the central historic district — about five miles southwest of the Santa Fe Plaza. The project is zoned for commercial uses and offers high-speed internet and custom-built interiors often outfitted with contemporary-style furnishings. Among the design features are cantilevers, high ceilings with exposed joists and HVAC ducting, and plenty of glass and steel. Hugh Driscoll designed Building 700 (pictured). "While some of the units were sold outright, Building 700 was one that was retained for leasing, so there was less customization of the interior," he said. "Most of the Lofts were wood-frame, but 700, because it was a little larger, is steel frame with light-gauge steel-stud walls. The overall aesthetic was contemporary, with a lot of exposed steel." Other architects involved on the various Lofts buildings included Gabriel Browne, Brad Cantrell, and Sarah Gage.

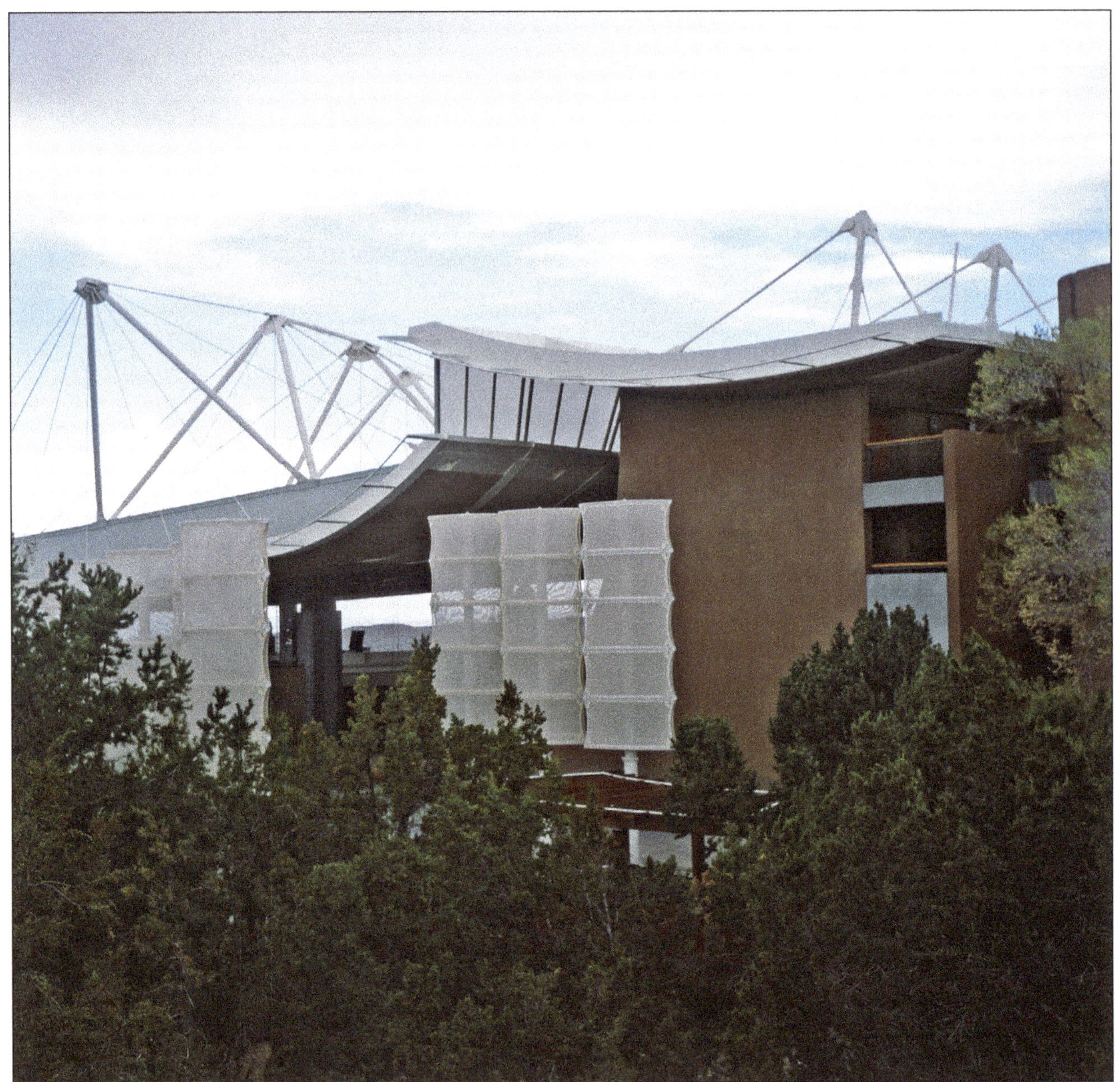

**Santa Fe Opera**. Here is a non-usual view of the modern SFO theater, compressed solely by means of camera viewpoint. Several of the important main features are shown, but the scale of the theater interior is hidden. The original open-air opera theater was designed by John W. McHugh and Van Dorn Hooker and opened in 1957. When it burned down a decade later, McHugh and Bradley Kidder fashioned a new building with a dramatically split roof. The present theater dates to a 1998 remodel by Polshek Partnership Architects, New York, working with acoustics specialists Purcell Noppe Associates. Eight sail-like weather-deflection banners on the south side protect the 2,128-seat theater. The sweeping stage roof is anchored to four massive columns from the previous theater. It is connected to the balcony roof by an 11-foot-high Teflon clerestory and both are suspended by means of a rod-and-mast system; this obviates the need for pillars and thus improves audience views of the opera stage. A 1998 story in *Civil Engineering* said that because there are no side walls, the composition, shape, and positioning of the stage-roof ceiling were critical to the acoustics of the renowned theater.

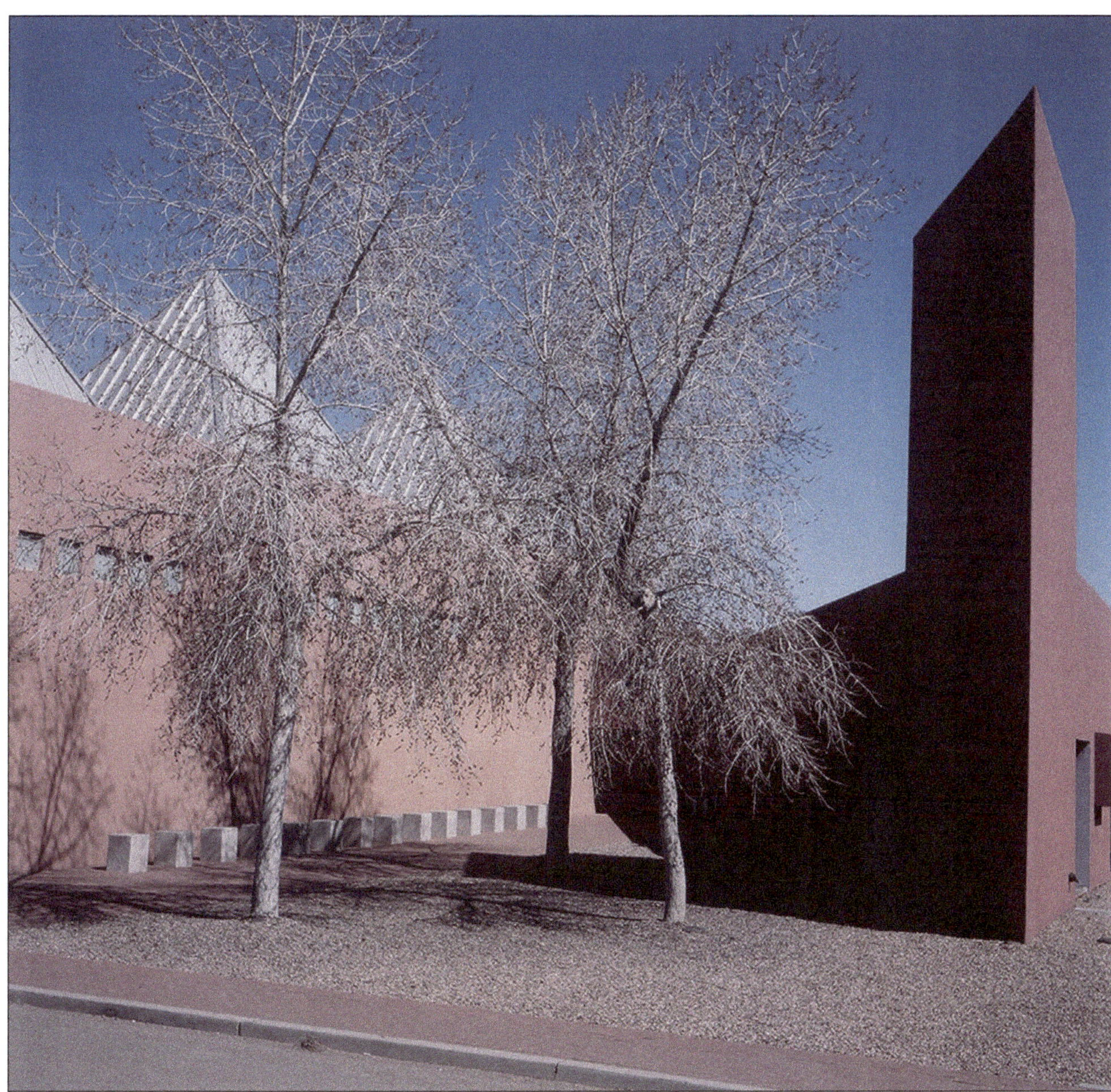

**Santa Fe Art Institute**, 1600 St. Michael's Drive. Red, yellow, purple, and orange surfaces enliven the spaces in this $12 million facility by Legorreta Arquitectos, Mexico City (with Santa Fe's Lloyd & Tryk Architects as the local firm on the project.) Ricardo Legorreta encouraged intimacy, including by breaking the functions into five building components: four for the (now-defunct) College of Santa Fe's Visual Arts Center and one, the largest, for the art institute. The towers, glass pyramids, pillars, and dynamic walls having ranks of small square openings along the tops generate engaging contrasts and shadows. Legorreta told Pasatiempo magazine (*Santa Fe New Mexican*) that the importance of the wall — the supremacy of solid over void — comes from the Islamic world and relates to a history of protection but also of mystery and the way Islamic peoples love discovering spaces. In a video about the 1999 project, he discusses the "way of living, more than shapes and forms," and stresses that he wanted to emphasize light, space, mystery, and movement "in order to really encourage the imagination." He desired that people should "be happy with the building, and happy in the building, more than being shocked or impressed."

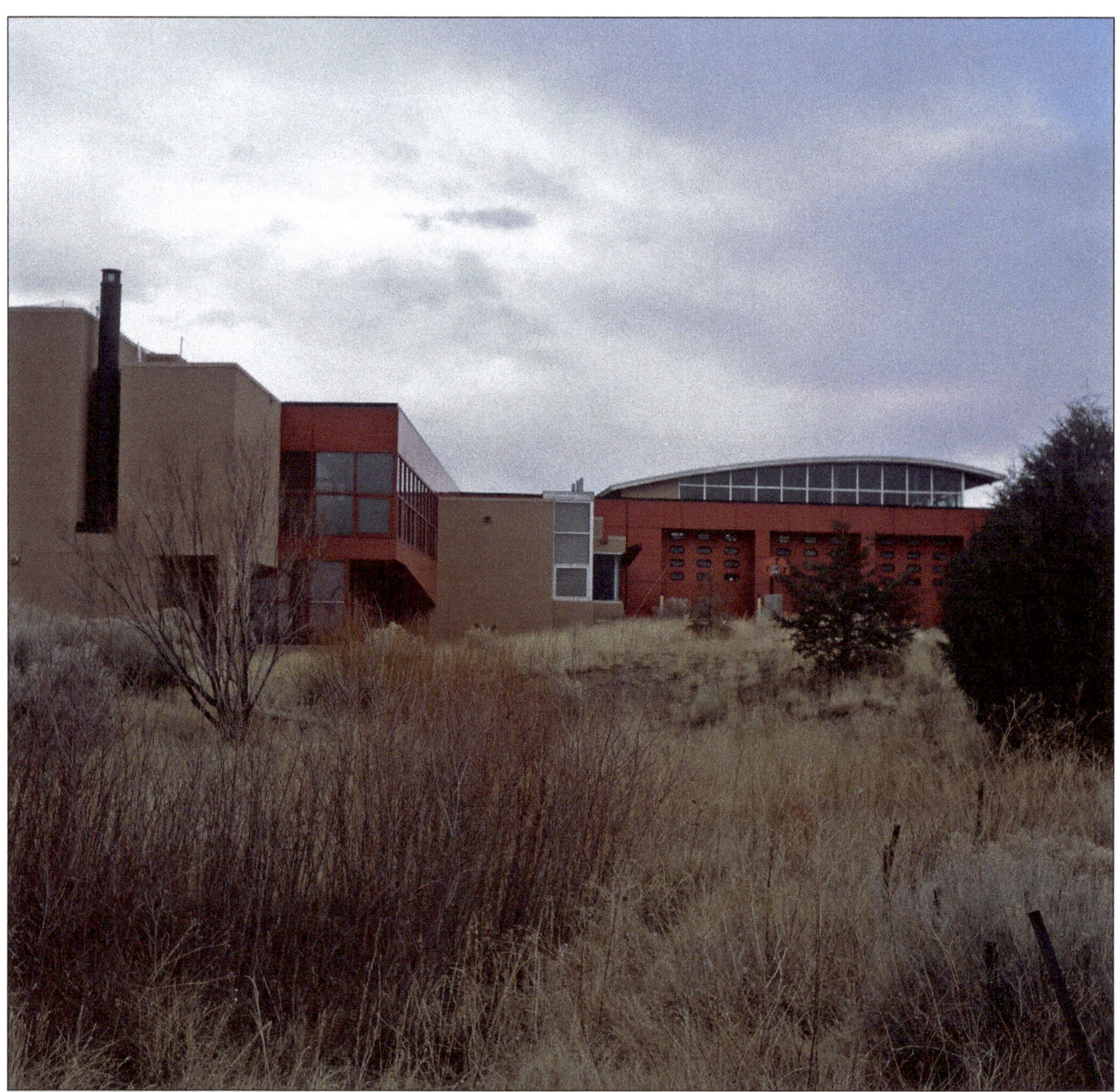

**Fire Station No. 7**, 2391 Richards Avenue, opened in 1999 near the rodeo grounds on Santa Fe's burgeoning south side. The station has a stylish, contemporary look, but architect Michael Freeman said the station's functions and resource efficiency were the priorities. The design incorporates suggestions from firefighters around the country who were asked what they would preserve or change in their own fire stations. This one, with three half-story levels stepping down the sloped building site, offers quick access to the truck bay from all areas. One afternoon earlier in his career, Freeman talked with the celebrated architect Louis I. Kahn, including about honest materials, an idea that is echoed in the red garage doors and glossy-red panels — a reminder of the fire trucks at the ready inside — that alternate with brown stucco and glass on the exterior.

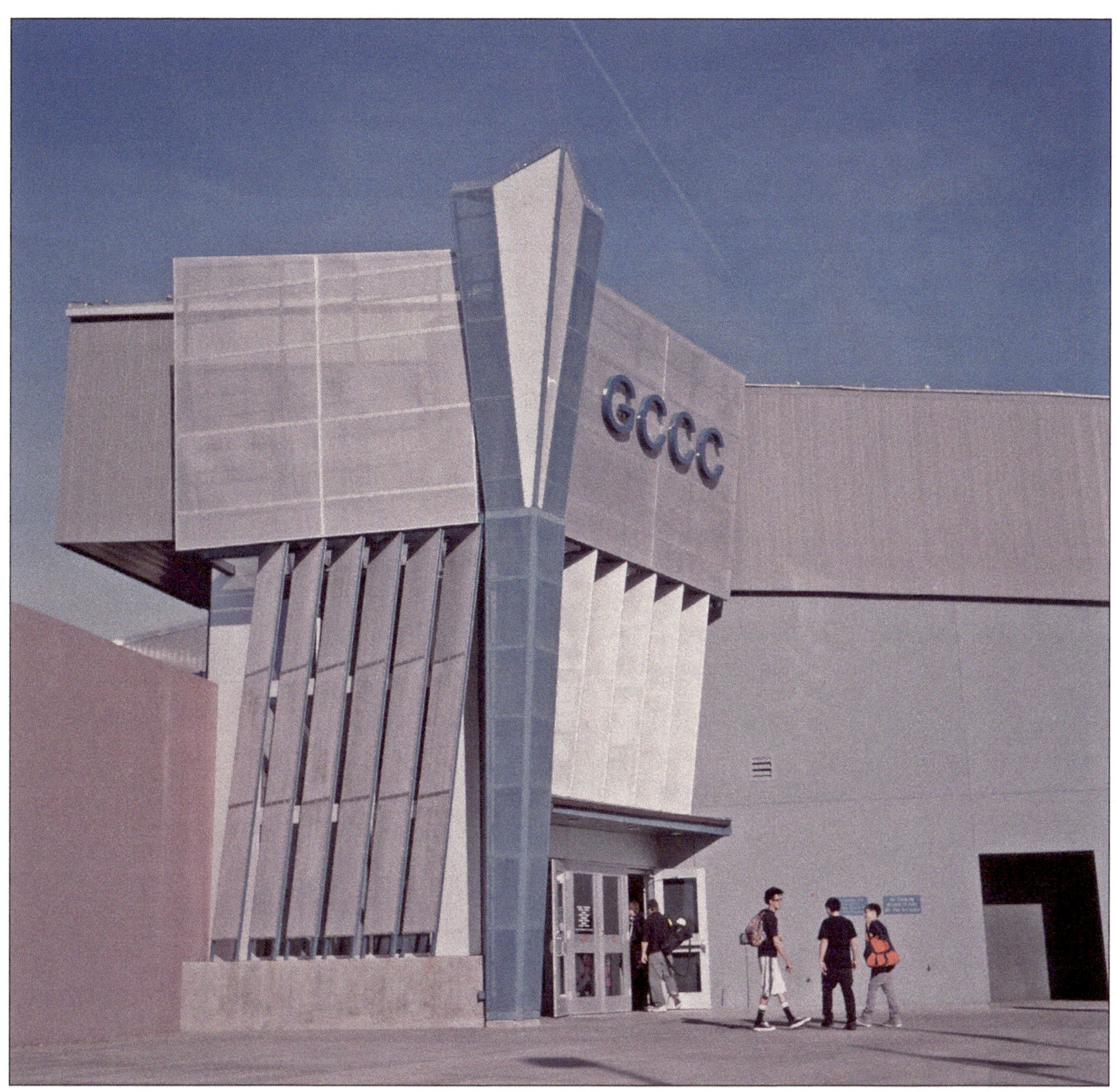


**Genoveva Chavez Community Center**, 3221 W. Rodeo Road. The $21 million, 170,000-square-foot recreation center with its burnished-concrete walls and vast roof curving nearly to the ground on one side opened in early 2000. It holds a multi-pool natatorium; an NHL-size ice arena; basketball, volleyball, and racquetball courts; and an elevated three-lane track around the perimeter of the gym. The entrance structure shown here was designed by Alexander Dzurec; the overall plan was by Mazria Riskin Odems Inc. "A major concern," Ed Mazria wrote in a statement of his design philosophy, "was how to make a 4-acre, 7-story building a distinct yet integrated part of the Santa Fe landscape ... We chose to create, through abstraction, the familiar form of a gently rolling hill." Mazria is now known nationally for his Architecture 2030 project, which poses an environmentally significant challenge to architects, builders, and owners: "All new buildings, developments, and major renovations shall be carbon-neutral by 2030."

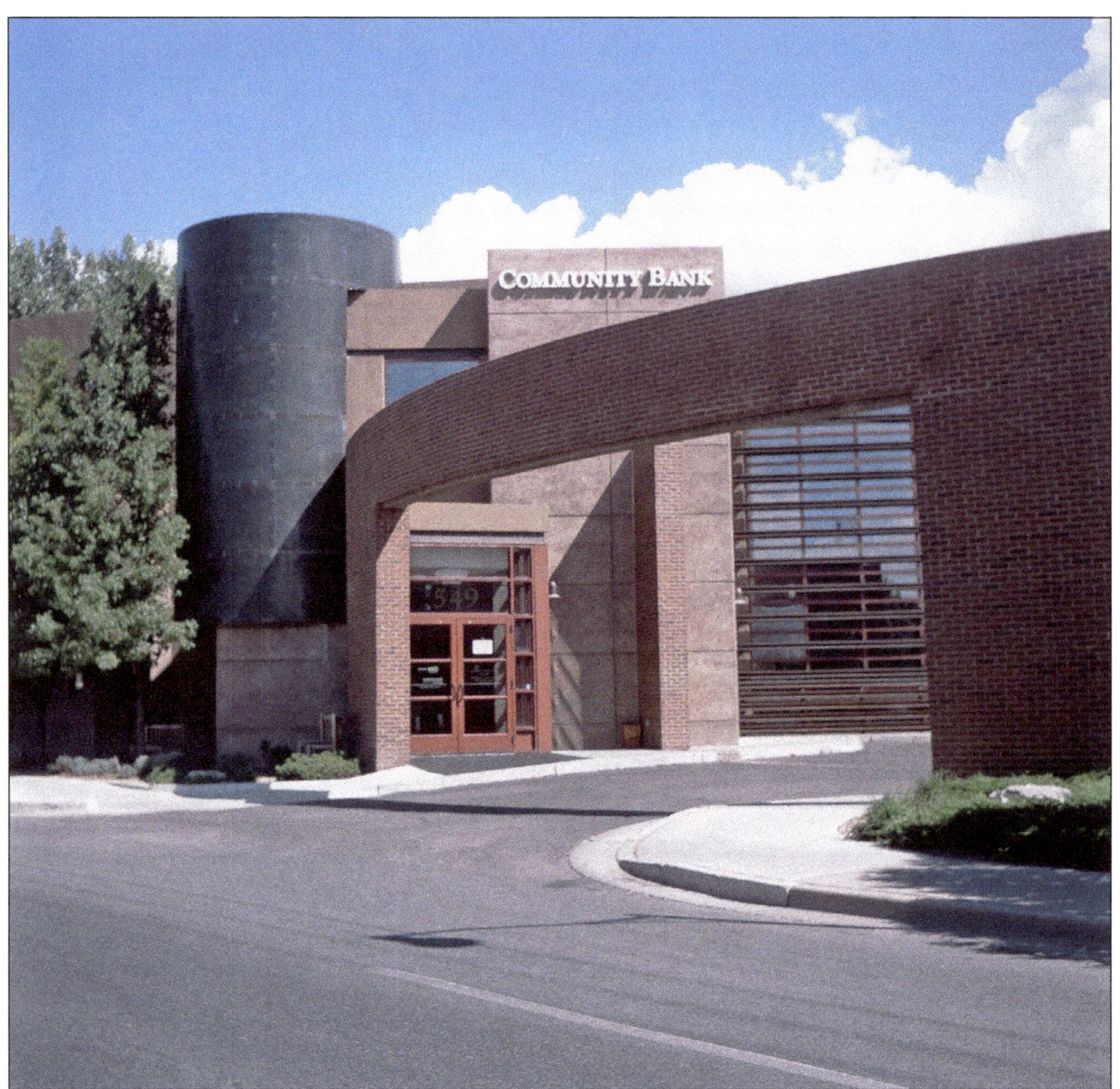


A new building for **Community Bank** was built in 2001 at 549 S. Guadalupe Street in the revitalized railyard district. A Santa Fe ordinance requires archaeological surveys before new construction; this one turned up the buried foundation of an old railroad turntable that the New Mexico Central Railroad employed to move locomotives into an adjacent roundhouse for servicing. The plans by architects Jon Dick and Aaron Bohrer, with assisting architect Tom Easterson-Bond, called for the part of the building holding the bank lobby to be "rotated." In a trench just outside, patrons could see a portion of the turntable foundations several feet below grade. Other historical references are the window blinds made of actual iron rail sections and a projecting elevator shaft housed in a curved steel cylinder fashioned to recall the old railroad water towers.

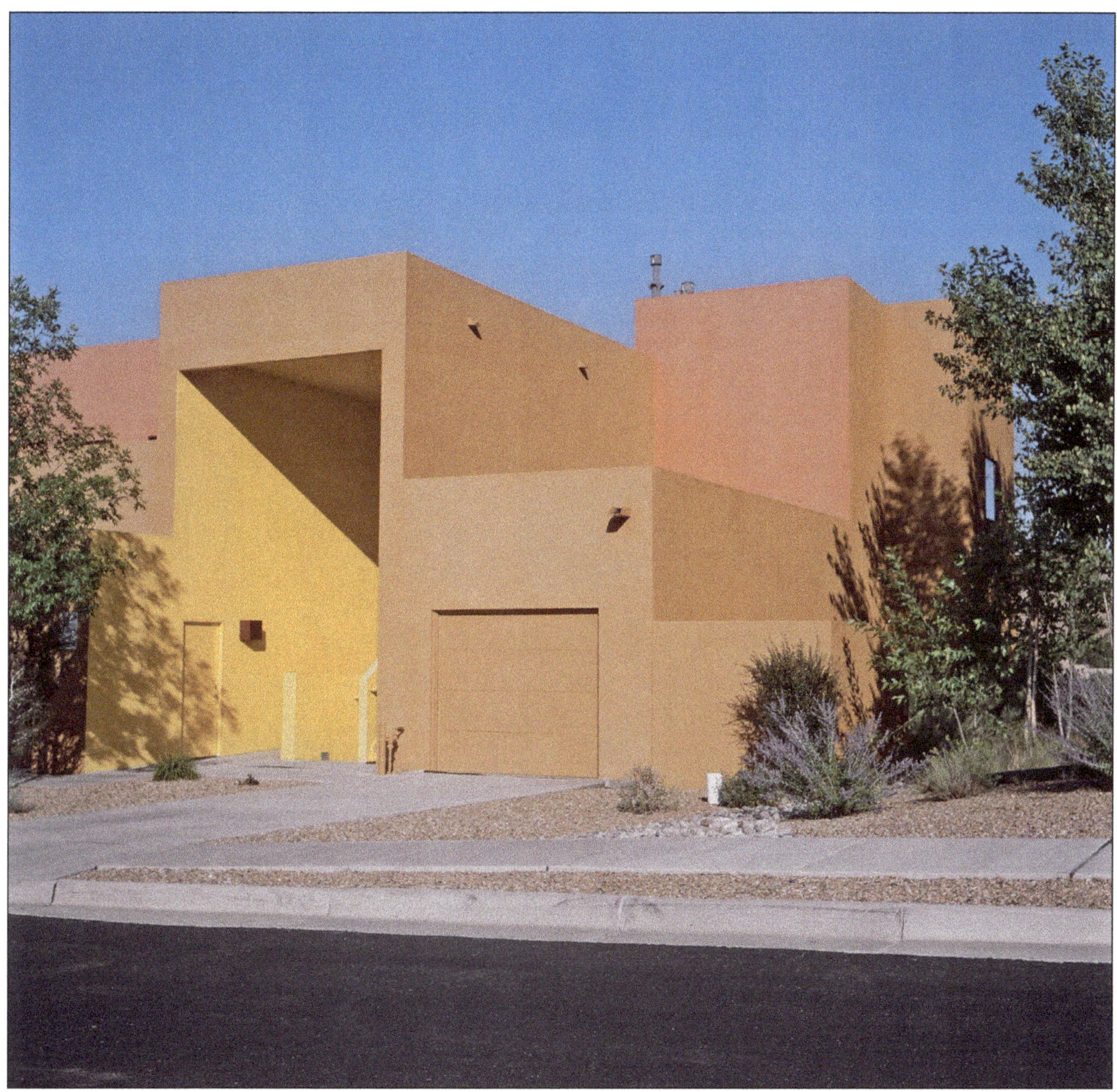

**Zocalo** is a subdivision on Santa Fe's north side that is named after the town squares that are typical south of the border. Ricardo Legorreta of Mexico City designed the 320-unit condominium project in clusters around small plazas. "The detailing of windows, doors, kitchens and materials were standardized while we sought the variety and interest of a modern village," says the architect's firm. You can see, in the building geometries, a relation to the Pueblo style, but Legorreta was a disciple of Luis Barragan, and there's a definite modernist flavor in these bold, boxy shapes. Legorreta believed that art should be a part of our daily lives; his love for color is wonderfully evident here. Contrasting a city full of earthy browns, the main Zocalo building masses are Tabasco red and pumpkin, and there are splashes of blue, yellow, pink, and purple in balconies, entryways, and other more private areas. Zocalo sales began in 2002; Dekker/Perich/Sabatini, Albuquerque, was executive architect on the project.

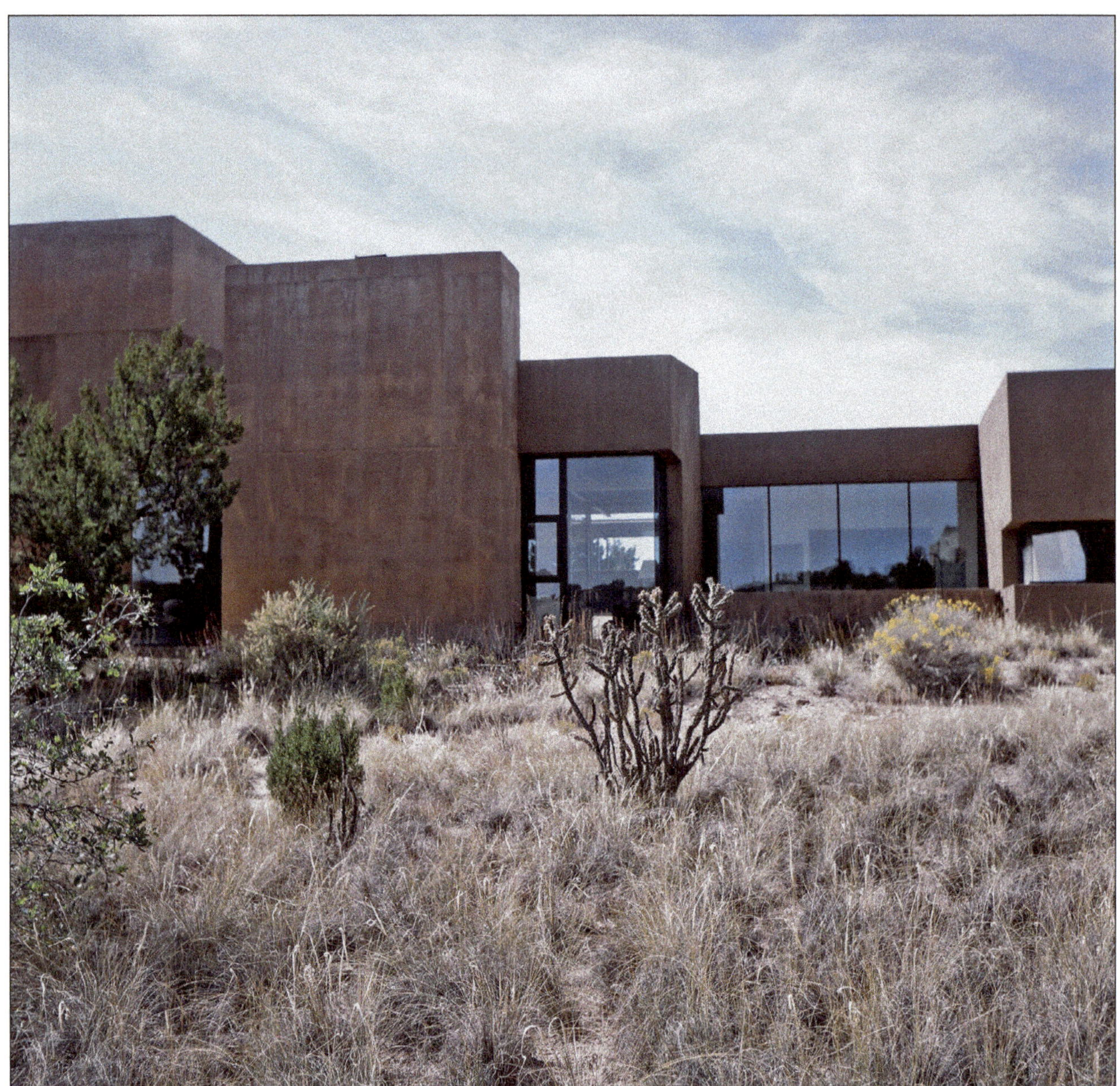

**Shadow House** on Brahma Lane was designed by Antoine Predock. The Albuquerque architect is known for his Spencer Theater in Ruidoso; the Austin City Hall; the San Diego Padres Petco Park; George Pearl Hall, home of the University of New Mexico's School of Architecture + Planning; and the awe-inspiring and architecturally awesome Canadian Museum for Human Rights, among many other projects. The 2000-2002 Shadow House, "low-lying and earth-toned, responds to the horizontality and fracturing of the surrounding mesas," according to the 2006 book *Antoine Predock Architect 4*. "The Shadow House is an abstract journey through the high desert, a convergence of earth, wind, fire, and water, bridging sunrise and sunset." Speaking of the "high desert" (Santa Fe is sited on an arid plateau, nearly a mile and a half above sea level, but it is not technically desert), the foreground here shows typical native flora, including, at center, a common cactus variously called tree cholla, cane cholla, and walkingstick cholla. The wonderful interior of this abode includes a 23-foot tower-foyer with a large, suspended glass prism; a 720-square-foot water-activated sloped stone "courtyard"; and a galaxy of steel blinds and trellises that play light and shadow from both sun and moon on assertively honest walls of form-marked concrete.

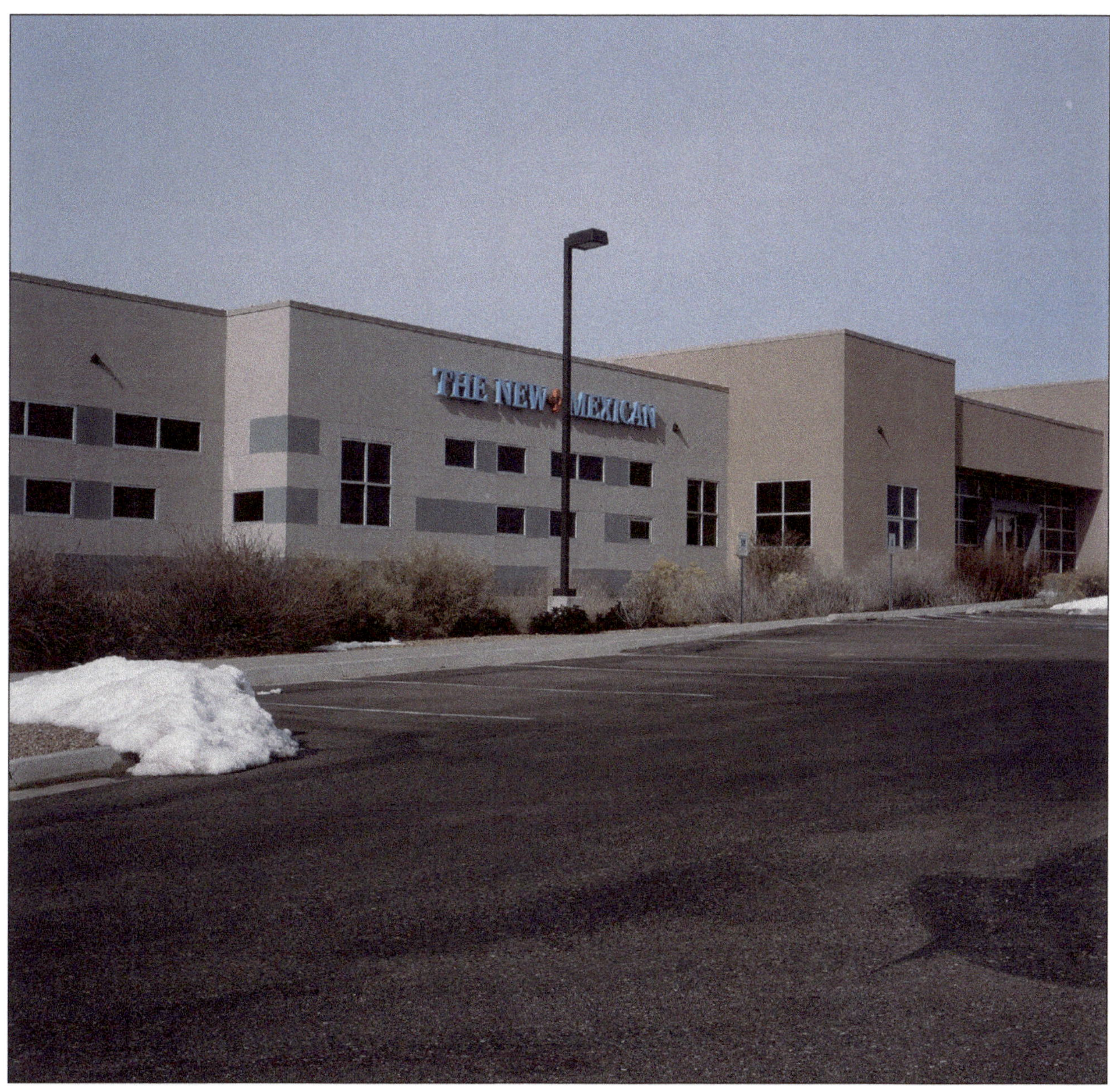


**Santa Fe New Mexican printing/circulation facility**, 1 New Mexican Plaza. The local newspaper's owner, Robin McKinney Martin, built this satellite office on the south side of the city, near Interstate 25, in 2004. The $21.5 million, 61,518-square-foot building was designed by Spears Architects in collaboration with Robert Dashiell, Inc, of Norfolk, Va. The program includes offices for production and circulation staff, a capacious room for the KBA Comet printing press and related operations, and facilities for newsprint delivery and newspaper distribution. "Using earthen colors found from the surrounding areas, the building complements the color palette of Northern New Mexico and sits in the landscape with splendor and ease," according to a Spears statement. Contemporary design was chosen for its relative affordability and as a symbol of the daily's progressive character. The arrangement of windows and adjacent gray panels and bands on the exterior was meant to evoke news type.

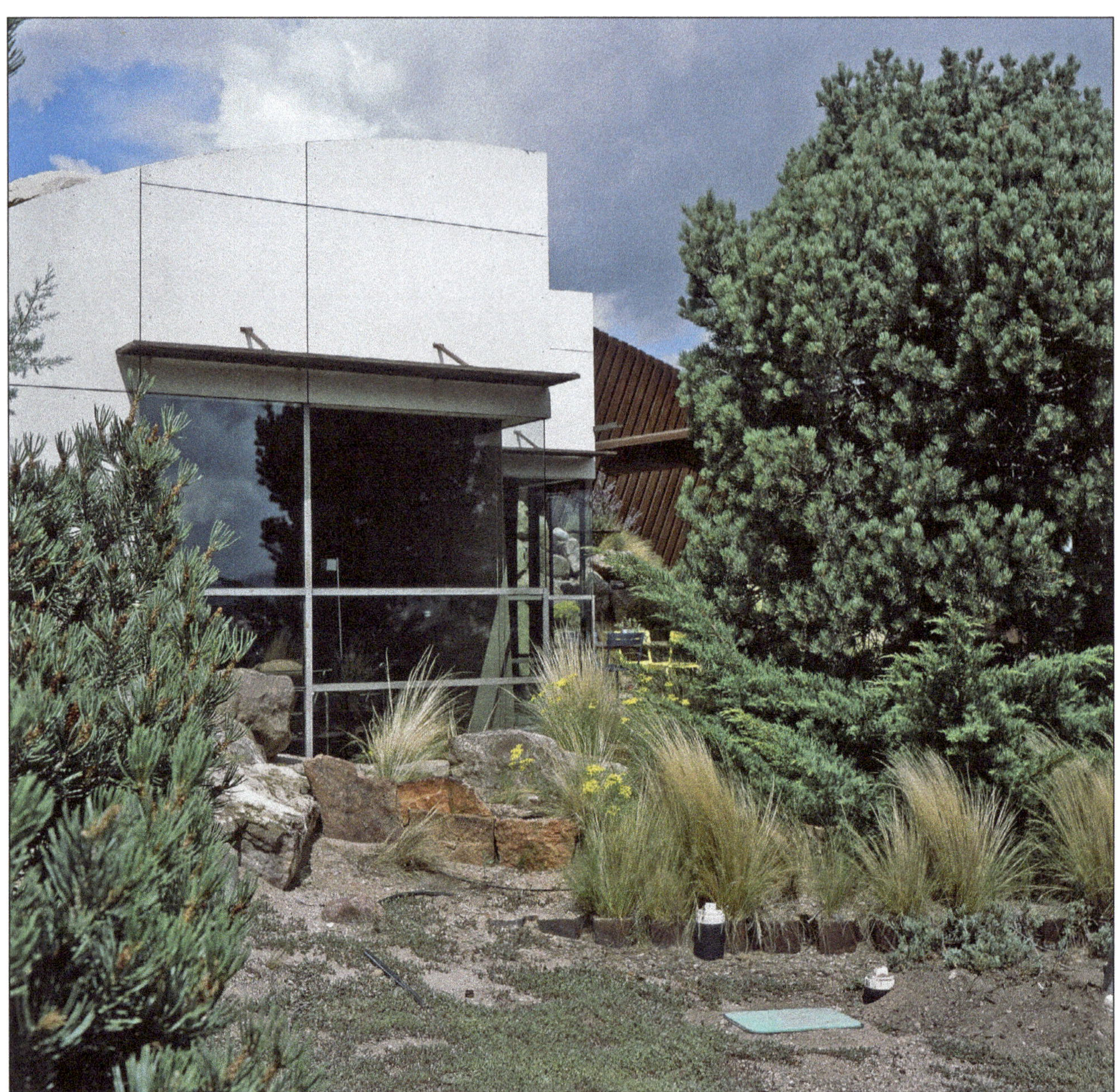

**Jeff Harnar house** on N. El Rancho Road. This exhilaratingly labyrinthine residence was designed and built by architect Harnar (1954-2006) as a home for himself and his wife, Lori. Just three miles from the Santa Fe Plaza, it is a small (1,650 square feet) masterpiece of contemporary design and original thinking. The house's walls of fiber-cement panels and steel-framed sheets of glass are joined outside by rusted-metal shades and cylinders. On the interior, most fiber-cement walls are ivory, but some are slate gray — and various panels push-spring out to reveal storage spaces or a television hollow. There are few doors; private rooms seem to be "hidden" around corners. The wood-paneled kitchen and concrete-topped island are subtly wedge-shaped, while the wall panels in the master bedroom are energetically canted. "I think architecture, like art, is a reflection of the times, of the culture, of the place where it was created, and of the people it was created for, and essentially that's what guides me," Harnar told me (for *The Santa Fe New Mexican*) in 2004. Four years later, during an event held at this house for the Jeff Harnar Award for Contemporary Architecture, architect Steve Oles called the building "a fantastic piece of art."

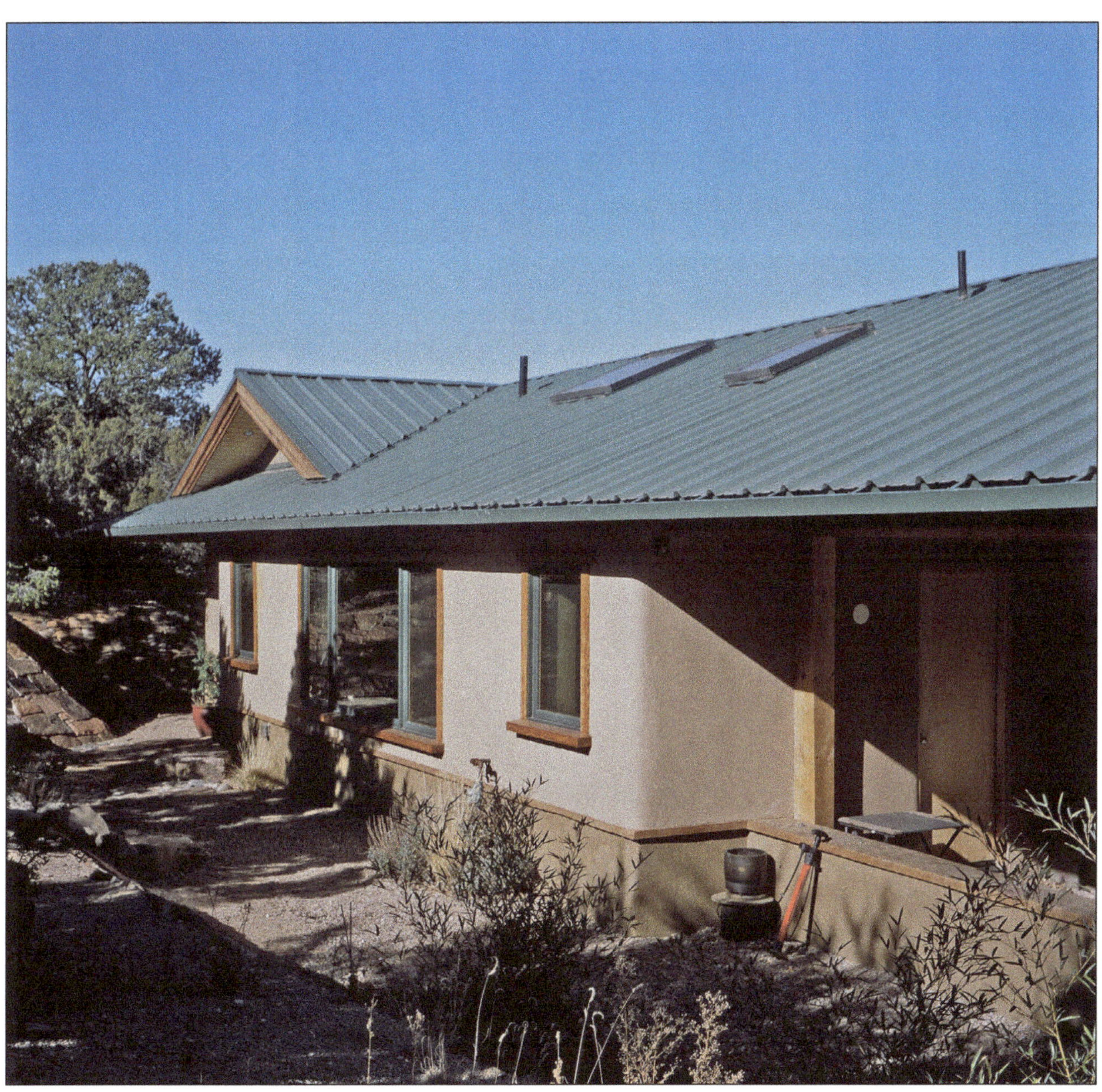

**Little guest house/yoga studio**, off of Old Santa Fe Trail. This 2009 building and the 2003 main house are by architect Paula Baker LaPorte and her husband, builder Robert LaPorte. Like their other small, elegant "EcoNest" homes, it features timber-frame construction with 12-inch clay/straw walls finished with natural clay plasters on the inside and lime plasters on the exterior. Earlier in her career, Baker realized she was suffering from toxic chemicals in building materials. She became a devotee of Building Biology, a construction philosophy and science that originated in Germany in the early 1960s. She teamed up with physician Erica Elliott and environmental health scientist John Banta to write *Prescriptions for a Healthy House: A Practical Guide for Architects, Builders and Homeowners* (1997). Baker practiced in Santa Fe for many years and wrote a monthly column titled "Healthy Home Corner" for *The New Mexican's* Santa Fe Real Estate Guide magazine from 2008 to 2010. The couple now lives and works in Oregon.

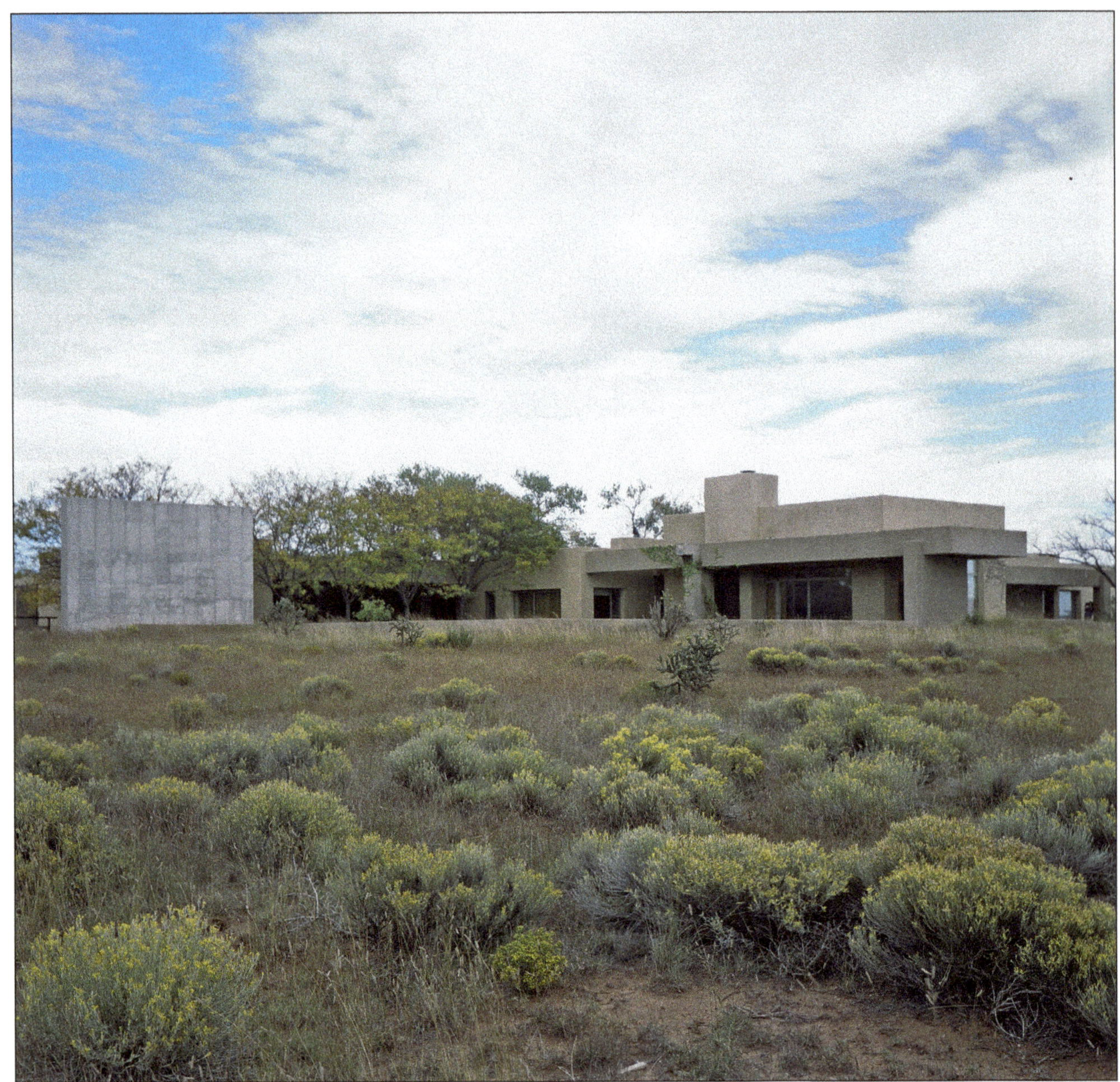

**Saddleback Ranch** in Galisteo won the inaugural Jeff Harnar Award for Contemporary Architecture in 2007. A creative product of architect Suby Bowden, interior designer Joe D'Urso, landscape architect Faith Okuma, and other collaborators, it was built as the residence of Emily Fisher-Landau and Sheldon Landau. The home, surrounded by thousands of acres of ranch land, has a broad concrete patio and pool protected from wind by a tall slab of form-marked concrete. Traditional stucco contrasts with the naked-concrete surfaces. "We did that as brutal as we could while still maintaining some elegance," Bowden said. Cantilevered planes relate to the Frank Lloyd Wright house that Fisher-Landau owned, and adored, in Rye, New York. Her desire for a massive character was satisfied with the triple-adobe walls and the concrete columns and beams. Gorgeous interior woodwork built by David Kozlowski, Greg Pratt, and Tod Williams includes gridwork panels, doors, and dividers that accentuate the hues in the fine plastered walls.

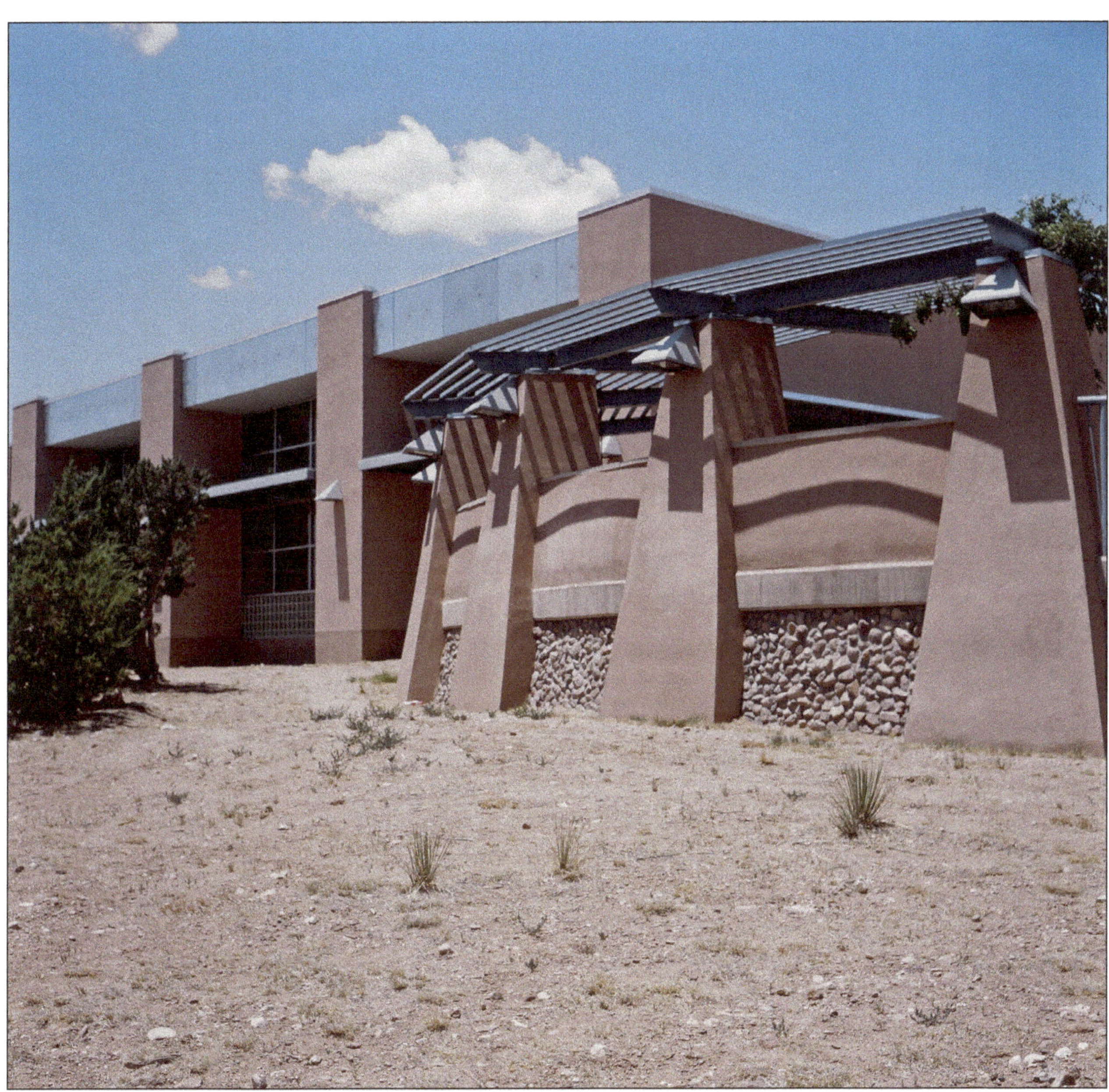

**Southside Library**, 6599 Jaguar Drive, opened in 2007 in the large Tierra Contenta subdivision in south Santa Fe. The 25,000-square-foot library was designed by Isaac Benton of Integrated Design & Architecture, Albuquerque, in partnership with Harvey Monroe of Terraplen Architects and Planners, Santa Fe. This photo of the southeast corner shows a long, glazed wall topped with a fascia of steel panels designed by Jimmy Romero, an artist known for his works in the stamped-tin tradition that dates to Spanish Colonial times. The central library section is flanked by rounded patios with river-stone veneer along the bottom, which was meant to create a transition to the landscape. The north-facing library front features a central entrance beneath a tall porch roof. Sustainable-design points show in the ample daylighting, passive-solar heating, and large silver-steel cisterns that store rainwater for irrigating landscaping.

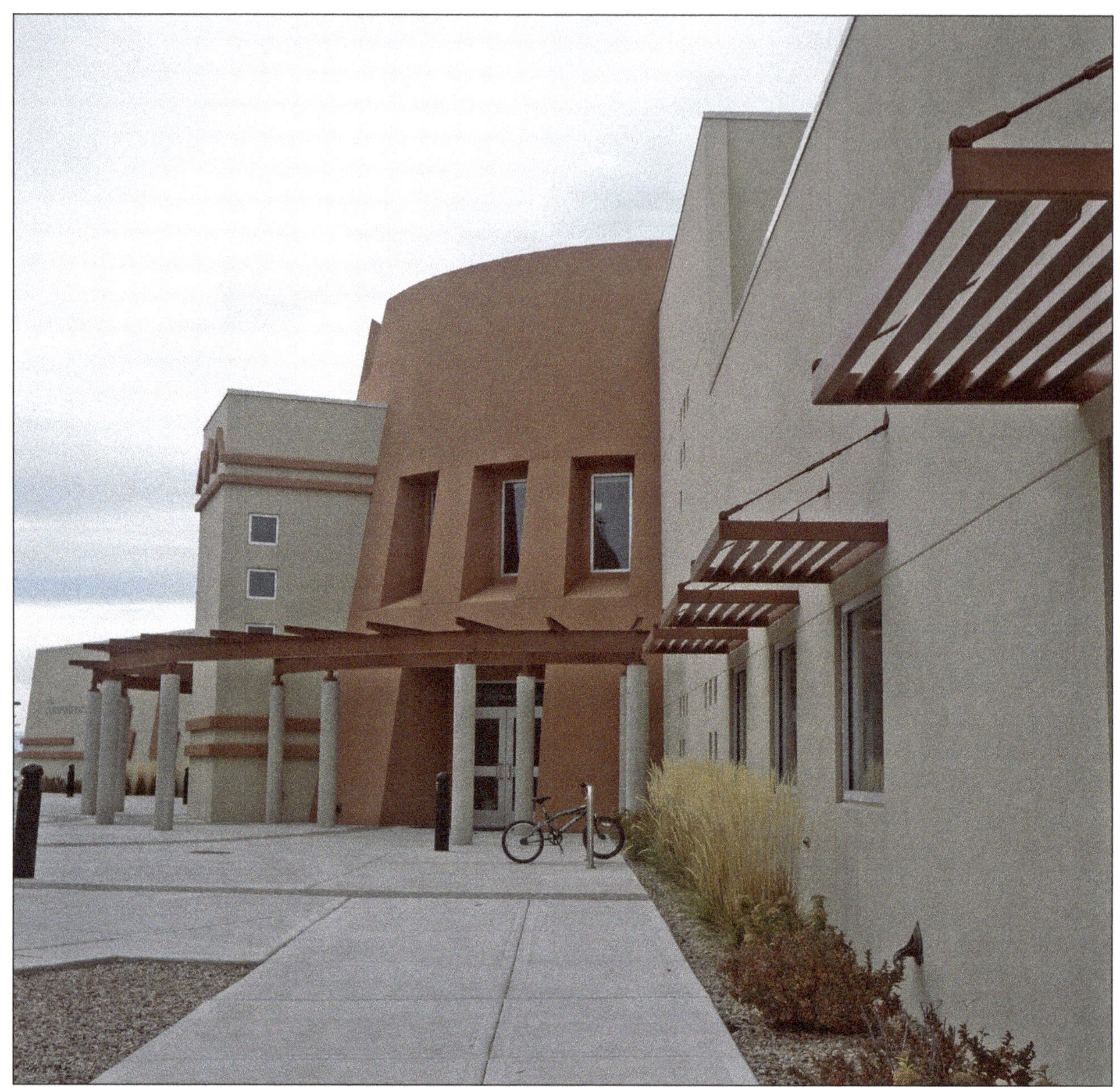

**IAIA Center for Lifelong Education**, 83 A Van Nu Po. This is one of the prominent buildings on the campus of the Institute of American Indian Arts that was designed by Diné architect Dyron Murphy. It articulates off of a circular plan with a large, central Dance Circle plaza in the center. Closer in, there are long, curved trellises marking concentric circles "like a stone dropped in a pond," as Paul Fragua describes them. Fragua (Jemez Pueblo) was project coordinator during the 1990s planning and development of the campus. That circular layout is a vestige of the original plan by noted Canadian architect Douglas Cardinal (Blackfoot-Métis); many other of his design elements were dropped as too expensive. Other buildings on the stunning IAIA campus were designed by Weller Architects, Sinkpe Architects Planners, and BPLW Architects.

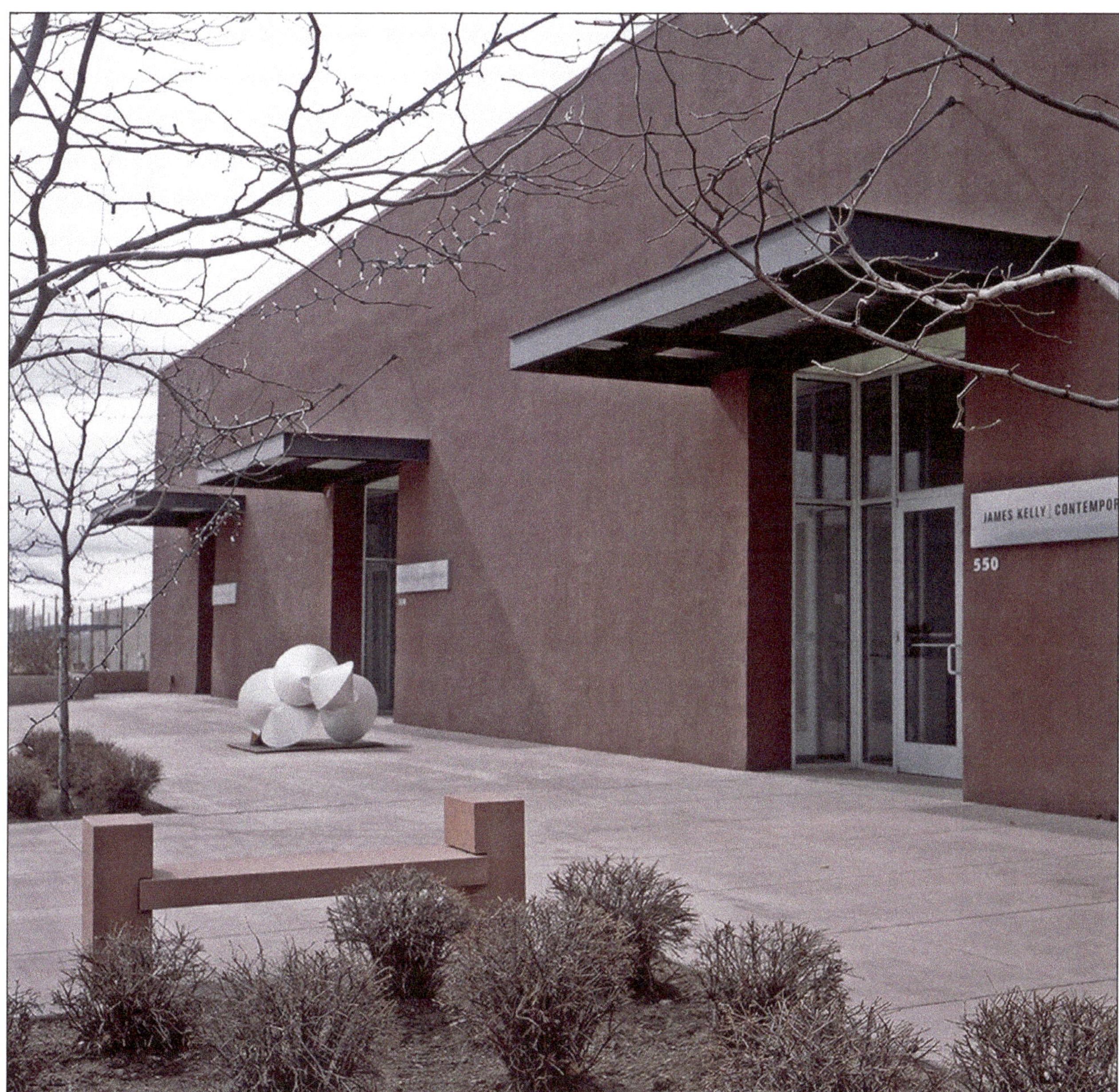


**Railyard Galleries** on S. Guadalupe Street at Paseo de Peralta began with an adaptive re-use project (which won a 2008 New Mexico Historic Preservation Award) by architects Devendra Narayan Contractor and Deirdre Harris. That was a remodel of a Sears warehouse built in the 1950s by Hansen Lumber. The scale and feeling of a warehouse were preserved, including by leaving the heavy wood posts and ceiling joists visible, but the building was updated with beautifully contrasting steel and glass elements. The project was one of the early achievements in the city's substantial revitalization of the 1880-1940 railroad district a half-mile southwest of the Santa Fe Plaza. Contractor next replaced the old Morelli Building, which was actually two structures up against one another. The new galleries honor that separation and benefited from a study the team undertook of historic materials and precise building placements. The two halves of the new building differ in setbacks, roof heights, and finish, one having corrugated-metal paneling and the other (shown here) stucco in a red that echoes the district's old brick buildings and railroad boxcars. The hanging canopies seen here are permitted shade structures in the Santa Fe Railyard, but the *portales* common in the downtown historic district are not.

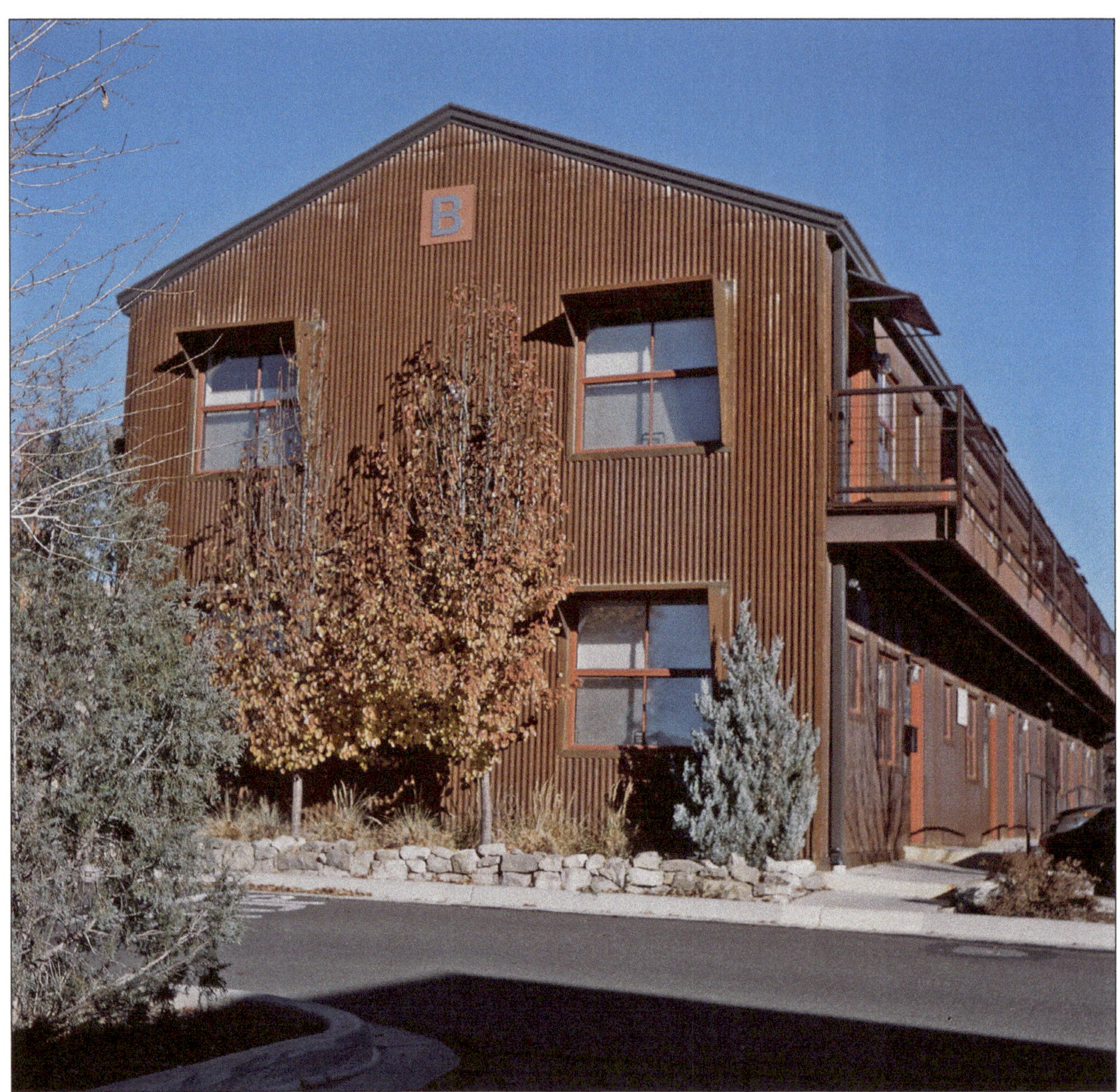


**Lena Street Lofts**, 1600 Lena Street. In December 2009, Ellis/Browning Architects Ltd. won an American Institute of Architects-Santa Fe "Citation Award" for this project. Lisette Ellis and her husband and partner Joe Browning offered their thanks to developers/builders/owners Rick and Rachel Brenner "for their commitment to this vision of an affordable industrial village." The lofts, occupying both new buildings and a remodeled structure, provide spaces for Iconik Coffee Roasters, HoCoFab Furniture, and many other businesses. The exteriors are characterized by red-rusted metal siding and continuous second-floor balconies with steel-and-cable railings.

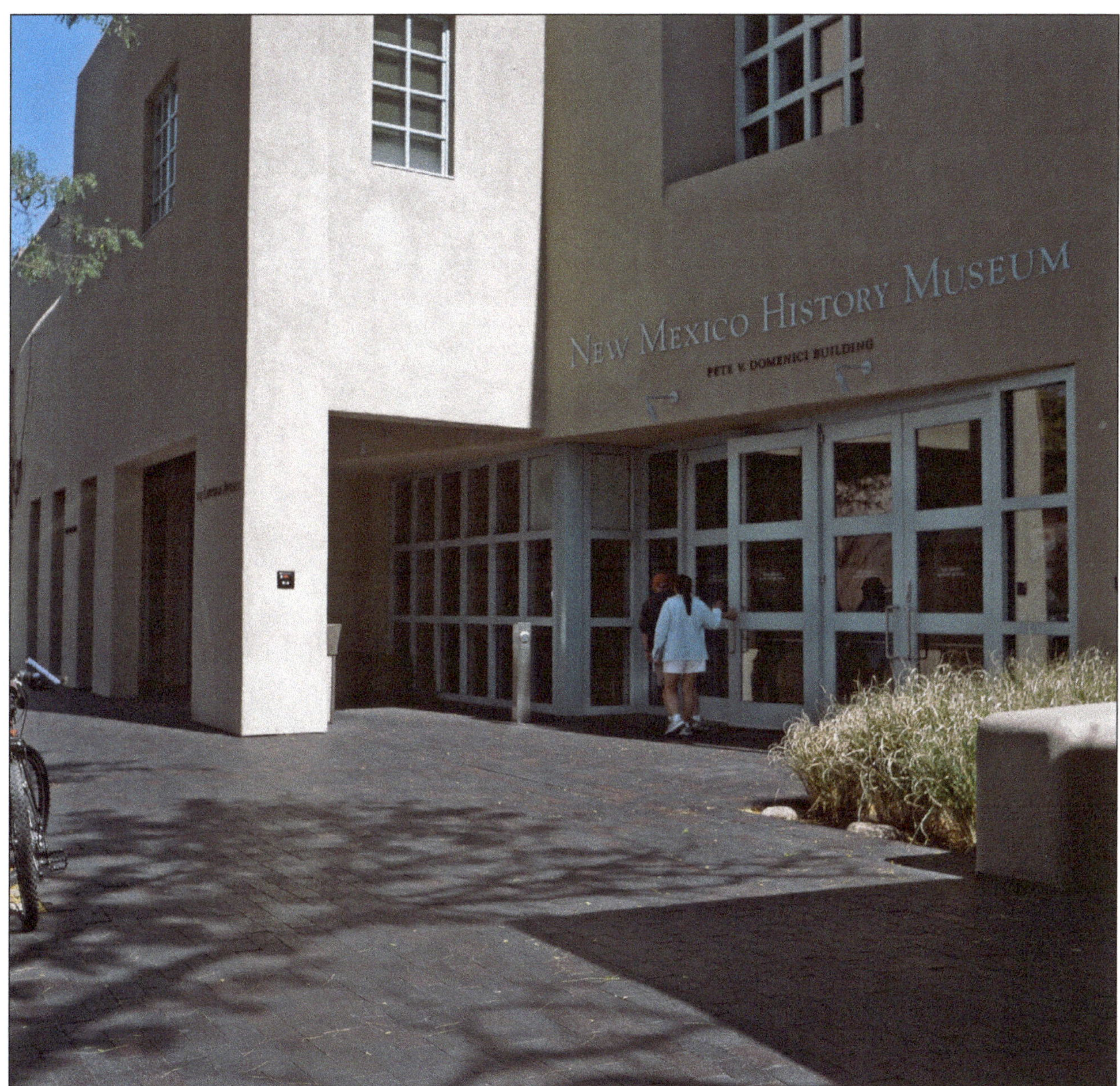


**New Mexico History Museum**, 113 Lincoln Avenue. The first part of this $35 million museum project was the demolition of the 1912 Elks Building and most of the 1909 National Guard Armory; preserved was a meeting room for the Palace of the Governors that had been remodeled by John Gaw Meem in 1939. Architects Conron & Woods of Santa Fe and Dagit-Saylor of Philadelphia had to "keyhole" the history museum in between the meeting room and the Fray Angélico Chávez History Library. Contractors exercised special care in both demolition and construction vibrations in order not to threaten the venerable Palace — and the museum was given a glassy breezeway that affords patrons close views of the cobble foundation in the north wall of the Palace courtyard buildings. The 2008 museum totals 96,000 square feet, plus a state-of-the-art storage vault of nearly 8,400 square feet. Walls were constructed using the Nudura brand of insulating concrete forms. The main museum entrance on Lincoln Avenue is inset at one end of a softly bowed and nicely varied facade that includes a partial collonade effect that plays off a more formal feature of that sort on the First Interstate Building to the north. On Washington Avenue, a taller, harder-edged mass featuring door/window grids on both stories distinguishes the History Museum from its close neighbors. Higher masses are set back to avoid a dominating effect at the street.

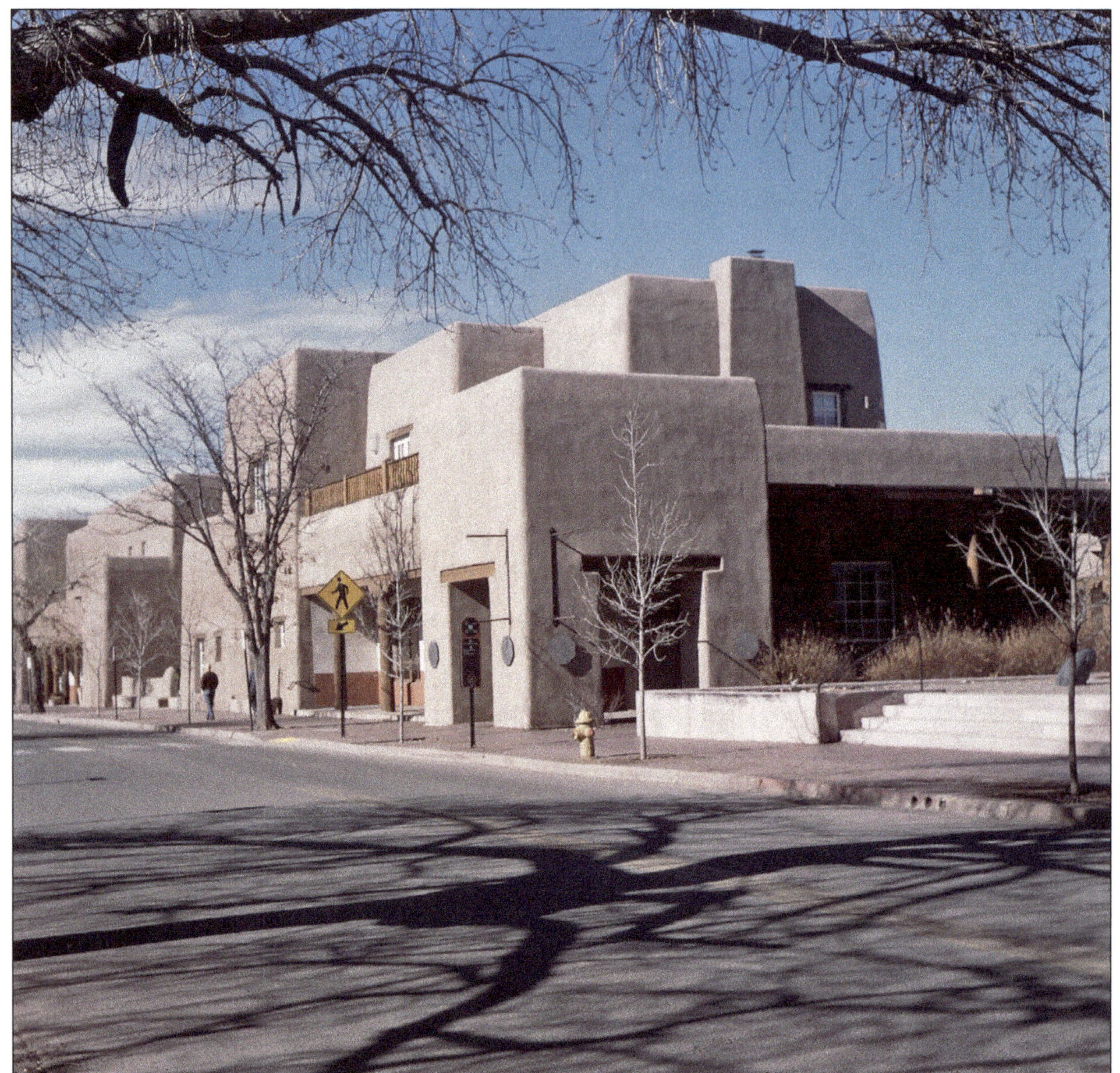

**Santa Fe Community Convention Center**, 201 W. Marcy Street, is both imposing and inviting. The steel-framed, stuccoed structure of 74,360 square feet was designed by Spears Architects in association with the Denver firm Fentress Architects. The four-year building project started with an archaeological survey (mandatory in downtown Santa Fe) that uncovered Indian architectural features and cultural artifacts dating back to the 400s. The 2008 civic center boasts long *portales* on three sides, those along Marcy Street and Grant Avenue designed as a friendlier gesture for pedestrians than long, blank walls. The walls within them sport painted wainscots, terra-cotta red facing the streets and blue facing City Hall, varying from the light earth brown of the rest of the building. Beverley Spears explained that, while massing and detailing conform to Spanish-Pueblo Revival styling, the building's close placement at the street, the large courtyard, extensive *portales*, and the *zaguan* are Spanish Colonial Revival elements. The prominent arch entry is a result, in part, of her affection for Spanish Colonial architecture to the south — witness her photography-rich 2017 book *Early Churches of Mexico: An Architect's View* — and its role in the development of Santa Fe. Overall, the convention center's masses possess a pleasing variety, and the rhythm of the fenestration is not fussily symmetrical. The building boasts an inviting 6,600-square-foot courtyard.

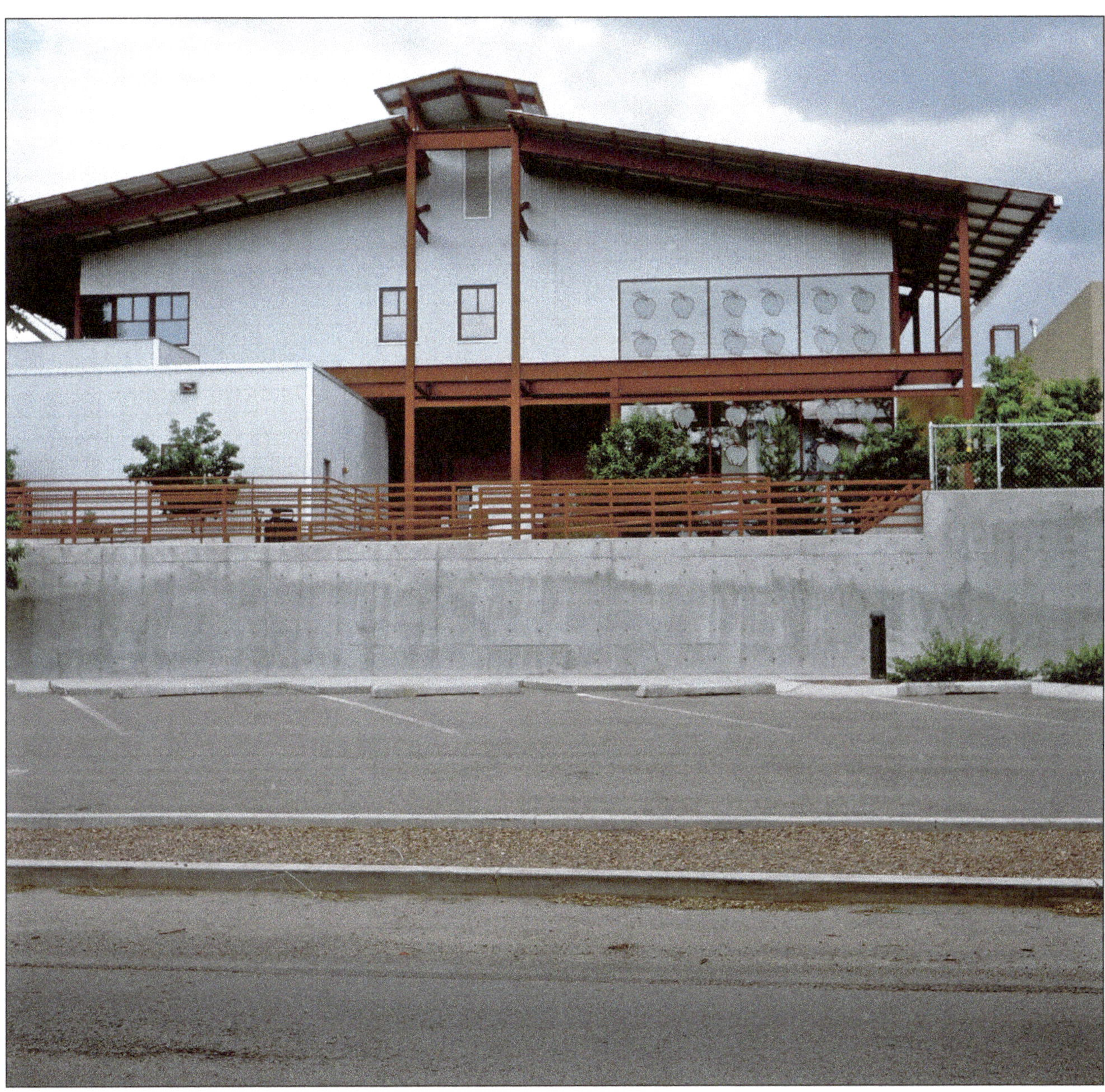

**Tesuque Elementary School addition**, 1555 Bishop's Lodge Road. This second-story addition was designed by Tom and Sara Easterson-Bond of WoodMetalConcrete Architecture. The traditional importance of agriculture in the community and region inspired the barn-like aspect with its a tall, pitched-roof facade and central "cap" roof that helps hide rooftop mechanicals. The architects worked within tight budget constraints to contrive a complex but pleasing variety, contrasting the silvery corrugated-metal skin with the red-steel structural members and including a bank of tall windows bearing etched images of apples; a kindergarten pod at front left to balance the brown gymnasium on the right side; and a short wall of naked, form-marked concrete at front. Tom Easterson-Bond told *The New Mexican* that a complicated structure is hidden beneath the 2008 building's boxy exterior: "This is one of those neat buildings that flexes and bends, so it's in tension and compression across a new concrete slab surface, which floats on steel members." The couple also renovated the circa-1930 adobe school to accommodate the school's library.

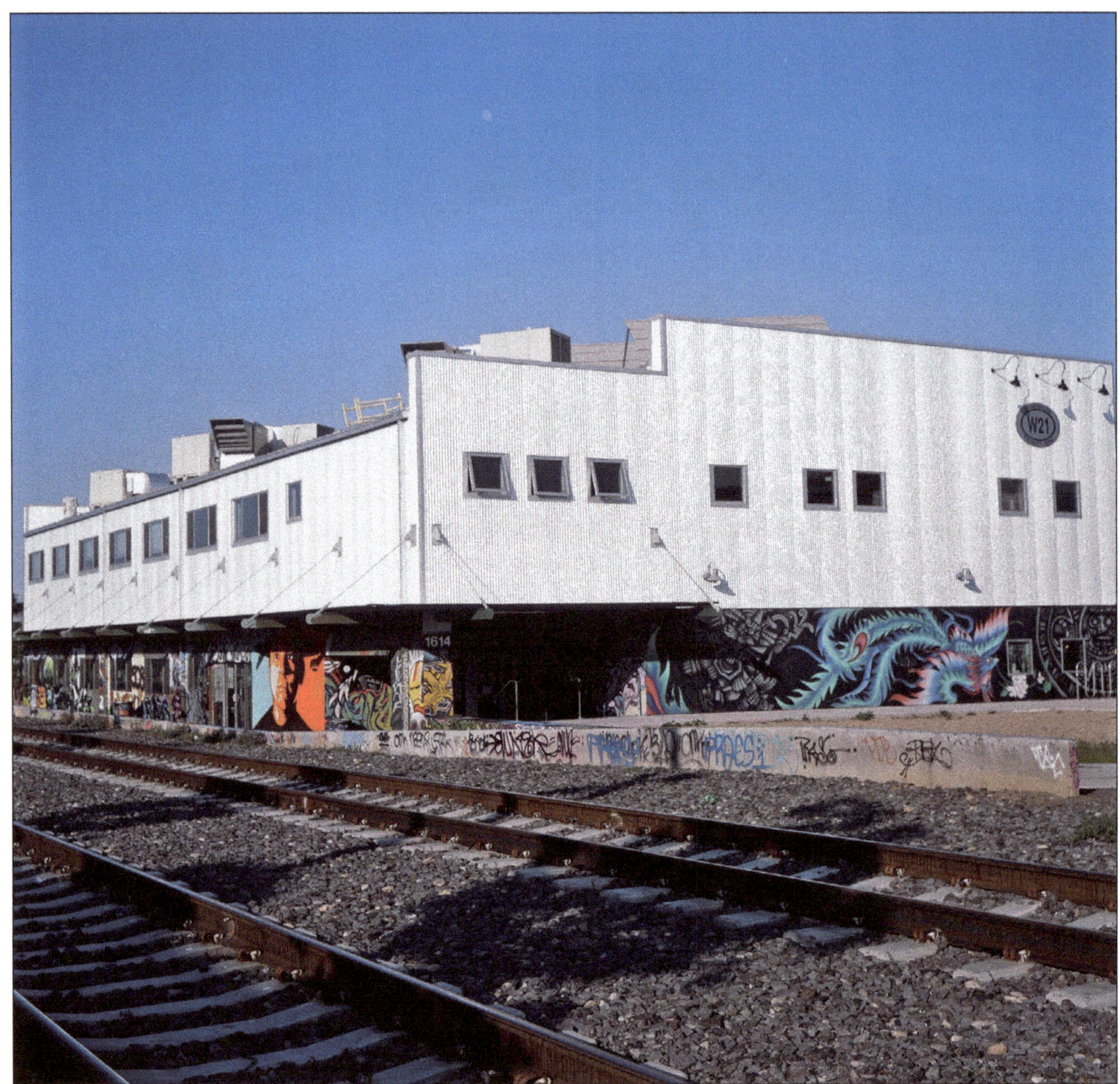


**Warehouse 21/Studio Center of Santa Fe**, 1614 Paseo de Peralta. The firm Mazria Odems Dzurec (and later Alexander Dzurec's Autotroph) designed this 2008 building as a flexible "core and shell structure" with performance spaces for art, music, and theater and to accommodate evolutionary changes in the program. That's a good thing, because in late 2017 Ana Gallegos y Reinhardt resigned as director after 21 years, and the advisory board she created moved to expand the teen center to also serve young peope in their 20s and 30s with artist studios, mentoring, and career training. Dzurec's exterior is corrugated metal — in sync with the Santa Fe Railyard's industrial vibe — with stucco at the ground level designed to provide a changing mural canvas for the participants. Sustainability elements in the 2008 building, which is more than four times larger than the original W21 digs in an old warehouse, include solar hot-water panels and "sunbender" skylight features to maximize daylighting. In October, 2019, it was announced that Warehouse 21, in this location since its founding in 1996, would depart by the year's end.

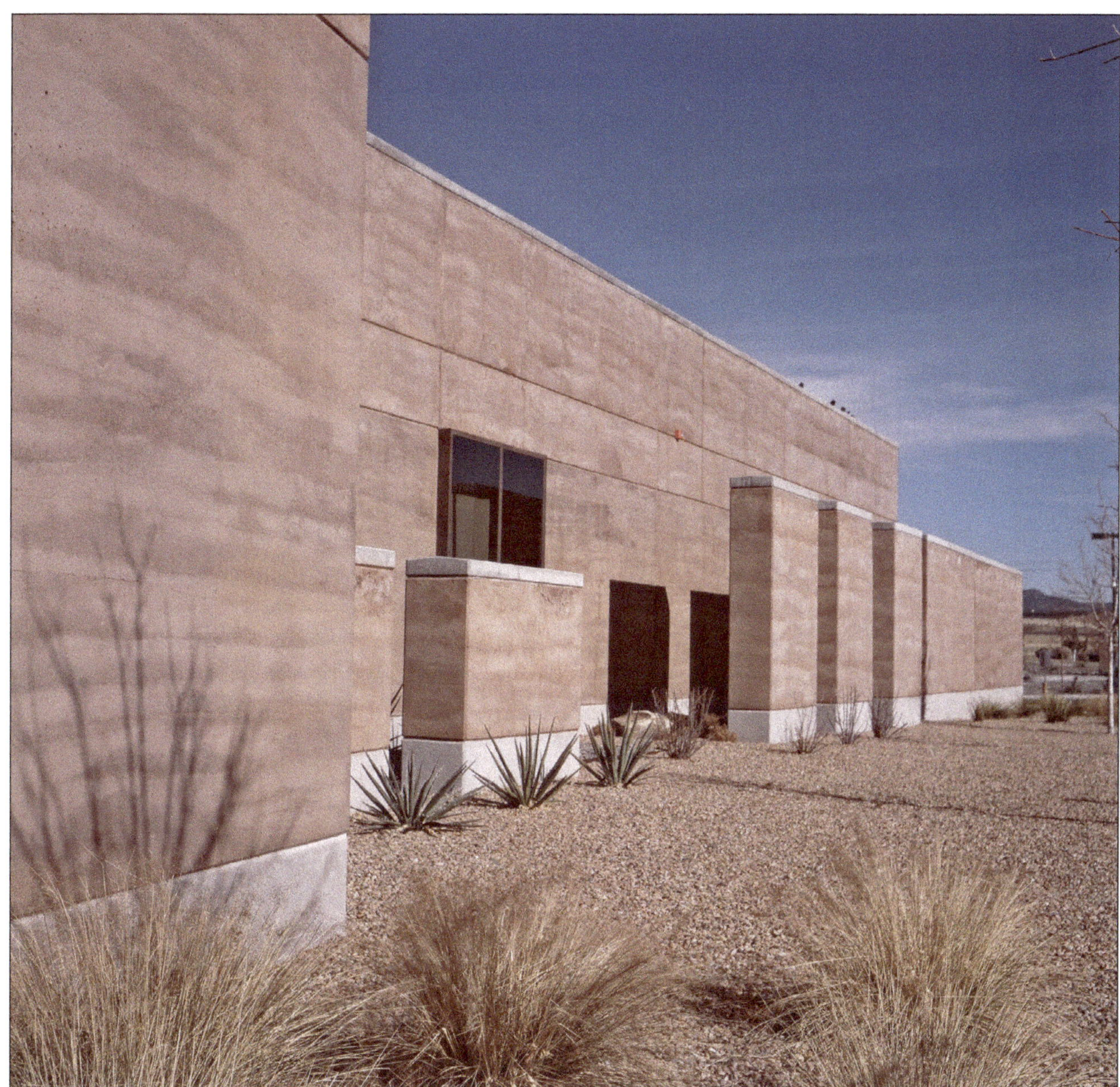

**PERA Building**, 33 Plaza La Prensa, is beautiful and interesting, for one reason because it is a contemporary government building boasting rammed-earth construction. The new headquarters of the state's Public Employees Retirement Association answered the mandate that local materials should be used. Conron & Woods Architects of Santa Fe and Leo A. Caly Company of Phoenix worked together on the design of this 35,000-square-foot building that combines modern steel framing and concrete stem walls and bond beams with 24-inch rammed-earth (*pisé de terre*) walls that offer excellent insulation and relate to important historic qualities. In a visit to the new building for a 2009 Pasatiempo story, architect Roy L. Woods said, "Adobe immediately came up, but since the 1930s we've been smearing concrete stucco on adobe buildings and hiding what they are." The design team liked the earth technique not only for its honesty but because its layering resembles the old Pueblo process of building puddled-adobe walls. Contrasting with the pinkish earth walls are rusted Corten beam trellises at the entry and in the courtyards — the office building has four *placitas* and so also relates to the region's Spanish architectural traditions.

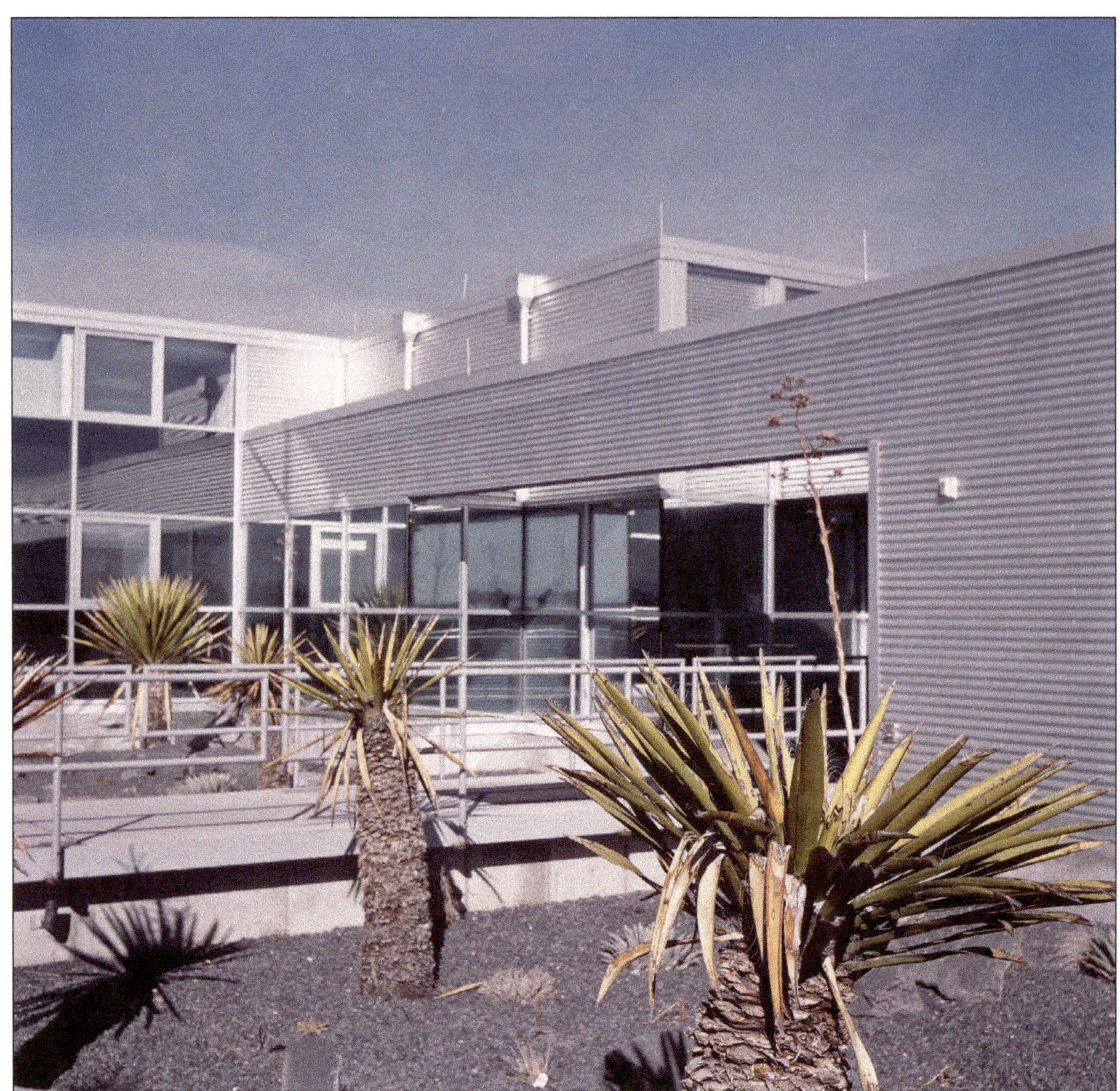

**Santa Fe County Public Works**, 424 N.M. 599. The series of bright, boxy, low-slung buildings was the vision of architect Michael Freeman. The exteriors are all glass and corrugated metal, a material that is made predominantly from recycled steel and is affordable, easy to install, and requires minimal maintenance. There are actually nine structures totaling about 45,000 square feet in the 2009 facility. Freeman located the Public Works Department's various divisions in wings, allowing for horizontal expansions that won't affect operations in neighboring divisions. Among the "green" features in the building's program are solar hydronic panels to heat water for vehicle-washing, strategic glazing for adequate daylighting, a smattering of concrete walls to provide thermal mass to moderate extreme outdoor temperatures, and an experimental wind generator to contribute operations electricity. Those concrete walls exhibit the marks left by the wall-casting forms. This is (in the late 2010s) an increasingly desirable aesthetic feature, but in this case it was also designed to broadcast "honesty," as it often was in midcentury Brutalist architecture — the architect liked the symbolic reference to the Public Works milieu.

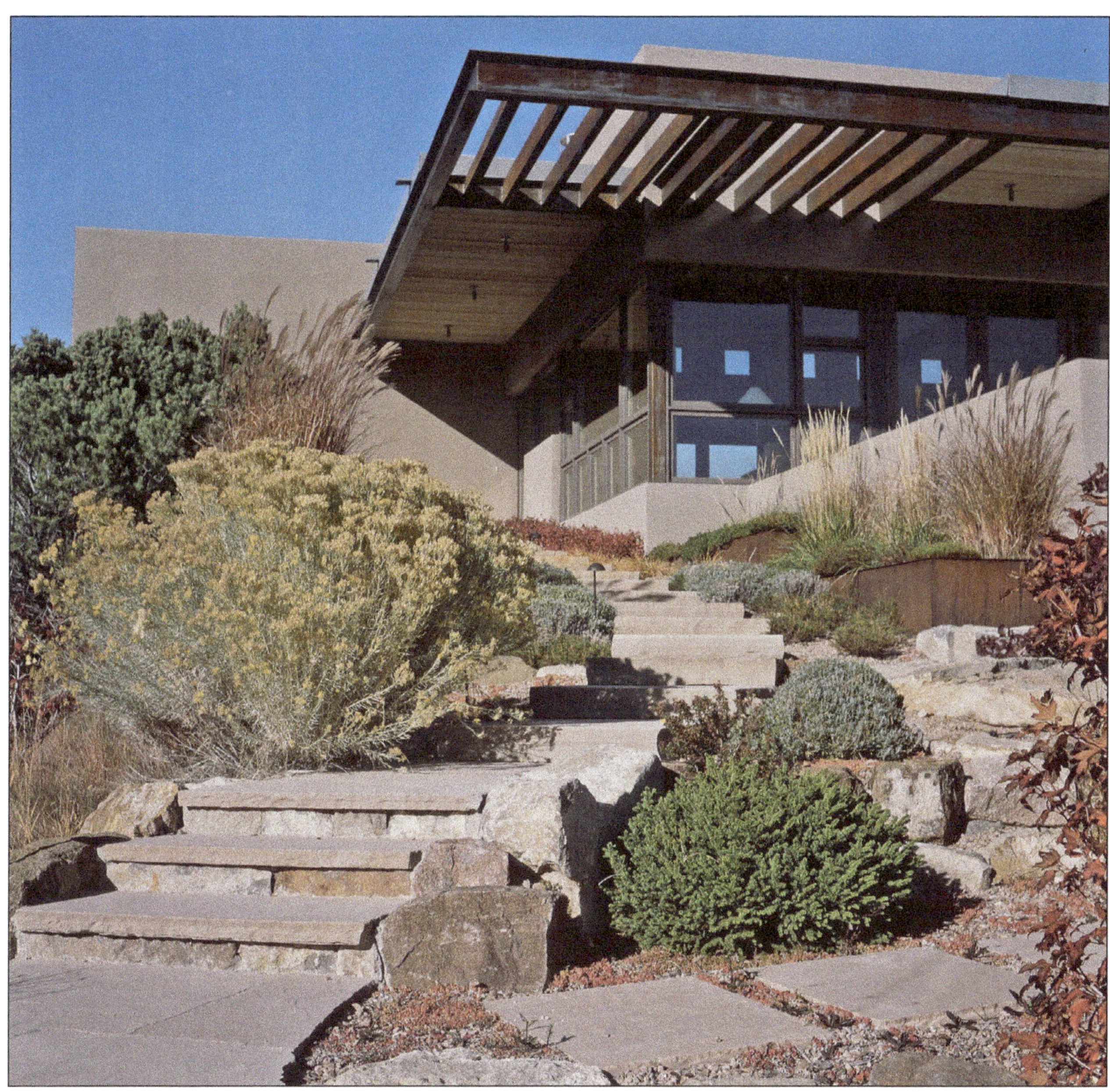

This house on **Indian Rock Lane** by architect Robert Zachry and builder Cal Thompson was designed for a challenging lot. It looks tucked into the slopy landscape and yet the house has strong universal design ("aging-in-place") credentials, with the main living area all on one level. Most of that is in one room more than 70 feet long and boasting a lovely palette: a floor of large-tile Israeli limestone, walls of hand-troweled plaster, and a ceiling of dark steel I-beams supporting whitewashed pine planks. The patio areas are also paved with primly tiled limestone. The outdoor area in this photo includes a patio partially covered by a cantilevered wood-and-steel roof and bordered by gravel troughs inside the containing walls. Some plantings are arrayed naturalistically, while others sprout from large, rusted steel vessels. The steps lead down to a guest parking area. A lower level of the residence holds guest rooms and a multipurpose room with bar.

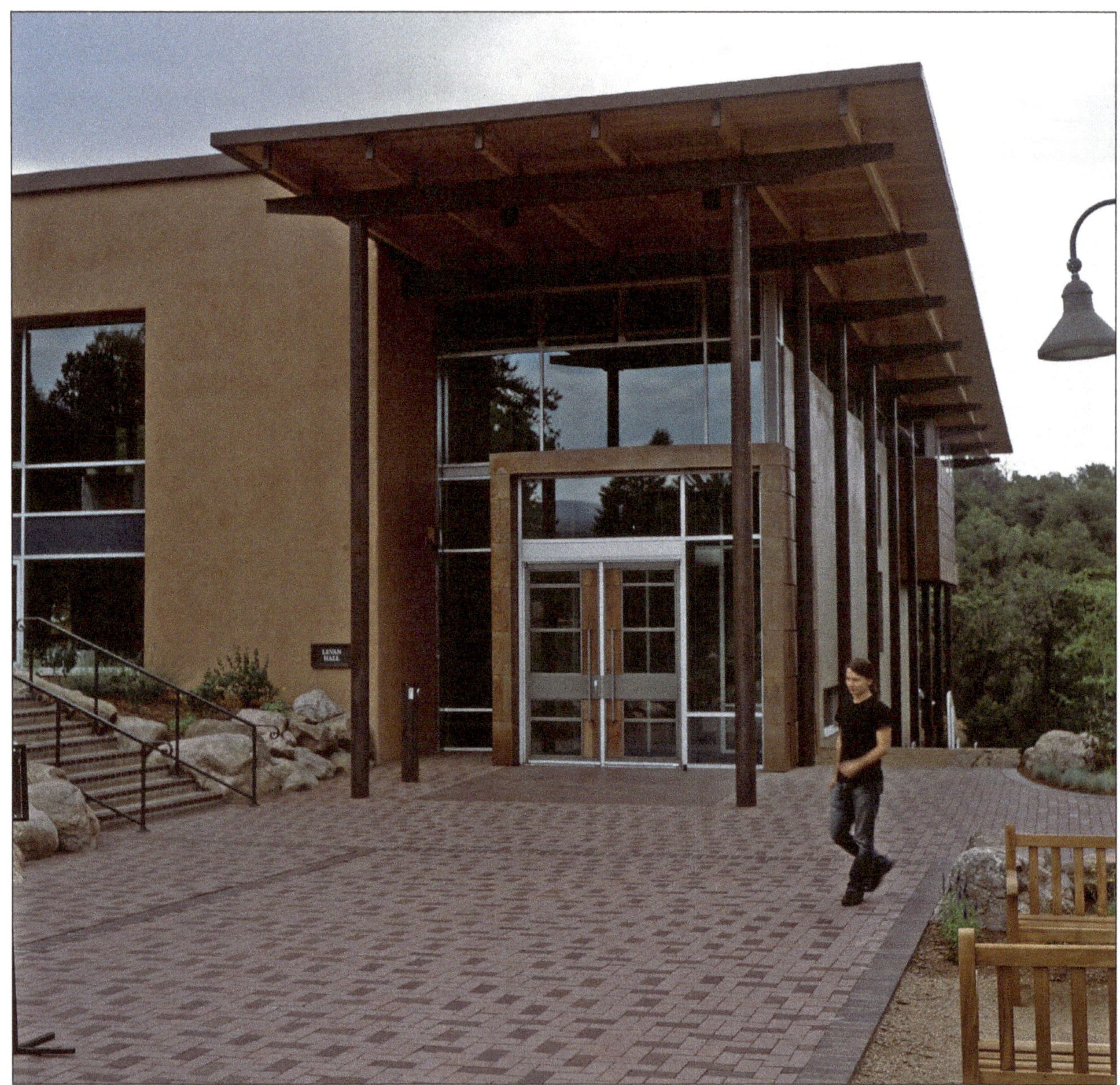


**Betty and Norman Levan Hall**, St. John's College, 1160 Camino Cruz Blanca, was designed by Lake|Flato Architects, San Antonio, and was completed in 2010. With its construction, the college's graduate program found a true home — it was previously splintered in a number of spaces around the Santa Fe campus. In an interview for the Santa Fe newspaper, the firm's David Lake told me that the dramatic, contemporary entrance — a two-story glazed *portal* — posed a desirable contrast to the historic buildings on campus. "I think Santa Fe needs to be a little more amenable to these, I think, poetic gestures, because we are building in the 21st century," he said. This was a LEED Gold project; among the green values are sustainable cork flooring, temperature-conditioning thermal mass in masonry walls, and large windows to reduce the need for daytime artificial lighting. In 2015, nearly 20 of the other buildings on the St. John's College campus, which were designed by John Gaw Meem associates Edward O. Holien and William R. Buckley, were listed on the National Register of Historic Places.

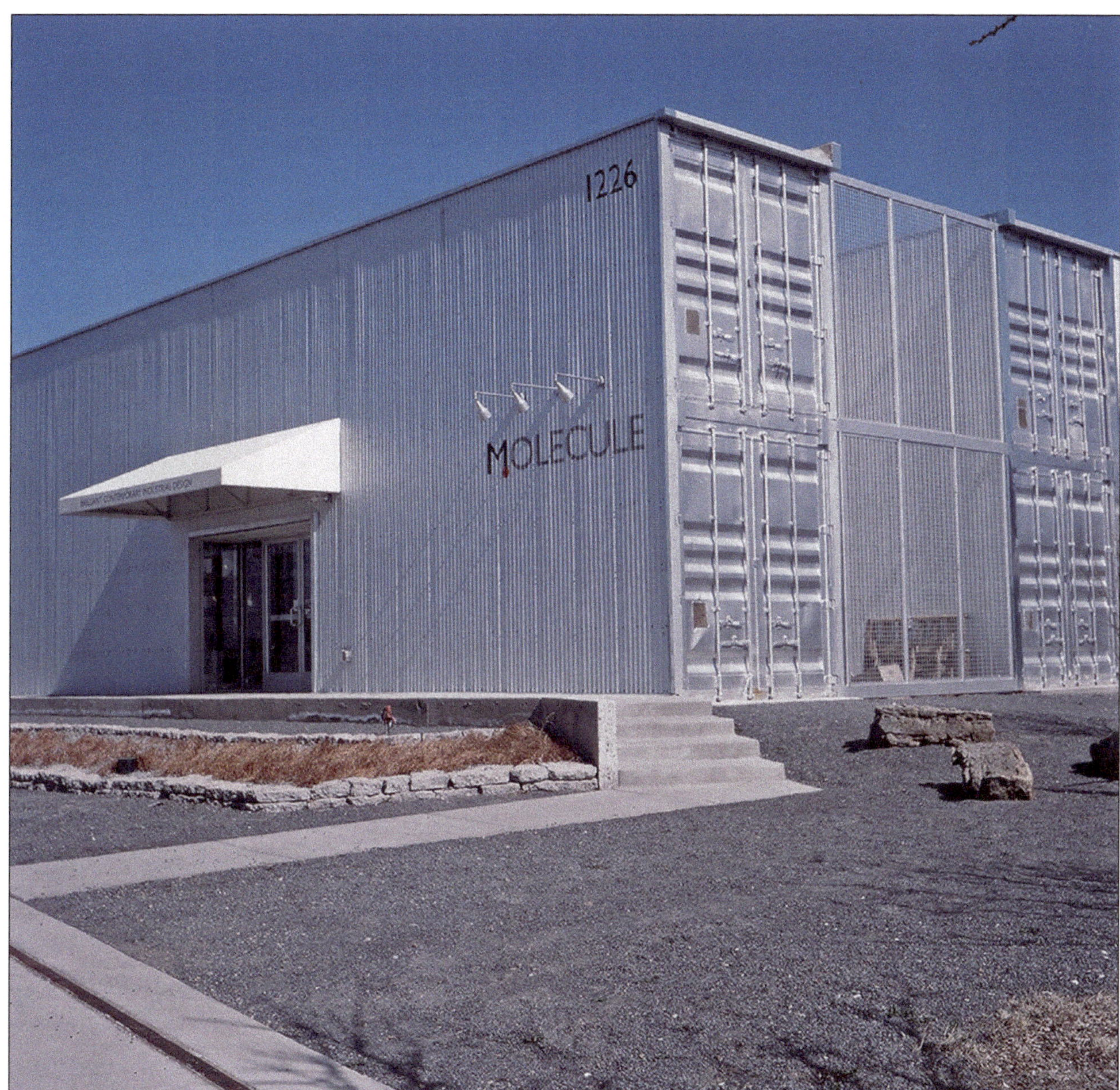


**Molecule Design**, 1226 Flagman Way. The modern-era trade imbalance has resulted in a surplus of intermodal shipping containers at U.S. ports. Adriana Siso recycled seven of these units (supplied by an Albuquerque dealer) for her beautiful Santa Fe showroom in the Baca Area of the Santa Fe Railyard. Two parallel 2-story sections of the building were built using four of the 40-foot containers. A broad space in between them was covered with translucent, white, polycarbonate material on steel framing to create a bright interior space. Siso constructed wing sections at the rear with three more shipping containers in this 2010 project that was permitted as "experimental" by the New Mexico Construction Industries Division. The showroom is insulated with several inches of sprayed foam beneath corrugated-metal sheeting on the long side surfaces. The ends of the shipping containers with their distinctive doors and locking bars were left undisguised.

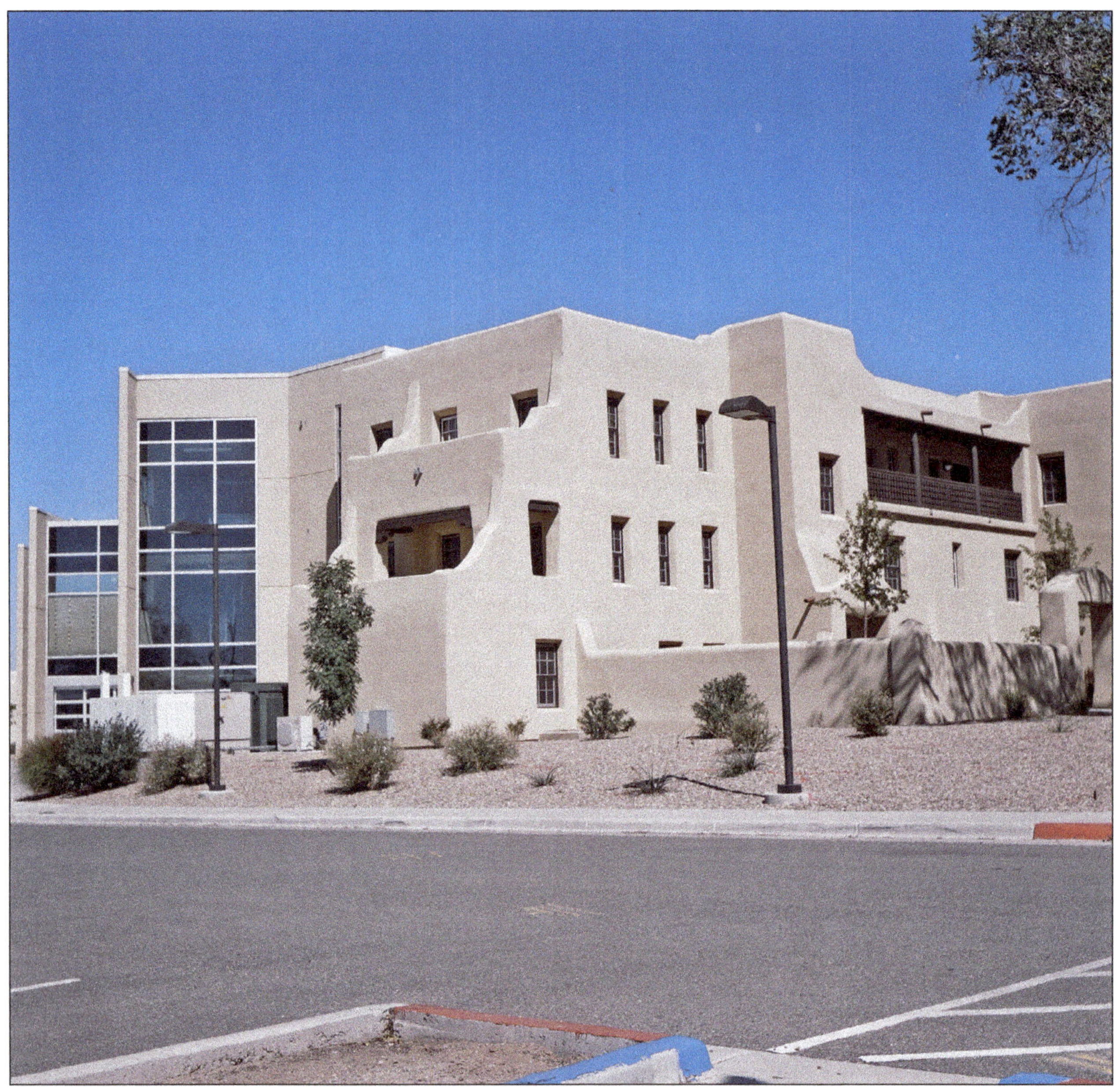

**New Mexico School For the Deaf**, 1060 Cerrillos Road, was established by the New Mexico Territorial Legislature in 1887, but it was already two years old. Lars and Belle Larson began teaching deaf students in an adobe house at the corner of Irvine and Dunlap streets in 1885. The original school house on today's campus of approximately 30 acres was built in 1891, then architect Isaac Rapp and contractor Antonio Windsor collaborated on a red-brick school building that opened in 1905. The oldest extant building is Rapp's Cartwright Hall (1916), which set a school precedent as an exemplar of the new Spanish-Pueblo Revival style. Cartwright, originally the girls' dormitory, was joined in 1928 by a boys' dorm, Connor Hall, designed by George Williamson. The school grew during the Depression years, aided by the Works Progress Administration, with the addition of the Maintenance Barn (John Gaw Meem, 1935) and Dillon Hall (Gordon Street, 1936). Extensive repairs and renovations in the early 1940s were led by Hugo Zehner of Meem and Zehner Architects and in 1978 by Kenneth Clark. In 2010, Kim Hooker of Studio Southwest Architects, Albuquerque, led a major reworking of Connor Hall (shown here), adding stucco-on-metal-frame wing-walls and remodeling classrooms to accommodate desks in crescents or circles rather than in rows (as had lamely been done in the old days), so deaf-signing students and teachers can easily see one another.

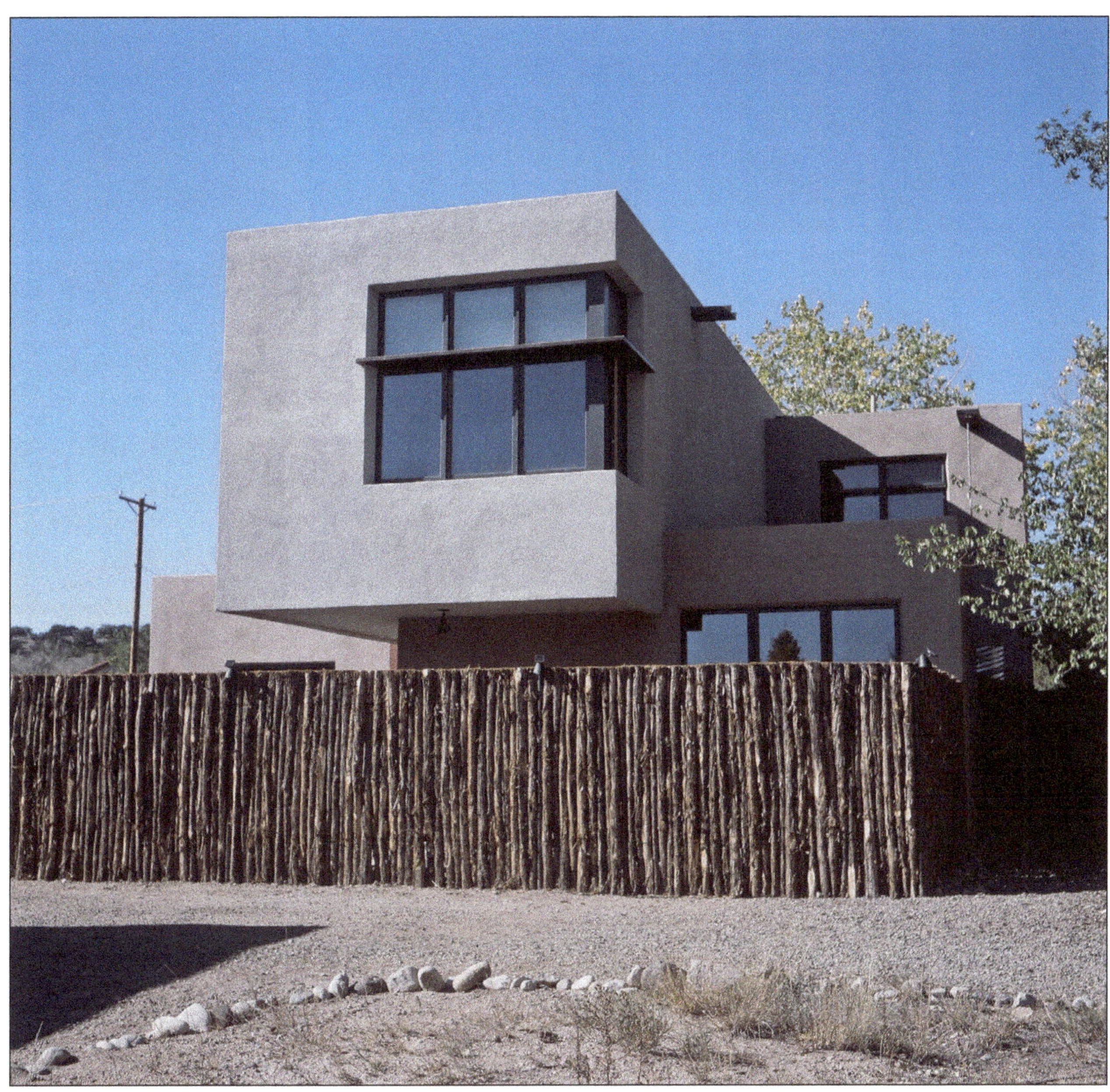

**Platinum Cantilever**, W. Alameda Street. Gabriel Browne, Praxis Design/Build, is responsible for this interesting home built to LEED Platinum standards, and at only about $189 per square foot. The clients wanted a 3-bedroom house on a 2,300-square-foot, L-shaped lot. Browne's solution was to invert the typical functions of a 2-story home. The master bedroom and studios, which are finished with tan-colored stucco, are situated on the ground floor. Above them is the cantilevered, gray-stuccoed, living room/kitchen/dining room mass with a large corner-slot window. A tall, narrow, red-colored rectangle holds the entry. A pair of tall rainwater-storage pipes in the courtyard are silvery corrugated steel, the same material the architect used in a distinctive bathroom shower. The yard is enclosed by a "coyote fence" made of *latillas* — poles of juniper or alder that were traditionally also used in roofs, laid above the *vigas*. This 2010 home is part of Tres Placitas del Rio, one of Santa Fe's oldest intentional "cohousing" communities, in which private residences are clustered around shared space.

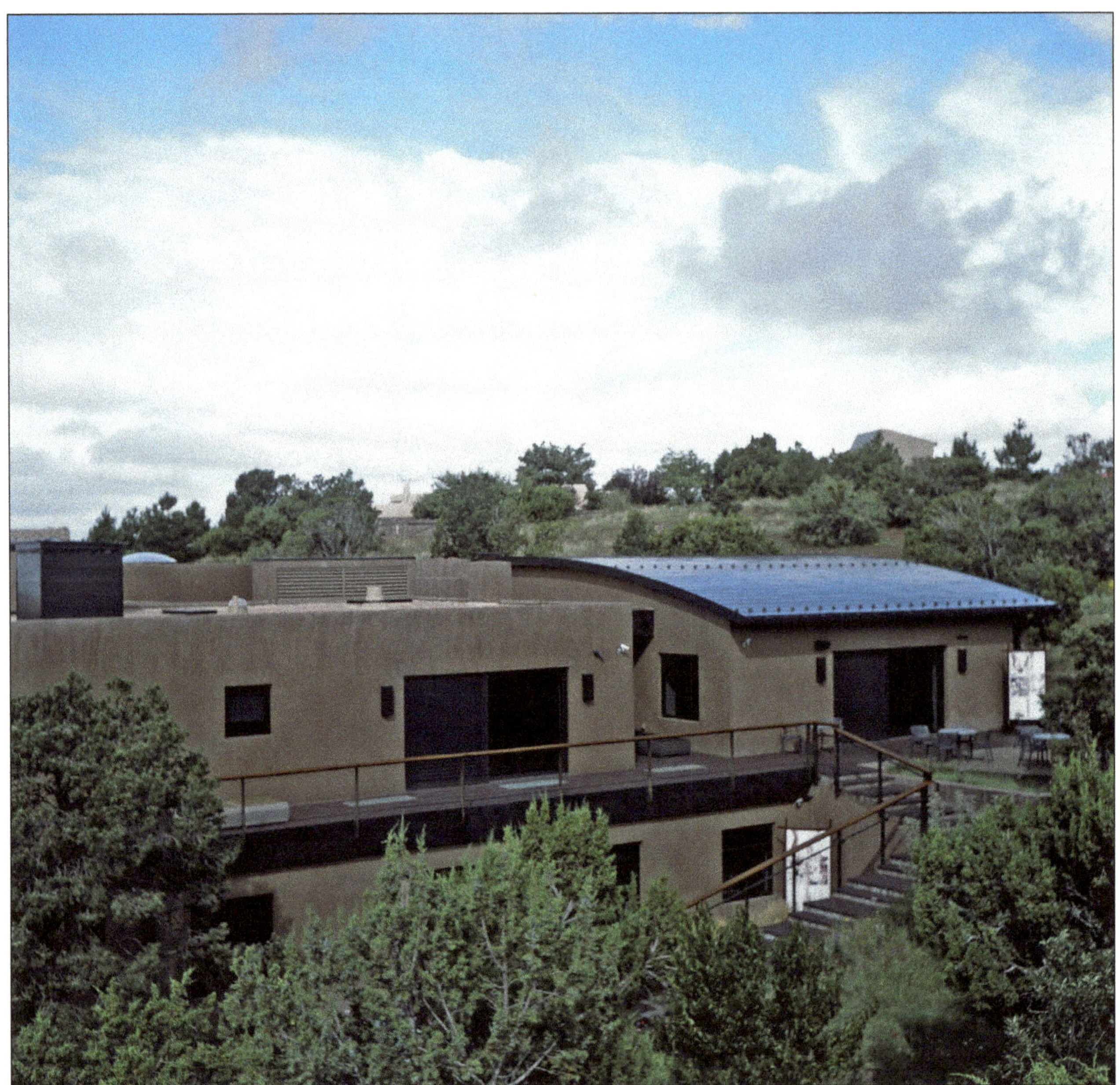

**Academy for the Love of Learning**, 133 Seton Village Road. Catherine Fletcher-Leriche, then with Spears Architects, had the lead on this Center at the Academy for the Love of Learning. The campus was developed on the site that long held the "Seton Castle" building erected in 1930 by naturalist and writer Ernest Thompson Seton; that structure burned down in 2005. The center has a circular, adobe meditation and contemplation room, but most of the walls were constructed of insulating concrete forms. Leriche involved *feng shui* practitioner Valmai Howe in the 2011 project design, which includes massive sliding doors that create expansive glass surfaces; a barrel roof; and a wraparound cable-rail balcony. A ground-source heat pump, wood flooring from sustainably harvested forests, photovoltaic and solar hydronic panels, and earth berming to moderate indoor temperatures earned the 14,000-square-foot building the "Gold" standard in the LEED green-building certification system.

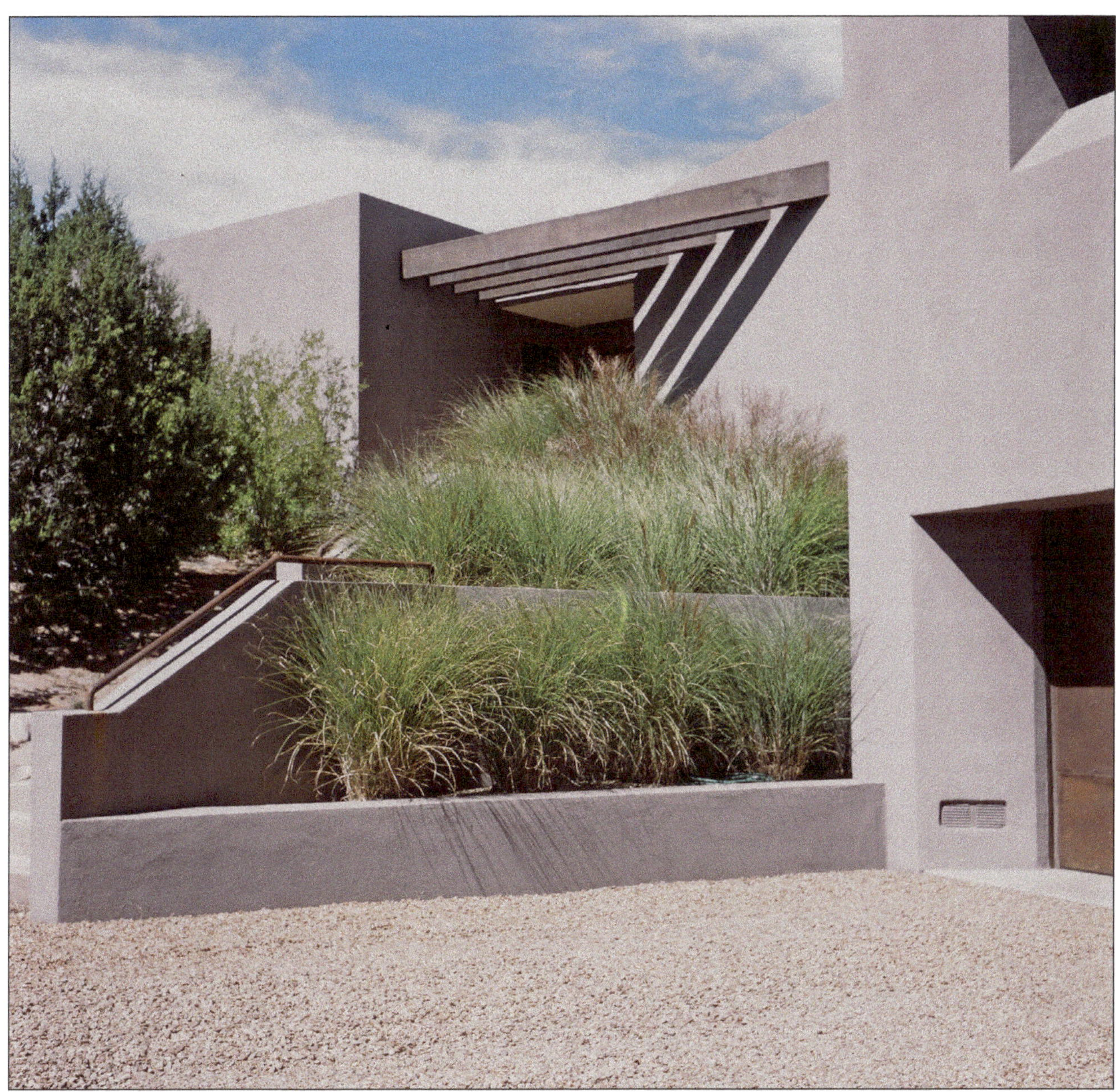

**Oles/Thompson residence** on City Lights. Architect Paul Stevenson "Steve" Oles (co-founder of the American Society of Architectural Illustrators) completed his Santa Fe house in 2011. Arriving, we see an assemblage of blocky forms with deeply chamfered openings, an entry stairway handsomely divided into three offset elements, and shadow-casting beams over the entry. In a meeting, Oles called it "a contemporary interpretation of the things that characterize New Mexico architecture." He also mentioned the virtue of "not leading with your strongest suit," referring to the semicircular portal (in the rear and not visible from the street) that, due to cantilevering, offers a splendid view uninterrupted by columns. The LEED "Silver" house has a central stone fireplace; actually, it's a triangular form that houses exterior and interior fireplaces and a water feature — made with an orphaned, 900-pound granite plinth from Kirtland Air Force Base — that is straight ahead when you come in the front door. "Wright believed heart and hearth as being basically synonomous," Oles said. "It's the anchor, and the fulcrum of the bi-axial plan of the house."

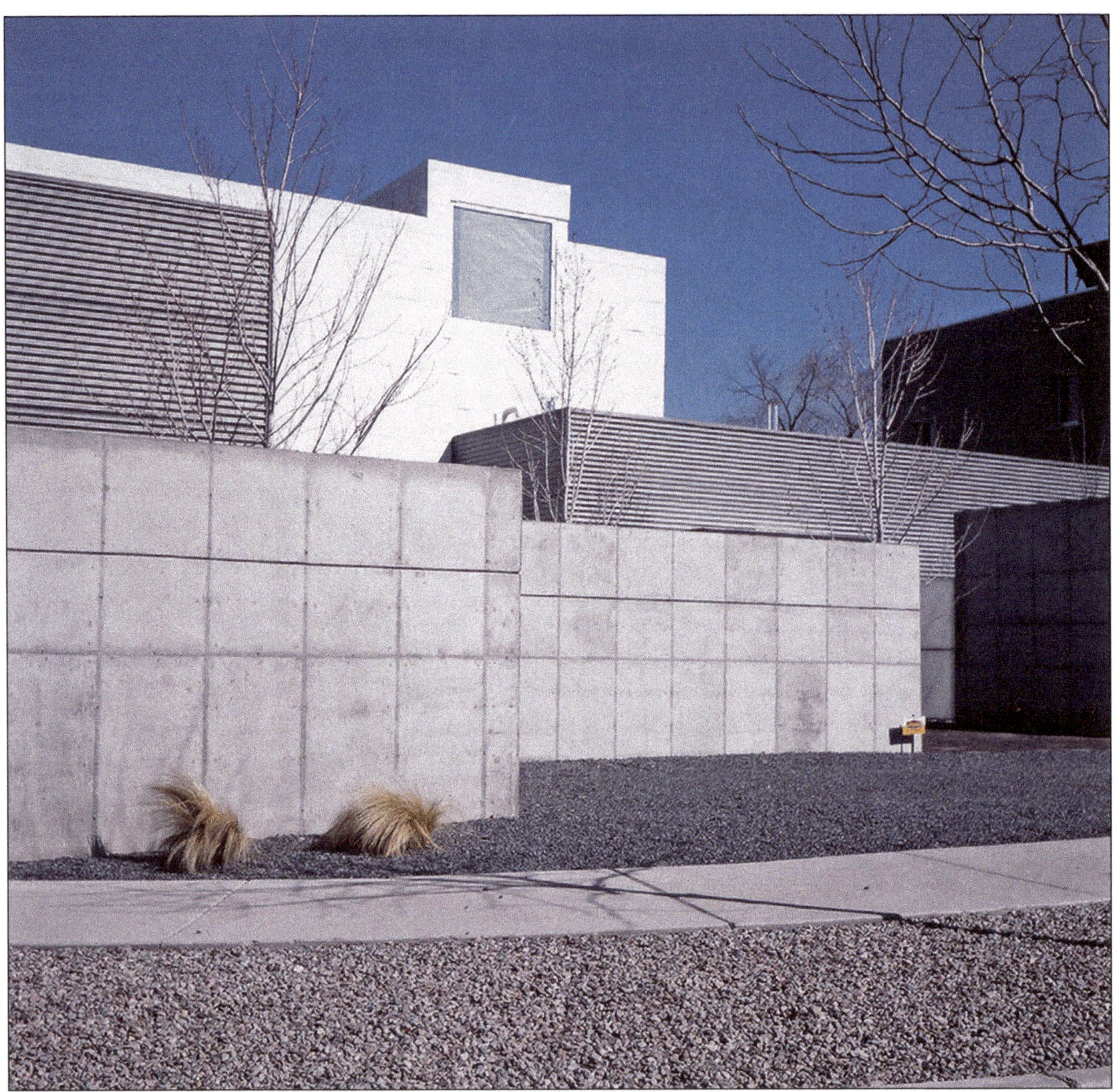

**Ricardo Mazal studio**, 926 Shoofly Street, in the Baca section of the Santa Fe Railyard, was completed in 2011. The artist worked with Jonah Stanford, principal of the design firm NEEDBASED, Inc. The exterior is an assemblage of boxlike forms in concrete; corrugated metal; flat, rhythmically placed steel panels; and glass. The interior is dominated by a bright studio space, about 40 feet square and 22 feet tall (to accommodate Mazal's large paintings) with clear white walls. Clerestories and skylights were computer-planned for a particular lighting profile. The idea from the beginning was for the big main cube and two other volumes, one for storage and the other finished as office space and a glassed-in kitchen. "Also important," Mazal said, "is the openness. You see no columns. It's entirely transparent inside, even in the patios [one of which has a small, deep lap pool]. I wanted patios, coming from Mexico. And I wanted big concrete walls. I wanted to get away from Santa Fe Style." For the walls, Stanford specified structural insulated panels (SIPs). The studio was designed, and plumbed, around the idea that in the future it could be converted into two living lofts.

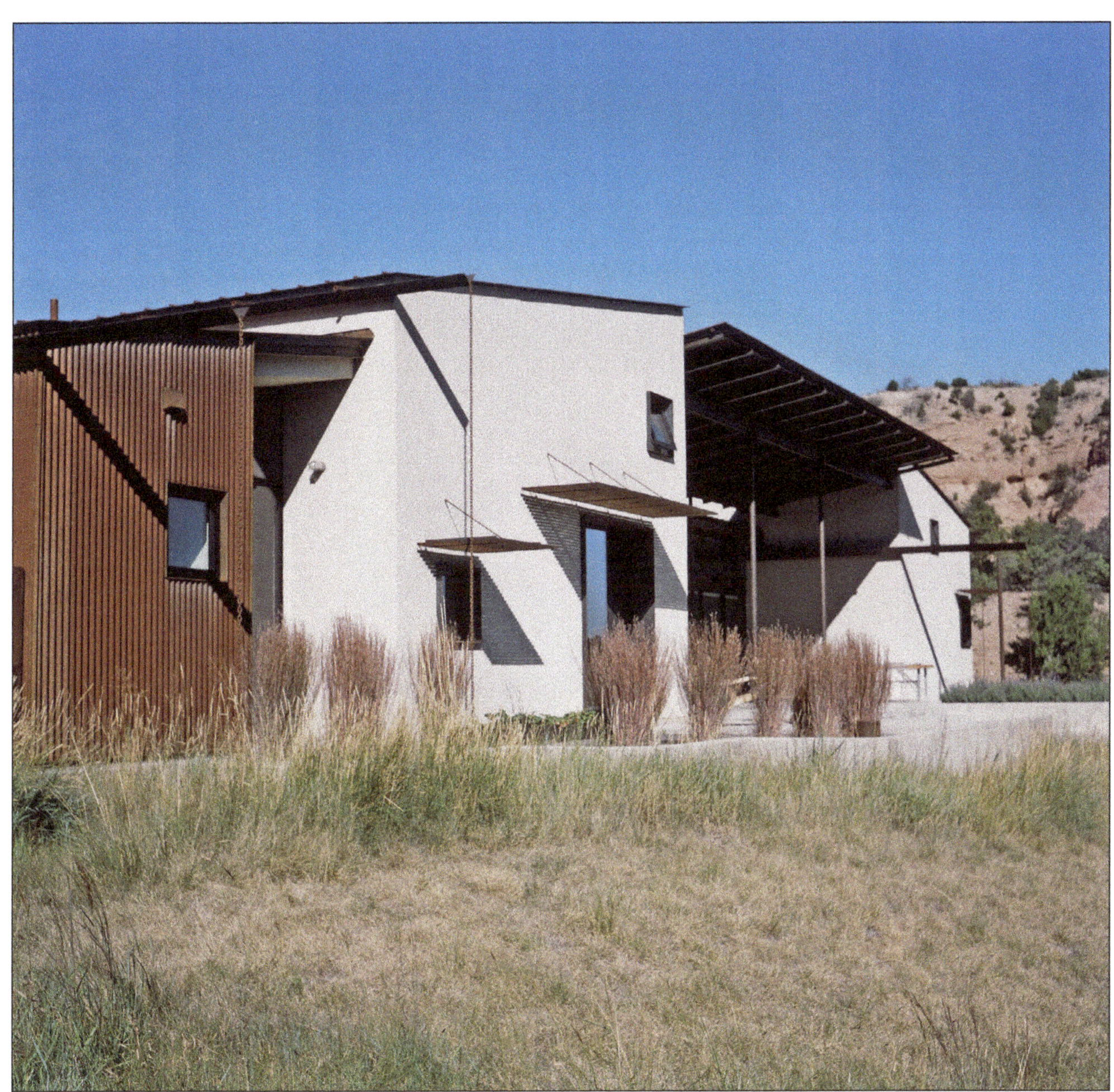

**Tesuque residence**. The owner of this house worked on the design with architect Mark Wellen of the Midland, Texas, firm Rhotenberry Wellen Architects. The builder was Denman & Associates, Santa Fe. Primary materials in this low-maintenance 2011 residence are metal — weathered corrugated steel covers much of the house and sections of steel bar grate serve as window shades — and wood, concrete, and glass; the house's highlight space is the glassy great room with floors of polished concrete. Two recycled shipping containers were altered (and adjoin a bathroom core) to serve as the guest house.

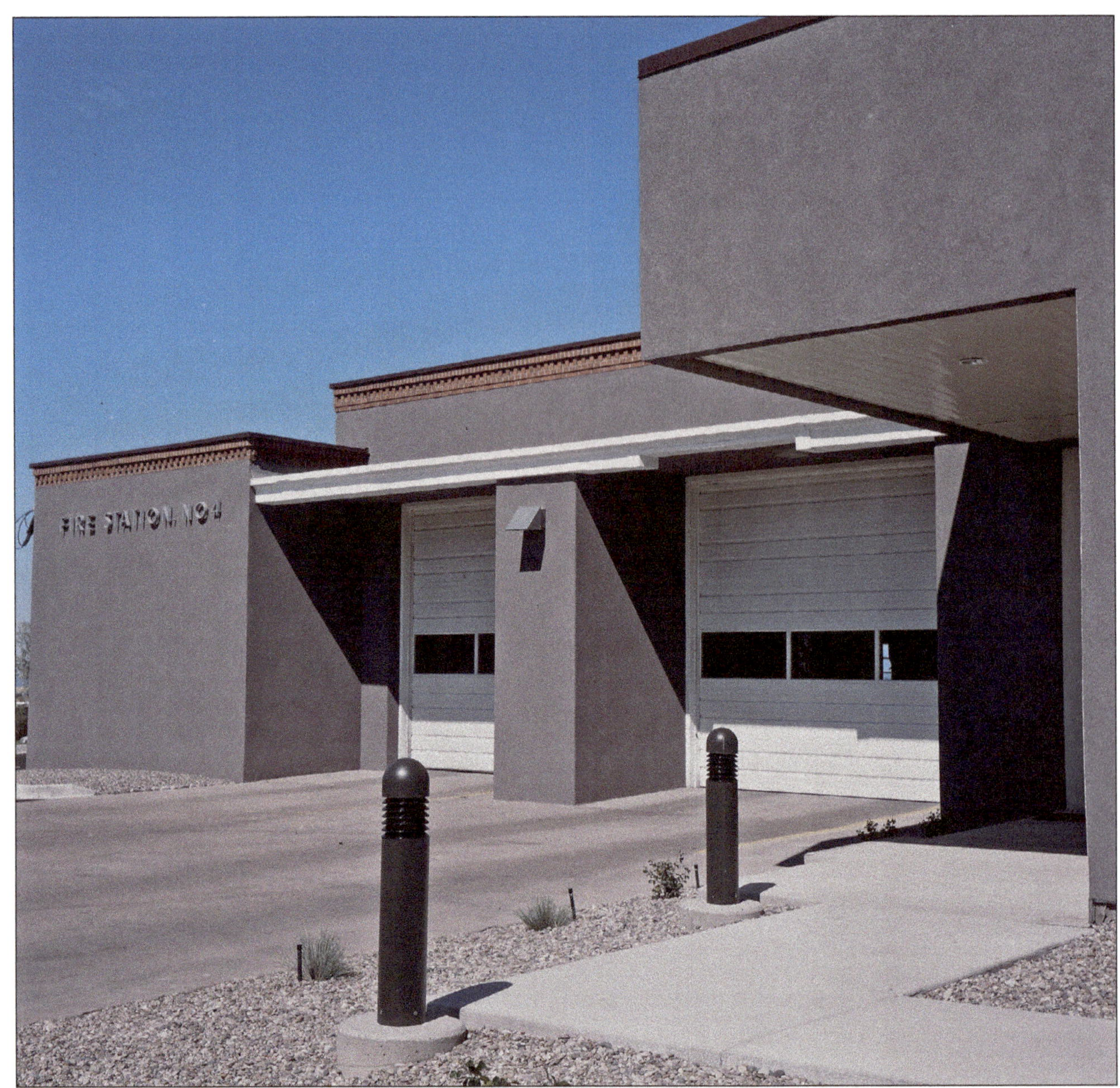


**Fire Station No. 4**, 1130 Arroyo Chamiso Road. Since 2005, Riskin Associates Architecture has designed four Santa Fe County fire stations ranging from 10,000 to 15,000 square feet, and has done additions and renovations on five more stations. Fire Station No. 4, completed in 2013, was one of the latter. Marci Riskin had to work with the existing pentile walls and a small site. She preserved basic elements of the building's Territorial Revival style, but added architectural interest in the various masses and shifted the stucco to a juicier hue.

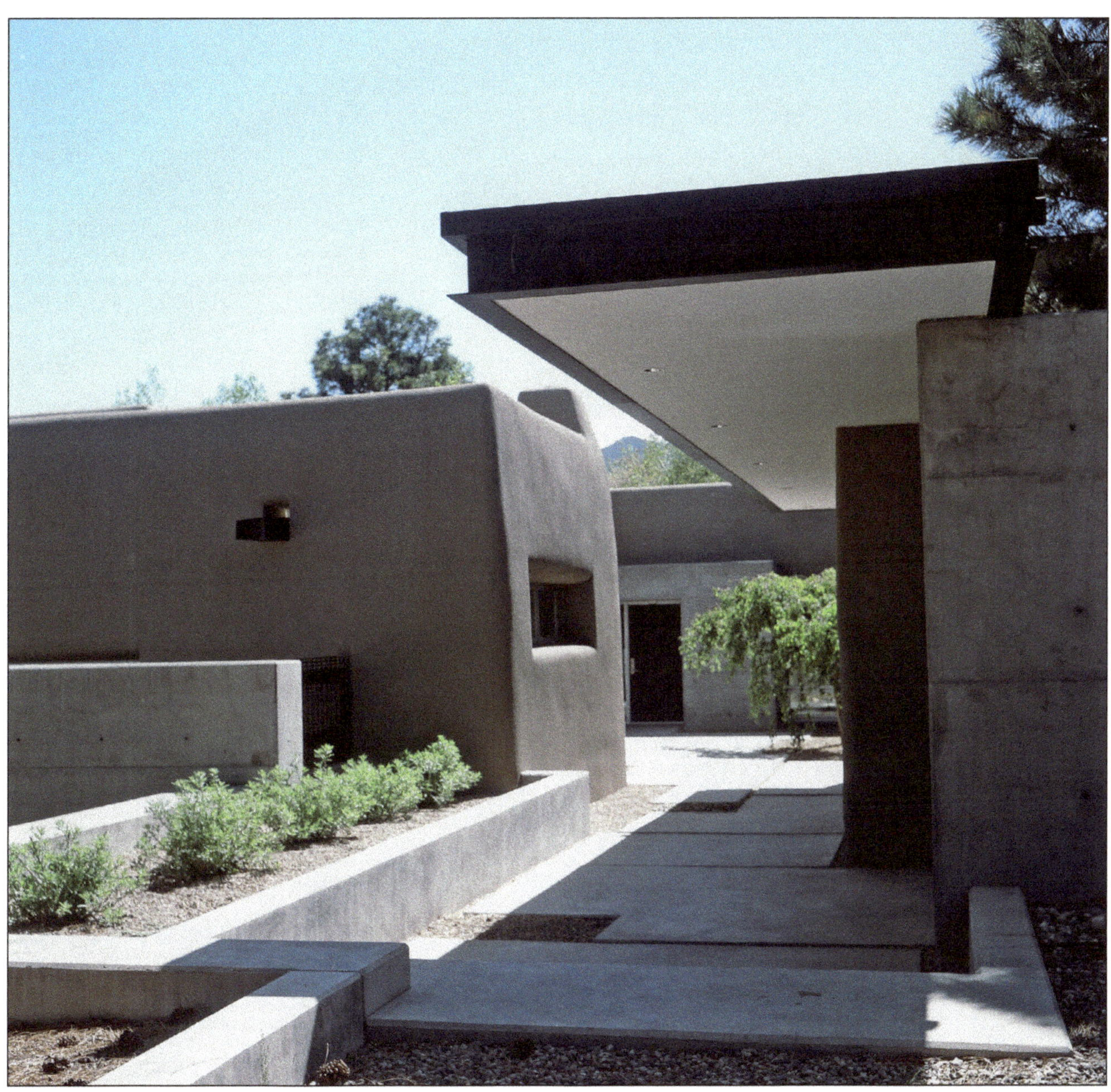

**Lumpkins/Jordan house**. William Lumpkins built this house on Camino Del Monte Sol for himself in about 1971. More than four decades later, it was remodeled and accentuated with new construction elements by architect Trey Jordan and contractor Tent Rock, Inc. "It had undergone two very bizarre renovations, one sort of cowboy with a corrugated-tin roof and the other a sort of Japanese tea house with green-glazed roof tile," Jordan said during a 2015 visit. "We do have his drawings, and anything that was original to the Lumpkins design we kept." The double-adobe Lumpkins sections, which are rounded and organic-looking, contrast beautifully with Jordan's sharp-cornered walls with exposed architectural concrete and steel grilles and cantilevers. "This is one thing I'm very interested in," Jordan said, "finding a historic building and keeping the parts of it that have integrity and being honest about the new chapter you're layering on top of it."

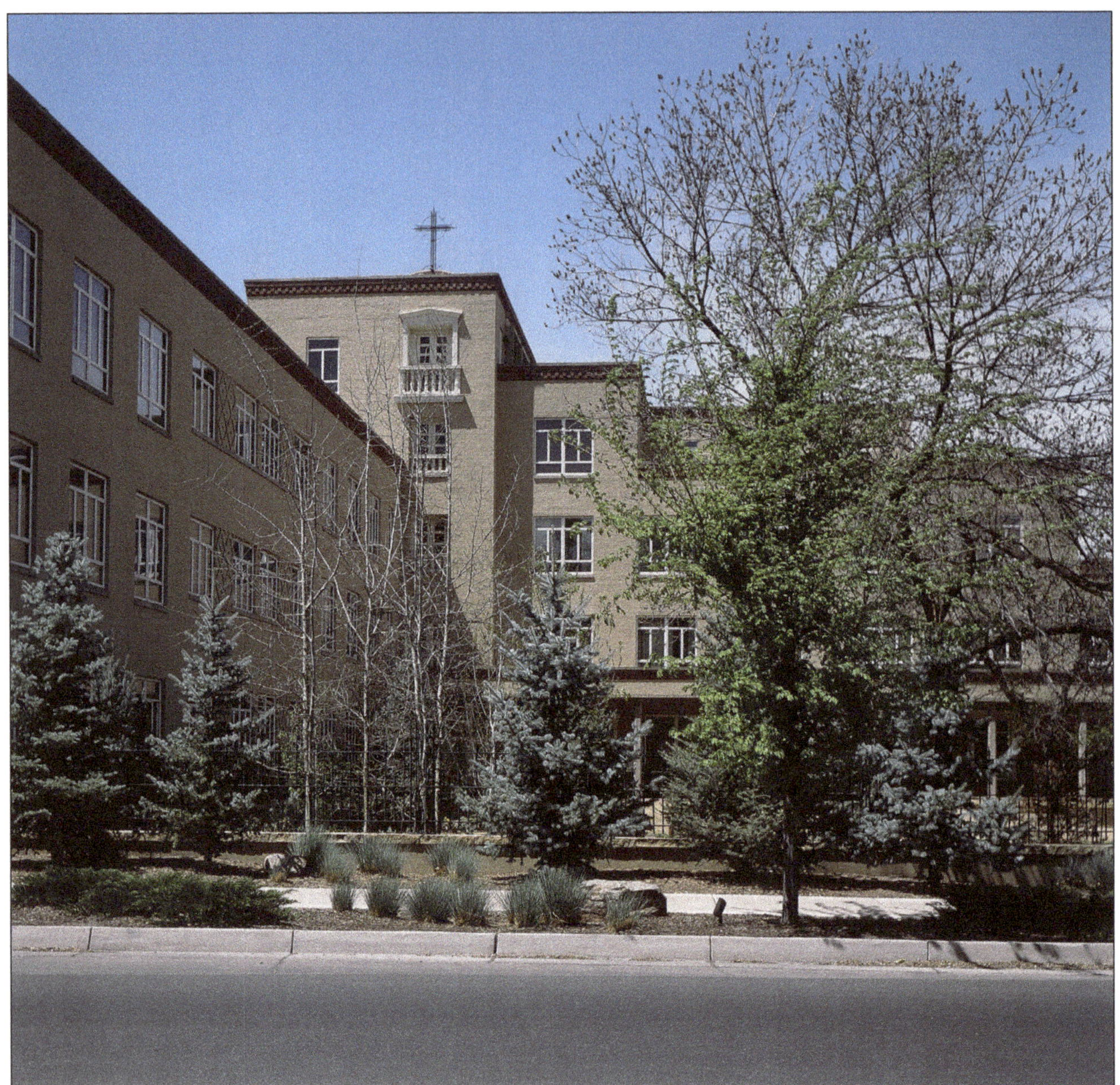

**Drury Plaza Hotel**, 828 Paseo de Peralta, opened in 2014 in the former St. Vincent Hospital building designed by John Gaw Meem. The old, painted-brick hospital was built on a budget, and this explains why the street facades are more decorative — including sections of ornamental brickwork between some windows — than the walls facing what used to be the parking lot. In his arrangement of masses and heights, Meem ingeniously fashioned an implied tower form (at left center in this photo) on an east-facing facade; at top is one of the building's fanciest windows, sporting a pediment with dentil cornice as well as a projecting 8-post balcony. The Drury Group's significant adaptive re-use project (with Santa Fe architect Mark Hogan) removed virtually all interior walls in the transformation to a 200-room hotel, which included an addition built of insulating concrete forms designed in harmony with the main building's Territorial Revival style. Laura Carpenter designed the wonderful Eloisa restaurant. This site first held the elaborate Second Empire-style St. Vincent Sanatorium, built in 1882 by Sister Blandina Segale and architect Projectus Mouly. It burned down in 1896 and Rapp & Rapp designed its more modest replacement; completed in 1910, it is now known as Marian Hall. It served as a convent after the adjacent Meem hospital opened in 1954, and just 23 years later the hospital was vacated when a new St. Vincent's opened two miles to the south.

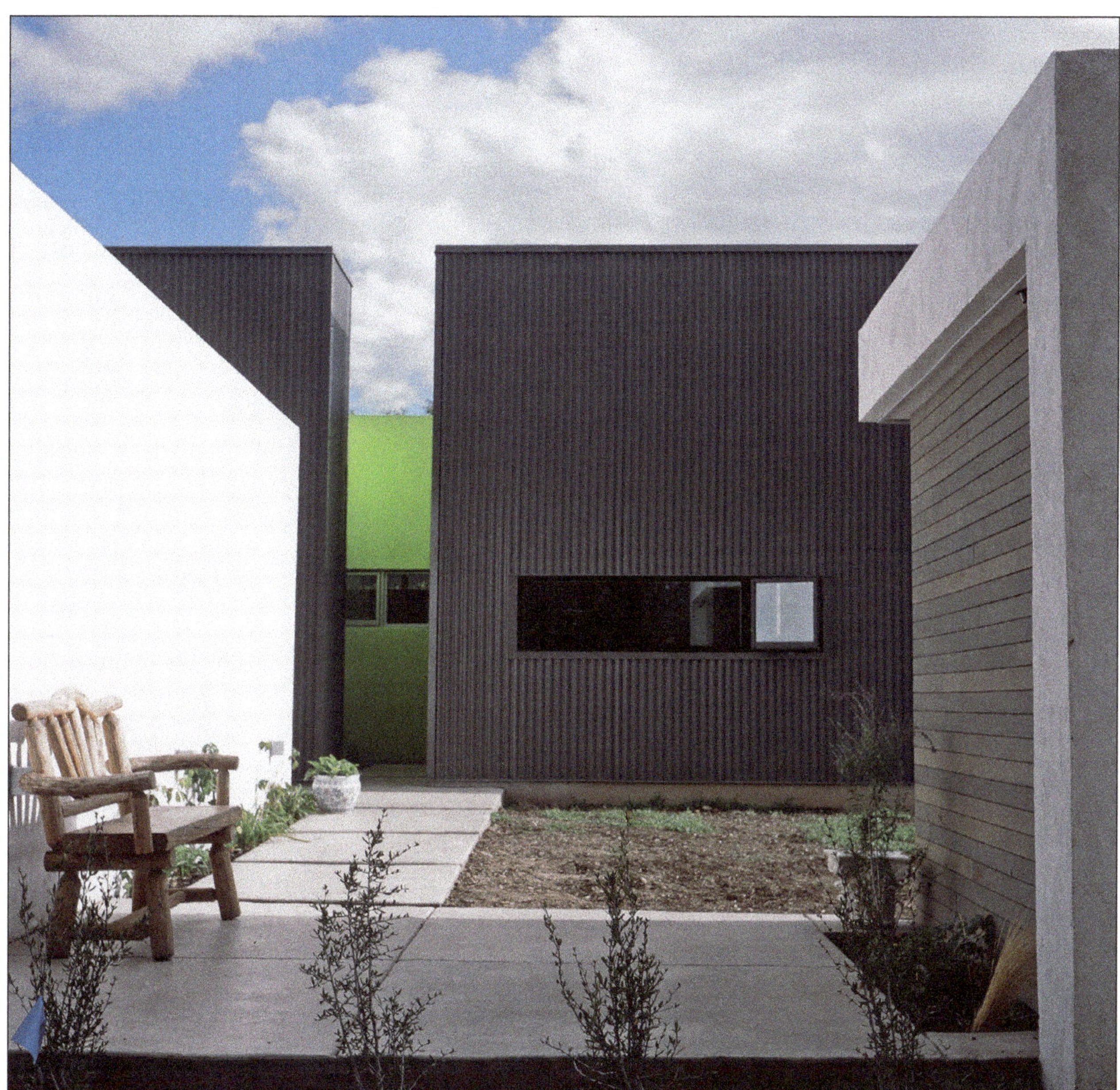

**Casa Tutti** on Montaño Street was built as a compact city infill project by owners Dee Bangert and architect Aaron Bohrer in collaboration with contractor Gerry Barber. This thoroughly modern residence, just 1,261 square feet, contrasts blocks and slabs of wood, dark gray metal, and light gray stucco with areas of bright color — including a lime-green wall and orange columns — placed out of the public view but enlivening the bright, efficient, open interior spaces and the courtyard and patio. The house won top awards for design, outdoor-living space, and energy and water efficiency in the local homebuilder association's 2015 Parade of Homes. This photo was taken in September 2015, not long after the residence was completed.

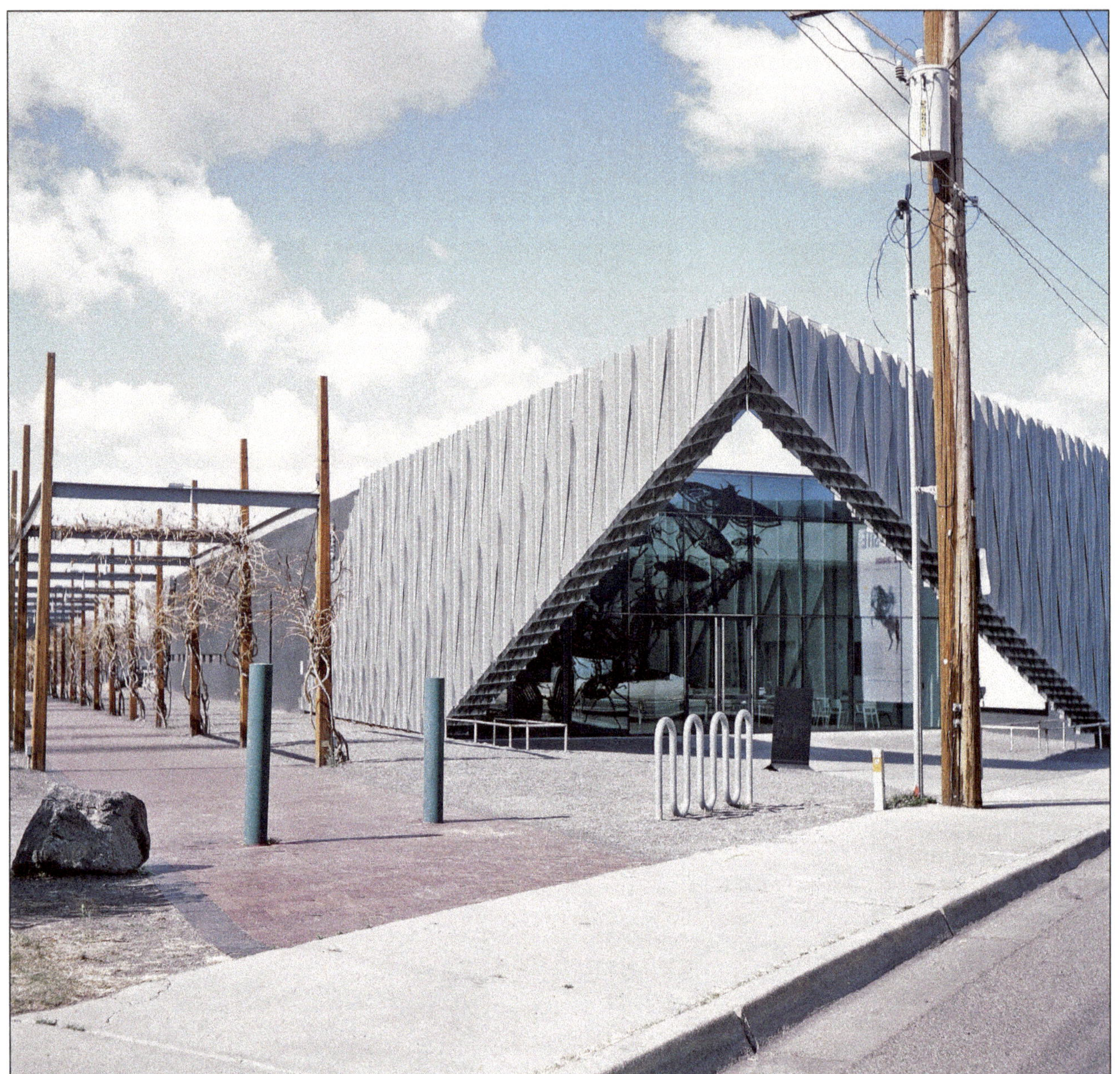

**SITE Santa Fe**, 1606 Paseo de Peralta. In 2017, local architect Greg Allegretti helped bring this dramatic design by SHoP Architects, New York, into reality. Santa Fe's contemporary-art museum dates to 1995, when Richard Gluckman (New York) renovated a 25-year-old Coors Beer warehouse. In the new millennium, SITE brought in architects Tod Williams and Billie Tsien, David Adjaye, and Greg Lynn to create innovative exterior and interior treatments for a series of exhibitions. The SHoP project added 10,000 square feet, including a climate-controlled gallery, an auditorium, the Sky Mezzanine gathering space, and an expanded, glass-fronted lobby. Outside, the building was tranformed with long wall sections of perforated-aluminum cladding that climax at front and rear in triangular "prow" features, and the stucco was contemporized with paint in SHoP's "Midnight Oil" color. Visible bolts between the cladding sections relate to the simple materials and construction strategies in the historic railyard district, according to the firm's project director, Ayumi Sugiyama. The structure at left is the Santa Fe Railyard Park entry *ramada*.

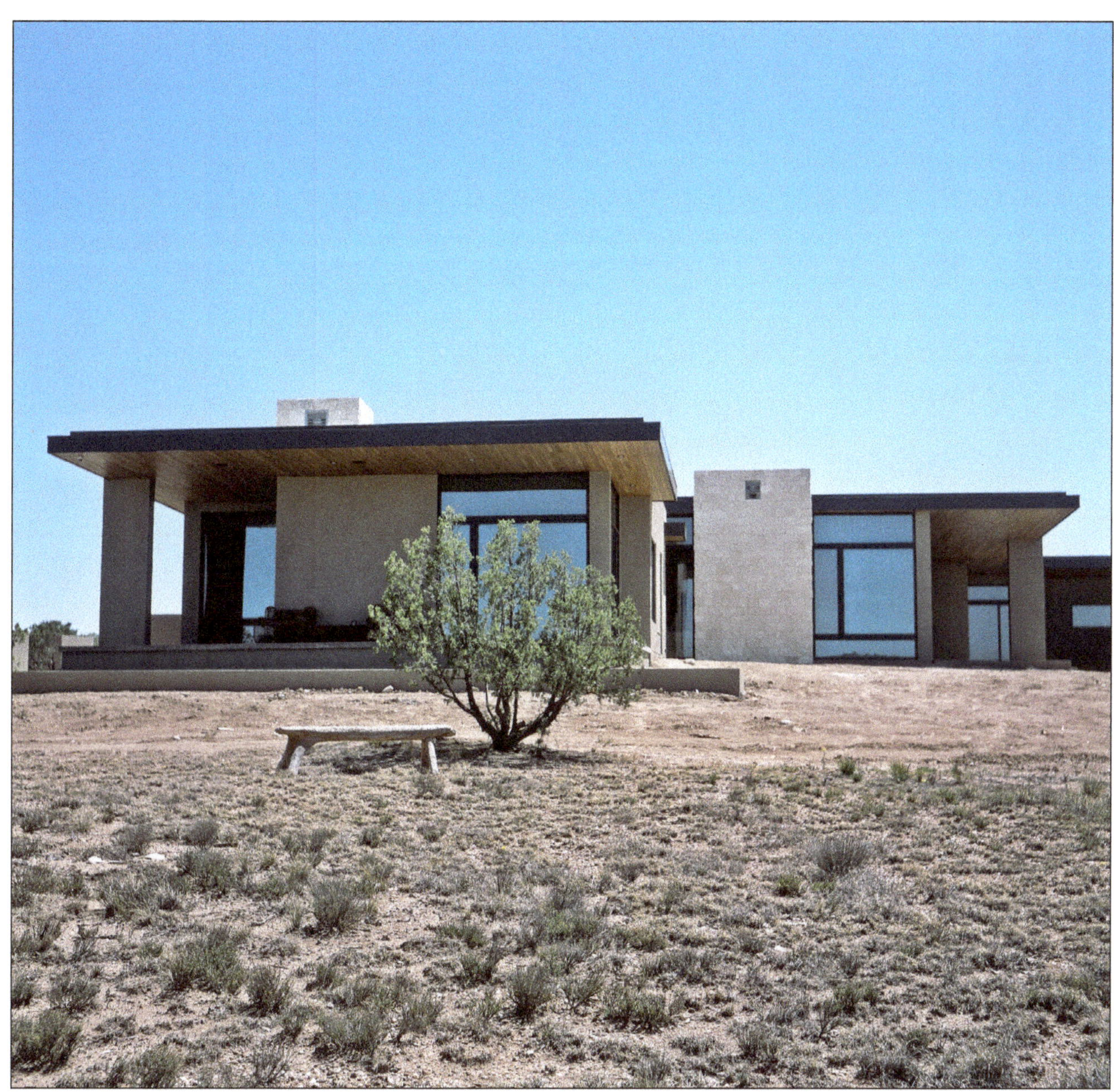

**Prull residence** on Camino Villenos. "We wanted something contemporary, but we wanted something that still fits into the landscape here," said Jodi Vevoda, wife of homebuilder Will Prull. On this, their own house, they worked with architect Craig Hoopes. The exterior (photographed shortly after completion) boasts sculptural wall elements of "Texas cream" limestone, a substantial proportion of glass, and a pleasing rhythm of solid versus void. Each large window is divided into a big pane framed by glazed horizontal "bands" (some operable for ventilation) at top, bottom and one side. During a walkthrough, Vevoda mentioned the surprise of "the reveal" inside. Hoopes explained: "The entry sequence is one of slowly revealing the outside. You come in and your focus is a stone wall with a fireplace, then as you walk down that gallery, the living room opens up with panoramas to the Jemez Mountains on one side and the Sangre de Cristos on the other. It is a sequence of unfolding." This residence is undeniably contemporary in design, yet features plastered walls and beamed ceilings, recalling Santa Fe Style. "Those things are part of our vocabulary, but it's how they're organized now that's different," Hoopes said. "But we're still trying to maintain that feel of belonging to the Southwest and belonging on the earth on which it's built. These are object houses in that they're unique, but they're not object houses as much as if to say, 'Look at me!'"

# Appendix 1

## About the photography

At some point in 2011, thinking about the visual element of this book idea, I wondered if I could do a survey of favorite buildings using my Rolleiflex twin-lens-reflex camera. It would be a particular challenge — not in using this camera, though, because we have a long history together, although most of it was in the 1980s. What would prove to be a bit problematic was the camera's square format. A huge majority of photographic compositions involving the dominant Spanish-Pueblo Revival and Territorial Revival buildings are logically horizontal. Historic adobe homes are typically long and low. That speaks to the fact that the material tends to get a bit unwieldy at heights over one story — and, anyway, this is the American West and there has always been, except in the center of established cities, plenty of space on the landscape for long and low. But just try to frame a pitilessly horizontal building in a square viewfinder!

You can walk backwards until you have the whole thing in frame, from side to side, but then there's a vast expanse of dirt or street or parking lot at the bottom of the frame, and quite a bit of sky — though sky expanses are rarely a problem for a photographer. Or else you can find a different perspective on the subject rather than full head-on, or you can focus on detail. You see herein more than a hundred attempts to attack these challenges; hopefully I succeed more often than not in capturing each of these esteemed hunks of Santa Fe architecture.

Then I thought that for this project I would for the first time load the Rolleiflex with color-transparency film rather than the black-and-white I always used before. In the process of making and evaluating the pictures, I've generally enjoyed the color approach, but I do miss the aesthetic edge of silver-based imagery, and being able to enhance contrast and mood to the extent one is able using colored filters with black-and-white film.

And as soon as I resolved to shoot color, I was saddened that for the first time in my life I was obliged to use something other than U.S.-made Kodak film. I shot hundreds of rolls of Tri-X, Plus-

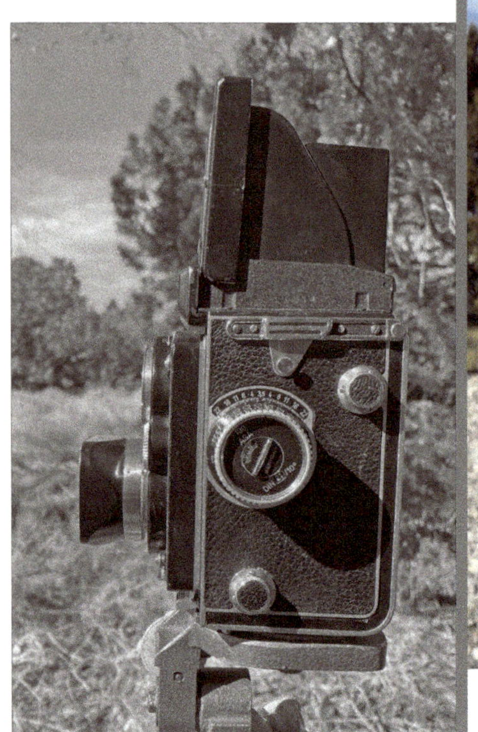

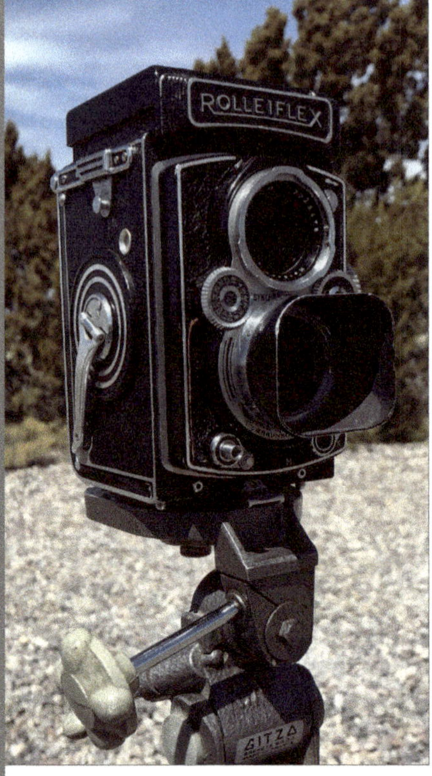


The Rolleiflex Automat

X, and Panatomic-X — and did my own developing and printing — when I lived in Los Angeles and the Seattle area from the late 1970s to the early 1990s. And I used a lot of Kodachrome and Ektachrome over the years. But by the time this project came along, those Kodak color films were depressingly defunct, victims of a diminishing market for film products following the "digital revolution." From the very small field of suitable films still available I chose Fujichrome Provia.

Another feature that can be considered a disadvantage in the antique Rolleiflex is that the focal length is fixed: there is no ability to zoom in or out for telephoto or wide-angle perspectives. You have to move around to find the shot you want. You must approach and compose the subject actively. Which actually is fun.

And the Rolleiflex is such a cool camera. Mine has a Zeiss Tessar lens, which is very good, optically. But what's most delightful is the fact that my camera (which was made in 1954, four years after I was made) is totally mechanical. There is nothing about it that requires a battery. (But I do not guess at exposures and my hand-held Pentax Spotmeter V light meter *is* battery-powered.)

The camera's multi-function viewing hood is an ingenious contraption, incorporating a shade for standard composition and focusing (in which you look down at the focusing groundglass while holding the camera at chest or belly level), and it also provides you with a framing device if you want to shoot using the camera at eye-level — and there are built-in magnifying lenses that you can flip into position to help you focus either way you shoot. Composing upside-down is also a breeze: if you want the highest angle on your subject, you can hold the Rollei at arm's length above your head and then frame, focus, and click while looking up into the viewfinder.

And now, here, I must make an assertion about the joy of film photography. I do not denigrate all digital image-making (which part of me stilll resists calling "photography") because I acknowledge its many advantages not only in convenience but in image quality. Those high-end, high-megapixel Nikons, Canons, Hasselblads, and even Leicas (sob!) achieve a thoroughly amazing (dare I say *unnatural*) resolution in detail, but at a price. There may be a discernible difference in the photographic print, akin to the one that some equally astute audiophiles notice between the vinyl record album and the CD. But there is most certainly a significant variation in attitude and approach. Let's think:

Film photographers well know the (scary) delight of anticipation, after making a photograph in the mind, then in the camera. You don't know what you have until you're working in the darkroom hours, days, or weeks later; or until you get the film back from the lab. Well, did you make your magic work? Were you successful in your evaluation of the scene or angle as "special" and in your approach and follow-through? Did your intuition and your application of the photographic tools come close to the ideals Ansel Adams conceived and practiced as "previsualization," with the beautiful gallery print a fulfilling performance? Or are the results so banal you wonder what the hell you were thinking?

By contrast, when you shoot with a digital camera, surprise is almost never a factor, because you can see the image you just captured on the viewing screen. Is there something deeper and maybe ultimately more meaningful about this difference? If I can know immediately whether what I just shot is good or poor, won't that allow me to fine-tune the whole process, and waste less time and money? Perhaps, but that surprise that I mentioned equals excitement and, I think, a measured refinement of the process of learning and *seeing.* — Paul Weideman

# Appendix 2

## Architects *(and masons and master builders)* Past

**Pedro de Peralta**. Governor 1609/1610-1613/1614 and possibly an "architect" of the Palace of the Governors

**Alonso Peinado**. A mission church founder in the early 1600s in this region, possibly involved in construction of small *jacal* chapel and/or the first *parroquia*

**Alonso de Benavides Peinado**. A missionary perhaps responsible for construction of San Miguel Chapel

**Andres Gonzales**. Master mason directed 1710 rebuilding of San Miguel Chapel

**Joab Houghton**. Trained as a civil engineer, he drew the plans for the first territorial capitol

**Dofflemeyer and Grace.** 1860s, including remodeling of the Spiegelberg store on the Plaza

**J.W. Corkins**. Named in 1870 *Santa Fe New Mexican* notice about plan for "Monumental School in the Plaza"

**John & M. McGee**. Architects and builders in Dec. 1870 *Santa Fe New Mexican* ad: "Plans and specifications furnished for all kinds of public and private buildings… Also, mills, furnaces, smelters, and desulphurisers erected."

**Antoine and Projectus Mouly**. Engaged 1870s-80s on cathedral project, Loretto Chapel

**Quintien (aka Quintus) Monier**. 1870s-90s, builder/mason on cathedral project, Loretto Chapel, St. Michael's College, 1881 Old Stone Dam, 1886 territorial capitol (in partnerships with William Colloudon and then Florence Donoghue), also a 1,585-foot stone fence for Santa Fe National Cemetery, and had a lime and brick kiln in Lamy. Michel Allaeys (of L'Association culturelle d'Aigueperse et ses environs) also listed "County Courthouse" in Monier's project list; presumably this was the 1887 building on the site of today's Coronado Building. The building that was Monier's home/office is now Southwestern Title & Escrow

**Francois Mallet**. 1870s cathedral project

**William Colloudon**. In partnership with Quintien Monier, involved in Loretto Chapel, St. Michael's College, and other projects

**Chas. Wheelock**. Sept. 6, 1880: "The New Mexican has received from Chas. Wheelock, the architect of Las Vegas, a photograph of the Palace Hotel as it will appear when completed... will be an exceedingly handsome building, three stories high, 90 x 150 feet, and ornamented by a great deal of fancy work."

**Wheeler & Randall**. Listed as Santa Fe architect in McKenney's Business Directory 1882-1883. A notice in the July 21, 1881, newspaper said, "Mr. N.H. Wheeler, the architect, has just let the contract for the building of the laundry for the Palace hotel." J.B. Randall probably designed the 1882 UNM Whitin Hall and may have designed Church of the Holy Faith

**Florence Donoghue**. Born in Dublin, he was a builder and brick manufacturer in Santa Fe. He constructed the First National Bank on the Plaza. Formed partnership with Quintien Monier in 1884 and together they built the territorial capitol. Donoghue completed an addition to the Spiegelberg Bros. store in August. 1884.

**Levi Ackroyd**. Mason and builder of Church of the Holy Faith, 1882

**F. McGregor**. Listed as a Santa Fe architect in McKenney's Business Directory 1882-1883, and advertised as "Draughtsman, Architect and Superintendent with Progress and Improvement Co., Santa Fe, New Mexico" in Nov. 8, 1881, issue of *Santa Fe Daily New Mexican*

**James Nichols** (1829-1885) built the Abraham Staab House and others having mansard roofs in Santa Fe

**T.N. Philpot**. Advertised as architect in *The New Mexican* late 1880s; had office in Sena Building

**D.D. Cobleigh**. Advertised as architect in *The New Mexican* late 1880s

**E.S. Jenison** of Chicago designed the 1886 capitol building

**Kirchner and Kirchner**, 1887, designed Santa Fe County courthouse (burned)

**Brigham**. References found for an "Architect Brigham," including 1886-1888 notices in the Santa Fe newpaper about designs for a boulevard between the Atchison, Topeka & Santa Fe Railway depot and the territorial penitentiary, and for beautifying the capital grounds

**Antonio Windsor**. Builder of Scottish Rite Temple, Women's Board of Trade Library, and Palen Hall at the Church of the Holy Faith. An 1888 ad in *The New Mexican* boasted "Close Figuring! Modern Methods! Skilled Mechanics!" and gave the location of Windsor's office as "Lower 'Frisco Street"

**Philip Hesch**. Builder of Hesch House, Eugenie Shonnard House

**Stanford White**, New York, designed Memorial Building of the Ramona Industrial School for Indian Girls

**Isaac Rapp**. Prolific architect in the area 1896-1921, responsible for 1900 State Capitol, First Ward School, New Mexico School for the Deaf, Marian Hall, Gross Kelly Warehouse, Sunmount Sanitorium, Fine Arts Museum, La Fonda, and other buildings in Santa Fe and before that in Las Vegas and in Trinidad, Colorado

**Charles F. Whittiesey**. 1902 notice in *Santa Fe New Mexican*: testing his machine for making building blocks from sand and Portland cement

**E.W. Hart**, 1907, Women's Board of Trade Library

**Goodwin, Earl E**. Advertised services in 1915 newspapers, but exact accomplishments are unknown

**Thomas MacLaren**: Circa 1915 Bronson Cutting House

**Trent Thomas**: 1920 Carlos Vierra residence, La Fonda (with Rapp), and was for a time Architect in Charge for the Historic American Buildings Survey, Southwest Unit

**Louis Simon**. Designed 1921 U.S. Post Office (now Museum of Contemporary Native Arts)

**John Gaw Meem**, working 1925 to 1959, resumé including Church of the Holy Faith Palen Hall, Manderfield School, La Fonda addition, Mary Vilura Conkey residence, Robert Tilney residence, Laboratory of Anthropology and Director's Residence, Amelia Hollenback residence, Federal Emergency Recovery Act (now Villagra) Building, Santa Fe Municipal Building (now Santa Fe Public Library), Cristo Rey Catholic Church, First Presbyterian Church, Imanuel Lutheran Church, Museum of International Folk Art, and many other Santa Fe houses, churches, and schools; also Zimmerman Library and dozens of other buildings for University of New Mexico, Albuquerque

**William Penhallow Henderson** working locally 1925-40, including on the Henderson house on Camino del Monte Sol, Sena Plaza second story and rear additions, El Delirio, Wheelwright Museum

**Katherine Stinson-Otero**. Pioneering American woman stunt pilot active as Santa Fe builder 1925-35: Dorothy McKibben House and many other residences, including in Plaza Chamisal

**Frank Applegate**. De la Pena House and other homes 1920s

**Miles Brittelle**, 1920s-1950s Brittelle & [John] Ginner, Santa Fe High School, Seth Hall

**T. Charles Gaastra**, 1920s Cassell Building, Gustave Baumann House, Bishop's Lodge

**A.C. Hendrickson**, 1920s various projects with Isaac Rapp

**Burnham Hoyt**, 1920s restorations of area mission churches

**George M. Williamson**, 1928 Connor Hall, New Mexico School for the Deaf; 1928 Seth Hall, Santa Fe High School

**A. Leicester Hyde**. Active in Meem firm from 1931

**Kenneth Clark**, 1930s-60s, First Presbyterian Church education building (with Philippe Register; razed 2004), collaboration with Meem on Plaza *portales*, 1940 Carlos Gilbert School (with W.C. Kruger)

**Bradley Kidder**, 1935-65, J.C. Penney store, 1967 Santa Fe Opera (with John McHugh)

**Willard Carl Kruger**, 1935-70 including Kruger office building, state penitentiary, New Mexico highways building, U.S. Post Office and Federal Office Building, State Capitol (Roundhouse), P.E.R.A. Building

**William Lumpkins**, 1935-95, Balcomb residence and other pioneering passive-solar homes, Donaciano Vigil House remodel, Teal residence (today's Eldorado Community Center), Rancho Encantado (destroyed for modern Encantado resort), DeVargas Center, conversion of La Fonda courtyard to La Plazuela restaurant

**Gordon Street**, 1930s, New Mexico Supreme Court, Harvey Jr. High School, New Mexico School for the Deaf buildings

**William E. Burk Jr.**, 1938 Beers Motor Company

**Cecil Doty**, 1939 National Park Service building

**Mary Colter**, 1926-1929 La Fonda interior renovation for Fred Harvey Co., 1940 La Fonda remodel including La Cantinita (today's French Pastry Shop)

**Allen Stamm**, 1940-80 builder of thousands of Santa Fe homes in the Spanish-Pueblo Revival style in Casa Mañana, Casa Linda, Casa Alegre, Casa Solana, and other neighborhoods

**Leo Wolmagood**, 1945-55, Cristo Rey School

**John McHugh** joined Meem firm in 1946; private practice 1955-1991. Santa Fe Opera 1957 and 1967, Immaculate Heart of Mary Seminary chapel, St. Francis Cathedral restoration, residences

**Holabird & Root & Burgee**, Chicago. 1949 addition to La Fonda

**Charles Royall Lugton** Schools architect practicing in Santa Fe 1949-72, in partnership for a period with Alfred Millington

**Earl (Pat) Wood**, 1950-70, with W.C. Kruger, Kenneth Clark, Ken DeLapp. Projects included Plaza Letrado, Vermejo Park Apartments, Coronado Condominiums, DeFouri Street bridge

**Ken DeLapp**, 1950s-80s DeLapp Engineering, work on Felipe Delgado House, Inn at Loretto, Capital High School

**John Conron**, 1954 Centerline Building (a remodel), Palace of the Governors adobe preservation; longtime editor *New Mexico Architecture;* headed Architects Associated, which included David Lent, Robert Plettenberg, Philippe Register

**Robert Plettenberg,** 1950s missionized San Miguel Chapel tower; was on first Historic Santa Fe Foundation board of directors

**Truman Matthews** ca. 1940 in Meem office. Designed 1963 county juvenile detention home on Airport Road; worked with Meem and Thomas on Historic American Buildings Survey

**Peter Van Dresser**, 1955-75, passive-solar houses

**Phillipe Register**, 1955-85, including Agua Fria Elementary School; College of Santa Fe Benildus Hall, administration building, Fogelson Library Center, Greer Garson Theater, many dormitories and classroom buildings; state police headquarters and training center, Ghost Ranch center

**Alfred R. Millington,** substantial work on 1957 Historic Styles Ordinance; partnership with Leo J. Wolgamood for a period, and served on Santa Fe Planning Commission and Santa Fe City Council in 1950s, 1960s

**Van Dorn and Marjorie Mead Hooker**, both architects trained at University of Texas. Van Dorn established the firm of McHugh, Hooker, Bradley P. Kidder and Associates. He designed the first Santa Fe Opera (1857) with John McHugh and a residence in Santa Fe, many Albuquerque structures.

**William and Madge Buckley**, both architects. He did 1959 First Baptist Church (with Meem). She did homes, including with Stamm Builders

**Urban Weidner** designed new cathedral/chapel roof in the 1960s

**Paolo Soleri**. Designed and supervised building (with students) of singular 1966 earth-cast amphitheater at Santa Fe Indian School

**John B. Arrison** had Arrison Inc. in Santa Fe 1966-1990. State government and Santa Fe Community College buildings

**Betty Stewart**, renowned Santa Fe homebuilder 1968-80

**Richard Eugene Halford**, 1950s-90s, Casa Loma Apartments, La Esquina Building, Vistas de Santa Fe, San Francisco Street parking garage

**Jeremiah Iowa** (d. 1994) design resumé includes La Posada Resort, Santa Clara Pueblo Senior Center

**Irene Von Horvath**, 1953-2007, Santa Fe planning, including Historic Styles Ordinance and the Paseo de Peralta loop

**Sara Melton**, 1970-2006 longtime staunch advocate of Santa Fe's historic architecture; member of Old Santa Fe Association and Historic Santa Fe Foundation

**Ron Robles**, 1970s-1990s, including houses, Vanessie Restaurant, Allene Lapides Gallery (one of the designers who remodeled former Spanish Baptist Church for the gallery, then again for Georgia O'Keeffe Museum)

**Bernabe Romero** 1970s-2015, Cathedral Park; several schools, including Santo Niño Regional Catholic School; Palace of the Governors addition; Magers Field building

**Richard Dorman**, 1975-2010 in Santa Fe, office buildings in partnership with Larry Breen

**Jeff Harnar**, 1977-1983 design/build and 1984-2006 architecture, including remodel for Jean Cocteau Cinema, Santa Fe Children's Museum; Barrett, Podmore, and other residences

**Harvey Hoshour**, Museum of International Folk Art's Girard Wing

**Louis L. Weller**, Weller Architects, Albuquerque, 1980-present, including Institute of American Indian Arts library

**Burke Denman**, 1981-2016, sustainable-building practitioner (longtime president of Sustainable Communities/ZERI-NM). Ironstone Gardens, Santa Fe Stoneworks, Bioneers office, and residences, including Jane Fonda house on the Pecos River

**Bill Agnew**, 1984-2013 Ventana de Vida senior apartments, Bradbury Science Museum in Los Alamos, restoration of a historic adobe farmhouse in Jaconita

**L.D. Burke**, 1989-2000, author of distinctive buildings including Pink Church, The Nunnery, Fortaleza Coyote, The Granaries; and cowboy furniture designer extraordinaire

**Alfred Von Bachmayr** , 1993-2010. Designs for Habitat for Humanity, various innovative, low-cost projects in Third World

**Larry Andren**, 1996-2017. Artist and architect known for beautiful, site-sensitive homes in Billings, Scottsdale, and Santa Fe — including more than five dozen in the Las Campanas and Monte Sereno subdivisions.

# Glossary

*acequia* – ditch constructed to convey river water to agricultural fields, orchards

adobe - sun-dried earthen bricks; mud used to make bricks and to plaster walls; also, a house made of adobe bricks

*alacena* - cupboard built into an interior adobe wall

*araña* – traditional wooden cross- or spider-shaped candle chandelier

*arroyo* - natural watercourse, usually dry; a gully

*banco* - long adobe (or facsimile) bench built along the base of a wall

*bulto* - three-dimensional *santo*, traditionally a carved and painted wooden statue

buttress - an exterior mass of adobe or other material built as an abutment to a wall for support

*campanario* - bell tower, belfry

*camposanto* – community cemetery adjacent to church

*canal (canales)* - trough extending out from parapet of flat roof, originally designed to drain rainwater and help protect adobe wall from water erosion

*cedro* – (See *raja*)

coping: protective and decorative brick course on top of parapet

corbel – scroll-shaped wood bracket used to support a *viga* or beam

elevation – view of building façade as seen from ground level

*enjarradora* - woman expert at wall-plastering

*ermita* – small chapel or shrine

*espadaña* – bell gable, wall belfry, often a cutout near top of curvilinear church facade

*farolito* – small paper lantern, traditionally a candle in sand in small brown bag, used in streetside rows during the holidays

*fogón* - corner fireplace (today usually called "kiva fireplace")

*horno* - outdoor adobe oven

kiva - Pueblo ceremonial space

*latillas* – juniper, alder, or willow saplings laid horizontal to, or herringbone-style on, *vigas* for roof decking. (See also *rajas*.)

*jacal* – wall-construction method using vertical timbers chinked with mud and stone; also known as wattle-and-daub construction

*jaspe* – gypsum-based whitewash

mansard - hip-roof variation with double-slope profile on each side, the lower slopes much steeper than the upper

*manta* – in old New Mexico Hispano homes, cloth stretched beneath *vigas*, sometimes hardened with flour-water mixture, to create a "ceiling"

*nicho* - niche in interior adobe wall used for display of *santos* and other artworks

parapet – low retaining wall around perimeter of flat roof

*parroquia* – parish church

pediment - shallow triangular ornamental wood piece atop a window or door

pentile - heavy, hollow clay blocks produced at the New Mexico Penitentiary from about 1915 and into the 1940s, used as a wall-building material

pintle hinge - no-hardware device, with projecting pintles carved as part of door and fitting into holes in lintel and bottom plate or sill

pithouse - ancient Indian dwelling dug into the earth, with covering of branches and mud

*placita* – courtyard within an L, a U, or a complete square of rooms or buildings

plan – building view as seen from above

plaza – public square

*portal* (*portales*) – long porch with beamed roof supported by corbels and *zapatas* on posts

*raja* – thin juniper (colloquially "cedar") trunks split and used like *latilla* as roof decking atop *vigas*

*ramada* — arbor; partial shade structure

*reredos* - altar screen

*retablo* - two-dimensional *santo*, traditionally a painted figure on a wooden board; also a decorative altar screen

*sala* – parlor, living room

*santero* – maker of *retablos*, *bultos*, and other religious artworks

*santo* – artwork depicting a saint

Spanish Pueblo Revival style - Building type with walls of earth-colored adobe (or facsimile), flat roof with *canales*, often with *vigas* projecting from exterior walls; typically one story

Territorial Revival style – Spanish-Pueblo-style house modified with sharper edges; brick coping along roofline; and white-painted, milled-woodwork details such as pedimented lintels on window frames and square portal posts

*terrón (terrones)* - sod brick cut from *cienega* (marsh)

*torreon* - defensive tower

*torta* – packed mud traditionally used over *viga/latilla* roof decking

*trastero* – freestanding closet

truth window - small area on a wall in which the plaster has been omitted or removed so visitors can see the adobes or other construction material

*vara* – old Spanish measure equal to 33.6 inches

*viga* - debarked log used as ceiling beam

*zaguan* - covered, horse-accessible entrance from street to *placita* or patio; a vestibule

*zambullo* - early door form employing pintle hinges

*zapata* – similar to corbel but double-ended, used to support beam joint on post

# Acknowledgments

Alan "Mac" Watson, Jake Barrow, Ed Crocker, Elaine Bergman, John Murphey, Charles Coffman, David Rasch, Lani McCulley, Kim Shanahan — for a wealth of good information about building and buildings over the decades

Daniel Kosharek, Hannah Abelbeck, Patricia Hewitt, and Tomas Jaehn of the New Mexico History Museum/Palace of the Governors Photo Archives and Fray Angélico Chávez History Library — for significant assistance researching the history of Santa Fe's built environment over the years

*The Santa Fe New Mexican* and owner Robin McKinney Martin — for indispensable source material (and for my longtime employment). And my editors at Pasatiempo — Denise Kusel, Hollis Walker, Camille Flores, and especially Kristina Melcher — for encouraging articles about (and my self-education in) architecture and design

Ronald J Stern, superintendent, New Mexico School for the Deaf — for access to school grounds

Owner Patrick Christopher — for access to, and tour of, Donaciano Vigil House

Peter Wirth — for text of "The Regional New Mexican Architecture," presented by his grandfather, John Gaw Meem, to an American Institute of Architects meeting in Santa Fe in 1953

Owner Jerry Ruther — for access to Bart Prince house

Office of Antoine Predock and homeowner Seymour Grufferman — for access to Shadow House

Owner Tias Little — for access to Paula Baker-designed house

Museum of Contemporary Native Arts security — for access to MoCNA roof to photograph Cathedral Basilica

Owner Andrea Soiero — for access to, and tour of, Wright Pottery House

Owner Curtiss Brennan — for access to the Dorothy McKibben House

Dora Cde Baca and Frosty Poston, for access to a second-floor window at the New Mexico Finance Authority to photograph the Loretto Chapel (ultimately not used because of busy foreground elements)

Owners Dan and Terri Guy — for access to, and tour of, their Katherine Stinson-Otero home, and for additional information about the builder

Pat Taylor, contractor and adobe preservation specialist — for help on technical issues related to adobe architecture

Office of the New Mexico State Historian website

Owner James Mayer — for access to, and tour of, the Gregorio Crespín House

Owner Armin Rembe — for access to, and tour of, the José Dolores García House

Mac Watson, the late William Baxter, François-Marie Patorni, Michel Debatisse, and the late Michel Allaeys (L'Association culturelle d'Aigueperse et ses environs) — for help in zeroing in on the accomplishments of Quintien Monier

Owner Dee Bangert — for access to, and tour of, Casa Tutti

Owner Steve Oles — for access to, and tour of, his home on City Lights

Archaeologist Cherie Scheick — for repeated access to her Agua Fria Schoolhouse Pueblo excavations, and later discussions about her work there

Owner Burke Denman — for access to, and tour of, the Hayt-Wientge Mansion

National Park Service — for access and permission to shoot NPS Building

Owners Stephen and Erin Crozier and architect Trey Jordan — for access to, and tour of, the Croziers' Camino Del Monte Sol residence

Santa Fe Indian School — for access and permission to photograph Paolo Soleri Amphitheater

Academy for the Love of Learning — for access and permission to photograph Academy Center

School for Advanced Research — for access and permission to photograph the SAR administration building

Owner Lori Harnar — for access to, and tour of, the Jeff Harnar residence

Archdiocese of Santa Fe — for access and permission to photograph the Cristo Rey church interior

St Michael's College — for access to San Miguel Chapel

Suby Bowden, AIA — for access to, and a tour of, her Saddleback Ranch house; and for her advice on elements of the book's text and back cover

Kim Kurian — for photographing the author and for her assistance scouting out Santa Fe Opera shooting locations

Jeff Acker — for his keen proofreading of the book

Molly Boyle — for cogent suggestions regarding the cover, the introduction, and the organization of the text

Taura Katerina Costidis — for her artful work on the front cover

Roget's Thesaurus — for assistance in avoiding excessive monotony in the text

# Bibliography and Sources

First, dozens of articles in the *Santa Fe New Mexican*, such as "Prize Winning Plan for Plaza Submitted by John Meem in McCormick Competition," published on June 10, 1931.

*All Trails Lead to Santa Fe: An Anthology Commemorating the 400th Anniversary of the Founding of Santa Fe, New Mexico in 1610* (Sunstone Press, 2010)

Anaya, Rudolfo A.; Sandoval, Richard C., illustrations. *The Farolitos of Christmas: A New Mexico Christmas Story* (*New Mexico Magazine*, 1987)

Badner, Jessica A.; Barbour, Matthew J.; and Wenker, Chris T. *Archaeology Notes 422: From Acequias to Industry: the Archaeology of Neighborhood and Infrastructure at the Santa Fe Railyard* (Museum of New Mexico Office of Archaeological Studies, 2014)

Barbour, Matthew; Akins, Nancy; Post, Stephen S.; and Lentz, Stephen. *Archaeology Notes 410: Settlers and Soldiers: The Historic Component at El Pueblo de Santa Fe, LA 1051* (Museum of New Mexico Office of Archaeological Studies, 2011)

Baxter, John O. "The Second Ward School," *Bulletin* of the Historic Santa Fe Foundation, Vol. 3, No. 2, June/July 1977

Belshaw, Michael. *Camino del Monte Sol Architectural Historic Survey* (City of Santa Fe, 1984)

Berger, William M. *Berger's Tourists' Guide to New Mexico: including descriptions of towns, pueblos, churches, pictures, statues, ruins and antiquities ; together with mountains, cañons, springs, and other places of interest...* (1883)

Boyd, E. "Domestic Architecture in New Mexico" in *El Palacio* Vol. 79 No. 3 (December 1973)

Bullock, Alice. "Early Urban" in the *Santa Fe New Mexican* Oct. 8, 1972

Bunting, Bainbridge. "Take a Trip with NMA: An architectural guide to Northern New Mexico" in *New Mexico Architecture*, Vol. 12, Nos. 9 and 10, Sept.-Oct. 1970

Bunting, Bainbridge. *Early Architecture in New Mexico* (University of New Mexico Press, 1976)

Bunting, Bainbridge. *Taos Adobes: Spanish Colonial and Territorial Architecture of the Taos Valley* (Fort Burgwin Research Center and Museum of New Mexico Press, 1964)

Chapman, Kate; and Stewart, Dorothy N. *Adobe Notes or How To Keep the Weather Out With Just Plain Mud* (Laughing Horse Press, Taos, 1930)

Chauvenet, Beatrice. *Holy Faith in Santa Fe: The Story of a Pioneer Parish* (Episcopal Church of the Holy Faith, 1977)

Chávez, Angélico. *Our Lady of the Conquest* (Historical Society of New Mexico, 1948)

Chávez, Thomas E. *An Illustrated History of New Mexico* (University Press of Colorado, 1992)

Chávez, Thomas E. *New Mexico Past and Future* (University of New Mexico Press, 2006)

City of Santa Fe historic-inventory-survey files on various properties

City of Santa Fe Planning Division. *Historic Building Inventory Manual: A Citizen's Guide to Conducting Architectural Survey in Santa Fe* (1997)

Colby, Catherine. *Architecture Report: 518 Alto Street, Santa Fe, New Mexico*, for the Historic Santa Fe Foundation, 2011

Colby, Catherine. *The Delgado House Architectural History Report* for the Historic Santa Fe Foundation, March 2013

Colby, Catherine. "Katherine Stinson Otero: From Pilot to Builder" (2016 draft)

Conron, John P., and Christopher, R. Patrick. "The Architecture of Santa Fe: A Survey of Styles" in *New Mexico Architecture* 20, no. 5, September-October 1978

Cornerstones Community Partnerships. *Adobe Conservation: A Preservation Handbook* (Sunstone Press, Santa Fe, 2006)

Creamer, Winifred. *The Architecture of Arroyo Hondo Pueblo* (SAR Press, 1993)

Davis, W.W.H. *El Gringo: New Mexico and Her People* (1857)

Diehl, Allison Cohen and Michael W. "Building Tucson in the Nineteenth and Twentieth Centuries," Center for Desert Archaeology, in *Archaeology in Tucson*, Vol. 10, No. 3, Summer 1996

Early, James. *Presidio, Mission and Pueblo: Spanish Architecture and Urbanism in the United States* (Southern Methodist University Press, 2004)

Frank, Larry, and Miller, Skip Keith. *A Land So Remote* (Red Crane Books, 2001)

Hammett, Kingsley. *Santa Fe: A Walk Through Time* (Gibbs Smith, 2004)

Harrelson, Barbara J. *From Every Window: A Glimpse of the Past* (La Fonda, 2011)

*Historic Districts Handbook: A Guide to Historic Preservation and Design Regulations in Santa Fe* (City of Santa Fe Planning Division, 1989)

Kammer, David. National Register of Historic Places multiple properties nomination: Buildings Designed by John Gaw Meem, 2002

Kessell, John L. *The Missions of New Mexico Since 1776* (University of New Mexico Press, 1980)

King, Bruce. *Cowboy in the Roundhouse: A Political Life* (Sunstone Press, 1998)

Kubler, George. *The religious architecture of New Mexico in the colonial period and since the American occupation* (1940)

La Farge, John Pen. "Santa Fe becoming exclusive, but for whom?" in *Santa Fe New Mexican*, Feb. 6, 1983

La Farge, John Pen. *Turn Left at the Sleeping Dog: Scripting the Santa Fe Legend, 1920-1955* (University of New Mexico Press, 2001)

Labinsky, Daria, and Hieronymus, Stan. *Frank Applegate of Santa Fe: Artist and Preservationist* (LPD Press, 2001)

Lakatos, Stephen A. *Archaeology Notes 424: Data Recovery Results from the First Judicial District Courthouse Complex, LA 156207, Santa Fe County, New Mexico* (Museum of New Mexico Office of Archaeological Studies, 2011)

Lehmberg, Stanford. *Churches for the Southwest: The Ecclesiastical Architecture of John Gaw Meem* (W.W. Norton, 2005)

Lewis, Nancy Owen. "Chasing the Cure in New Mexico: The Lungers and Their Legacy" in *El Palacio*, Vol. 113, No. 4 (Winter 2008)

Lewis, Nancy Owen. *Chasing the Cure in New Mexico: Tuberculosis and the Quest for Health* (Museum of New Mexico Press, 2016)

Loomis, Sylvia, editor. *Old Santa Fe Today* (Historic Santa Fe Foundation, 1972)

Loomis, Sylvia. Interview with John Gaw Meem for New Deal and the Arts Project, Archives of American Art, Smithsonian Institution, 1964

Lucero, Thomas L., and Steele, Thomas J. *Religious Architecture in Hispano New Mexico* (LPD Press, 2005)

Lumpkins, William. *La Casa Adobe* (Ancient City Press, 1986)

Mather, Christine; and Woods, Sharon. *Santa Fe Style* (Rizzoli International Publications, 2001)

McAlester, Virginia Savage. *A Field Guide to American Houses* (Knopf, 2013)

McCord, Richard. *No Halls of Ivy: The Gritty Story of The College of Santa Fe* (Lasallian Christian Brothers, 2013)

McHugh, John W. "Old Santa Fe and What To Do About It" in *New Mexico Architecture*, Vol. 12, Nos. 1 and 2, Jan-Feb 1970

Mead, Christopher Curtis. *The Architecture of Bart Prince: A Pragmatics of Place* (W.W. Norton & Company, 1999, 2010)

Meyer, Marian. *A Century of Progress: History of the New Mexico School for the Deaf* (NMSD, 1989)

Montaño, Mary. *Tradiciones Nuevomexicanas: Hispano Arts and Culture of New Mexico* (University of New Mexico Press, 2001)

Morrow Reardon Wilkinson Miller Ltd. *Santa Fe Plaza: Cultural Landscape Report* (City of Santa Fe, 2006)

National Park Service: El Camino Real de Tierra Adentro website

National Park Service: Santa Fe National Historic Trail website

New Mexico Historic Preservation Division. *Recording a Vanishing Legacy: The Historic American Buildings Survey in New Mexico 1933-Today* (Museum of New Mexico Press, 2001)

New Mexico Historical Review

New Mexico Office of the State Historian website

Noble, David Grant, editor. *Santa Fe: History of An Ancient City* (School for Advanced Research, 2008)

Nusbaum, Rosemary. *The City Different and the Palace* (1978)

Nusbaum, Rosemary. *Tierra Dulce: Reminiscences from the Jesse Nusbaum Papers* (Sunstone Press, 1980)

Palace of the Governors/New Mexico History Museum and New Mexico Digital Collections

Paul, Peter D., and Pratt, Boyd. "New Mexico's Capitols: Search for a Regional Symbol" (1999 draft document at Fray Angélico Chávez History Library, Santa Fe)

Pierson, Heather L., Bechtol, Gayla, et al. *Historic Districts Handbook: A Guide to Preservation and Design Regulations in Santa Fe* (City of Santa Fe, 1989)

Post, Stephen S. *Archaeology Notes 442: Archaeological and Historical Study of the School for Advanced Research Campus at 660, 666, and 679 Garcia Street, Santa Fe, New Mexico* (Museum of New Mexico Office of Archaeological Studies, 2011)

Post, Stephen S., and Oakes, Yvonne R. *Archaeology Notes 311: A Data Recovery Plan for Excavation at the New Mexico Museum of History Site: 700 Years of Human Occupation Near the Palace of the Governors in Santa Fe, New Mexico* (Museum of New Mexico Office of Archaeological Studies, 2002)

Pratt, Boyd C. "A Brief History of the Practice of Architecture in New Mexico" in *New Mexico Architecture*, Nov.-Dec. 1989

Pratt, Boyd C.; Lazzell, Carleen; Wilson, Chris. "Directory of Historic New Mexico Architects" (1988 draft)

Prince, L. Bradford. *Old Fort Marcy, Santa Fe, New Mexico: Historical Sketch and Panoramic View of Santa Fe and its Vicinity* (1912)

Prince, Le Baron Bradford. *A Concise History of New Mexico* (1912)

*Representative New Mexicans: The National Newspaper Reference Book of the New State containing Photographs and Biographies of over Four Hundred Men Residents of New Mexico, compiled and published by C.S. Peterson, Denver*, 1912

Ruminer, John. *109 East Palace Avenue: A Microcosm of Santa Fe's Four Hundred Year History* (Los Alamos Historical Society, 2014)

Russell, Marian. *Land of Enchantment: Memoirs of Marian Russell Along the Santa Fe Trail* (1954)

*Santa Fe Railyard Master Plan and Design Guidelines* (City of Santa Fe, 2002)

Secord, Paul R. *Santa Fe's Historic Hotels* (Arcadia Publishing, 2013)

Segale, Sister Blandina. *At the End of the Santa Fe Trail* (1932)

Seth, Sandra and Laurel. *Adobe! Homes and Interiors of Taos, Santa Fe and the Southwest* (Architectural Book Publishing Company, 1988)

Shapiro, Jason. *Before Santa Fe: Archaeology of the City Different* (Museum of New Mexico Press, 2008)

Sheppard, Carl D. *Creator of the Santa Fe Style: Isaac Hamilton Rapp, Architect* (University of New Mexico Press, 1988)

Sherman, John. *Santa Fe: A Pictorial History* (Donning Co., 1983)

Shiskin, J.K. *An Early History of the Museum of New Mexico Fine Arts Building: "The new museum is a wonder..."* (Museum of New Mexico Press, 1968)

Simmons, Marc. *The Sena Family: Blacksmiths of Santa Fe* (Press of the Palace of the Governors, 1981)

Simmons, Marc. Trail Dust: "N.M. Capitol Evolved from Palace of the Governors to Roundhouse" in *Santa Fe New Mexican*, June 9, 2001

Simmons, Marc. Trail Dust: "Lamy's Legacy" in *Santa Fe New Mexican*, Jan. 3, 2009

Simmons, Marc. Trail Dust: "Letter gives glimpse of territorial life in New Mexico" in *Santa Fe New Mexican*, May 31, 2013

Spears, Beverley. *American Adobes: Rural Houses of Northern New Mexico* (Ancient City Press, Santa Fe, 1986)

Spears, Beverley, and Sze, Corinne. *Santa Fe Historic Neighborhood Study* (City of Santa Fe, 1988)

Spears, Beverley. Westside-Guadalupe Streetscape and Design Ordinance Report (City of Santa Fe, 1987)

Stedman, Myrtle and Wilfred. *Adobe Architecture* (Sunstone Press, 1973)

Sze, Corinne P. Elizabeth and Henry Berchtold House listing nomination for Historic Santa Fe Foundation, December 6, 2001

Sze, Corinne, and Henry, Patti. National Historic Landmark Inventory/Nomination: Palace of the Governors, 1999

Sze, Corinne. "A History of the Catron Block," in *Bulletin* of the Historic Santa Fe Foundation, Vol. 14, No. 1, September 1986

Sze, Corinne. "Santa Fe's Railroad Era Plaza" in *Bulletin* of the Historic Santa Fe Foundation, February 1992 Vol. 20 No. 1, February 1992

Sze, Corinne. "The Santa Fe Railway's Santa Fe Passenger Depot" in *Bulletin* of the Santa Fe Foundation, Vol. 20, No. 1, February 1992

Sze, Corinne. Fairview Cemetery history

Sze, Corinne. *Within Adobe Walls: A Santa Fe Journal: Selections from the Charlotte White Journals* (Historic Santa Fe Foundation, 2001)

The Laws of the Indies (1573) c/o The Codes Project, funded by the National Endowment for the Arts, Duany Plater-Zyberk & Co., National Science Foundation, and the GeoDa Center, Arizona State University

Traugott, Joseph. *Pueblo Architecture and Modern Adobes: the Residential Designs of William Lumpkins* (Museum of New Mexico Press, 1998)

Treib, Marc. *Sanctuaries of Spanish New Mexico* (University of California Press, 1993)

Twitchell, Ralph Emerson. *Old Santa Fe: The Story of New Mexico's Ancient Capital* (Santa Fe New Mexican Publishing Corp., 1925)

University of New Mexico Center for Southwest Research and Rocky Mountain Online Archive

Van Dresser, Peter. *Passive Solar House Basics* (Gibbs Smith, 1977)

Vierra, Carlos. "Our Native Architecture in its Relation to Santa Fe" in *El Palacio*, Vol. IV, No. 1, January 1917

Watson Conserves. *The Santa Fe Depot of 1909, The Atchison, Topeka and Santa Fe Railway Passenger Depot in Santa Fe, New Mexico: A Conditions Assessment Report and Preservation Plan for 2009*

Weideman, Paul. "William Penhallow Henderson: artist, builder, furniture-maker," in *Bulletin* of the Historic Santa Fe Foundation, Vol. 31, No. 1, Summer 2007

Weideman, Paul. "The Jane & Gustave Baumann House," in *Bulletin* of the Historic Santa Fe Foundation, Vol. 32, No. 1, Spring 2010

Weigle, Marta. *Hispanic Villages of Northern New Mexico: A reprint of Volume II of the 1935 Tewa Basin Study, with supplementary materials* (Ancient City Press, 1994)

Weigle, Marta. *Telling New Mexico: A New History* (Museum of New Mexico Press, 2009)

Wikipedia: dozens — nay, scores — of searches for basic information and to point the way to primary source materials

Wilson, Chris, and Horn, Oliver. *The Roque Lobato House, Santa Fe, New Mexico* (Schenck Southwest Publishing, 2014)

Wilson, Chris. *Facing Southwest: The Life & Houses of John Gaw Meem* (W.W. Norton, 2001)

Wilson, Chris. *The Myth of Santa Fe: Creating a Modern Tradition* (University of New Mexico Press, 1997)

*Windmills and Dreams: A History of the Eldorado Community and Neighboring Areas* (Eldorado Community Improvement Association, 1997)

Wingert-Playdon, Kate. *John Gaw Meem at Acoma: The Restoration of San Esteban del Rey Mission* (University of New Mexico Press, 2012)

Wirth, Nancy Meem, editor. Chili Club Papers by John Gaw Meem, 1939-1976. Santa Fe: n.p., 1994

# Index

*Page numbers in Italics = reference photos/graphics*
***Bold italics = Rolleiflex photos***

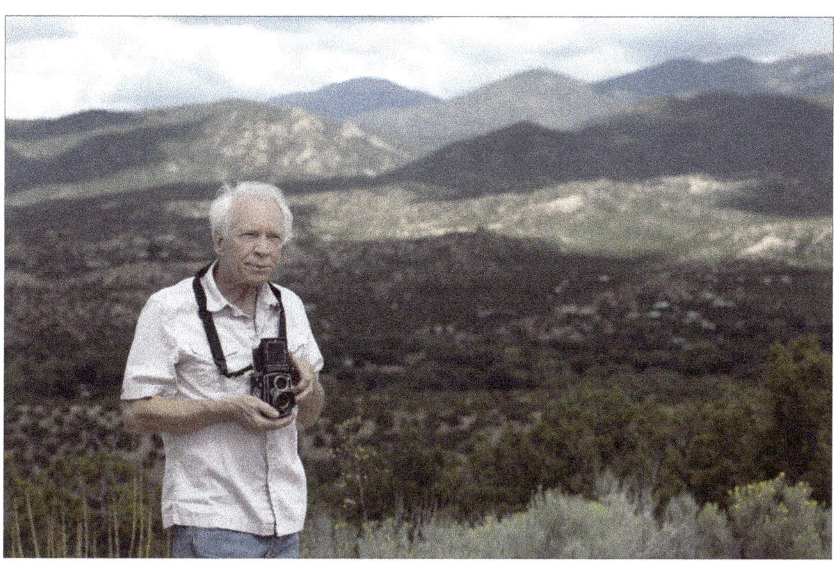

PHOTO BY KIM KURIAN

**Paul Weideman** was born in Indianapolis and grew up in Ohio, Michigan, and in Southern Rhodesia, Africa (age 11-15). He earned bachelor's degrees in biology (Western Michigan University, Kalamazoo) and editorial journalism (University of Washington, Seattle) and has worked as a journalist since 1984, the last twenty-five years in Northern New Mexico. In 1996, he married Mary Margaret Vigil, whose parents were members of multigenerational Santa Fe families. His record of writing about architecture in *The Santa Fe New Mexican's* weekly arts magazine, Pasatiempo, and its monthly Home/Santa Fe Real Estate Guide magazine was recognized with a special Service Award by the Santa Fe chapter of the American Institute of Architects in 2017.

www.ingramcontent.com/pod-product-compliance
Lightning Source LLC
LaVergne TN
LVHW060630110826
845147LV00014B/882

* 9 7 8 0 5 7 8 6 0 6 9 0 3 *